OVER A BARREL

OVER A BARREL

The Costs of U.S. Foreign Oil Dependence

John S. Duffield

STANFORD LAW AND POLITICS
An imprint of Stanford University Press
Stanford, California
2008

Stanford University Press
Stanford, California

©2008 by the Board of Trustees of the Leland Stanford Junior University.
All rights reserved.

Printed in the United States of America on acid-free, archival-quality paper.

Library of Congress Cataloging-in-Publication Data
Duffield, John S.
   Over a barrel : the costs of U.S. foreign oil dependence / John S. Duffield.
      p. cm.
   Includes bibliographical references and index.
   ISBN 978-0-8047-5499-6 (cloth : alk. paper)
   1. Petroleum industry and trade--Government policy--United States. 2. Petroleum industry and trade--Political aspects--United States. 3. Petroleum conservation--United States. 4. Imports--United States. I. Title.

HD9566.D82 2008
338.2'72820973--dc22   2007027396
Typeset by Bruce Lundquist in 10/14 Minion

To Elizabeth and Stuart

Contents

Tables, Figures, and Maps

Tables

Figures

Maps

Preface

WHAT A DIFFERENCE a few years can make. When I began to conceptualize this project in 2003, few people evidenced concern about U.S. foreign oil dependence. That changed, however, as the price of a barrel of oil passed the $30 mark, then more than doubled over the next two and a half years. Now it seems that the perils of dependence on foreign oil are recognized by almost everyone, and hardly a day goes by without the appearance of some new proposal for addressing them.

Alas, academic books are not often known for the timeliness of their contributions to policy debates, and given how quickly the public discussion has moved, this book may be no exception. Yet I believe that a careful scholarly analysis can still make a useful contribution, in part because the challenges posed by foreign oil dependence are complicated and will not be quickly resolved. Above all, we still need a full accounting of the costs to the United States of its foreign oil dependence, which is the principal goal of this book. Such an assessment is a necessary foundation for effective action. As the book tries to make clear, the costs have stemmed not just from the fact that the United States imports so much oil but also from the policies that concerns about high oil prices and unreliable foreign supplies have spawned. Thus attempts to reduce the costs should address those policy responses as well as the underlying economic conditions that prompted them. The book also emphasizes that the proper focus of efforts to reduce the economic costs and risks of foreign oil dependence should not be imports per se but the more general dependence of the U.S. economy on oil, regardless of its place of origin.

The relatively rapid completion of this project was greatly facilitated by a number of institutions and individuals. I would not have been able to write this book as quickly as I did without the generous financial support of Georgia State University (GSU) and the German Marshall Fund of the United States. A Research Initiation Grant from GSU enabled me to start work on the project during the fall of 2003. The College of Arts and Sciences at GSU then awarded me a professional leave that allowed me to write full-time during the 2005 calendar year. During the second half of that year, a research fellowship from the German Marshall Fund of the United States supported me.

While working on this book, I was ably assisted by many research assistants: Josephine Dawuni, Adam DiGiovanni, Sean Ding, Michael McPherson, Raluca Miller, Sara Miller, Kris Sauriol, and Jonathan West. I also thank Michael McPherson for commenting on a draft of the entire manuscript.

A number of experts provided helpful comments on different parts of the manuscript. They include my GSU colleagues Charles Hankla, Michael Herb, Jennifer McCoy, and Carrie Manning, as well as Michael O'Hanlon of the Brookings Institution. In addition to these experts, Rachel Bronson, Chip Carey, Gregory Gause, Mary Matthews, Ed Morse, William Quandt, Ruhi Ramazani, Michael E. Smith, and Dona Stewart also helped by answering specific queries, providing documents and data, and suggesting additional sources. Although not experts, my parents, Richard and Mary Rose Duffield, offered encouragement throughout the research and writing process, and my mother took time to read the manuscript, flagging a number of typographical errors. Although the assistance of all these individuals was invaluable, I alone am responsible for the accuracy of the facts and judgments that follow.

I am grateful to my editor at Stanford University Press, Amanda Moran, for the early interest that she took in this project and for her assistance in moving the manuscript expeditiously through the review and approval process. From there, Mariana Raykov, my production editor, saw to it that the manuscript was smoothly and rapidly converted into book form.

Last but not least, I owe a special thanks to my wife, Cheryl, and to my children, who lovingly tolerated my preoccupation with completing the project and who did not complain too vociferously each time I slipped off to the basement study to work on the manuscript. I hope that my children in particular will understand, someday if not right away, that in writing this book,

I aspired to make the world at least a slightly better place for them and others of their generation, even as so much more remains to be done. That is why I dedicate the book to them.

JSD
Decatur, Georgia
February 2007

Abbreviations

ANWR	Arctic National Wildlife Refuge
AWACS	Airborne Warning and Control System
BTC	Baku-Tbilisi-Ceyhan
CAFE	Corporate Average Fuel Economy
CBO	Congressional Budget Office
CENTCOM	U.S. Central Command
CIA	U.S. Central Intelligence Agency
CRS	Congressional Research Service
DOD	U.S. Department of Defense
DOE	U.S. Department of Energy
DOT	U.S. Department of Transportation
DSCA	Defense Security Cooperation Agency
EIA	Energy Information Administration
EPA	U.S. Environmental Protection Agency
EPCA	Energy Policy and Conservation Act (1975)
ESLC	Energy Security Leadership Council
FBI	Federal Bureau of Investigation
FFV	flexible-fuel vehicle

FSU	former Soviet Union
FY	fiscal year
GAO	U.S. General Accounting Office/Governmental Accountability Office
GDP	gross domestic product
GNP	gross national product
GVWR	gross vehicle weight rating
ICTA	International Center for Technology Assessment
IEA	International Energy Agency (Paris)
IEP	International Energy Program
IISS	International Institute for Strategic Studies
IMF	International Monetary Fund
IOC	International Oil Companies
LMSR	large, medium-speed, roll-on/roll-off transport ship
LPG	liquefied petroleum gases
LNG	liquified natural gas
MAB	Marine Amphibious Brigade
MAF	Marine Amphibious Force
MBD	million barrels per day
MEF	Marine Expeditionary Force
MIDEASTFOR	Middle East Force
mpg	miles per gallon
MPS	Maritime Prepositioning Ships
MRC	major regional conflict
MSP	minimum safeguard price
NATO	North Atlantic Treaty Organization
NAVCENT	U.S. Naval Forces Central Command
NCTAUS	National Commission on Terrorist Attacks Upon the United States
NIC	National Intelligence Council

NGL	natural gas liquids
NRC	National Research Council
NRDC	Natural Resources Defense Council
NSC	National Security Council
NSDD	National Security Decision Directive
NSF	National Science Foundation
NTPF	Near-Term Prepositioning Force
O&M	operations and maintenance
OECD	Organization for Economic Cooperation and Development
OPEC	Organization of the Petroleum Exporting Countries
OPIC	Overseas Private Investment Corporation
ORNL	Oak Ridge National Laboratory
OSD	Office of the Secretary of Defense
OTA	Office of Technology Assessment
OUD	Office of the Undersecretary of Defense
PdVSA	Petróleos de Venezuela S.A.
RDJTF	Rapid Deployment Joint Task Force
RO/RO	roll-on/roll-off
RRF	Ready Reserve Force
SFC	Synthetic Fuels Corporation
SPR	Strategic Petroleum Reserve
SUV	sport utility vehicle
TAPS	Trans Alaska Pipeline System
UAE	United Arab Emirates
USAF	U.S. Air Force
VMT	vehicle miles traveled

OVER A BARREL

1 Introduction

The Benefits and Costs of Foreign Oil Dependence

> We have a serious problem. America is addicted to oil, which is often
> imported from unstable parts of the world.
> > *President George W. Bush, January 31, 2006*

THE UNITED STATES is highly dependent on foreign oil. Until the late 1940s, it was a net oil exporter. Today, however, well over half of the crude oil and petroleum products consumed in America come from abroad. The flood of imports now stands at more than twelve million barrels per day (MBD), or more than six hundred gallons for every man, woman, and child each year. The U.S. government projects that this deluge will only continue to increase, reaching between thirteen and fifteen MBD by 2015 and then seventeen to twenty-one MBD by 2030, when imports will account for as much as two-thirds of all consumption (EIA 2006a, 115, tab. 24).

Imports are not the only form of U.S. foreign oil dependence. World markets largely determine the prices of oil and petroleum products in the United States. As most American consumers well know, when the world price of oil goes up, so do the prices of gasoline, heating oil, and other petroleum products at home. Because so much economic activity now crosses national boundaries, moreover, the health of the U.S. economy is closely bound up with the economic well-being of a number of other countries that are themselves large oil importers. When U.S. economic partners are hurt by high oil prices, the American economy inevitably suffers as well.

This substantial and growing reliance on foreign oil provides a number of economic benefits. Theoretically, the price of every barrel of oil that comes from abroad is less than what it would cost to produce an additional barrel in the United States or to reduce U.S. oil consumption by an equivalent amount.

But America's foreign oil dependence also comes at a cost, much of which is not reflected in the price that motorists pay at the pump.

What precisely are the costs of U.S. foreign oil dependence? Unfortunately, no one has offered a satisfactory answer to this vital question. Over the years, a number of relatively specialized and technical reports have addressed various aspects of the topic, such as the economic costs of oil shocks or the military costs of defending the Persian Gulf. But few of these studies have been widely circulated, most are quite dated, and none addresses the full gamut of relevant issues. Despite all the ink that has been spilled on the subject of oil, a comprehensive analysis of the costs of U.S. foreign oil dependence has not yet been written.

That is the purpose of this book. It seeks to identify and make explicit the full range of costs associated with U.S. foreign oil dependence and to provide, where possible, reasonable estimates of those costs. A secondary objective is to suggest some of the most promising ways of reducing these costs, but a thorough treatment of that issue would require a separate study. The bulk of the book is therefore devoted to the logically prior goal of determining just what and how big are the costs of foreign oil dependence. Unless it can be shown that these costs are substantial, there will be little reason or incentive to modify current U.S. policies.

Along the way, I hope to offer clear, accessible, yet authoritative answers to the questions many Americans have about the subject: Just how dependent is the United States on foreign oil? What economic problems does this dependence pose? What efforts has the U.S. government made, both at home and abroad, to reduce the economic costs and risks of foreign oil dependence? What additional costs have those policies imposed? And what more might be done to address them?

The book makes three interrelated arguments. First, despite their importance, the costs to the United States of foreign oil dependence have gone largely unrecognized by the general public. To be sure, public opinion polls have sometimes registered heightened concern about dependence on foreign oil, especially in recent years, but such concerns are typically linked to high gasoline prices and do not necessarily reflect a broader appreciation of the problem (Yankelovich 2006; Public Agenda 2006). In fact, although some costs, like the annual bill for oil imports, are obvious and quantifiable, a number of others are not so apparent or easy to measure. For example, it is difficult to put a price tag on the costs of coddling oil-rich authoritarian regimes at the expense of promoting representative government, human rights, and other important values. Thus costs have often been incurred even when oil—and gasoline—prices have been relatively low and stable.

Second, the costs of U.S. foreign oil dependence have been substantial. Since the 1970s, the economic costs alone have run in the trillions of dollars. The magnitude of these costs provides a compelling reason for taking measures to reduce them, especially where doing so does not eliminate the benefits of foreign oil dependence.

Third, the policies that the United States has in fact adopted in response to its foreign oil dependence have only increased the overall costs. Successive U.S. administrations have tended to neglect the opportunities at home to reduce the economic costs by limiting demand. Instead, they have emphasized foreign and military policies designed to promote the development of new sources of foreign oil, to protect existing supplies, and to ensure access to them both. But this strategy has proved to be both highly expensive and largely unsuccessful. Many of the costs cannot be quantified, but those that can be have amounted to at least tens of billions of dollars per year. Yet more than three decades after the first oil shock of 1973, we find that the international situation is little improved. The world oil market is tight and likely to remain so for the foreseeable future, oil prices have flirted with the record highs of the early 1980s, and the risk of potentially costly supply disruptions is as great as it has been in many years.

One positive consequence of this otherwise bleak assessment is that the costs of foreign oil dependence can still be reduced substantially at relatively little expense. A large part of the solution lies in bringing down the overall level of oil dependence of the U.S. economy. This approach was pursued with some success during the late 1970s and early 1980s, but the opportunities for reducing oil consumption remain largely untapped. At least as important, however, is the need to rethink and revise the expensive foreign and military policies and commitments that have developed around U.S. foreign oil dependence over the past three decades.

The Benefits of Foreign Oil Dependence

Although the focus of this book is the costs of foreign oil dependence, there is no denying that this dependence has also yielded substantial economic and other benefits to the United States. Most obvious are the benefits of importing oil. Typically, countries import either when the goods in question are un-available at home or when their cost is lower than that of domestically pro-duced equivalents. Thus American consumers and businesses profit from oil imports because "they pay less for energy than they would if they were to rely more extensively on higher-cost domestic oil or alternative fuels" (GAO 1996, 19). Overall energy prices are lower than if the United States had to rely on its own energy resources, resulting in greater economic output for a given level of energy consumption.

Unfortunately, it is not possible to determine these benefits directly. One can measure them only indirectly by estimating the harm that would be caused by reducing imports from existing levels, which would in turn in-volve some combination of a decline in consumption and a greater reliance on more expensive domestic sources of energy. A 1995 U.S. government study attempted to do just that. It considered the hypothetical effects of higher oil prices (caused either by a gradual decline in world production or the grad-ual introduction of a comparable oil import fee) on both imports and U.S. gross domestic product (GDP). The study found that a price increase of $10 per barrel above the forecast price would cause GDP to decline by about $50 billion after ten years, while a $20 increase would result in an annual GDP loss of about $100 billion. On the basis of these calculations, it concluded that the then-current level of imports provided hundreds of billions of dol-lars in economic benefits each year. Only in the event that the proceeds of an import fee were used entirely to reduce the federal budget deficit was the long-term effect on GDP of a reduction in imports predicted to be negligible (GAO 1996).[1]

The importation of oil also has strategic benefits. By using petroleum from abroad, the United States is able to extend the life of its domestic reserves. Today, the preservation of national oil production potential is not regarded as being as important as it was in the past. Indeed, the U.S. government has recently sold or leased most of the naval petroleum reserves established in the early 1900s. Nevertheless, there are good strategic reasons to postpone the day when the United States is unable to produce significant amounts of oil. The gradual exhaustion of domestic oil reserves will increasingly limit U.S. energy options, and the United States could once again find itself in a position where it would have to rely more heavily on domestic output. The use of imported oil allows the United States to conserve its own energy resources to meet fu-ture needs and emergencies.

The large volume of oil imports is closely related to the liberalization of the U.S. market for oil and petroleum products, which has conferred yet other benefits. In order to understand these benefits, it is useful first to consider the consequences of market restrictions. Since World War II, the United States has experimented with market restrictions on two principal occasions, each time with mixed results. In 1959, the Eisenhower administration imposed oil import quotas to protect domestic producers from less expensive imports from the Middle East and Venezuela. These controls, which were maintained in one form or another for fourteen years, kept domestic oil prices well above the world market price—60 to 70 percent higher in some cases—even as it stimulated domestic production (Yergin 1991, 539). Nevertheless, by the early 1970s, oil was in short supply and the quota system was abolished.

At almost the same time, the Nixon administration imposed price controls on domestic crude oil and petroleum products. These controls helped to shield U.S. consumers from the sharp rise in world oil prices that accompanied the first oil shock in 1973. Unfortunately, they also stimulated consumption while discouraging conservation and domestic production, causing imports actually to rise. Because of the strength of consumer interest in maintaining controls, not until 1979 did the U.S. government begin to lift them.

Since the early 1980s, both imports and the prices of oil and petroleum products have been unregulated in the United States. The price and import levels have been determined primarily by market forces. Although the resulting fluctuations have had various disadvantages, the liberalization of the U.S. oil market—and increasingly other energy markets—has helped to ensure that energy resources have been put to their most productive uses.

The Costs of Foreign Oil Dependence

For some, U.S. foreign oil dependence would appear to be an unqualified boon. As one commentator bluntly put the matter, "Oil imports aren't a problem" (Taylor 2001). Nevertheless, it is essential to recognize that U.S. foreign oil dependence has also imposed substantial costs. Although these costs have assumed a variety of forms, they can be grouped into two broad categories: (1) the actual and potential economic costs that result from foreign oil dependence, and (2) the costs of the various U.S. government policies—economic, diplomatic, military, and others—that have been undertaken in response to the economic costs and risks. All of these elements must be considered when attempting to assess the overall burdens of foreign oil dependence.

Perhaps most familiar are the actual and potential economic costs, some of which have been directly experienced by American consumers and producers in the form of gasoline shortages and sharp price increases. The economic costs and risks can be further subdivided into two groups: the recurring costs associated with importing large and growing volumes of oil, and the less predictable harm caused by periodic oil supply disruptions and price shocks, both in the past and possibly in the future. Although economists have carefully examined these costs, there is disagreement about just how big they are. Nevertheless, most would agree that the total economic costs to the United States of foreign oil dependence have been substantial, with estimates running as high as $7 trillion for the period 1970 to 1999 alone.

Given the magnitude of these costs, the United States has had a strong interest in reducing them. And especially since the first oil shock in 1973, successive administrations have made a variety of efforts to do so, both at home and abroad. These policies can be grouped into three general categories. One includes efforts to reduce foreign oil dependence by limiting imports and oil consumption more generally. Another category comprises measures intended to mitigate the impact of oil shocks independently of any reduction in oil imports and consumption that might be achieved. The third involves policies aimed at reducing the size and likelihood of future oil shocks and ensuring reliable access to adequate supplies of foreign oil at reasonable prices. These policies, while at least partly successful, have generated substantial additional costs of their own.

What steps has the U.S. government taken to reduce foreign oil dependence? The efforts within this area have been the most diverse. They have included taxes, automotive speed limits, fuel economy standards, subsidies and incentives to develop substitutes for oil and to increase oil production within the United States, as well as research and development of alternative fuels and energy sources. But overall, the attempts to limit American oil consumption and imports have also been the most modest. For example, the U.S. government has never imposed a substantial gasoline tax or oil import fee, and it has never invested heavily in mass transit for the purpose of reducing oil use in the transportation sector. Other programs that were attempted, such as the production of synthetic fuels and related federal research and development efforts, have been scaled back in size or abandoned altogether. Since the early

1980s, the use of economic policy instruments to reduce foreign oil dependence has rarely, if ever, assumed a high priority. Thus the costs have been small, but so have the results.

Somewhat more successful have been U.S. policies intended to mitigate the economic impact of oil shocks. Most important among these have been the maintenance of price controls in the 1970s and, especially, the establishment of a Strategic Petroleum Reserve (SPR) of hundreds of thousands of barrels that could be released in the event of a disruption in oil supplies. The SPR has proved a valuable insurance policy at a total cost of at most $125 billion over three decades, and possibly much less. Nevertheless, the size and composition of the SPR have not been significantly updated to reflect changing strategic and economic circumstances, and American efforts to develop complementary cooperative arrangements with other oil consuming nations through the International Energy Agency (IEA) have added little to the U.S. capacity to lessen the effects of an oil shock by itself.

A third set of measures has been intended to reduce the risk and magnitude of future oil shocks and, more generally, to ensure dependable access to adequate amounts of oil from abroad at reasonable prices. These primarily external policies have been by far the most costly.

The United States and its economic and security partners have faced two general types of threats to the steady flow of oil from foreign sources. Initially, U.S. policymakers were primarily concerned with the possibility that hostile oil producing states would intentionally cut production or otherwise withhold oil from consumers, as exemplified by the 1973 Arab oil embargo. Since the Iranian Revolution in the late 1970s, however, the principal focus has been an unintended supply disruption of major proportions. The potential causes of such a disruption have been numerous, but among the greatest sources of concern have been perceived Soviet hegemonic aspirations in the Persian Gulf, intraregional struggles for dominance, such as the Iran-Iraq War and Iraq's invasion of Kuwait, internal political conflicts, and terrorist attacks on major oil facilities.

In response to these threats, successive U.S. administrations have pursued a variety of more specific objectives, which have varied according to the circumstances. In some cases, they have sought to convince existing oil producers to refrain from politically motivated embargoes or production cuts and, instead, to produce at levels that would result in moderate oil prices and to increase output above normal levels whenever necessary to compensate for unexpected supply disruptions. Elsewhere, the United States has worked to diversify the sources of foreign oil by promoting the development of additional oil resources. As the 1991 National Security Strategy noted, "Diversification of both productive and spare capacity is important to providing a cushion to the oil market. Increased production . . . from other areas would also contribute to the security of oil supplies" (Bush 1991b). And the United States has sought to strengthen and stabilize oil producers in the face of external or internal threats.

A final objective has been to protect directly, if necessary, critical oil supplies and the pipelines and sea lanes that connect them to world markets. This goal was articulated perhaps most prominently by President Jimmy Carter in January 1980 following the Soviet invasion of Afghanistan, when he famously declared, "An attempt by any outside force to gain control of the Persian Gulf region will be regarded as an assault on the vital interests of the United States of America, and such an assault will be repelled by any means necessary, including military force."[2] But it has been a staple of statements of U.S. national security policy ever since. For example, the 1991 National Security Strategy of the first Bush administration stated, "The concentration of 65 percent of the world's known oil reserves in the Persian Gulf means we must continue to ensure reliable access to competitively priced oil and a prompt, adequate response to any major oil supply disruption" (Bush 1991b, 22). Likewise, the 1998 national security strategy of the Clinton administration noted, "Conservation and energy research notwithstanding, the United States will continue to have a vital interest in ensuring access to foreign oil sources. We must continue to be mindful of the need for regional stability and security in key producing areas to ensure our access to and the free flow of these resources" (Clinton 1998, 32–33; see also Clinton 2000).

In pursuit of these goals, the United States has made use of the full range of external policy instruments, including diplomacy, military and economy assistance, and, not least, the application of military power. The nature and magnitude of American actions have varied from region to region and over time, as both the demand for oil and threats to its supply have waxed and waned. The principal focus of these efforts has been the Persian Gulf, but other regions have also figured importantly in U.S. policy, especially in more recent years. Overall, the level of effort has been considerable.

In part because of the emphasis they have received, these external policy measures have arguably enjoyed some measure of success. The world has not seen another oil embargo since the early 1970s or a major oil supply disruption since Iraq's 1990 invasion of Kuwait. But they have also generated substantial additional costs of their own. Most apparent have been the direct financial outlays these policies have entailed, especially for but not limited to military programs and operations. Less obviously, the costs have included constraints on American freedom of action and the compromise, if not the outright sacrifice, of other valued policy goals. No less important have been the many unintended consequences of U.S. actions that have, collectively, increased the threat to the United States and its interests.

Limitations of the Book

Although this book covers a wide range of topics, its scope is importantly limited in a number of respects. Five such limitations deserve explicit mention.

First, the book concerns only the costs of foreign oil dependence to the United States, rather than to other states, insofar as these can be isolated. Clearly, reliance on oil from foreign sources has imposed costs on a number of countries as well as on the broader international community. Arguably, however, the most fruitful place to begin an accounting of these costs is with the United States. As the largest consumer and importer of oil, the United States has paid the highest economic price. And how U.S. policymakers have responded to the economic costs and risks of foreign oil dependence has been especially consequential not only for the United States itself but for the world as a whole.

Second, the book is limited to the costs of dependence on foreign oil, to the exclusion of other foreign energy supplies. Such a distinction might be harder to justify in the case of some other countries, such as those in Europe and Japan, which have imported substantial quantities of coal, natural gas, and electricity. Dependence on energy sources of any kind from abroad is likely to result in certain costs. In the case of the United States, however, virtually all of the costs have been associated with oil. The only other form of energy that the United States imports in substantial quantities is natural gas. Yet gas imports, though growing, still amount to significantly less than 20 percent of total consumption, and most arrive via secure pipelines from Canada, which poses none of the problems that are characteristic of many oil exporting countries. In addition, the international natural gas market remains highly segmented, so that supply disruptions in one part of the world may have relatively little effect on prices in another. This situation is beginning to change with a growing trade in liquified natural gas (LNG), but U.S. imports of LNG in 2005 still met less than 3 percent of domestic demand. Nevertheless, the potential implications of continued increases in U.S. dependence on foreign natural gas will be considered in the last chapter.

Third, the book looks only at the costs that can be related to the international dimensions of oil dependence. Thus it disregards some of the costs that result from the U.S. economy's more general reliance on oil. Of particular concern in recent years has been the impact of burning fossil fuels on the global climate. But the widespread use of oil and petroleum products has long imposed a number of additional substantial environmental, health, and other social costs that have not been reflected in their price to consumers. According to one 1998 estimate, these additional costs amounted to between $232 and $943 billion per year, increasing the "real price of gasoline" by two to eight dollars per gallon (ICTA 1998, 34).

Fourth, the book does not consider some of the political and strategic costs associated with the transfer of hundreds of billions of dollars in oil revenues to exporting countries, especially when oil prices are high. After the first oil shock, Western policymakers were concerned about the effect that the sudden accumulation of unprecedented numbers of "petrodollars" by states in the Persian Gulf and elsewhere would have on the global financial system and searched for ways to "recycle" them (Spiro 1999). Since then, the focus has shifted to the negative impact of outsized revenues on the oil exporting countries themselves and their policies, or what Thomas Friedman has termed "petrolism" (Friedman 2006d). In many countries, this windfall has fostered corruption, stunted political development, and, paradoxically, even contributed to economic decline (Karl 1997). It has also empowered some states, such as Iran and Sudan, to engage in activities that are inimical to American interests and made them less vulnerable to external pressures. Of particular concern in recent years has been the use of Saudi oil wealth to promote a version of Islam, Wahhabism, that is hostile to the West and, directly or indirectly, to finance international terrorist organizations like al Qaeda (see, for example, Brisard 2002; Greenberg 2003; Greenberg 2004). As Fareed Zakaria has observed, "In almost every region, efforts to produce a more stable, peaceful and open world order are being compromised and complicated by high oil prices" (Zakaria 2005).

Although these consequences are important, they can be attributed only in part to the United States and its policies. Traditionally, only a small percentage of oil exports from the Middle East, for example, have been destined for the American market. More important, high oil prices and revenues are not something over which the United States can exert direct control. Rather, they are determined most immediately by world market conditions, including overall demand, supply, and the availability of spare production capacity. To be sure, as the world's single largest consumer and importer of oil, the United States has done more than any other country to shape global demand. Thus if Americans consumed and imported less, both prices and oil revenues would fall somewhat. But lower prices would in turn stimulate demand elsewhere while discouraging exploration and new investment in production capacity, thereby partially offsetting the positive effects of U.S. reductions.

In addition, the negative strategic consequences of oil revenues have varied substantially over the years. In the face of the sharp price hikes of recent years, it is easy to forget that for nearly a decade and a half, from the mid-1980s until the end of the 1990s, oil prices and the revenues earned by oil exporters remained relatively low. Yet throughout this period, the United States continued to incur high costs as a result of its foreign oil dependence.

Finally, it is important to note that the temporal scope of the study is restricted to the period since 1973. The United States has a long history of involvement with oil producing countries and regions, especially Latin America and the Persian Gulf, and it has been a net importer of oil since the late 1940s. Until the early 1970s, however, the economic costs and risks of foreign oil dependence were of little concern to policymakers in Washington, and both U.S. domestic and foreign energy policies were driven primarily by other considerations. These included supporting U.S.-based international oil companies in their efforts to gain oil concessions abroad, promoting the economic growth of America's economic and security partners, and protecting domestic producers from cheap foreign oil by imposing import quotas.

Why could the United States afford to be complacent? Through the late 1960s, imports accounted for less than 20 percent of total U.S. consumption. More important, the international oil market was generally characterized by a glut, which kept prices low. During the 1960s, world prices held steady at $1.80 a barrel, or approximately $10 per barrel in today's money (BP 2006). And in the event of a major supply disruption anywhere in the world, American oil producers had the capacity quickly to increase output in order to prevent a shortage. Thus the United States even encouraged Europe and Japan to become still more dependent on foreign oil as a means of hastening their postwar economic recoveries.

This complacency was reinforced by the experience of 1967, when Arab countries attempted to impose an oil embargo on the United States, Britain, and West Germany in response to the Arab-Israeli War of that year. Because of concurrent domestic disturbances in several oil exporting countries, Middle East oil production initially dropped by as much as six MBD before stabilizing at about 1.5 MBD below previous levels, equivalent to the amount of Arab oil that normally went to the three embargoed countries. Almost one MBD of this loss was quickly made up for by a surge in U.S. production, however, and increased output by Venezuela, Iran, and Indonesia more than compensated for the rest. The available supplies were redistributed where needed, and within a month, it was clear that the embargo was a failure (Yergin 1991, 555–57; Little 2002, 63–64; J. Pollack 2002, 82). Thus the 1967 oil crisis prompted no significant changes in the policies of the United States and its allies. Oil imports continued to grow as if there were no reason to be concerned.

By the early 1970s, however, the conditions that had allowed the United States to benefit from foreign oil dependence at little or no cost were no longer present. Because of rapidly growing demand in the United States and other industrialized countries, oil markets were tightening. Between 1965 and 1973 alone, world consumption grew by some 80 percent. And by 1972, U.S. producers were pumping at maximum capacity, which eliminated their ability to provide a supply cushion in the event of an emergency (Rutledge 2005, 8 and 43). In May of the following year, President Nixon ended the oil import quota that had been established in 1959. At the same time, the governments of a number of oil producing states were increasingly challenging the pricing policies and even the ownership positions of the major international oil companies that operated on their territories.

The full implications of these altered circumstances were driven home in 1973, when the next Arab oil embargo and production cutbacks resulted in shortages and a quadrupling of world oil prices. For the first time, the United States was not able to deal with a serious supply disruption. Since then, Americans have paid a high economic cost for foreign oil dependence, while reducing these costs has been an important goal of U.S. policy.

Organization

Just how dependent is the United States on foreign oil, and how did it become so dependent? Chapter 2 explores the nature and magnitude of U.S. foreign oil dependence. It explains that foreign oil dependence can take several distinct forms. Most familiar is the dependence that comes from importing significant amounts of foreign oil. Another, less obvious form of dependence results from allowing the domestic price of oil and petroleum products to be determined by world markets. Both of these forms of foreign oil dependence derive in turn from the economy's general reliance on oil, which currently meets about 40 percent of America's energy needs. Finally, the United States is indirectly dependent insofar as its major economic and security partners also rely heavily on foreign oil to power their economies. The chapter pays particular attention to the overall degree of oil dependence of the American economy and the level of oil imports, since these are the aspects of foreign oil dependence over which U.S. policy can exert the greatest degree of influence. After discussing the principal uses of oil, Chapter 2 describes the historical patterns of U.S. oil consumption, production, and the resulting need for ever-growing amounts of imports.

Why does U.S. foreign oil dependence matter? It would not be an issue but for the fact that it can have economic costs, and these costs can be substantial. Chapter 3 examines these actual and potential economic costs in some detail. It reviews the estimates that professional economists have generated and considers how important the costs are likely to be in the future. Although economists have often disagreed about the precise nature and magnitude of these economic costs, they have frequently put them in the range of tens of billions of dollars per year. The chapter first considers the routine and recurring costs associated with paying for oil imports, such as the transfer of wealth abroad and the consequent decrease in potential U.S. economic output. It then analyzes the costs that can follow unexpected supply disruptions and accompanying price increases, or "oil shocks." After reviewing the history of oil shocks, how they can hurt the economy, and estimates of their costs, Chapter 3 concludes with a discussion of the factors that will determine the likelihood, magnitude, and impact of future oil supply interruptions.

Chapter 4 examines the various economic policies that the United States has adopted since the early 1970s in response to foreign oil dependence and their costs. The first section looks at domestic efforts to reduce foreign oil dependence by limiting U.S. oil imports and consumption. Among the measures considered are those intended to discourage demand by making oil and petroleum products more expensive, to promote conservation and the more efficient use of oil, to substitute alternative fuels and energy sources, and to increase domestic oil production. The next section considers how the United States has attempted to mitigate the economic impact of oil shocks, chiefly through the use of price controls and the creation of the Strategic Petroleum Reserve. A final section describes how the United States has sought to achieve these goals in cooperation with other consumer countries. Although these measures, taken together, have reduced somewhat the economic costs and risks of foreign oil dependence, overall they have been quite modest in nature.

The next three chapters address the external policy measures that the United States has undertaken to reduce the likelihood and magnitude of oil shocks and the additional costs that those policies have entailed. Chapter 5 considers how dependence on oil from abroad has shaped U.S. foreign policy toward actual and potential oil producing regions of the world. It examines the ways in which the United States has sought to use diplomacy, economic and military assistance, and arms sales to strengthen and influence governments in a position to determine world oil supplies and prices. The chapter pays particular attention to the Persian Gulf, which has been and will remain the world's single largest source of petroleum exports. But it also looks at three other regions of increasing importance to the United States: Latin America, the Caspian Sea, and sub-Saharan Africa. The chapter shows that these efforts have been far from cost-free and that, in many cases, they have conflicted with other important U.S. policy objectives, such as the promotion of democracy, protection of human rights, good governance, and economic development.

Chapter 6 continues the examination of external responses to foreign oil dependence by considering the impact that it has had on American military policy. In contrast to the previous chapter, here the focus is exclusively on the Persian Gulf, which is where by far the most substantial military efforts have been directed and thus the military costs have been the highest. The chapter employs two complementary methods. The marginal cost approach involves identifying the specific programs, capabilities, and activities that the United States has undertaken for the purposes of protecting and ensuring access to foreign oil supplies and then adding up their costs. The total cost approach involves dividing the number of basic combat units in each service into the entire manpower and budget of that service and then multiplying the cost of each unit by the number of units attributable to oil-related missions. The chapter also considers the costs of the various military operations that the United States has conducted in the region to protect, directly or indirectly, American oil interests there. It finds that the total price tag of these military efforts has amounted to tens of billions of dollars per year since the early 1980s.

The scope of Chapters 5 and 6 is limited to the costs that American policy-makers knowingly incurred or should have been able to anticipate in choosing to pursue these courses of action. But U.S. foreign and military policies have frequently resulted in unintended consequences. Above all, they have undermined what were nominally friendly regimes, created new enemies, and empowered potentially hostile actors, thereby actually increasing the severity of the threats to U.S. interests, both oil-related and otherwise. These unintended consequences and the additional, unexpected costs they have imposed are the subject of Chapter 7.

Chapter 8 first summarizes the various costs, both material and intangible, that can be attributed to U.S. foreign oil dependence and the policies that it has spawned. It argues that although these costs have been often overlooked, they have been substantial. Just those costs that can be quantified have easily amounted to tens, and possibly hundreds, of billions of dollars each year. And the costs are likely to grow only larger in the coming years, should there be no significant reduction in U.S. foreign oil dependence or change in American policies. The chapter then reviews the principal options that exist for reducing the costs of foreign oil dependence and past policy responses, grouping them into three broad categories that parallel the discussion above. First, the United States could make renewed efforts to reduce oil consumption and, indirectly, its dependence on foreign oil. Second, it could increase its capacity to mitigate, if not neutralize, the impact of future oil shocks. And third, it could review its foreign and military policies toward oil producing regions with an eye toward ensuring their cost-effectiveness. Since these external policies have been the most costly of all the responses pursued by successive administrations, modifications in them to eliminate elements that were counterproductive or unnecessary to enhance energy security or to bring the costs in line with the benefits could yield the largest savings.

2 Taking the Measure of U.S. Foreign Oil Dependence

For too long our nation has been dependent on foreign oil.
President George W. Bush, January 23, 2007

J UST HOW DEPENDENT is the United States on foreign oil, and how did it get to be that way? Before we can assess the costs, it is important to understand the nature and magnitude of U.S. foreign oil dependence. To begin, we must recognize that foreign oil dependence can take several distinct forms. Most obvious is the dependence that results from importing significant amounts of oil and petroleum products from other countries and regions, or "import dependence." Another is the dependence that results from allowing the domestic price of oil and petroleum products to be determined by world markets, or "market dependence." Both of these forms of foreign oil dependence derive in turn from the American economy's general reliance on oil. Finally, the United States is indirectly dependent on foreign oil insofar as the economies of its major trading and security partners are themselves characterized by import and market dependence.

Particular attention should be paid to the overall degree of oil dependence of the American economy and the level of oil imports, since these are the aspects of foreign oil dependence over which U.S. policy can exert the greatest amount of influence. The United States has long supported the liberalization of international commerce. Thus it seems highly unlikely that it would ever again choose either to isolate its economy from the world oil market or to restrict trade and financial flows to and from other highly oil-dependent states.

U.S. Oil Dependence

The American economy is heavily dependent on oil.[1] In fact, oil has long been the single most important U.S. energy source, and it still accounts for some 40 percent of primary energy consumption in the United States. In contrast, coal and natural gas each provide about 23 percent, and nuclear power another 8 percent. All other energy sources, including hydro, wind, and solar power, still amount to just 6 percent (see Figures 2.1 and 2.2).[2]

Major Uses of Oil in the U.S. Economy

Why is oil so important to the U.S. economy? For the same reasons it has been described as "the world's most valuable energy resource" (Rutledge 2005, 1). Not only has oil been abundant, but it has the best physical characteristics of any energy resource. It is highly compact, yielding the greatest amount of energy per unit of weight and volume. In addition, as a liquid at standard temperatures and pressures, it is relatively easy to handle and transport. As a result

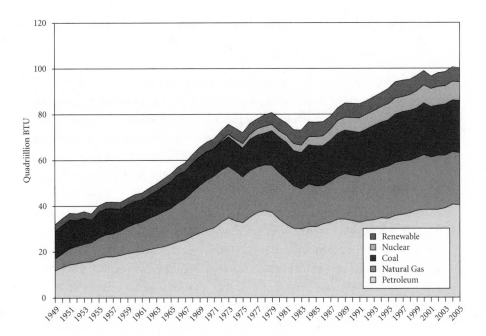

FIGURE 2.1 U.S. Energy Consumption, 1949–2005
SOURCE: EIA 2005b, tab. 13.

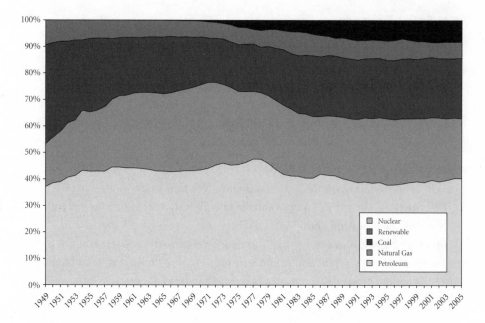

FIGURE 2.2 Shares of U.S. Energy Consumption by Fuel, 1949–2005
SOURCE: EIA 2005b, tab. 1.3.

of these desirable characteristics, oil and petroleum products enjoy a wide range of applications, the most important of which are transportation, steam and power generation, feed stocks for industry, and space and water heating.

Petroleum products fall into three main categories: fuels, finished nonfuel products such as solvents and lubricants, and feedstocks for the petrochemical and other industries. These can be further subdivided into a number of distinct products, as shown in Table 2.1.

Obviously, the vast majority of petroleum products are various forms of fuel. This dominance of fuel is reflected in the main uses to which oil products are put. By far the most important end-use sector is transportation, which accounts for about two-thirds of the demand (motor gasoline, diesel fuel, jet fuel). Next come industrial uses, which account for another quarter of all oil consumption (liquified petroleum gases [LPG], diesel fuel, petroleum coke). But of that 25 percent, approximately half takes the form of fuel while the other half is used as feedstocks (Lovins et al. 2004, 93). The remaining tenth goes for residential and commercial applications, mainly water and space heating (heating oil, LPG), and electric power generation (residual fuel oil).

TABLE 2.1 Principal U.S. Petroleum Products (2005)

Product	Amount (millions of barrel per day)	Percentage of Total
Motor gasoline	9.13	44.2
Distillate fuel oils (diesel fuel and heating oil)	4.11	19.9
Liquified petroleum gases (propane, butane, etc.)	2.02	9.8
Jet fuel	1.63	7.9
Residual fuel oil	0.91	4.4
Asphalt and road oil	0.54	2.6
Petroleum coke	0.51	2.5
Lubricants	0.14	0.7
Total	20.6	100.0

SOURCE: EIA 2005b, tab. 5.11.

U.S. Oil Consumption

Given its many desirable characteristics and applications, just how much oil do Americans use? Currently, the United States consumes more than 20 MBD of petroleum products, or approximately seven and a half billion barrels per year. This amounts to some three gallons a day for every man, woman, and child. The United States is by far the largest oil consuming nation, accounting for one-quarter of global demand.

With one principal exception, U.S. oil use has risen steadily in the past century. It grew especially rapidly during the postwar era. Between 1949 and 1973, consumption tripled from 5.8 MBD to 17.3 MBD, representing an annual growth rate of nearly 4.7 percent. After the first oil shock in 1973, demand briefly dropped but then resumed its climb, reaching 18.8 MBD in 1978. Only after the second oil shock, beginning in late 1978, did U.S. consumption decline substantially, reaching a temporary low of 15.2 MBD in 1983. Since then, however, it has increased almost every year, surpassing the 20 MBD mark in 2003.

Most of this growth has been driven by the transportation sector, which accounts for about 27 percent of all U.S. energy demand. Oil use in most other end-use sectors has actually declined dramatically over the past three decades (see Figure 2.3 and Tables 2.2 and 2.3). In the residential and commercial sectors, the amount of energy coming from petroleum dropped from 18.2 percent in 1973 to 11.8 percent in 1980, where it has more or less remained. In the electric power sector, it has fallen even more sharply, from nearly 18 percent in 1973 to just 3 percent in recent years. As a result, oil consumption in the residential and commercial sectors combined fell by half between 1973 and 1993 in both absolute and relative terms, while it has come down by two-thirds in the electric power sector. Only in the industrial sector, where feedstocks constitute the single largest category of petroleum use (OTA 1991, 32), has demand grown in absolute terms, while staying roughly constant (between 24 and 29 percent) as a share of total oil consumption.

How have these impressive reductions been achieved? In the residential and commercial sectors, the primary mechanisms have been gains in efficiency and greater use of electricity and natural gas for heating. In electric power generation, coal, nuclear, and natural gas units have replaced most older, oil-fired capacity. Even the industrial sector has largely displaced oil as a source of energy. The vast majority of the oil is used either as a feedstock or for on-site transportation and construction equipment (OTA 1991, 33–34; Plotkin and Greene 1997, 1179–80).

In contrast, oil use in the transportation sector has grown substantially in both absolute and percentage terms, from slightly more than half of total

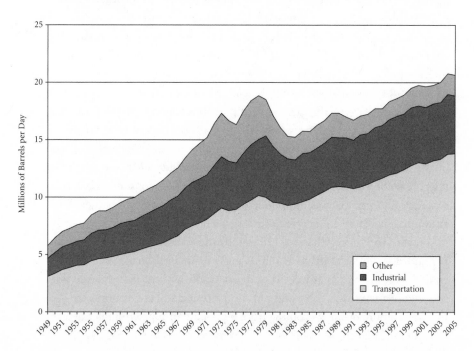

FIGURE 2.3 U.S. Petroleum Consumption, 1949–2005
SOURCE: EIA 2005b, tabs. 5.13a–d.

TABLE 2.2 U.S. Petroleum Consumption by End-Use Sector
(millions of barrels per day)

End-Use Sector	1973	1983	1993	2003
Transportation	9.05 (52.3%)	9.41 (52.3%)	11.12 (64.5%)	13.33 (66.4%)
Industry	4.48 (25.9%)	3.85 (25.3%)	4.44 (25.7%)	4.99 (24.8%)
Residential	1.49 (8.6%)	0.74 (4.9%)	0.80 (4.6%)	0.86 (4.4%)
Commercial	0.75 (4.3%)	0.55 (3.6%)	0.38 (2.2%)	0.38 (1.9%)
Electric power	1.54 (8.9%)	0.68 (4.4%)	0.49 (2.9%)	0.53 (2.7%)

SOURCE: EIA 2005b, tabs. 5.13a–d.

TABLE 2.3 Share of Energy from Petroleum by End-Use Sector

End-Use Sector	1973	1980	1999	2003
Transportation	95.8	96.5	97.4	96.4
Industry	27.9	31.1	36.9	29.1
Residential and commercial	18.2	11.8	11.7	11.6
Electric utilities	17.8	10.7	2.8	3.1

SOURCES: Davis 2000, tab. 2.4 (for 1980 and 1999); Davis and Diegel 2004, tab. 2.2 (for 1973 and 2003).

oil consumption in 1973 to two-thirds today. The size of that increase alone, approximately 4.5 MBD (50 percent), is greater than the current oil consumption of every country but China and Japan. Within the transportation sector, automobiles and light trucks are responsible for approximately 60 percent of all petroleum use, while medium and heavy trucks account for another 20 percent (Davis and Diegel 2004, tabs. 2.4, 2.5).

What accounts for this tremendous growth? Most directly, it can be attributed to an increase in both the number of vehicles on American roads and, secondarily, the amount each vehicle is used. Not only has the U.S. population grown, but the number of vehicles per 1,000 inhabitants increased from 481 in 1970 to 766 in 2002. Concomitantly, miles driven per capita rose from 5,441 in 1970 to 9,903 in 2002. As a result, total vehicle miles traveled in the United States more than doubled between 1975 and 2002, from 1.33 trillion to 2.86 trillion, an average annual growth rate of nearly 3 percent (Davis and Diegel 2004, tabs. 3.5, 8.1). Meanwhile, average fuel economy—the number of miles driven per gallon—increased in the late 1970s and early 1980s, but it has stagnated in more recent years and even begun to decline with the growing popularity of larger minivans and sport utility vehicles. Finally, there have been few commercially available substitutes for petroleum-derived motor vehicle fuels. Oil still supplies more than 95 percent of transportation energy needs.

Consequently, motor gasoline consumption in the United States rose by more than one-third between 1982 and 2002, from 98.5 to 133 billion gallons, and total highway fuel use increased by nearly one-half, from 113 to 168 billion gallons, over the same period (Davis and Diegel 2004, tab. 2.9; see also EIA 2005b, 147; ICTA 2005, 1). Today, American cars and light trucks alone consume 10 percent of all the oil used in the world (NRC 2002, 20), and Americans use ten times more gasoline per person than the global average (Egan 2004). Even in comparison with other industrialized countries, the United States stands out. Per capita demand for gasoline and diesel in the United States is three times greater than in Japan and two and a half times higher than in Britain, France, and Germany (Rutledge 2005, 11).

In the future, U.S. oil consumption is expected only to grow. In 2006, the Energy Information Administration (EIA) of the U.S. Department of Energy projected that total petroleum demand would rise from 20.7 MBD in 2004 to 27.6 MBD in 2030 in the reference case, which is based on business-as-usual trend estimates (EIA 2006a, ii). This would represent an increase of 33 percent, or an average annual growth rate of 1.1 percent. Even assuming high oil prices, the EIA estimated that consumption in 2030 would reach 25.2 MBD. And virtually all of this growth—more than 80 percent—would occur in the transportation sector. According to the EIA, refined petroleum products supplied to the transportation sector would increase from 13.7 MBD to 19.8 MBD in the reference case and 18.0 MBD in the case of high oil prices. In either case, transportation would account for more than 70 percent of all U.S. oil consumption (EIA 2006a, 179, tab. C4).[3]

Import Dependence

Without America's substantial reliance on oil, it could not be dependent on foreign oil. But foreign oil dependence is not a necessary consequence of oil use. Even at current levels of consumption, foreign oil dependence would not be an issue if the United States imported little or no oil and if the U.S. oil market was isolated from the rest of the world. In fact, neither of these conditions holds. The United States is a substantial net importer of oil, and domestic prices for petroleum and petroleum products are highly sensitive to international market conditions.

The United States now meets some 60 percent of its oil needs, or more than 12 MBD, via imports. Why is this the case? The basic cause is simple. U.S. oil consumption far exceeds domestic oil production. As a result, the United States has increasingly had to turn to foreign sources of oil in order to satisfy demand.

Stagnation and Decline of U.S. Oil Production

Commercial production began in Pennsylvania in 1859.[4] Since then, approximately three million wells have been drilled in the contiguous forty-eight states and Alaska (IEA 1998b, 47). Cumulative oil output now stands at approximately 200 billion barrels, the greatest of any country in the world. During most of the twentieth century, the United States was the world's largest oil producer. It was only surpassed by the Soviet Union in the mid-1970s. Although the United States moved temporarily ahead of Russia following the dissolution of the Soviet Union at the end of 1991, Saudi Arabia has consistently pumped more oil since then.

U.S. petroleum production grew fairly steadily until 1970, when total output reached 11.3 MBD. At that point, output in the lower forty-eight states peaked and began to decline. In 1977, oil from Alaska's North Slope began to make its way to market via the Trans Alaska Pipeline System (TAPS), eventually reaching 2.0 MBD in the late 1980s. As a result, overall production recovered somewhat and enjoyed a secondary peak of 10.6 MBD in 1985. Since then, however, the trend lines have been steadily downward, with production dropping below 7 MBD in 2005, the lowest level in more than five decades (see Figure 2.4).

This decline can be seen in both the number of producing oil wells and in average well productivity. The former reached an all-time high of 647,000 in 1985 before steadily dropping to 506,000 in 2005, while the latter peaked at 18.6 barrels per day per well in 1972 and then fell to 10.1 barrels per day per well in 2004 (EIA 2006b, 129, tab. 5.2). More fundamentally, decline in production reflects the depletion of the most important existing oil fields and the failure to find significant new ones. By the end of the twentieth century, more than 80 percent of the oil in the ten largest fields ever discovered in the United States had been removed. The famous East Texas oil fields, which once held more than 5 billion barrels, had been all but exhausted, and some three-quarters of the estimated 13 billion barrels of recoverable reserves in Prudhoe Bay, Alaska,

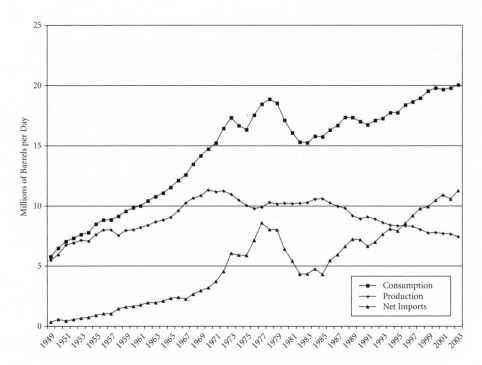

FIGURE 2.4 U.S. Petroleum Consumption, Production, and Imports, 1949–2005
SOURCE: EIA 2005b, tabs. 5.1.

which were not tapped until the 1970s, had already been pumped. Overall, as the 1990s came to an end, cumulative U.S. crude oil production had reached approximately 190 billion barrels, while remaining proved crude oil reserves stood at only 22 billion barrels (EIA 1999, 13–14). In 2005, overall U.S. petroleum reserves, including natural gas liquids and gas condensate, totaled less than 30 billion barrels, or just 2.4 percent of global reserves.[5]

This downward trend is expected to continue indefinitely. Small new discoveries of oil continue to be made, and improvements in production techniques steadily increase the amount of oil that can be recovered from a given formation. As a result, total proved U.S. petroleum reserves have remained roughly constant since the early 1990s. Nevertheless, each additional barrel of oil is, on average, more expensive to produce.

Thus the EIA projects that U.S. petroleum output, after rising slightly in response to higher world prices, will decline to 6.4 MBD by 2030.[6] This figure assumes no significant production at that time in the Arctic National Wildlife Refuge (ANWR) in Alaska, which could eventually reach rates of 1.0 to 1.35 MBD. But the EIA has estimated that production would not begin in the refuge until seven to twelve years after final approval is given by the U.S. government and that peak levels of production would not be reached until twenty to thirty years later, or sometime in the 2030s at the earliest (EIA 2005a, 101; EIA 2000). Of late, moreover, major oil companies have shown little interest in drilling there (Gerth 2005a).

Resulting Growth of U.S. Oil Imports

As a result, U.S. oil production has not been able to keep pace with oil consumption. In fact, the United States became a net importer of oil as early as 1946. For more than two decades thereafter, American imports of petroleum and petroleum products grew only slowly, remaining less than one-fifth of total oil consumption. In 1969, however, the amount of oil that came from abroad passed the 20 percent mark and then accelerated rapidly, peaking at more than 46 percent of consumption and 8.6 MBD in 1977. The level of imports held steady for two years after the 1973 oil shock because of the resulting economic recession. But between 1975 and 1977, it jumped sharply as a result of renewed demand and declining domestic production (EIA 2006b, 139, tab. 5.7).

The high oil prices of the late 1970s and early 1980s stimulated energy conservation and improvements in energy efficiency. At the same time, U.S. production enjoyed a resurgence following the opening of the Alaska pipeline in 1977. As a result, net U.S. oil imports declined by more than half between 1977 and 1982, to just 4.3 MBD, a figure that represented less than 30 percent of consumption.

Since 1985, however, rising consumption and declining domestic production have resulted in a steady two-decade-long rise in imports. In 1997, they reached a new high and, for the first time, provided for more than half of American demand. Now, net U.S. imports stand at more than 12 MBD and constitute some 60 percent of all oil use. Indeed, they amount to approximately 15 percent of total world output. Despite its still prodigious level of domestic petroleum production, the United States imports twice as much petroleum as Japan, which has no oil resources of its own, and more than all the countries of Europe outside the former Soviet Union combined. Only China, with more than three times the population and a much more rapid rate of economic growth, has the potential to rival the United States as an oil importer, and then only decades in the future (BP 2006) (see Figure 2.5).

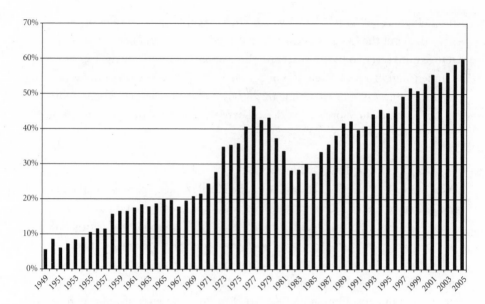

FIGURE 2.5 Imports as Share of U.S. Oil Consumption, 1949–2005
SOURCE: EIA 2005b, tabs. 5.1.

Where do U.S. imports come from? In 2005, more than half of the foreign crude oil and petroleum products consumed in the United States originated in just four countries: Canada (16.0 percent); Saudi Arabia (12.3 percent); Venezuela (12.1 percent), and Mexico (11.2 percent). Some 44 percent of all imports came from the members of the Organization of the Petroleum Exporting Countries (OPEC), which include Saudi Arabia and Venezuela, and a little less than half of that share (18.6 percent of the total) originated in the Persian Gulf. Since 1988, the shares of U.S. imports from OPEC and the Persian Gulf have averaged about 47 and 21 percent, respectively (EIA 2006b, 139, tab. 5.7). In comparison, other parts of the world are much more dependent on Middle East oil. In 2005, 82 percent of Japan's oil came from the region, as did nearly four-fifths of the imports to the rest of Asia (excluding China) (BP 2006).

Parallel to the projections of continued growth in U.S. oil consumption and continued decline in production, net U.S. imports are expected to rise substantially in future years. In 2006, the EIA projected that they would increase at an average annual rate of 1.4 percent in the reference case, reaching 14.4 MBD in 2020 and 17.2 MBD in 2030. Paradoxically, the EIA also estimated that net imports will be significantly higher, from 19.7 to 21.1 MBD in 2030, regardless of whether world oil prices are lower or higher than expected (EIA 2006a, 115, tab. 24).[7] Other recent twenty-year forecasts have predicted even higher levels, ranging from 19.2 to 22.3 MBD (EIA 2005a, 120, tab. 37).

Market Dependence

The source of U.S. oil imports was much more of a concern three decades ago than it is today. In 1973, it was possible for Arab oil producers to impose an embargo on exports to the United States. Even then, however, international oil companies were able to mitigate the impact of the embargo by redirecting supplies from other sources. Such a scenario is all but unimaginable now, moreover, given subsequent changes in world markets. The system of long-term contracts, which prevailed through the 1970s, has been replaced by a much more flexible market system, which allows oil shipments to be rerouted quickly in response to changes in supply and demand. As commodities, oil and petroleum products are fungible and will move to buyers willing to pay the highest price (Franssen 2003).

Thus an equally if not more important form of U.S. foreign oil dependence is the integration of American markets for crude oil and petroleum products into the corresponding world markets. During the 1970s, the United States maintained price controls on most domestically produced oil. As a result, the price of imported crude oil averaged about 50 percent higher than its domestic counterpart.[8] These price controls buffered American consumers somewhat from the first two oil shocks. But they also had the undesirable effect of discouraging both energy conservation and domestic production, thereby contributing to significantly higher levels of imports than might otherwise have been expected during the second half of the 1970s. Overall, these and other negative consequences were regarded as outweighing the benefits, and the Carter and Reagan administrations lifted price controls between 1979 and 1981.

Since then, the prices of oil and oil products in the United States have closely reflected those on world markets, which are determined by global conditions of supply and demand.[9] Thus even if the United States did not import a single barrel of oil, its economy could still be greatly affected by developments abroad. Because oil is traded on global markets, anything that affects supply or demand anywhere affects prices everywhere (Taylor and Van Doren 2005; see also Goldwyn and Billig 2005, 514). Indeed, economists argue, "The principal economic cost of an oil supply disruption arises because of the economic harm caused by an oil price shock, and this harm will occur whether or not the United States imports any oil" (Bohi and Toman 1996, 53). As a 1996 study by the U.S. General Accounting Office (GAO, now called the Government Accountability Office) noted:

> The integration of the U.S. oil market into the world oil market means that the United States cannot isolate itself from the effects of oil supply disruptions. As long as oil prices are set in the marketplace, oil price changes in one part of the world affect oil prices everywhere, including the United States. Reducing oil imports would not reduce the negative effects of oil price increases. (GAO 1996, 34)

Thus unless the United States were to reestablish oil price controls, higher prices resulting from a supply disruption overseas would hurt the U.S. economy just as much as regions that are even more dependent on foreign imports. Even with price controls on domestically produced oil, the U.S. government could do nothing about higher prices for imports short of doling out massive subsidies. As a result, the GAO study concluded, "Unless the United States were to shift fundamentally away from a market-based economy and ban all oil imports and exports, reducing oil imports could not substantially reduce the effects of oil supply disruptions on the U.S. economy" (GAO 1996, 34). And given that the share of oil imported today is much higher than it was in the early 1970s, the ability to isolate the American market is more limited than ever. It is simply not practical to consider making the United States independent of the global oil market in the foreseeable future (Yergin 2005, 55).

Indirect Foreign Oil Dependence

Even if the United States could somehow close off its oil markets, it would not be able to isolate itself completely from the effects of global oil supply disruptions and the resulting price hikes. It would still feel the impact of such disruptions on the economies of other countries. Not only has the United States relied heavily on foreign oil to meet its own energy needs, but so have many of its major economic and security partners. As a result, the United States is indirectly dependent on foreign oil. Any rise in prices or downturn in demand abroad that resulted from an oil shock would eventually ripple through the U.S. economy. "The interdependence of Western economies is such," notes one longtime student of American oil diplomacy, "that a disruption of oil supplies to heavily import-dependent Europe or Japan would have a negative impact on U.S. export earnings, prices and overall production and employment levels" (Bahgat 2001, 2; see also Cordesman 2003, 135–37).

Compared with the United States, Europe and Japan were relatively late to convert from coal to oil. But by the 1960s, they were quickly making up for lost time. Between 1965 and 1973 alone, oil consumption grew by more than 50 percent in Britain and Canada, more than doubled in France, Germany, and Italy, and more than tripled in Japan. During the same period, oil as a percentage of total energy consumption rose from 38 to 50 percent in Britain, 47 to 68 percent in France, 42 to 57 percent in West Germany, 66 to 76 percent in Italy, and 59 to 78 percent in Japan (BP 2006).

Since the first oil shock, oil consumption has either stagnated or declined in most of the industrialized countries. Canada and Britain have joined Mexico as net oil exporters, at least temporarily.[10] Nevertheless, many of America's trading and security partners remain heavily dependent on foreign oil, despite the fact that their oil use per capita is much lower than in the United States. With extremely limited energy resources of their own, Japan and South Korea rely on imported oil to meet nearly half of their energy needs. Notwithstanding North Sea oil production, the countries of Europe currently import approximately half of the oil they use from other regions, and three of the four largest European economies—those of France, Germany, and Italy—are almost entirely dependent on foreign oil. Even China, which until the mid-1990s was a net exporter, now takes approximately 50 percent of its oil from abroad, and that share has been growing rapidly. None of these countries, including the exporters, would be spared the impact of an oil price shock.

Conclusion

Even if the United States imported not a single drop of oil, it would still be highly dependent on foreign oil. Through the integration of its markets for oil and petroleum products in the corresponding world oil market and its high degree of economic and security interdependence with other oil using countries, it would still be vulnerable to the negative effects of oil market disruptions. This vulnerability is greatly amplified, however, by the status of the United States as by far the world's largest consumer and importer of oil. The next chapter examines the actual and potential economic costs of U.S. foreign oil dependence.

3   The Economic Costs and Risks of
U.S. Foreign Oil Dependence

*Oil dependence ranks among the most significant economic problems the
United States has faced over the past 30 years.*

David Greene and Nataliya Tishchishyna, "Costs of Oil Dependence"

U.S. FOREIGN OIL dependence would not matter but for the fact
that it can have economic costs, and these costs can be substantial. This was not always the case. For many years after World War II, the
growing level of U.S. reliance on oil from abroad imposed few economic costs.
For one reason, the international price of oil was relatively low. Throughout
the 1960s, it hovered around $10 per barrel in current dollars. In addition, the
United States and friendly countries maintained sufficient excess production
capacity so as to be able to compensate for almost any disruption of foreign
oil supplies. Thus neither the nationalization of Iran's oil industry in 1951, the
Suez crisis of 1956, nor the Arab-Israeli War of 1967 had a significant impact on
American oil supplies and prices. Following the first "oil shock" in 1973, however, the world price of oil rose substantially, eventually reaching approximately $90 per barrel in current dollars, and became much more volatile. Just
as important, that U.S. producers no longer possessed the ability to make up
for any loss of output or exports from oil producing states became evident at
that time.

As a result of those changes, U.S. foreign oil dependence has imposed significant economic costs and risks for more than three decades. Some are the
routine and recurring costs associated with paying for oil imports, such as
the transfer of wealth abroad and a decrease in potential domestic economic
output. Other costs are the result of unexpected supply disruptions and the
accompanying sharp price increases. As the 1996 National Security Strategy

noted, "The experiences of the two oil shocks and the Gulf War show that an interruption of oil supplies can have a significant impact on the economies of the United States and its allies" (Clinton 1996). With few exceptions, the principal disagreement among professional economists concerns the size of these costs and risks, not whether they exist.

This chapter examines these actual and potential economic costs of U.S. foreign oil dependence in some detail. It considers the full range of economic costs, and not just external costs. The latter refer to the spillover costs of one person's activities on another person's welfare, which are typically ignored by the market in the determination of prices (Bohi and Toman 1996, 2, 10). Thus some economic costs and risks are already reflected in the price of oil, but others are not, and even those that are accounted for need to be made explicit.

Recurring Economic Costs

Every day, millions of barrels of crude oil and petroleum products arrive in the United States from abroad via tanker and pipeline. And every day, hundreds of millions of dollars flow out of the country to pay for those imports (see Figure 3.1).

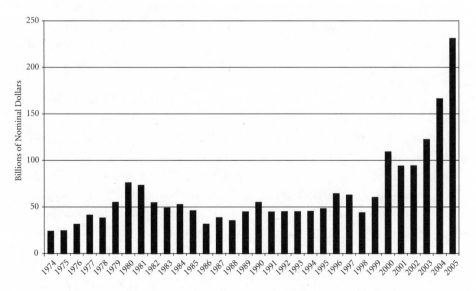

FIGURE 3.1 Cost of Net U.S. Petroleum Imports, 1974–2005
SOURCE: EIA 2007b, tab. 1.5.

Since the early 1970s, crude oil and petroleum products have accounted for a substantial amount of all U.S. imports, reaching nearly one-third of the total in 1980. Although this share dropped to well below 10 percent in the late 1980s and again in the 1990s as a result of temporary declines in both oil prices and the level of imports, it has grown steadily in recent years, reaching 15 percent in 2005. Net oil imports have also represented a large fraction of the U.S. trade deficit, fluctuating between 20 and 42 percent during the past decade. In 2000, the bill for petroleum imports passed 1 percent of U.S. gross national product (GNP) for the first time since 1985 (Holdren 2001, 44). Altogether, according to one estimate, Americans sent $2.2 trillion abroad for oil between 1975 and 2003 (Lovins et al. 2004, 15).

Wealth Transfers Abroad

Some fraction of this steady outflow of dollars represents a net transfer of wealth abroad. If world oil prices were set by market forces alone, then the amount paid would closely reflect the marginal cost of producing and transporting the last barrel of oil. For several reasons, however, the world oil market is less than fully competitive. In many oil producing countries, governments rather than market forces determine the amount of oil produced. In addition, oil exporting states have often attempted to coordinate output levels in order to influence world prices. This coordination has taken place primarily through the Organization of the Petroleum Exporting Countries (OPEC), whose twelve current members include ten of the world's thirteen largest oil exporters. But it has sometimes also involved important non-OPEC exporters, such as Mexico and Russia.

The net result is that world oil prices have typically been higher than they would have been in the presence of perfectly competitive oil markets. And as long as U.S. oil prices are set by world markets and world prices are artificially high, consumers will transfer wealth to producers, both at home and abroad. The size of the transfer to foreign producers, which is of primary concern here, is equal to the quantity of U.S. oil imports times the difference between the actual price and the competitive market price (Greene, Jones, and Leiby 1998, 60). Initially, this transfer takes the form of financial exchanges, but eventually, oil exporters may be expected to claim payment in real terms by purchasing goods and services from the United States. Thus more domestic output will have to go to exports, leaving fewer goods and services for consumption at home (Mork 1982, 89).

The principal question is not whether oil prices have been higher than competitive levels, but just how big this difference has been. Estimates of the competitive market price rest heavily on a number of assumptions. As a result, economists have disagreed over whether the difference is significant or minimal (Leiby et al. 1997, S–6). Nevertheless, the lack of consensus has not prevented economists from attempting to measure it. A 1993 Oak Ridge National Laboratory (ORNL) study chose $9.10 per barrel in 1990 dollars as a reasonable estimate for the period 1972–91. Using that figure, it calculated that the annual transfer of wealth to foreign suppliers during those two decades added up to $1.2 trillion, or a present value of $1.9 trillion, in 1990 dollars. Even if the competitive market price were assumed to have risen by 2 percent a year, the net wealth transfer would still have amounted to $1.0 trillion, or a present value of $1.76 trillion, in 1990 dollars (Greene and Leiby 1993, 30, 35–37). A later Oak Ridge study, using three different indicators, produced a slightly lower but still substantial estimate. It put the competitive market value at $11.27 per barrel for the years 1970 and 1999 and estimated the total wealth transfer abroad over that period at $1.16 trillion in 1998 dollars (Greene and Tishchishyna 2001, 17, 24). Thus if these government studies are reasonably accurate, U.S. consumers have transferred significantly more than $1 trillion to foreign oil producers so far, and the figure is still growing.

Loss of Potential Gross Domestic Product

The overall economic effect of chronic foreign oil dependence, as a consequence of both higher than competitive prices and the transfer of wealth abroad, is a decrease in potential total economic output, as measured by gross domestic product (GDP).[1] Higher oil prices crowd out other opportunities for consumption and saving (Toman 2002, 21). As a result, "the economy can produce somewhat less with the same endowment of capital, labor, materials, and other energy resources. Even if all resources were fully employed in the best uses, the potential to produce is reduced because oil is more scarce. The loss of potential GDP persists as long as oil prices remain elevated" (Greene and Tishchishyna 2001, 16).

How large have these losses been? According to the 1993 Oak Ridge study, the total potential GDP loss from 1972 to 1991 came to between $1.4 and $2.1 trillion, or a present value of between $2 and $3 trillion, in 1990 dollars, assuming a competitive market price of $9.10. Again, even if the competitive price were assumed to have risen by 2 percent per year, the potential GDP loss would still have been a hefty $1.2 to $1.8 trillion (Greene and Leiby 1993).

This finding is similar to that of a 1995 analysis by the U.S. General Accounting Office (GAO), which estimated that a sustained $10 increase in the price of oil would cause GDP to decline by about $50 billion per year (GAO 1996). The later Oak Ridge study put the overall GDP loss between 1970 and 1999, during which world oil prices averaged about $16.30 above the competitive price, at about $1.2 trillion in undiscounted 1998 dollars, or $40 billion per year (Greene and Tishchishyna 2001, 23–24).

Future Recurring Costs

There are good reasons to expect that the recurring economic costs to the United States of foreign oil dependence will be even higher in future years. First, net U.S. imports of petroleum and petroleum products are projected to rise substantially from the current level of more than twelve million barrels of oil per day (MBD) during the next two decades. Depending on oil prices, the most recent U.S. government projections for imports range between 13.2 and 15.3 MBD for 2015 and between 17.2 and 21.1 MBD for 2030, and these estimates are lower than those of recent years (EIA 2006a, 115, tab. 24).[2]

Second, although world oil prices are unlikely to sustain the peaks of more than seventy dollars per barrel experienced in 2006, most observers expect them to remain relatively high by historical standards and possibly to reach even higher levels (for example, Morgenson 2004; Rutledge 2005, 199; IMF 2005b, 169; Deutsch and Schlesinger 2006, 20). The basic problem is that global production is likely to have difficulty keeping up with rising demand, resulting in a tight market and continued upward pressure on prices over at least the medium term (West 2004; IMF 2005a, 18). In mid-2006, the EIA projected that world oil consumption would grow by roughly 1.4 MBD every year over the next two and a half decades, reaching a total of 118 MBD in 2030. This would represent a nearly 50 percent increase over the 2004 level of about 80 MBD. The International Energy Agency (IEA), the International Monetary Fund (IMF), and private groups have predicted similar or higher rates of increase. Even in the case of low economic growth, the EIA projected consumption would rise to more than 103 MBD in 2030, a still hefty 30 percent increase.[3]

Most of this growth is expected to occur in developing countries, led by China and India. Chinese oil consumption has more than doubled in the past decade, from just 3.4 MBD in 1995 to 7 MBD in 2005 (BP 2006). In 2002, China surpassed Japan as the second largest oil user, and its demand for oil seems unlikely to slow anytime soon. The EIA projects that Chinese consumption will reach 10.0 MBD in 2015 and 15.0 MBD in 2030, an annual growth rate of 3.8 percent. Oil consumption has also grown rapidly in India, from 1.3 MBD in 1993 to 2.6 MBD in 2004 (BP 2006). The EIA projects that it will continue to rise by an average of 2.4 percent per year, reaching 3.3 MBD in 2015 and 4.5 MBD in 2030 (see Table 3.1).

Oil use is also expected to increase in the industrialized world, although the majority of this growth will likely be due to the United States. The EIA projects that U.S. demand will increase from slightly more than 20 MBD to 23.5 MBD in 2015 and then 27.6 MBD in 2030, an annual average of 1.2 percent. Similar or higher rates of growth are also expected in South Korea, the former Soviet Union and Eastern Europe, and Latin America. But consumption in Western Europe is projected to rise by less than 1 MBD, while that in Japan will not grow at all (EIA 2006c, 87, tab. A4).

The EIA also projects that world oil production will rise equally fast (EIA 2006c, 158, tab. E4). But many observers are not so optimistic. During the 1980s and 1990s, the world oil market was able to count on a substantial amount of surplus production capacity to meet increases in demand. During the last several years, however, most countries, including the members of OPEC, have been producing at or close to their full capacity, and the level of output in many of the world's largest non-OPEC oil fields has already peaked. For example, Alaskan oil production has been declining since 1988, and the

TABLE 3.1 Projections of World Oil Consumption (June 2006)
(millions of barrels per day)

Region/Country	2003	2015	2025	2030	Average Annual Change (%) 2003–2030
OECD	48.5	53.9	57.4	59.7	0.8%
United States	20.1	23.5	26.1	27.6	1.2%
Non-OECD	31.6	44.5	53.3	58.2	2.3%
China	5.6	10.0	13.2	15.0	3.8%
India	2.3	3.3	4.1	4.5	2.4%
Eastern Europe/ Former Soviet Union	4.9	6.0	6.7	7.1	1.4%
Total	80.1	98.3	110.7	118.0	1.4%

SOURCE: EIA 2006c, tab. A4.

IEA expects North Sea production to fall by almost half, to three MBD, in 2020 (Mouawad 2005a; see also IEA 2004c, 107). Yet because oil prices have been relatively low for much of the period since 1985, investment in the oil industry has lagged. As a result, the IEA estimated in 2004 that some $2.2 trillion would need to be invested in exploration and development by 2030, or an average of $80 billion per year, if expected demand was to be met (Stevens 2004).

Whether the oil industry will actually be able and willing to make the necessary investment, however, is in doubt. According to the IEA, the industry increased investment in oil and natural production by just 5 percent between 2000 and 2005, after accounting for inflation, despite high prices (Bahree 2006). Indeed, private oil companies have reportedly cut investment in exploration during the last decade after a string of mergers led them to focus on cost-cutting and higher returns to shareholders (Mouawad 2004).[4]

Another brake on investment is that the international oil companies (IOCs) enjoy access to only a very small and declining share of the world's oil reserves. It is widely believed that where IOCs have remained in or been allowed back into a country, both oil production and capacity have grown substantially. Their expertise and access to capital have been instrumental in achieving many of the recent production gains in places such as Venezuela, Nigeria, Algeria, and the United Arab Emirates (Sieminski 2005, 38). According to one estimate, however, Western oil companies as a whole have unrestricted access to only 6 percent of known reserves, mainly in North America and Europe, and are able to invest in countries that possess an additional 11 percent of reserves through joint ventures or production sharing agreements (Mouawad 2006). Even then, important producers such as Venezuela and Russia have recently sought to change the terms of previous agreements with private companies, calling into question their attractiveness as destinations for future private investment.

Instead, much will depend on the behavior of state-owned or national oil companies (NOCs), which control the vast majority of the world's oil reserves. Yet they may be no more willing or able to sink substantial additional funds into new production capacity. Given the experience of many with overinvestment in the 1970s, such producers may follow a cautious approach to investment decisions (IMF 2005a, 14). Of perhaps even greater concern is the fact that "with the exception of Saudi Aramco, no national oil company in any OPEC country has a good track record in the exploration and development business. The harsh reality is that it has been difficult for national oil companies of the Persian Gulf oil states to muster the capital, technology, and human resource capabilities to find and develop significant volumes of oil" (Barnes and Jaffe 2006, 149; see also Sieminski 2005, 37). Finally, pressing social needs generated by rapidly growing populations and, in some cases, large government debts have greatly limited the funds available for investment in the oil sector, even at a time of record high revenues (IMF 2005a, 15; Barnes and Jaffe 2006, 149).[5] As former Federal Reserve Chairman Alan Greenspan recently concluded, "Unless those policies, political institutions, and attitudes change, it is difficult to envision a rate of reinvestment by these economies adequate to meet rising world oil demand" (Greenspan 2006, 7).

The most critical player in this regard is Saudi Arabia, which has been the single largest oil producer for more than a decade and sits on nearly one-quarter of the world's proven reserves. In 2004, the state-owned oil company, Saudi Aramco, announced plans to boost production capacity from 10.5 MBD to 12.5 MBD by 2009 and claimed that it was studying scenarios for raising production to 15 MBD (Morrison 2004; Dickey 2006). At about the same time, the EIA projected that Saudi production capacity would rise to 14.4 MBD in 2015 and then to an impressive 22.5 MBD in 2025 (EIA 2004b, 213). More recently, however, some experts have raised doubts about the ability of Saudi Arabia to sustain production at much more than current rates, even after investing tens of billions of dollars (Gerth 2005b; Simmons 2005; Barnes and Jaffe 2006, 149). And perhaps in response to such doubts, in 2006, the EIA revised its projections of Saudi production capacity in 2025 dramatically downward, to just 15.1 MBD (EIA 2006c, 155, tab. E1).

As a result of these trends and expectations, a number of analysts expect prices to stay relatively high in the coming years. As one recent study concluded, "While the world will not soon 'run out of oil,' new supplies are almost surely going to be more difficult and expensive to produce than in the past" (Deutsch and Schlesinger 2006, 20). In addition, the Saudis, who have traditionally played a key role in keeping prices stable and relatively low, appear to support higher prices than they have in the past (Rutledge 2005, 199; Mouawad 2005c; Bronson 2006).

To be sure, recent price spikes reflect more than the overall balance of supply and demand. They also include a scarcity, risk, or "fear" premium, estimated to be at least $5 to $10 and perhaps as much as $15 to $20 dollar per

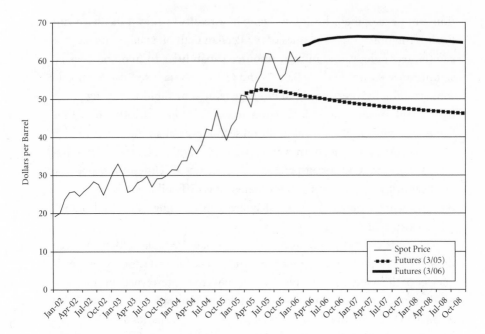

FIGURE 3.2 Crude Oil Spot Prices and Futures, 2002–2006
SOURCE: IMF 2006, fig. 1.20.

barrel (Morrison 2004; Lauerman 2005, 1; Yergin 2006), owing to a heightened possibility of supply disruptions because of political turmoil and conflict in many oil producing regions. But supply disruptions are a serious concern only when the system lacks sufficient spare production capacity to compensate for unexpected losses. And such excess capacity, which has been steadily drawn on to meet rising demand, now stands at its lowest level in more than thirty years and is not expected to increase significantly in the foreseeable future, resulting in an oil market that continues to be tight (IMF 2005a, 10, 18; IMF 2005b, 170; Deutsch and Schlesinger 2006, 17).[6]

The likelihood of sustained high prices is also suggested by dramatic recent rises in oil futures contracts. From 1986 until 2002, the price of longer-term futures stayed between $18 and $21 per barrel, even as market prices fluctuated between a low of $10 and a high of $30 (Horsnell 2004). Since 2003, however, long-term futures prices have risen steadily, surpassing $30 per barrel in mid-2004 and then $40, $50, $60, and even $70 per barrel in rapid succession during the following two years (see Figure 3.2) (Norris 2006).

The Economic Costs of Oil Shocks

In addition to the recurring economic costs associated with high levels of imports, the United States has been subjected to several oil shocks involving sharp increases in the price of oil and some restrictions on supply. Although infrequent, these shocks have imposed substantial short-term adjustment costs on the U.S. economy and could do so again in the future.

The History of Oil Shocks

Traditionally, oil shocks have been precipitated by sudden and unexpected disruptions in the supply of oil. Since 1970, there have been four particularly severe supply disruptions. These have had differing impacts on the price of oil and on the U.S. economy (see Table 3.2).[7]

The first important supply disruption and price shock occurred in late 1973. After being fixed at $1.80 per barrel through the 1960s, the posted price on which long-term contracts for internationally traded oil were based rose to $3 between 1970 and 1973 under growing pressure from the OPEC countries (Yergin 1991, 577–84). But it was poised to go much higher. Following the U.S. intervention in

TABLE 3.2 Major Oil Supply Disruptions Since 1973

	First Oil Crisis (10/73)	Second Oil Crisis (12/78)	Iran-Iraq War (10/80)	Iraq-Kuwait War (8/90)
Cause	Arab production decrease	Iranian production decrease	Loss of Iraqi and Iranian production	Loss of Iraqi and Kuwaiti exports
Duration	6 months	4 months	5 months	7 months
Net supply decrease (duration)	4.3-4.5 MBD (2 months) 2.2-2.6 MBD (2 months)	5.3-5.6 MBD (2 months) 3.8 MBD (2 months)	3.7-4.1 MBD (2 months) 2.5-3.0 MBD (3 months)	5.0-5.3 MBD (2 months) 4.0-4.7 MBD (3 months)
Maximum price increase	$3.01 (10/73)– $11.65 (1/74)	$14.94 (12/78)– $30.75 (1/80)	$34.63 (10/80)– $39 (2/81)	$16.54 (7/90)– $32.88 (10/90)
Global excess production capacity	3.75 MBD	4.55 MBD	6.70 MBD	6.20 MBD
OECD petroleum stocks (days)	Public: 0 Private: 70	7 65	9 77	25 61

SOURCES: Morse and Jaffe 2001, append. B. Price data: Yergin 1991; EIA 2006d.

the Arab-Israeli War that October, OPEC unilaterally raised the posted price by some 70 percent, to $5.12 per barrel. Simultaneously, the Arab members of the organization agreed to scale back oil production by 5 percent per month until Israel withdrew its forces from Arab territories, and several embargoed all oil shipments to the United States. As a result, by December 1973, Arab oil output had declined by five MBD, or nearly 10 percent of free world production.[8] At that time, the Arab states decided to defer making any further cuts, but OPEC took advantage of the leverage that the supply reduction had provided to boost the price to $11.65, a nearly fourfold increase over early October. The following March, the Arab oil ministers agreed to end the embargo and restore production to pre-October volumes, but the posted price remained at the new, much higher level (Long 1985, 24; Yergin 1991, 606–8, 614; Miglietta 2002, 274).

The second oil crisis began in October 1978, when Iranian oil workers went on strike. Up to that point, Iran had been the fourth largest oil producer, after the Soviet Union, the United States, and Saudi Arabia. By the end of the year, however, its production had dropped sharply, from approximately 6 MBD to less than 1 MBD, and its exports had fallen from 4.5 MBD to nothing. Because other states increased their output in order to compensate for the decline, overall noncommunist production decreased by only 2 MBD, or about 4 percent. But because many oil companies, independent refiners, and governments responded by building up their inventories, the net shortfall amounted to as much as 5 MBD, which was comparable in size to the previous oil shock. To make matters worse, Saudi Arabia, after raising its output from 8.3 MBD in September to 10.4 MBD in December, reduced production to 9.8 MBD during the first quarter of 1979 and then temporarily lowered it by another 1 MBD during the second quarter, generating additional fears of a shortage. As a result of such fears, prices on the spot oil market more than tripled between October 1978 and November 1979, from $13 to a temporary high of $41 dollars per barrel, notwithstanding the fact that overall global production was higher in 1979 than it had been the previous year. The higher spot prices in turn facilitated a steady ratcheting up of OPEC contract prices, which rose from less than $14 at the end of 1978 to an average of nearly $29 a year later and eventually stabilized at more than $34 dollars per barrel in mid-1980. In absolute terms, this price hike was even greater than that of the first oil shock (Yergin 1991, 678–96; Quandt 1982, 14; Rustow 1982, 183–84; Long 1985, 27–28).

Hardly had the second oil crisis subsided when another shock rippled through the system with the outbreak of the Iran-Iraq War in September 1980.

Each party to the conflict quickly targeted the other's oil production and export facilities in the Persian Gulf. In addition, Syria shut down the Iraqi pipeline through its territory, leaving Turkey as the only outlet for Iraq's exports. Altogether, the war temporarily removed as much as 4 MBD from the market, or some 8 percent of free world demand. In response, spot prices jumped as high as $42 dollars per barrel, and most OPEC countries raised their official contract prices to $36 per barrel. One reason for the relatively modest size of the price increase in comparison with the previous two oil shocks was that, this time, Saudi Arabia quickly stepped up its own output by nearly 1 MBD, and it temporarily refused to raise the posted price of its oil above $32 per barrel. In addition, demand in the industrialized countries was already dropping sharply as a result of the earlier price increases, and oil companies could draw on the substantial stocks they had accumulated the previous year. Thus spot prices declined almost as quickly as they had risen, falling to $35.50 by the end of the year and then just $32.5 by mid-1981 (Yergin 1991, 711–14; Keohane 1984, 235; Long 1985, 29; Ikenberry 1988, 100).

The fourth noteworthy oil shock followed Iraq's invasion of Kuwait in August 1990. The invasion and subsequent UN sanctions removed 4 to 5 MBD in exports from the market, or roughly 7 percent of global production. In response, prices on the spot market doubled, from approximately $16.50 per barrel in July to nearly $33 in October. Nevertheless, the crisis was short lived. Once again, Saudi Arabia quickly ramped up its output, this time by 3 MBD, and other OPEC countries added another 1.2 MBD in production. By January 1991, prices had fallen back to prewar levels and the crisis was effectively over (see OTA 1991, 7; Greene, Jones, and Leiby 1998).

How Oil Shocks Hurt the Economy

As Philip Verleger has pointed out, with market mechanisms, the fundamental problem of disruptions is not physical shortages but price increases and their economic consequences (Verleger 1994, 7). Thus, broadly speaking, oil shocks can have three negative effects.

First, they may result, at least temporarily, in increased outlays for oil imports. Oil consumption and oil production are relatively unresponsive (inelastic) to price hikes in the short run.[9] Thus sudden reductions in supply can cause prices to rise dramatically, and it can take a while before higher prices result in significantly lower demand and greater levels of domestic supply. One reason for this lack of responsiveness is that increased oil production and the replacement of oil burning machinery with substitutes that are more efficient or use other energy sources require large capital investments and long lead times. In the meantime, consumers must pay inflated prices for the oil they continue to import, which effectively reduces their income and purchasing power. The country must export more goods and services to pay for each barrel of imported oil (Leiby et al. 1997, S–7; Bohi and Toman 1996, 74; Huntington 2005, 4).

Second, oil shocks may reduce over the longer term a country's potential economic output, assuming that prices remain at an elevated level. In response to higher energy prices, firms may use less energy, which reduces the amount of output that can be produced with a given amount of capital and labor. As a result, the productivity of both labor and capital declines (GAO 1996, 32). In a sense, this effect is no different from that of a more gradual price increase.

Thus the most distinctive cost of oil shocks is how they may temporarily cause economic output to fall below even the now diminished full potential, or what are called macroeconomic adjustment costs. As one study explains:

> In the short run, the economy must adjust by re-balancing outputs and inputs of labor, materials, energy, and capital in ways that may end up costing more than is necessary in the long-run (*more* than the loss of potential GNP). Wages and prices do not adjust immediately to the new price of oil for reasons such as cost-of-living provisions in labor contracts and entitlement programs. Substitution of other energy sources and other factors of production for oil take time because of the durability of . . . energy-using equipment. The GNP level that can be reached in the short-run is necessarily lower than that which could be reached if the economy were able to adjust to the long-run, optimal, prices and wages. (Leiby et al. 1997, S–8)

The magnitude of these costs depends on the size of the oil price increase as well as the vulnerability of the economy to adjustment losses for a price shock of a given size (Leiby et al. 1997, S–9). Because these costs result from the economy's inability to respond quickly, they are temporary and are believed to dissipate within three to five years (Greene and Tishchishyna 2001, 16). In the meantime, however, the economy will experience inflationary pressures and increased unemployment (OTA 1991, 106).

It should be emphasized that these last two effects—loss of potential economic output and macroeconomic adjustment costs—are independent of the level of U.S. oil imports. Rather, they are primarily a function of the size of the price rise and the nation's overall oil consumption. As long as market forces prevail, a decrease in imports not accompanied by a comparable decrease in consumption would not substantially lower the costs of an oil shock. U.S. participation in the world oil market means that the United States cannot isolate itself from the effects of oil supply disruptions (GAO 1996, 3, 32–35; see also Mork 1982, 95; Bohi and Toman 1996, 53).

Costs of Past Oil Shocks

How much have oil shocks hurt the U.S. economy? Some analysts, including former Federal Reserve Chairman Alan Greenspan, have noted a striking correlation between oil supply disruptions and economic downturns (Hamilton 1983; Greenspan 2002). As one study concludes, "Significant oil price shocks preceded every recession of the past three decades and every one of the three significant oil price spikes (1973–74, 1979–80, 1990–91) was followed by a recession" (Greene and Tishchishyna 2001, 28).

The recessions associated with the oil shocks of the 1970s were especially severe. For example, after growing between 5 and 6 percent in 1972 and 1973, real U.S. GNP fell by 0.6 percent in 1974 and by an additional 1.1 percent the following year before recovering. Inflation nearly doubled from 3.3 percent in 1972 to 6.2 percent in 1973, and then again to 11.0 percent in 1974. Meanwhile, unemployment jumped from an annual average of just 4.9 percent in 1973 to 8.5 percent two years later, a postwar record (Mork 1982, 85).

Economic studies have offered varying estimates of the size of the actual economic costs of oil shocks. Some have focused on the resulting decline in the share of economic output. For example, the National Petroleum Council calculated that the 1973–74 Arab oil embargo resulted in a reduction in real GNP of 2.7 percent and that the 1979 Iranian revolution triggered a 3.6 percent fall in real GNP (OTA 1991, 12). Another set of analyses found that U.S. GDP fell by 2.5 percent in 1974, 5 percent in 1975, and 4.5 percent in 1976 and that the second oil crisis caused a decrease in GDP of 1 percent in 1979 and 4 percent in 1980 (Greene, Jones, and Leiby 1998, 60; see also Hickman, Huntington, and Sweeney 1987, 10–11).

Other studies have sought to measure the total macroeconomic adjustment costs imposed by oil shocks over the decades since 1973. These estimates have been on the order of $1 to $3 trillion, although most of the costs were in fact incurred during the years following the first two oil shocks. For example, an earlier, but perhaps the most detailed, analysis found that from 1972 to 1991 the macroeconomic adjustment costs totaled between $800 million and $1.3 trillion, or a net present value of about $1.4 to $2.3 trillion (in 1990 dollars). But these costs peaked at $76 billion in 1974 and again at $124 billion in 1980 (1990 dollars).[10]

To be sure, some economists have questioned whether oil shocks by themselves have had a significantly negative impact on the U.S. economy (for example, Bohi and Toman 1996; Barsky and Kilian 2004). Douglas Bohi in particular has argued that energy prices appear to have had little to do with macroeconomic failures during the 1970s. Rather, in his view, unenlightened monetary policies intended to prevent inflation could explain the sharp drops in GDP that occurred in the United States, as suggested by the fact that not all advanced industrialized countries experienced a recession after the 1979–80 price shock (Bohi 1989; Bohi 1991). More generally, too much attention to the period 1973–85, when the price of oil rose well above historic norms, could provide a distorted picture of how the oil market has performed both before and after the shocks of that era (Bohi and Toman 1996, 32).

Estimates of the Costs of Future Oil Shocks

Such skepticism is not widely shared, however. According to a recent survey, the most thorough research to date has found that postshock recessions are indeed largely attributable to jumps in oil prices and could not have been avoided by different monetary policy responses (Jones, Leiby, and Paik 2004, 27). Thus many economists have attempted, since at least the early 1980s, to estimate the possible costs of future oil shocks. Given the potential consequences, the interest in such forecasting is understandable.

Unfortunately, these predictions, while suggestive, have varied substantially. One reason for this variance is that they have not always focused on the same consequences. Some studies have attempted to measure the total future costs of occasional supply disruptions over a number of years. For example, a 1990 U.S. Department of Energy (DOE) study put the net present value of three hypothetical disruptions between 1990 and 2020 at $650 billion, or an average of $22 billion per year. Similarly, a 1993 Oak Ridge study calculated that the net present value of GNP losses and economic adjustment costs from hypothetical supply disruptions between 1993 and 2010 could be $400 billion, or again about $22 billion per year (GAO 1996, 33). A 1992 report by the Congressional Research Service arrived at a somewhat lower but still substantial estimate of $6 to $9 billion for the average annual cost of the risk of supply disruptions (CRS 1992, 8).

More common have been efforts to measure the potential loss of economic output from a single hypothetical oil shock. Even these efforts, however, have employed widely differing theoretical models and assumptions. Particularly important variables are the expected size and duration of the supply disruption, oil's share of GDP and energy consumption, the responsiveness of supply and demand to changes in energy prices, and the policy responses undertaken by government. In addition, studies have used varying impact measures and calculated costs in terms of different reference points, making comparisons even more difficult.

One of the first attempts employed a computerized macroeconomic model developed at the Massachusetts Institute of Technology that had previously been used successfully to analyze the effects of the oil shocks of the 1970s (Mork 1982, 98–101). This study assumed a one-year oil supply disruption of 10 MBD occurring unexpectedly in 1985, which would cause the overall price of energy to rise by about 35 percent in real terms in the first year, 17 percent in the second year, and 5 percent in the third. This analysis predicted that real GNP would fall by 7.9 percent ($121 billion in 1972 dollars) in the first year, 4.1 percent ($64.3 billion) in second, and 2.8 percent ($45.3 billion) in third. The total economic cost was put at $260 billion in 1972 dollars.[11]

A 1984 study by the U.S. government's Office of Technology Assessment (OTA) estimated the impact of prolonged global supply shortfall of 9–10 MBD that resulted in a 3 MBD reduction in the amount of oil available in the United States. On the assumption that domestic producers were able to replace the entire U.S. shortfall by the end of five years, the study calculated that economic output would fall by an annual average of about 3.5 percent, with a maximum loss of 5 percent occurring in the second year after the start of the supply disruption. In the event that only half of the initial shortfall was replaced, the estimated average GNP loss amounted to 6.2 percent, with a maximum of 10 percent occurring in the second year (OTA 1991, 107).

A study conducted at about the same time by the Energy Modeling Forum at Stanford University produced similar, if slightly lower, results. It employed fourteen different widely used models of the aggregate U.S. economy to predict the effects of a hypothetical 50 percent increase in oil prices (from $36 to $54 in 1983 dollars) that persisted over four years. The median estimates for the drop in real economic output (GNP) were 1.4 percent ($47 billion in 1983 dollars) in the first year, 2.9 percent ($97 billion) in the second year, 2.5 percent in the third year, and 2.1 percent in the fourth year. Total projected

GNP losses during the four-year period ranged from $142 to $609 billion, with an average loss of $328 billion in 1983 dollars. Most of this drop in real output could be attributed to temporary declines in aggregate demand that would push the economy well below the full-employment level. In addition, the hypothetical oil shock was expected to result in a further $125 billion (1983 dollars) on average in losses due to the increased cost of oil imports. More U.S. exports would be required to pay for each imported barrel of oil, leaving fewer domestic goods for internal use (Hickman, Huntington, and Sweeney 1987; see also Bohi and Toman 1996, 48–50; Greene and Leiby 1993, 35, 39–40).

A second OTA study, published in 1991 immediately after the Gulf War, examined the impact of a major supply disruption in which the entire Persian Gulf oil production—then approximately 16 MBD—was removed from the world market for five years, resulting in an initial loss of about 4 MBD to the U.S. economy. Assuming that no major effort was made to replace U.S. oil use, it found that such a disruption would cause oil prices to more than double, rising from an assumed baseline of $22 to $49.70 after two years and then drop to $43.5 after five years. As a result, real GNP would decline by 5 percent after two years and remain 2 percent below the initial baseline after five years. In a second scenario, the study assumed that an aggressive U.S. policy to replace oil use resulted in a reduction in demand of 1.4 MBD in the second year and 3.0 MBD in the fifth year. In that case, it estimated that GNP would still fall by 4.6 percent after two years and 1.6 percent after five years (OTA 1991, 108–11).

One of the most recent studies analyzed the effects of a hypothetical two-year supply disruption in 2005–2006 that was similar in size to those of 1973–74 and 1978–79. It assumed a reduction in OPEC supply of 4.2 MBD, or 5 percent of world production, in 2005, followed by the loss of an additional 2.8 MBD in 2006 and then a gradual increase in OPEC production by 0.7 MBD per year until 2010. It calculated that oil prices would more than double initially and that the U.S. economy would lose a total of $520 billion in 1993 dollars (Greene, Jones, and Leiby 1998).

In sum, a number of studies have shown that any future oil shock would have a significant negative impact on the U.S. economy. Just how big this impact could be has been a matter of disagreement, but estimates of the economic losses have consistently run in the hundreds of billions of dollars and reached as high as $1 trillion when inflation is taken into account. Recent economic analyses suggest the following rules of thumb. Assuming an oil price of $58 per barrel and global consumption of 85 MBD, oil prices would rise by 9.1 percent for each 1 MDB net oil disruption, although increases anywhere in the range of 6.1 percent to 18.2 percent could not be ruled out (Huntington 2005, 6–7). In turn, U.S. GDP would decline by between 0.024 percent and 0.055 percent for each 1.0 percent rise in oil prices during the first year or two following an oil shock (Jones, Leiby, and Paik 2004, 28; Jimenez-Rodriguez and Sanchez 2005; Huntington 2005, 32–33). Thus a major supply disruption of 5 MBD could cause oil prices to rise by 30 to 90 percent and cut U.S. output by between 0.72 percent and 5 percent, or roughly $86 to $600 billion per year, assuming a GDP of $12 trillion.

Factors Influencing the Costs of Future Oil Shocks

Needless to say, estimating the economic costs of future oil shocks may be more of an art than a science. Much uncertainty necessarily surrounds the process. To make matters worse, many of the factors that can influence those costs have changed significantly over the years and continue to do so. For analytical purposes, the most important factors can be grouped into two main categories: those that would determine the magnitude and likelihood of an oil shock and those that would determine the economic impact of a shock of a particular size and duration (see Table 3.3).

Size and Likelihood of an Oil Shock

Future oil shocks cannot be ruled out. Indeed, we can be virtually certain that another major supply disruption will someday occur. The difficulty lies in predicting when it will happen and how big it will be.

TABLE 3.3 Factors Influencing the Economic Costs of Future Oil Shocks

Size and Likelihood of an Oil Shock
  Geographical Concentration of Supply
  Stability of Oil Producing Countries and Regions
  Availability of Spare Production Capacity
  Strategic Petroleum Stocks
  Market Mechanisms

Economic Impact of an Oil Shock
  Oil Intensity of the U.S. Economy
  Government Policy Responses
  Demand Elasticity of Oil

Geographical Concentration of Supply   Two closely related determinants are
the degree of geographical concentration of global oil production and the
stability of the most important oil producing countries and regions. If oil
production is concentrated in just a few places, then the risk of a major supply
disruption depends heavily on the stability of those areas. If, by contrast, oil
production is widely dispersed geographically, then instability in one or even
several oil producing countries may not pose a significant risk of a major
supply disruption.

Since the oil shocks of the 1970s, the world's oil supply has arguably become more diversified. In the mid-1970s, it was highly concentrated in OPEC
countries in general and the Persian Gulf states in particular.[12] At that time,
OPEC oil output reached more than 50 percent of the world total and more
than 60 percent of production outside the Soviet Union. At the same time, oil
production in the Persian Gulf reached 37 percent of the global total and more
than 44 percent of non-Soviet production. Saudi Arabia's share of world and
noncommunist oil production peaked slightly later, in 1981 following the outbreak of the Iran-Iraq War, when it reached more than 17 percent and nearly
22 percent, respectively (see Figure 3.3).

The high oil prices of the mid- to late 1970s and early 1980s, however, eventually led to a significant decline in global demand as well as increased oil
production in other regions. As a result, the OPEC and Persian Gulf shares of
world oil production dropped precipitously. By 1985, OPEC output had sunk to
29 percent of the world total and 37 percent of that outside the Soviet Union.
Production by the Persian Gulf states dropped to just 18 percent of global supply and 23 percent of non-Soviet production. Saudi Arabia's respective shares
fell to just 6.3 and 7.9 percent.

Meanwhile, the share of the world's oil supply coming from other regions
grew substantially. The percentage produced by members of the Organization
for Economic Cooperation and Development (OECD), which includes the most
developed countries, grew from a low of 22.6 percent in 1976 to a high of 34.9
percent in 1985, thanks in large part to the arrival of oil from the North Sea and
Alaska's North Slope. As a share of non-Soviet oil production, OECD output
went from 27 to 41 percent during the same time period. Output in the Soviet
Union, which became a significant exporter, also grew markedly. As a share of
total world production, it rose from less than 15 percent in 1973 to nearly 22 percent in 1983. And output from the rest of the developing world doubled as a share
of total world oil production, rising from 7.5 percent in 1973 to 15 percent in 1985.

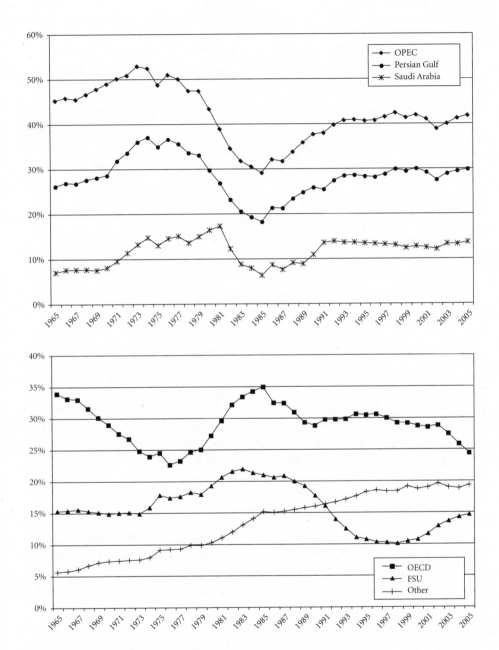

FIGURE 3.3 Distribution of World Oil Production, 1965–2005

SOURCE: BP 2006.

Since the mid-1980s, however, oil production has once again become more concentrated in OPEC, the Persian Gulf, and Saudi Arabia, although not to the extent of the mid-1970s. Since the early 1990s, OPEC's share of world oil production has hovered around 40 percent, that of the Persian Gulf states has fluctuated between 27 and 30 percent, and that of Saudi Arabia has generally stood between 12 and 14 percent. This shift back to greater reliance on the Persian Gulf and OPEC owes to the collapse of oil production in the former Soviet Union, which fell by more than 40 percent between 1987 and 1996, and stagnation in the oil output of the OECD countries even as world demand grew by more than one-third. The principal exception to this renewed concentration in OPEC and the Persian Gulf is continued growth in the share of oil produced in non-OPEC developing countries, which now stands at about 20 percent of global output. Nevertheless, these countries combined, which include China, India, Brazil, Argentina, Malaysia, Angola, Egypt, and Oman, produce only 50 percent more oil than does Saudi Arabia alone.

The concentration of the world's oil supply in OPEC countries and the Persian Gulf in particular is expected only to increase in future years. In 2005, the EIA projected that OPEC's share of conventional oil production would rise to more than 45 percent in 2025, while that of the Persian Gulf would reach nearly 35 percent (EIA 2005c, 160–62). Others have predicted that in 2030, OPEC will control more than half of the global oil supply, while significantly more than 40 percent will come from the Persian Gulf (Sieminksi 2005, 28; Mouawad 2005b; IMF 2005a, 10). Likewise, the EIA has projected that the share of all oil exports coming from the Persian Gulf, currently about 40 percent, will increase to 66 percent, and possibly as high as 76 percent, by 2025 (EIA 2003, 53).

The main reason for these trends is that nearly two-thirds of the world's proved oil reserves are located in the Gulf. According to recent estimates, Saudi Arabia alone possesses approximately 264 billion barrels of proved reserves, or about 22 percent of the world total of 1.2 trillion barrels. Iraq, Iran, Kuwait, and the United Arab Emirates all have roughly 100 billion or more barrels of proved reserves, or another 10 percent of global reserves each (BP 2006).

To be sure, considerable uncertainty surrounds these figures. Some appear to be rather arbitrary. In the mid- to late 1980s, each of the major Persian Gulf producers hiked its reserve estimates dramatically, and as recently as 2002, Iran unilaterally declared a 30 billion barrel increase, to as many as 130 billion barrels, in the size of its proved reserves. These figures also exclude nonconventional sources of oil, such as tar sands, which may give Canada as much as 170 billion more barrels in effective oil reserves. Finally, much of the Persian Gulf, including large parts of Iraq, has not been thoroughly explored. But further exploration is likely to result only in higher estimates.

Stability of Oil Producing Countries and Regions   Given the present and likely future distribution of oil production, what is the probability of a major supply disruption? In the past, much attention was focused on the danger that one or more oil producing states might seek to limit exports in order to apply political pressure to consuming countries. The classic example of the use of the so-called oil weapon was the 1973 Arab oil embargo. Since then, however, this threat has become much less credible as exporters have become increasingly dependent on oil revenues and, by extension, the economic well-being of their customers. Instead, the principal threats to the steady flow of oil are most likely to stem from conflicts within oil producing states and regions.

Some of the largest supply disruptions in the past have been the result of international conflicts. The problems began even before the oil shocks of the 1970s. During the 1956 Suez crisis, Egypt blocked the canal and sabotaged the pipeline that brought Iraqi oil to the Mediterranean, interrupting the normal supply route for three-quarters of Western Europe's oil (Yergin 1991, 490–91). During the 1967 Arab-Israeli War, the flow of Arab oil was temporarily reduced by 60 percent, and the overall initial loss of Middle East oil amounted to 6 MBD, or roughly one-sixth of world consumption (Yergin 1991, 555).[13] These events were followed by the outbreak of the Iran-Iraq War in 1980 and the Iraqi invasion of Kuwait in 1990, both of which removed large amounts of oil from the market. Even the Arab oil embargo might not have occurred, moreover, but for the U.S. intervention on behalf of Israel in the 1973 October War.

Whether interstate conflict will cause a major oil supply disruption in the future is difficult to say. Few observers would be so bold as to predict an imminent war involving a major oil producing state. Certainly, the removal from power of Saddam Hussein, who had been responsible for the most recent wars in the Persian Gulf, has at least temporarily reduced the risk of aggression there. Yet relations among many of the critical oil producers in the region remain less than harmonious.

At least two more general considerations would seem to ensure that conflict involving oil producing states will remain a real possibility for the foreseeable future. One is the intrinsic and easily exploitable value of oil, which will continue to make it a tempting target for aggression. As Michael Klare has argued, "Conflicts over oil will constitute a significant feature of the global security environment in the decades to come" (Klare 2001, 27). The other factor is the absence of liberal democracy in many oil exporting states. As a general rule, nondemocratic or democratizing regimes are more prone to fight one another than are their democratic counterparts (Russett and Oneal 2001; Mansfield and Snyder 1995).

The fact that so many oil exporters lack liberal norms and democratic institutions also has a bearing on the second likely principal cause of future oil shocks: internal conflict. In fact, a majority of the global supply disruptions since 1951 have had domestic origins. For example, Iran's nationalization of its oil fields in the early 1950s resulted in a supply shortfall of some 0.7 MBD, or approximately 5 percent of world consumption at the time, for a period of forty-four months. The second oil shock was precipitated by the Iranian Revolution, which saw widespread strikes by Iranian oil workers. And in early 2003, unrest in Venezuela caused that country's production to drop briefly by more than 2.5 MBD, while a major strike in Nigeria knocked as much as 800,000 barrels per day off the market.[14]

Thus, in the future, major supply disruptions are perhaps most likely to be the result of domestic political conflict, whether in the form of civil wars, coups, revolutions, strikes, terrorist attacks, or something else. Time and space constraints do not permit a detailed, country-by-country analysis of the risks of internal conflict. Suffice it to say that many of the leading current and future oil exporters have experienced various forms of instability and internal unrest, and they seem likely to continue to do so until they develop strong, democratic governments characterized by the rule of law and respect for human rights. Approximately one-half of all oil exports are currently from states that rank low in terms of political stability (see Table 3.4). Looking to the future, only 9 percent of world oil reserves are held by countries considered "free" by Freedom House, the leading non-governmental organization devoted to tracking the progress of democracy around the world (Lovins et al. 2004, 18). As a result, conclude two expert observers, "The danger of an oil disruption is high and increasing, as the world grows more dependent on unstable states both inside and outside OPEC for the security of its energy supply" (Kalicki and Goldwyn 2005, 4).

Of particular concern, of course, is Saudi Arabia, which has been the

TABLE 3.4 Leading Net Petroleum Exporters, 2003

Country	Political Stability*	Failed States Index 2006** (ranking)	Oil Production (MBD)	Net Oil Exports (MBD)	Proved Oil Reserves (billions of barrels)
Saudi Arabia	9	77.2 (73)	9.9	8.3	262.7
Russia	6	87.1 (43)	8.4	5.8	72.5
Norway	0	16.8 (146)	3.3	3.0	10.1
Iran	8	84 (53)	3.9	2.5	133.3
Venezuela	8	81.2 (64)	2.6	2.3	77.2
UAE	4	Not rated	2.7	2.3	97.8
Kuwait	4	60.8 (105)	2.3	2.0	99.0
Nigeria	8	94.4 (21)	2.2	1.9	35.3
Mexico	4	73.1 (85)	3.8	1.8	16.0
Libya	5	68.5 (95)	1.5	1.3	39.1
Algeria	7	77.8 (72)	1.4	1.2	11.8
Iraq	10	109 (4)	1.3	1.0	115.0
Total			43.3	33.4	969.8

*Political stability is measured on an 11-point scale, with 10 representing the lowest level of stability and 0 the highest.
**The Failed States Index rates countries on twelve indicators of state failure, with a maximum score of 120 points. One hundred forty-six states were rated in 2006.
SOURCES: EIA 2004c; BP 2006; Economist Intelligence Unit 2004; Fund for Peace 2006.

world's largest exporter for the past several decades. Large-scale internal turmoil there would have profound repercussions for the world economy. Analysts have long debated whether the Saudi ruling family would be able to retain its grip on power, and they continue to disagree on the matter. For example, a 2002 CIA memo reportedly described the House of Saud as "inherently fragile" and voiced "serious concerns about [the country's] long-term stability" (Sennott 2002), while Saudi expert F. Gregory Gause has recently argued that "the short- and medium-term prognosis for the regime's stability is quite good" (Gause 2002, 42). At a minimum, one can say that many of the ingredients for domestic unrest are present there. The regime is widely viewed as corrupt and alienated from the country's rank and file and even the educated middle class (see, for example, Hersh 2001; Yetiv 2004, 34). At the same time, a rapidly growing population and, until recently, suppressed oil revenues have resulted in declining living standards and widespread unemployment, further fueling the level of public discontent. As one recent analysis concludes, the threats arising from within have become more serious since the 1970s (Yetiv 2004, 28).

A relatively new element in the equation is the possibility of terrorism directed at oil facilities, in Saudi Arabia and elsewhere. Osama bin Laden has urged his followers to attack Persian Gulf oil facilities on the grounds that they are "the most powerful weapons against the United States," and the Saudi arm of al Qaeda has called on fighters to target Saudi oil supplies.[15] In fact, terrorists struck a French oil tanker in 2002, and more recent attacks on targets related to the oil industry in Saudi Arabia have been widely attributed to al Qaeda or independent terrorist groups that it has inspired (Sachs 2004; Clawson and Henderson 2005, 8).

Some have questioned whether even determined terrorist strikes against critical oil installations could ever succeed in Saudi Arabia. The regime has devoted substantial sums to providing security. But a successful attack cannot be completely ruled out, and it could have profound consequences. The Saudi oil industry is highly concentrated. About half of Saudi oil production comes from one oil field, and two-thirds of Saudi oil goes through a single processing complex at Abqaiaq and just two offshore terminals. As a result, simple attacks on a few key facilities, such as pipeline nodes, could disrupt a significant portion of the world's oil supply for at least a couple of months and perhaps for as long as two years.[16] Thus, according to Seymour Hersh, by late 2001, current and former U.S. intelligence and military officials had portrayed the growing instability of the Saudi regime—and the vulnerability of its oil reserves to terrorist attack—as the most immediate threat to American economic and political interests in the Middle East (Hersh 2001).

Elsewhere, where fewer resources have been available to protect oil facilities, attacks against them have been very successful. During the first two years after the U.S. invasion of Iraq, the oil infrastructure there was subjected to nearly two hundred significant acts of sabotage by those opposed to the U.S. occupation or seeking to destabilize the new Iraqi regime.[17] Likewise, the main oil pipelines in Colombia have suffered extensive bombing (Lovins et al. 2004, 18; Klare 2004a, 128, 140–42). Overall, concludes Steve Yetiv in a comprehensive study of the stability of the world oil market, "the potential for terrorism against the global oil infrastructure has grown over time" (Yetiv 2004, 218).

Availability of Spare Production Capacity Of course, whether a supply disruption, whatever its origins, would cause an oil price shock would depend on the magnitude of the loss and the ability to compensate for it with oil from other sources. In theory, the loss of oil from one country or region could be made up for either by an increase in production elsewhere, releases from petroleum stocks, or some combination of the two. Thus an additional important determinant of the risk of oil shocks is the amount, distribution, and responsiveness of spare production capacity in the world. The decline in world oil consumption in the late 1970s and early 1980s inadvertently resulted in a substantial cushion of production capacity, which peaked at an estimated 9 to 15 MBD, or as much as one-quarter of world consumption, in 1985 (Morse and Jaffe 2001, 19; *Economist* 2005). This excess capacity has been drawn upon on several occasions to compensate for supply disruptions, most notably following the Iraqi invasion of Kuwait (see Figure 3.4).

Because the price of oil collapsed in the mid-1980s and stayed relatively low thereafter, however, producers have had little incentive until recently to invest in additional production capacity. Thus as demand recovered in the late 1980s and the early 1990s, the once substantial cushion of spare capacity was gradually whittled away. Although the total amount stood as high as 6 to 7 MBD

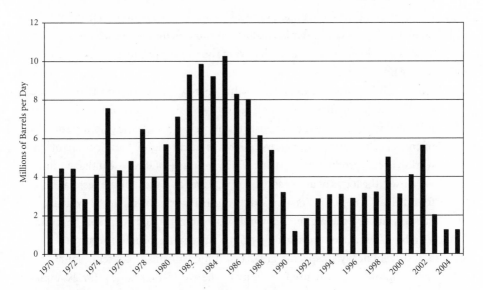

FIGURE 3.4 OPEC Spare Production Capacity, 1970–2005
SOURCE: IMF 2006, fig. 1.21.

in the early part of this decade, more recent jumps in consumption have left little production capacity to spare to blunt a major supply disruption. Indeed, according to a number of estimates, all the OPEC countries combined retained as little as 1.0 MBD in excess capacity in 2004 and 2005.[18]

. According to the chief economist of the IEA, Fatih Birol, 5 MBD of spare capacity is needed to put the world into the "comfort zone."[19] Absent a significant reduction in demand for oil as a result of sustained high prices or a global economic recession, as occurred in the late 1990s, however, the situation is unlikely to improve notably in the foreseeable future. The IMF has recently observed that spare capacity may remain low through at least 2010, as the current set of capacity expansion and replacement projects is expected just to keep pace with demand. And given their experience with an abundance of excess capacity in the 1980s, it is doubtful that OPEC countries will invest heavily in dedicated spare capacity (IMF 2005a, 10 and 18; West 2005, 213).

As a result, in the words of former Algerian oil minister Sadek Boussena, "One can expect an extended period of just-in-time supply—sufficient, certainly, to cover average demand, but inadequate to cover unexpected supply or demand fluctuations" (Boussena 2004). The oil market is likely to remain tight and vulnerable to shocks. Indeed, as Alan Greenspan observed in mid-2006, "The balance of world oil supply and demand has become so precarious that even small acts of sabotage or local insurrection have a significant impact on oil prices. . . . The buffer between supply and demand is much too small to absorb shutdowns of even a small part of the world's production" (Greenspan 2006, 6).[20]

The ability of the limited remaining spare capacity promptly to replace lost production is further constrained by two other factors. First, much of it is located in precisely the oil exporting countries that are the primary sources of concern. Traditionally, Saudi Arabia has held roughly half or more of the world's excess production capacity, which would be of little use if that country were itself the locus of an oil supply disruption, and most of the rest has been found elsewhere in the Persian Gulf. Thus little or none might be available if Saudi Arabia or the region as a whole was subject to a disruption.[21] Second, a high percentage of the spare capacity that remains produces crude oil that is relatively heavy in specific gravity and high in sulfur content (sour) and thus cannot be readily used in many of the world's refineries (for example, IEA 2004c, 111; Lovins et al. 2004, 9). Consequently, it could not necessarily provide quick relief in response to an emergent oil shortage.

Strategic Petroleum Stocks   Ameliorating this worrisome situation somewhat is the establishment of strategic stocks of petroleum in many advanced industrialized countries since the oil shocks of the 1970s. These government-controlled reserves now amount to more than 1.4 billion barrels. The U.S. Strategic Petroleum Reserve (SPR) alone contains nearly 700 million barrels, or the equivalent of roughly two months of U.S. imports. In combination with the private holdings of oil companies and other commercial entities, these stocks provide the OECD states with a potential total reserve of some 4 billion barrels of oil that could be drawn on in an emergency (see Figure 3.5).

As helpful as they may be, strategic reserves do not represent a foolproof solution to the problem of supply disruptions for several reasons. First, after a rapid buildup in the 1970s and early 1980s, total OECD petroleum stocks have grown relatively little in absolute terms, and they have actually declined in relation to total world oil consumption. As the SPR was filled, privately held commercial inventories in the United States fell by approximately 300 million barrels. During the last two decades, moreover, China and other developing countries have become significant users of oil without adding measurably to

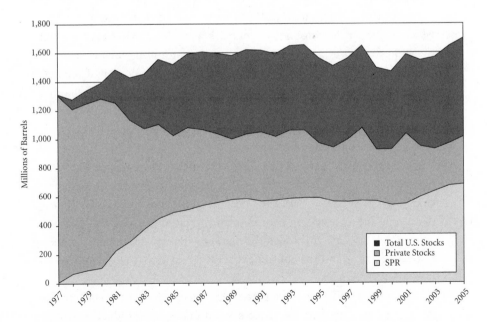

FIGURE 3.5 U.S. Petroleum Stocks, 1977–2005
SOURCES: EIA 2005b, tab. 5.15; EIA 2007b, tab. 11.3.

world stockpiles. Second, except in extreme circumstances, governments can exert little influence over the release of oil from private commercial stocks, and even the coordination of government releases is uncertain. Third, the strategic reserves are limited in the rate that they can be used. It is estimated that the SPR can be drawn down at a top rate of just 4.3 MBD, and then only for ninety days, while the maximum theoretical rate for the OECD as a whole, assuming successful coordination, is about 8 MBD (Lovins et al. 2004, 10). Fourth, even ample crude oil stocks do not guarantee the presence of adequate reserves of particular petroleum products, notably gasoline, to smooth out any possible fluctuations in supply and demand. This limitation was made evident when Hurricane Katrina shut down refineries and pipelines along the U.S. Gulf Coast in 2005, causing gasoline prices to jump by approximately 50 percent in the United States.

Market Mechanisms   A further positive development has been changes in the oil market since the 1970s, which have made the price of oil less susceptible to major spikes (Bohi and Toman 1996, 82–84, 87; Moore, Behrens, and Blodgett 1997). One was the shift from primary reliance on long-term contracts, which specify the volume to be delivered and fix the price for a period of time, to a more flexible pricing system based on the spot market, which is a better indicator of current market conditions (EIA 1999, 53). Until the end of the 1970s, no more than 10 percent of internationally traded oil was sold on the spot market, which served the narrow function of balancing the input and output mixes of refiners. By 1983, however, more than half of all oil was either traded on the spot market or sold at prices that were keyed to the spot market price, and the percentage continued to rise (Yergin 1991, 722). Not only has the volume of the spot market grown immensely, but also the market has broadened to serve the needs of all segments of the petroleum industry. Compared to the more rigid distribution channels characteristic of earlier years, the centrality of the spot market has enhanced the fungibility of crude oil and petroleum products in world markets and hence the efficiency with which the market will allocate supplies according to relative prices and the consumer's willingness to pay (Bohi and Toman 1986, 42–43; Yergin 2006).

The other stabilizing development was the creation in the late 1970s and 1980s of futures markets for crude oil and petroleum products. A futures contract is an agreement between a seller to deliver and a buyer to accept a commodity on a designated date in the future for a specified price. Futures markets allow producers and consumers to hedge against uncertainty in price or supply and, in particular, to mitigate the impact of possible unfavorable changes in market conditions (EIA 1999, 55; GAO 1996, 40). As a result, the futures markets in crude oil and petroleum products have reduced the need physically to hold inventories on speculative grounds, thereby contributing to greater overall stability of demand, which can in turn dampen price rises (Moore, Behrens, and Blodgett 1997). Remember that it was the buildup in inventories in response to the Iranian Revolution that more than any other single factor was responsible for the following price shock.

In sum, it is difficult to provide an overall assessment of the risk of a major oil supply disruption. Some developments over the past three decades appear to have reduced the risk, while others would seem to have increased it. A decade ago, a Congressional Research Service study concluded that the danger of another oil shock had declined substantially (Moore, Behrens, and Blodgett 1997). Just a few years later, however, veteran industry analysts Ed Morse and Amy Myers Jaffe judged that "with spare capacity scarce and Middle East tensions high, chances are greater than at any point in the last two decades of an oil supply disruption that would even more severely test the nation's security and prosperity" (Morse and Jaffe 2001, 9).

A sophisticated 2005 study attempted to quantify the probability of a supply disruption over the next ten years. Drawing on the judgments of more than two dozen oil market and energy security experts, it put the likelihood of a disruption of 2 MBD or more lasting at least one month at approximately 80 percent, of a similar-sized disruption that lasted at least six months at approximately 70 percent, and of a 5 MBD disruption for at least one month at 50 percent (Beccue and Huntington 2005). For the time being, the heightened danger of another oil shock is reflected in the "risk premium" that has added as much as 15 to 20 dollars to the price of a barrel of oil over the last several years (Morrison 2004; Lauerman 2005, 1; Yergin 2006). How long this situation will last and how it will end, whether in a gradual loosening of the market or a new oil crisis, is impossible to tell.

Economic Impact of an Oil Shock

Should another oil shock occur, what impact would it have on the U.S. economy? Obviously, the effects would depend on the duration and magnitude of the supply disruption and the resulting increases in world prices. But they would also be shaped by the characteristics of the economy itself. In this regard, developments over the past several decades have had mixed implications.

Oil Intensity of the U.S. Economy   On the positive side, the U.S. economy is less vulnerable to oil shocks than it was three decades ago because it has become much more energy efficient. The amount of energy needed to generate one dollar of economic output fell by 43 percent between 1975 and 2003 (Lovins et al. 2004, 43). The amount of oil per dollar of GDP, or "oil intensity," has declined even more, by approximately half, as oil has fallen from nearly 48 percent of total energy consumption in the United States in 1978 to around 40 percent today. The relative decline in the importance of energy-intensive manufacturing in the U.S. economy and the concomitant rise of the service industry mean that energy in general and oil in particular are not as important as they once were for economic growth. Moreover, some sectors, led by electricity generation, have shifted almost entirely away from the use of oil.

As a result of these changes, oil constitutes a much smaller share of the U.S. economy than it did three decades ago. The fraction of GDP spent on oil fell from a high of around 8 percent in 1980 to only 2 percent in the early 2000s, or about where it was before the first oil shock despite the fact that real oil prices were roughly twice as high (NRC 2002, 13). Nevertheless, the declines in U.S. energy and oil intensity have slowed substantially since the mid-1980s, and oil's share of U.S. GDP has risen commensurately with the recent runup in oil prices.

Government Policy Responses   A second reason for optimism is that economists and policymakers may have drawn useful lessons from past experiences with supply disruptions that will enable them to manage more effectively any that might occur in the future. One influential argument circulating in professional economic circles is that inappropriate monetary policy responses were largely to blame for the recessions that occurred in the wake of the first oil shocks. When inflation and inflation-related fears were high in the 1970s and early 1980s, the U.S. Federal Reserve Board felt compelled to react to high oil prices by raising interests rates, thereby slowing the economy. Thus anti-inflationary U.S. monetary policy was at least a contributory factor in the recessions that followed the oil shocks of 1973 and 1979 (Bohi 1989; Bohi 1991; Barsky and Kilian 2004; Andrews 2004).

Demand Elasticity of Oil   The demand for oil remains relatively unresponsive to price increases, however, and there are solid grounds for believing that it has become even more price inelastic over the years. The main reason for this trend is that oil use has become increasingly concentrated in the transportation sector, which now accounts for some two-thirds of all petroleum consumption. Oil has been replaced by other energy sources in the sectors where this could be done so relatively easily, such as electric power generation. In contrast, transportation remains more than 95 percent dependent on oil, and it has historically demonstrated the least ability to respond to price shocks by switching to alternative fuels. If oil substitutability is in fact lower in the transportation and sector than in others, then the overall substitutability of oil in the economy may have decreased (Greene, Jones, and Leiby 1998, 61; Greene and Tishchishyna 2001, 13 and 21). According to one authoritative estimate, the price elasticity of demand for oil is about 0.05 in the short term (Huntington 2005, 5–6). If the price rises by 1 percent, then demand will fall by only one-twentieth of a percent. Thus a supply disruption that causes the price of oil to double will also cause spending on oil to nearly double at least temporarily (Perry 2001).

Conclusion

Foreign oil dependence has imposed a number of costs on the U.S. economy, especially since 1973. These costs include the recurring expenses attributable to importing large quantities of oil from abroad as well as the episodic economic burdens imposed by oil supply disruptions. A 1993 Oak Ridge study estimated the combined cost of wealth transfers, potential losses in GNP, and macroeconomic adjustment costs at $4.1 trillion in 1990 dollars for the period from 1972 to 1991 (Greene and Leiby 1993). A 2001 calculation put the total cost for the thirty-year period 1970–99 at $7 trillion in 1998 dollars ($8.4 trillion in 2005 dollars) (Greene and Tishchishyna 2001, 22 and 28). As long as the United States consumes and imports large amounts of oil and allows the price to be set on world markets, these costs will only continue to mount.

Given the magnitude of these costs, the United States has had a strong interest in limiting its oil consumption and imports and in mitigating the economic consequences of oil shocks. Beyond that, it has had an interest in preventing or at least reducing the likelihood and magnitude of possible future supply disruptions. To these ends, the United States has pursued a number of policies, both at home and abroad, during the past three decades. Some of the fruits of these policies, in the form of the SPR and the decline in U.S. oil intensity, have been suggested above. But it remains to describe in detail these policies and the additional costs they have imposed.

4 U.S. Economic Policy Responses and Their Costs

We have only two modes—complacency and panic.

James Schlesinger, first U.S. Secretary of Energy and former
Secretary of Defense and Director of Central Intelligence, 2005

SINCE THE OIL SHOCKS of the 1970s, foreign oil dependence has posed significant economic costs and risks to the United States. In response, successive administrations have pursued a number of economic policy measures—both at home and in cooperation with other industrialized countries—intended to reduce these actual and potential economic costs. These policies have had two general goals: (1) reduce U.S. foreign oil dependence, especially import dependence, by limiting American oil consumption and increasing domestic oil production, and (2) mitigate the economic impact of future oil supply disruptions independently of any reduction in imports and consumption that might be achieved.

These economic measures have reduced somewhat the economic costs and risks of foreign oil dependence. As a general rule, however, they have been quite modest in nature and have imposed only small financial burdens. In particular, the United States has done relatively little to reduce overall oil consumption. For example, the U.S. government has never imposed a substantial gasoline tax or oil import fee, nor has it ever invested heavily in mass transit for the purpose of reducing demand in the transportation sector. All the most important initiatives, moreover, were begun in the 1970s. Some of those initial responses, such as fuel economy standards for light-duty vehicles and the Strategic Petroleum Reserve, have been maintained, although they have not been substantially updated to reflect changing circumstances.[1] Other early policy responses, such as the production of synthetic fuels and related federal research and development efforts, have been scaled back in size or abandoned altogether. Since the early 1980s, the use of economic policy instruments to reduce the costs and risks of foreign oil dependence has rarely, if ever, assumed a high priority.

This chapter examines the various economic policies that have been adopted since the early 1970s in response to U.S. foreign oil dependence and the benefits and costs of those policies. The chapter is limited in two respects. First, it considers only federal policy, neglecting any efforts that have been made at the state and local levels. Second, it focuses on the policies that have been enacted, paying little or no attention to the many proposals that were never adopted.[2]

Efforts to Reduce U.S. Oil Consumption and Imports

The United States has little control over the degree to which it is indirectly dependent on foreign oil via trade and financial ties with its principal economic and security partners. Likewise, short of isolating the American markets for crude oil and petroleum products from the broader world markets, there is nothing that the United States can do about market dependence. Thus the principal strategy available for reducing foreign oil dependence has been to limit imports and to cut back on oil consumption more generally. Imports are responsible for recurring economic costs, while a high level of consumption augments both the magnitude of oil imports, other things being equal, and the vulnerability of the economy to oil shocks, given the integration of U.S. and world oil markets.

Several general approaches exist for reducing oil consumption and, indirectly, imports: discouraging demand by making oil and petroleum products more expensive through taxes and other fees, promoting conservation and the more efficient use of oil, and substituting alternative fuels and energy sources. In addition, the level of oil imports can be attacked directly by imposing tariffs and quantitative limits on them and by increasing domestic oil production.

Since the 1970s, the U.S. government has employed virtually all these approaches, although to widely varying degrees. Overall, however, the United States has made only modest efforts to cut oil use and imports, despite repeated calls for energy independence. The primary focus of American policy has been on reducing fuel consumption in the transportation sector, particularly by light-duty vehicles, where the biggest gains were to be made. Yet even in this area, U.S. actions have been limited largely to promoting vehicle fuel economy rather than discouraging demand via higher prices or the development of alternative motor fuels (see also Plotkin and Greene 1997, 1179–80).

Discouraging Demand

In 1959, the United States imposed a mandatory quota on oil imports. The purpose, however, was not to minimize foreign oil dependence but to protect U.S. domestic producers from lower-priced oil from abroad. As demand began to outstrip domestic production in the late 1960s and early 1970s, the quotas were progressively raised and then lifted altogether in April 1973, just months before the first oil shock (Rustow 1982, 166; Yergin 1991, 590).

Thus rather than quotas, the United States has confined itself since then to the use of taxes and fees to limit imports and to discourage oil consumption more generally. Yet even at the height of the oil crises of the 1970s, it never made a serious effort to do so. The principal exception occurred in 1975, when President Gerald Ford imposed a special duty on imported oil, which eventually amounted to $2 per barrel. In fact, however, the fee was intended to serve as a political bargaining chip as Ford sought congressional approval of his proposed energy program, which included an excise tax on domestic oil. When Congress finally passed the Energy Policy and Conservation Act that December, the administration dropped the special fee, even though the legislation lacked the desired excise tax (Bohi and Russell 1978, 242–44).

In contrast, the United States has imposed excise taxes on gasoline, diesel, and other liquid fuels used in transportation. But the federal gas tax long preceded the oil shocks, dating to 1932, and though the size of the tax has increased several times since 1973, it has never been justified as a means of discouraging demand. Rather, its primary purpose has been to fund the federal highway program through the Highway Trust Fund and, since 1983, mass transit as well as to raise general revenues for the government.[3] Although several presidents have proposed raising the gas tax in order to reduce consumption, this idea has never garnered favor in Congress. Indeed, so unlikely have been the prospects for congressional support that when Ford, soon after taking office in 1974, set a goal of cutting oil imports by one million barrels per day (MBD) by the end of the following year, he explicitly ruled out the imposition of any additional gas tax for that purpose (Bohi and Russell 1978, 241).

Of course, fuel taxes with other objectives could still have the effect of discouraging consumption if they were set at a high enough level. In fact, however, the U.S. taxes on gasoline and diesel have been among the very lowest in the industrialized world. Indeed, the real value of the gas tax has generally been at or below where it stood in 1970, notwithstanding a more than threefold increase in nominal terms (see Figure 4.1). In 2005, the average total tax for a gallon of gas in the United States was about 46 cents, including the federal tax of 18.4 cents as well as state and local taxes. In contrast, drivers in Japan, France, Germany, and the United Kingdom paid an average of $2.15, $3.77, $4.01, and $4.22 in taxes per gallon, respectively (Hoo and Ebel 2006).

Promoting Energy Conservation and Efficiency

Rather than discouraging demand, U.S. efforts to reduce oil imports and consumption have emphasized conservation and energy efficiency. And the bulk of these efforts has been concentrated in the transportation sector. This focus

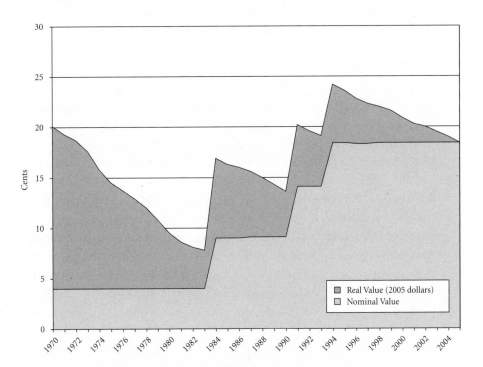

FIGURE 4.1 Nominal and Real Value of Federal Excise Tax on Gasoline, 1970–2005

has made sense for two related reasons. Transportation was already responsible for more than 50 percent of all oil consumption in 1973, and that share has only grown in the intervening years, to approximately two-thirds of U.S. oil demand today. In addition, the sector was and has remained almost entirely dependent on oil. As a result, few immediate opportunities have existed for switching to other energy sources, as was possible in the residential, commercial, electric power, and, to a lesser extent, industrial sectors.

One early response to the first oil shock was to achieve an immediate increase in automotive fuel economy by restricting the speed at which people could drive. In early 1974, the Nixon administration imposed a fifty-five-mile-per-hour federal speed limit. At the time, a government study found that reducing the average vehicle's speed from seventy to fifty-five miles per hour could result in a fuel economy gain of 24 percent (Davis and Diegel 2004, tab. 4.24). In practice, the gains were probably lower, but according to one estimate, the speed limit saved 2.5 billion gallons of gasoline and diesel fuel, or 2.2 percent of total motor fuel consumption, in 1983. Because of falling gasoline prices, however, the standard was relaxed in 1987 to allow states to set limits as high as 65 miles per hour, and it was fully repealed in 1995 (Mouawad and Romero 2005).

In addition, the federal government has occasionally used financial incentives to promote fuel economy. Most notable among these has been the so-called gas-guzzler tax, an excise tax on the purchase of new passenger cars that consume disproportionately large amounts of gasoline. The tax first applied to cars manufactured in automobile model year (MY) 1980 and was phased in over the following decade. The fuel economy level at which the tax takes effect rose from 15.0 miles per gallon (mpg) to 22.5 mpg, and the size of the penalty, which depends on how far a car falls below the threshold, increased substantially. Today, the tax ranges from a minimum of $1,000 to a maximum of $7,700 for a car with a fuel economy rating under 12.5 mpg (NRC 2002, 21; Davis and Diegel 2004, tab. 4.21). Receipts grew rapidly as the tax was phased in, reaching a high of nearly $148 million in 1986. After that, however, they declined more or less steadily until 1998, when they amounted to only $48 million, before rising again in the next several years (Davis and Diegel 2004, tab. 4.22). The substantial decline between 1986 and 1998 suggests that the tax successfully deterred manufacturers from producing highly inefficient cars. But it may also reflect the principal limitation of the tax: it does not apply to sport utility vehicles (SUVs), minivans, and pickups, which have comprised an ever-increasing share of the light-duty vehicle fleet.

At about the same time, the U.S. government also began to promote conservation, at least indirectly, by providing support for public transportation. For many years, federal transportation funding was used almost exclusively for roads programs. When Congress decided to raise the gas tax from four to nine cents per gallon in 1983, however, it dedicated one cent, or 20 percent of the increase, to a newly established Mass Transit Account within the Highway Trust Fund. Subsequently, each time there has been an increase in the amount of gas tax going into the highway fund, one-fifth of the total has been allocated to mass transit. Since 1997, the overall share of the gas tax devoted to the account has been 15.5 percent, or 2.86 cents per gallon (Buechner n.d.).

As a result, federal funding of public transportation has grown steadily and substantially during the past two decades. From an initial level of approximately $1 billion per year in the 1980s, it has risen to several billion dollars per year. Of the $27.7 billion remaining in the Highway Trust Fund at the end of fiscal year (FY) 2001, $7.4 billion was designated for the Mass Transit Account (CBO 2002, 4). According to a 1996 Department of Transportation estimate, mass transit reduced auto fuel consumption by approximately 1.5 billion gallons annually, or 0.1 MBD (DOT 1996). How much of this savings could be attributed to federal spending, which accounts for only a fraction of all spending on mass transit, however, is difficult to determine.

The measure that has had by far the biggest impact on oil consumption in the transportation sector was the imposition of fuel economy standards for most of the vehicles sold in the United States. The Energy Policy and Conservation Act of 1975 set up the Corporate Average Fuel Economy (CAFE) program, which required automakers to increase the average fuel economy of new light-duty vehicles with the goal of essentially doubling it in a decade (Kenderdine and Moniz 2005, 425). The program established distinct standards for passenger cars and light-duty trucks. Initially, it also distinguished between two-wheel- and four-wheel-drive trucks, and it required that each manufacturer meet the standards separately for both its imported and its domestic fleets—the so-called two-fleet rule—where a domestic vehicle was defined as one for which at least 75 percent of the parts were manufactured in the United States. In the 1990s, however, both distinctions were eliminated for light trucks.

Congress itself set the initial fuel economy standard for passenger cars, which rose from 18 mpg in MY 1978 to 27.5 mpg in MY 1985. Since then, the standard has been set by the Department of Transportation (DOT), which slightly relaxed it for model years 1986 through 1989 before restoring it to 27.5 mpg in MY 1990, where it has remained. DOT has also set the standards for light trucks, which began at 17.2 mpg for two-wheel-drive vehicles in MY 1979 and rose to a temporary peak of 20.5 mpg in MY 1987. After dropping to as low as 20 mpg in the early 1990s, the light-truck standard was gradually raised to 20.7 mpg in MY 1996, where it stayed for nearly a decade. The 1985 standard for passenger cars implied a doubling in the overall fuel economy of American-made automobiles, which had averaged only about 14 mpg over the period 1965–75 and had dropped as low as 12.9 mpg in 1974. The standards eventually set for light trucks implied an approximately 50 percent increase in fuel economy (OTA 1982, 41; NRC 2002, 1–3; Bamberger 2003; CBO 2002, 3; NHTSA 2005).

Compliance with the CAFE standards is measured by calculating the sales-weighted average of the fuel economies of a given manufacturer's product line. Domestically produced and imported passenger car fleets continue to be calculated separately. As originally enacted, the penalty for noncompliance was $5—later increased to $5.50—for every 0.1 mpg that the fleet average falls below the standard, multiplied by the number of vehicles sold in the corresponding fleet that year. If a manufacturer exceeds the standard in one year, however, it may earn credits that can be used to offset shortfalls in other years without penalty (Bamberger 2003; Greene 1990; CBO 2002, 3; NHTSA 2005). Total fines collected grew steadily in the mid-1980s and since then have fluctuated between $20 and $50 million per year (Davis and Diegel 2004, tab. 4.20).

Since the CAFE program was established, the fuel economy of light-duty vehicles on American roads has improved substantially. Between 1975 and 1988, the fuel economy of passenger cars manufactured in the United States nearly doubled, to 28.8 mpg, while that for those imported from abroad increased by roughly one-third. During the same period, the fuel economy of new light trucks rose by more than 50 percent, peaking at 21.7 mpg in 1987. Taken together, new light-duty vehicle fuel economy increased from 15.3 mpg in 1975 to 26.2 mpg in 1987, a gain of more than 70 percent. As a result of these improvements, the average fuel economy for all passenger cars in use—both old and new—increased from 13.4 mpg in 1973 to 21.4 mpg in 1999, while the estimated on-road fuel economy of light trucks rose from 10.5 mpg to 17.1 mpg over the same period. Overall light-duty vehicle on-road fuel economy increased from

13.2 mpg in 1975 to 19.6 mpg in 1999, a gain of 48 percent (NRC 2002, 14–17; Bamberger 2003, 6; Davis and Diegel 2004, tabs. 4.18, 4.19) (see Figure 4.2).

There is some question, however, as to how much of the improvement can be attributed to the CAFE standards alone. A 2002 study by the National Research Council (NRC) noted that isolating the effects of the standards from other factors affecting U.S. light-duty vehicles during the past twenty-five years is a difficult analytic task and that there had been no comprehensive assessment of what would have happened had fuel economy standards not been in effect (NRC 2002, 3, 13). As a result, some have maintained that these improvements would have happened anyway as a consequence of rising oil prices during the 1970s and early 1980s, while others have argued that the CAFE program played the leading role—and was perhaps twice as important as high gas prices—in bringing about the increases in fuel economy (Greene 1990; Greene 1998, 610). Most analyses have found, however, that the standards did exert a significant independent influence and that they have been especially important at setting a fuel economy floor in more recent years

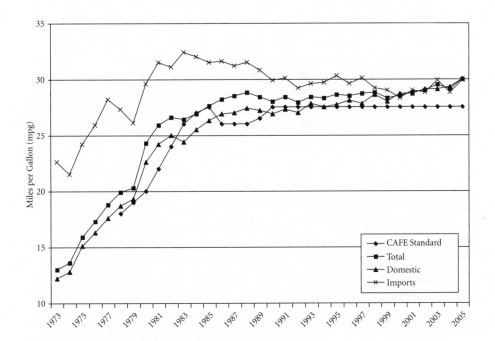

FIGURE 4.2 Passenger Car Fuel Economy, 1973–2005
SOURCE: http://www.nhtsa.dot.gov/Cars/rules/CAFE/CAFEData.htm (accessed Nov. 21, 2006).

(Plotkin and Greene 1997, 1182–83; IEA 1998b, 32; NRC 2002, 14–15; Bamberger 2003, 6). As the 2002 NRC study concluded:

> The CAFE program has clearly contributed to increased fuel economy of the nation's light-duty vehicle fleet during the past 22 years. During the 1970s, high fuel prices and a desire on the part of automakers to reduce costs by reducing the weight of vehicles contributed to improved fuel economy [but] the CAFE standards reinforced that effect, [and] the CAFE program has been particularly effective in keeping fuel economy above the levels to which it might have fallen when real gasoline prices began their long decline in the early 1980s. (NRC 2002, 3)

What impact, then, has better fuel economy and, indirectly, the CAFE program had on U.S. oil consumption? Fuel use by passenger cars and light trucks is roughly one-quarter lower than it would have been had fuel economy not improved since 1975. In 2000, this translated into an estimated annual reduction of 43 billion gallons of gasoline, compared with actual consumption of 129 billion gallons that year, or 2.8 MBD in U.S. oil consumption, about 14 percent of total demand. And with the price of oil averaging just over $28 per barrel in 2000, it meant a savings to consumers of nearly $30 billion. In addition, given that U.S. consumption represents such a large share of the global market, a difference of that magnitude could have meant a reduction in world prices of 4 to 6 percent, implying additional savings of $1.00 to $1.80 for each of the 3.8 billion barrels of oil imported that year (NRC 2002, 19–20; Davis and Diegel 2004, tab. 2.9). Other studies have offered higher figures, on the order of 30 percent, for the resulting reduction in gasoline consumption (for example, Greene 1998, 595; ESLC 2006, 32). In view of the fact that oil prices and miles driven have only increased in more recent years, current savings are sure to be even greater.

What have been the costs of the CAFE program? In contrast to many of the other energy programs adopted by the U.S. government, the establishment of fuel economy standards entailed no additional federal expenditures, but it may have imposed some economic and social costs. For example, the standards may have required auto manufacturers to make greater capital investments than they otherwise would have. According to a 1982 estimate by the U.S. Office of Technology Assessment, however, the additional investment needed to achieve even steadily rising fuel economy standards would have amounted to only $300 to $700 million per year (OTA 1982, 76–77). By the mid-1980s, moreover, most of the gains in fuel economy had already been achieved. The program may have also made automobile travel somewhat less safe. For example, the NRC has estimated that the downweighting and down-sizing of automobiles that occurred in the late 1970s and early 1980s probably resulted in an additional 1,300 to 2,600 traffic fatalities in 1993 (NRC 2002, 3). But not all of these deaths can be directly attributed to the fuel economy stan-dards, and since the late 1980s vehicles have become heavier on average.

Despite, or perhaps because of, the impressive increases that were made in fuel economy in the late 1970s and early 1980s, the CAFE standards remained virtually unchanged for two decades. The standard for passenger cars is the same as it was in MY 1985, and that for light trucks increased by only 0.2 mpg between 1987 and 2004. The Reagan administration sought, unsuccessfully, to discontinue the program. It argued that the standards were no longer neces-sary in a deregulated market and that their principal effect was to limit the ability of U.S. auto manufacturers to meet consumer demand for a full line of vehicles and to compete against foreign manufacturers (DOE 1988, 42 and 49). Then from 1996 until 2000, Congress prohibited the DOT from not only updating the standards but even studying possible changes (NRC 2002, 1). Not until 2003 did the DOT issue new standards for light trucks, which provided for an increase from 20.7 mpg to 22.2 mpg over several years ending in MY 2007 (NHTSA 2005), and in 2006, the DOT announced a fundamental revi-sion of the light-truck standard that it claimed would raise the average fuel economy for the covered vehicles to approximately 24 mpg in 2011 (Wald 2006; Meckler 2006).

During the nearly two decades that the standards were effectively frozen, overall fuel economy actually declined. The fuel economy of new passenger cars and light trucks, considered separately, has been essentially constant. But the average fuel economy of all new light-duty vehicles slipped nearly 8 per-cent, from a peak of 25.9 mpg in 1987 to 23.8 mpg in 1999, the lowest level since 1980.[4] The principal reason for this decline was a shift in the mix of vehicles on the road from traditional passenger cars toward SUVs, pickup trucks, and vans, which count as light trucks. In 1975, passenger cars, including station wagons, constituted 80 percent of the light-duty vehicle market, and as re-cently as 1990, they still accounted for 67 percent of vehicle sales. But with the introduction of the minivan in the mid-1980s, van sales grew rapidly, reach-ing 10 percent of all light-duty vehicle sales in 1990. Likewise, SUV purchases mushroomed from less than one million units in 1990 to more than four and a half million in 2004, and now constitute one-quarter of the total. As a result of these trends, the light-truck component of the market passed the 50 percent mark in 2000 and continued to grow (see Figure 4.3).[5]

The shift in actual miles driven and fuel use has been equally dramatic. Between 1978 and 1993, light-truck vehicle miles traveled (VMT) grew from 279 to 998 billion, an average annual increase of 5.2 percent, while passenger car VMT rose from 1,147 billion to 1,661 billion, or just 1.5 percent per year on average. Likewise, fuel use by light trucks jumped from 24.2 to 56.3 billion gallons, or 3.4 percent per year, while that by passenger cars actually declined, from 80.6 to 74.6 billion during the same twenty-five-year period.[6]

Finally, it is important to recognize the limits that have been built into the CAFE program from the very beginning. The standards have never applied to heavy trucks, which account for approximately 8 percent of all miles driven and approximately 20 percent of all transportation fuel use, and "light" trucks weighing more than eighty-five hundred pounds have been exempt. In addition, manufacturers can earn CAFE credits by producing flexible-fuel vehicles (FFVs) that can run interchangeably on gasoline or an alternative fuel, such as ethanol. But this provision has had, if anything, a negative effect on fuel

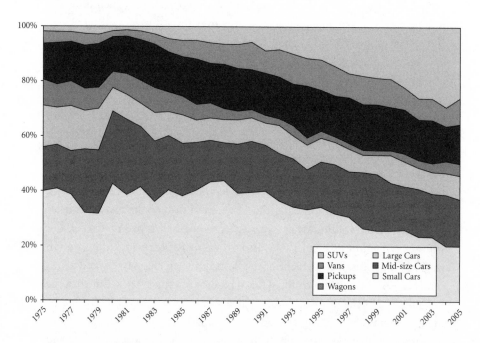

FIGURE 4.3 Light-Duty Vehicle Market Shares, 1975–2005

economy. FFVs seldom use any fuel other than gasoline, yet the credits enable manufacturers to increase their production of less-fuel-efficient vehicles (NRC 2002, 2–3). Not least important, official fuel economy ratings have been universally inflated. The actual fuel use of all vehicles has been about 15 to 20 percent higher than test results. Thus, according to several estimates, the entire personal vehicle fleet has averaged only 20 mpg to 21 mpg on the road in recent years (IEA 1998b, 31; Gerard and Lave 2003, 3; Hakim 2005).

Developing Substitutes for Oil

The United States has also made some efforts to develop and promote the adoption of substitutes for crude oil and its products. For example, during the energy crises of the 1970s, the government temporarily placed restrictions on the use of oil for electricity generation (Plotkin and Greene 1997, 1179). The most important of these efforts, however, have been the ambitious synthetic fuels (synfuels) program of the early 1980s and long-standing tax incentives intended to encourage the substitution of renewable alcohol fuels for gasoline and diesel. Nevertheless, the government synfuels program was abandoned after just five years, and the amount of U.S. oil consumption displaced by alcohol fuels only recently passed the 1 percent mark.

In 1980, Congress created the National Synfuels Production Program under the Energy Security Act of that year. Its purpose was to promote the rapid development of a major synfuels production capability using the extensive coal and oil shale resources of the United States. The legislation set specific production goals of 500,000 barrels per day by 1987 and 2 MBD by 1992, and it authorized $20 billion for the program (OTA 1982, 42–43; Cohen and Noll 1991, 288–89).

The synfuels program was designed to be different from both traditional research and development activities and prior federal energy research. Under the program, synfuel development was to proceed all the way to commercialization and was to be accomplished in the private sector with development-specific subsidies. To implement the program, the Department of Energy (DOE) was authorized to offer financial incentives, mainly in the form of purchase commitments and price guarantees, for the production of alternative or synthetic fuels. The Energy Security Act also created an autonomous Synthetic Fuels Corporation (SFC) as a quasi-investment bank to provide incentives to promote private ownership and operation of synfuels projects. Corporation funds could be used for financial assistance in the form of price guarantees, purchase agreements, and loan guarantees; direct loans; and support for joint ventures (OTA 1982, 42–43; Gaskins and Stram 1991).

Despite much initial fanfare, the SFC lasted only five and half years and is generally regarded as a failure. It was able to stimulate the continuing production of synthetic fuels in only four projects, two of which had been previously approved by the DOE. The most important projects, moreover, were limited to coal gasification. Viable commercialization of oil shale, which had the greatest potential to displace oil imports, was never achieved. When oil prices fell in the 1980s, commercial interest in synthetic fuels faded, and at the end of 1985, the SFC was closed down, twelve years ahead of schedule (OTA 1982, 42–43; Gaskins and Stram 1991).

In response to the energy crises of the 1970s, the United States also sought to encourage the substitution of renewable alcohol fuels for gasoline and diesel. Since the late 1970s, the federal tax code has contained five tax incentives that benefit alcohol fuels, including four tax subsidies for the production and use of alcohol transportation fuels. The most important of these subsidies has been a varying exemption from the excise tax on gasoline and diesel, which was most responsible for the development and growth of the alcohol fuels market until the mid-2000s.[7]

The Energy Tax Act of 1978 established a full excise tax exemption through 1984 for alcohol fuels, including gasohol, a blend of 90 percent gasoline and 10 percent ethanol. When the gasoline tax was raised from 4 to 9 cents per gallon in 1983, the gasohol exemption was increased to 5 cents, and then to 6 cents in 1984. Since 1990, gasohol has been exempt from 5.4 cents of the 18.4 cents per gallon excise tax. Mixtures containing a smaller percentage of ethanol, which are primarily intended to boost the octane level of gasoline in order to reduce ozone and carbon monoxide emissions, receive a prorated exemption. Straight alcohol fuels—mixtures that contain a minimum of 85 percent alcohol—also qualify for excise tax exemptions at rates ranging from 5.4 to 7.0 cents per gallon, but the market for these straight fuels has always been very small (Lazzari 1995; Lazzari 1999; Gielecki, Mayes, and Prete 2001).

The federal subsidy program has greatly stimulated the production of ethanol. Prior to the initiation of the program in 1979, the United States produced virtually no fuel ethanol. Subsequently, output grew steadily, reaching 175 million gallons in 1980, 870 million gallons in 1990, 1.6 billion gallons in 2000, and 3.9 billion gallons in 2005. During its first two decades, the excise tax exemption for alcohol motor fuels resulted in more than $8 billion in foregone federal revenues, and in 1999, the Energy Information Administration estimated that it was worth $725 million that year alone (Lazzari 1999; Gielecki,

Mayes, and Prete 2001; DiPardo 2002). Despite these impressive gains, the amount of ethanol produced did not reach 1 percent of total gasoline and diesel consumption until the early 2000s.[8] Nevertheless, ethanol production has accelerated in recent years and is expected to continue to grow, as the Energy Policy Act of 2005 mandates that 7.5 billion gallons of renewable fuels be included in all gasoline sold in the United States by 2012.

The other important tax incentive has been a federal tax deduction, enacted in 1992, for alternative fuel vehicles, including those that run on fuels containing at least 85 percent alcohol. For passenger cars and other qualifying vehicles under 10,000 pounds, purchasers can deduct up to $2,000 from their gross adjusted income. Larger deductions apply to heavier vehicles. Like the straight alcohol fuels on which they run, however, the market for these vehicles has remained very small. After 2000, this deduction was extended to gasoline-electric hybrid vehicles, but it was phased out in 2006.

Increasing Domestic Oil Production

Complementing these various efforts to reduce American oil consumption, the U.S. government has taken several steps to increase the level of domestic oil production as a means of displacing imported oil. Perhaps the most important of these was the passage of the Trans-Alaska Pipeline Authorization Act in November 1973, just a month after the beginning of the Arab oil embargo. Substantial amounts of oil had been discovered on Alaska's North Slope in 1968, but a variety of legal disputes had blocked the construction of a north-south pipeline across Alaska, which was deemed the most economic means of bringing the oil to market. The 1973 act, which passed by just one vote despite the heightened concern about oil prices and energy security, removed the last major legal hurdle. Construction on the pipeline began in April 1975 and was completed in May 1977, allowing oil to begin flowing the following month. When Alaskan crude production peaked at 2.0 MBD in 1988, it accounted for more than 20 percent of total U.S. petroleum output (and nearly one-quarter of crude oil production), although it has since fallen by more than half.

Other, less dramatic, steps to increase domestic oil production have included various tax incentives for oil and gas investment and the leasing of mineral rights on federal lands and the outer continental shelf. In addition, the government has reduced or waived royalties in an effort to encourage oil exploration and development when difficult physical conditions make the resources costly to develop and to ensure continuing production from marginal wells. For example, the Outer Continental Shelf Deep Water Royalty Relief Act of November 1995 reduced or eliminated royalties in existing leases for oil and gas resources in deep-water areas, and it suspended royalties on new leases in specified water depths in the Gulf of Mexico for five years. Likewise, the government issued new regulations in 1996 that lowered royalties on federal lands that produce heavy oil (IEA 1998b, 51). Overall, however, these measures have been able to do little to arrest the general decline in total U.S. oil production, which has dropped by more than 33 percent since 1973.[9]

Energy Research and Development

The federal government has supplemented and supported these economic policies and programs with investments in energy research and development (R&D). From 1974 through 2000, the federal government spent more than $100 billion in 2000 dollars for this purpose, mostly through DOE programs. This direct federal investment constituted about one-third of the nation's total expenditure on energy R&D, including that by the private and nongovernmental sectors (NRC 2001, 1–2).

Nevertheless, federal spending on energy research and development has been marked by multiple and changing goals, of which lowering oil dependence has been but one. Of course, reducing dependence on energy imports, especially oil, was a central tenet of energy policy during the 1970s and into the 1980s. During that period, the Ford administration assigned top priority to coal and uranium technologies as substitutes for high-priced oil and gas, while the subsequent Carter administration placed greater emphasis on energy conservation, renewable energy resources such as solar and wind, and increased fossil fuel production in the short- to medium-term. Parallel to the synfuels program, federal research and development also stressed the production of alternative liquid fuels from domestic sources such as coal and oil shale, and the government engaged in large and expensive demonstration projects (Barfield 1982, 5, 19–20; NRC 2001, 1, 9–10).

Beginning in the early 1980s, more faith was placed in market forces to resolve imbalances in energy supply and demand. The Reagan administration withdrew support for large demonstration and development projects and instead stressed long-term research and development. It also emphasized energy production over conservation and, within the production side, nuclear power over fossil fuels. After 1992, however, priorities shifted back in the direction of renewable energy resources and energy efficiency (Barfield 1982; NRC 2001, 10, 88–89).

Paralleling these shifting goals have been wide swings in the size of the federal energy R&D budget. Spending increased rapidly during the energy crises of the 1970s, from just $2 billion in 1973 to more than $7 billion in 1979 in 2000 dollars. During the following decade, however, it declined almost as quickly, to just $4 billion in 1983 and then to a low of $2.8 billion in 1987 (2000 dollars) (see Figure 4.4).

These shifting priorities are reflected in the experience of the Office of Fossil Energy within the DOE, which received $15 billion between 1978 and 2000. Fifty-eight percent of this money went for R&D in coal utilization and conversion, of which approximately one-half was spent on building and operating large commercial-sized demonstration plants for direct liquefaction and gasification between 1978 to 1981. Indeed, during that four-year period, when the overall level of spending was especially high, nearly three-quarters of the office's R&D budget was devoted to technologies for producing liquid and gas fuels from U.S. coal and oil shale in order to address the effects of the energy

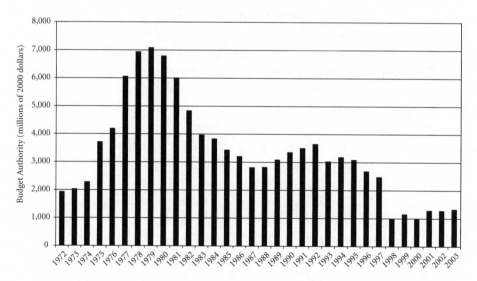

FIGURE 4.4 Federal Energy Research and Development, 1972–2003

NOTE: Beginning in FY1998, a number of DOE programs were reclassified from energy to general science and basic research.

SOURCE: NSF 2004, tab. 42.

crises (NRC 2001, 2, 5, 44, 46). In contrast, only 14 percent of the office's R&D money was spent on traditional oil and gas research (NRC 2001, 46).

What impact has federal spending on energy research and development had? It is difficult to quantify the contributions this investment may have made. A National Research Council study did conclude that energy efficiency programs have provided some national security benefits by decreasing oil use somewhat. But it also found that DOE research programs have proved disappointing in reducing petroleum dependence in the transportation sector (NRC 2001, 64). Likewise, it judged that the fossil energy programs of 1978 to 1986, which emphasized going directly from bench-scale to large-scale demonstrations to make synthetic fuels from coal and oil shale, yielded relatively small benefits that were less than the cost of the programs (NRC 2001, 63).

Efforts to Mitigate the Economic Impact of Oil Shocks

Despite repeated calls for energy independence over the years, the United States has never come even close to achieving that goal. Indeed, it may now be farther away than ever. Oil imports did fall by half between 1977 and 1982, to just 4.3 MBD, but the decline owed more to high prices, which suppressed demand and stimulated domestic production, than to government programs. Moreover, the percentage of total demand met by foreign oil never dropped below 27 percent, and since the mid-1980s imports have grown inexorably in both absolute terms and as a share of consumption.

Even though American foreign oil dependence could not be eliminated or even substantially reduced, the economic costs of oil shocks could at least be mitigated. Since the 1973 Arab oil embargo, the U.S. government has employed two main measures to buffer the economy against supply disruptions and sharp price hikes. During the 1970s, it maintained price controls on crude oil and many petroleum products, but this policy proved to be counterproductive and was eventually abandoned. Instead, the principal long-term response for reducing the impact of possible oil shocks has been the Strategic Petroleum Reserve.

Price Controls

The measure that did the most to mitigate the impact of the first oil shock was the maintenance of price controls on crude oil and many petroleum products. This was not their original purpose, however. The Nixon administration had initially imposed a ninety-day freeze on prices and wages in August 1971 in an attempt to arrest an inflationary spiral. The controls on oil and petroleum products had subsequently been modified several times and were still in effect at the time of the Arab oil embargo.

The most recent version, Phase IV, had been introduced in August 1973 and was intended to last only through the following April. It was designed to preserve some of the benefits of price controls while encouraging domestic oil production, which had been in decline since 1970. The Phase IV rules maintained ceilings on the retail prices of gasoline, diesel, and home heating oil, which together accounted for about 70 percent of refined products. At the same time, they introduced a novel two-tier pricing system for domestically produced crude oil. The price of crude from existing wells—"old" oil—continued to be frozen, while the price of new crude—defined as supplies that exceeded 1972 production levels—was permitted to rise to world levels. In addition, production from stripper wells, those producing less than ten barrels per day, was exempted from controls as was imported crude oil (de Marchi 1981, 456; Bohi and Russell 1978, 221–22).

After the first oil shock hit, these ceilings were maintained. And in December 1975, the Energy Policy and Conservation Act, which also established the CAFE program, extended them for at least another forty months and broadened them to include new oil and stripper-well oil, thereby reducing the weighted-average price ceiling for domestic crude oil by more than one dollar per barrel. Consequently, although the act also permitted the president to raise the average price by up to 3 percent per year plus an adjustment for inflation, price controls on crude oil and petroleum products were retained long after they were removed from the remainder of the economy (Bohi and Russell 1978, 229).

In the short term, the price controls had the desirable effect of limiting the impact of the first oil shock. They partially shielded consumers from the jump in world oil prices, greatly slowing the rise in the cost of both crude oil and petroleum products in the United States (see Table 4.1). Thus even as world oil prices quadrupled, the U.S. price of gasoline increased from about thirty-five cents per gallon before the embargo to slightly more than fifty cents in the mid-1970s. According to one estimate, the price controls saved consumers as much as $24 billion in 1975 (DOE 1988, 4; Ikenberry 1988, 166–71).

These benefits came, however, at a considerable cost. The price controls encouraged demand and discouraged conservation without greatly stimulating domestic oil production. As a result, oil consumption in the United States

TABLE 4.1 Prices for Crude Oil and Gasoline, 1968–1982

	Crude Oil Refiner Acquisition Costs (nominal dollars per barrel)		Gasoline Prices (nominal cents per gallon) 1968–1977: leaded regular 1978–1982: all grades
	Domestic	Imported	
1968	3.21	2.90	33.7
1969	3.37	2.80	34.8
1970	3.46	2.96	35.7
1971	3.68	3.17	36.4
1972	3.67	3.22	36.1
1973	4.17	4.08	38.8
1974	7.18	12.52	53.2
1975	8.39	13.93	56.7
1976	8.84	13.48	59
1977	9.55	14.53	62.2
1978	10.61	14.57	65.2
1979	14.27	21.67	88.2
1980	24.23	33.89	122.1
1981	34.33	37.05	135.3
1982	31.22	33.55	128.1

SOURCE: EIA 2005b, tabs. 5.21, 5.24.

rose by nearly 1.5 MBD, or more than 8 percent, between 1973 and 1978 even as it declined in Europe. And net U.S. imports grew even faster, from 6.0 MBD in 1973 to 8.6 MBD in 1977, a trend that was slowed only by the arrival of Alaskan oil on the market in substantial quantities that year.

Even before the embargo, price controls also created problems for many domestic refiners and marketers, who did not have equal access to cheaper oil. Many were largely or wholly dependent on unregulated domestic or imported crude, resulting in differences in their input costs. The sharp rise in world prices following the embargo only made matters worse, and regional price disparities and shortages followed (Bohi and Russell 1978, 222–24; Ikenberry 1988, 169–70).

In response to these problems, the government took steps toward preparing to ration gasoline in the event of a severe crisis. As early as November 1973, President Nixon ordered that contingency plans be prepared for formal

rationing to consumers and for special taxation of oil products, and he requested legislation granting the president authority to allocate or ration energy supplies, which Congress promptly granted. Likewise, the Energy Policy
and Conservation Act of 1975 requested that the president submit a gasoline
rationing plan to Congress for approval and granted the president standby
powers to impose gasoline rationing and other demand-restraint measures. It
was not until the final year of the Carter administration, as the second energy
crisis subsided, however, that a plan was approved by Congress and detailed
preparations for standby rationing could begin (Bohi and Russell 1978, 228–29,
237–38, 334; Yager 1981, 606–8; DOE 1988, 5; CBO 1981, 2).

More important, the price controls forced the government to adopt a
mandatory allocation program for refiners and marketers. At the beginning
of 1974, the Nixon administration implemented a set of guidelines for the allocation of both crude oil and refined products. A year later, the Ford administration developed a crude-oil cost equalization, or "entitlements," program
in a further attempt to eliminate disparities in input costs (Bohi and Russell
1978, 222–26; de Marchi 1981, 452). But these allocation schemes only made the
situation worse. Not only were they administratively burdensome, but by requiring companies to transfer increased supplies to competitors, they reduced
still further the incentives to find new oil (Bohi and Russell 1978, 333).

As a result of such problems, there was considerable interest in lifting the
price controls as soon as possible in order to let the market allocate supplies
and bring about an equilibrium between supply and demand. For more than
half a decade, however, Congress opposed doing so. Many feared that consumers would be hurt and that the big oil companies, which had been sus-
pected of engineering the energy crisis in the first place, would profit exces-
sively. It was not until April 1979 that President Carter was able to begin the
process of gradually lifting price controls on domestic crude and petroleum
products, with the goal of removing them completely by October 1981. Shortly
after taking office in January of that year, President Reagan ordered the immediate removal of all remaining controls.

The Strategic Petroleum Reserve

Instead of price controls, the principal U.S. policy for limiting the impact of oil
supply disruptions has been the maintenance of the Strategic Petroleum Reserve (SPR). The SPR was officially established in December 1975 by the Energy
Policy and Conservation Act (EPCA). The EPCA mandated the creation of a

strategic petroleum reserve with a capacity equivalent to ninety days of imports, then about 500 million barrels, within seven years.[10] In 1977, the Carter administration increased the goal to one billion barrels by 1985.[11]

The reserve is stored in underground salt domes along the Gulf Coast of Texas and Louisiana. The first storage sites were acquired in April 1977, and the first oil was delivered in July of that year. Today, the reserve consists of approximately sixty storage caverns located at four storage areas. Each cavern can hold approximately ten million barrels and measures about two hundred feet across and two thousand feet deep.[12]

The buildup of the SPR proceeded rapidly at first, with the fill rate reaching 300,000 barrels per day, or more than 100 million barrels per year, in 1978. During the second oil shock, when world prices doubled, purchases were greatly reduced, leaving the SPR with the equivalent of less than two weeks of imports (Alm, Colglazier, and Kates-Garnick 1981, 326f.). A more rapid pace was resumed in the early 1980s, and the size of the SPR passed the 500 million barrel mark in 1986. After that, its growth slowed again considerably, leaving a total of 585.7 million barrels at the time of the 1991 Gulf War. The SPR's holdings temporarily peaked in the mid-1990s at 592 million barrels, even though its potential storage capacity had reached as much as 750 million barrels, and then declined because of nonemergency oil sales and exchanges to approximately 540 million barrels in 2000 (see Figure 3.5).[13]

In November 2001, following the terrorist attacks of September 11 that year, President George W. Bush directed the DOE to fill the SPR to its full capacity in order to "maximize long-term protection against oil supply disruptions." As of late 2006, the reserve contained some 690 million barrels out of a potential storage capacity of 727 million barrels. Oil can be pumped from the reserve at a maximum rate of 4.3 MBD for ninety days, with oil beginning to arrive in the marketplace fifteen days after a presidential decision to initiate a drawdown. The withdrawal rate then declines to 3.2 MBD from days 91 to 120, to 2.2 MBD for days 121 to 150, and to 1.3 MBD for days 151 to 180.[14]

The SPR can lessen the impact of an oil shock in two ways. First, it can be used to replace any loss of supplies. As a result, its very presence can deter shortfalls created for political purposes, as during the 1973 Arab oil embargo. As an early study noted, the likelihood that a producer state would use its ability to manipulate oil supplies in an attempt to influence U.S. policy is directly related to its chances of success (Alm, Colglazier, and Kates-Garnick 1981, 326). With a large enough petroleum stockpile, the United States could compensate for virtually any intentional disruption. With the passage of time, however, another embargo has come to be viewed as highly unlikely.

Thus an even more important purpose of the SPR is to moderate prices during a supply disruption or other oil market crisis. The release of stockpile oil to the market can reduce fears of a shortage and thereby obviate the consumer panic that has often been responsible for driving up prices. Thus, some have argued, if a substantial strategic reserve had been available and used after the Iranian production cutback of 1978–79, virtually all of the resulting price increase could have been avoided (Alm, Colglazier, and Kates-Garnick 1981, 326).

Under what circumstances would stockpile oil be released? According to the EPCA, there is no preset "trigger" for withdrawing oil from the SPR. Instead, the president determines that a drawdown is required by "a severe energy supply interruption or by obligations of the United States" under the International Energy Agency. The EPCA defines a "severe energy supply interruption" as one which (1) "is, or is likely to be, of significant scope and duration, and of an emergency nature"; (2) "may cause major adverse impact on national safety or the national economy" (including an oil price spike), and (3) "results, or is likely to result, from an interruption in the supply of imported petroleum products, or from sabotage or an act of God." Should the president decide to order an emergency drawdown of the SPR, oil would be distributed mainly by competitive sale to the highest bidder.[15] In 1991, Congress granted the president authority to use the SPR for more limited supply disruptions. It approved the release of up to thirty million barrels during a two-month period without a declaration of a severe supply interruption or the need to meet international obligations (Goldwyn and Billig 2005, 512, 524).

In fact, the SPR has been used to address an actual or expected disruption of foreign oil supplies on just one occasion and only to a limited extent. In January 1991, on the eve of Operation Desert Storm, President George H. W. Bush ordered a limited drawdown of 33.75 million barrels in order to avert a possible price spike. In the event, however, world oil prices dropped quickly after the outbreak of hostilities, and only 17 million barrels were sold, as markets quickly perceived that the war would be brief and that Saudi oil supplies were not in danger (Delucchi 1998, 63–64; Goldwyn and Billig 2005, 512).

Nevertheless, the SPR has served as an insurance policy against supply disruptions, and in this capacity, it has been widely regarded as one of the most successful economic policy responses to U.S. foreign oil dependence.[16]

But at what price? Unfortunately, there is no single answer to this question, in part because analysts have used different methods to calculate the cost of the SPR. One method is simply to add up the annual government outlays. As of early 2005, the United States had invested about $4 billion in facilities and $16 billion in oil purchases.[17] The total for oil purchases would be higher but for the fact that the additions to the reserve since 2001 have been provided by domestic producers at no charge in lieu of royalty payments for production on federal lands. Thus the actual cost to the government, including foregone revenues, is somewhat greater. Annual operations and maintenance costs during the first decade or two averaged about $100 million, but they have grown larger in more recent years, approaching $200 million (Bohi and Toman 1996, 125; Leiby et al. 1997, S–12; Delucchi 1998, 66–67; ICTA 2005, 4). Thus altogether, direct government spending has totaled roughly $25 billion, not accounting for inflation, which would cause the figure to be higher.

A second approach assumes that all the money for capital investment and oil purchases is borrowed. It estimates an annualized cost that includes the interest that must be paid on this debt as well as operation and management expenses and capital depreciation. The two largest components of the annualized cost are the imputed interest charges on the more than $16 billion spent to purchase oil and the financing of the funds invested to build and maintain the capital infrastructure. Depending on the interest rate used, estimates for these carrying costs in the mid-1990s, when the size of the SPR stood at nearly 600 million barrels, ranged from $1 to $2 billion per year. To this figure must be added a further $100 to $200 million per year for the operating costs (Bohi and Toman 1996; Koplow and Martin 1998, 4.17–4.18). During twenty-five years, the overall cost would total roughly $25 to $50 billion.

A final approach assumes that the interest is not paid off every year but is capitalized through additional government borrowing. As one study has noted:

> Given the government's fiscal deficits throughout [the] SPR's life, the Treasury had to issue debt to provide [the] SPR's funding, and it had to pay interest on that debt. To pay the interest, the Treasury would have needed either to receive compensation for its investment [which it did not] or to issue more debt, effectively requiring it to pay interest on accrued interest. As the purpose of issuing the debt in the first place was to fund [the] SPR, this compounding of interest would be directly attributable to [the] SPR as well. (Koplow and Martin 1998, 4.22)

That study went on to calculate that the SPR would have been responsible for a total debt from direct investment and compounded interest on unpaid debt of $74.7 billion in 1995 and that the interest cost alone on this accrued debt was more than $5.2 billion that year (Koplow and Martin 1998, 4.23–4.24). By the mid-2000s, the total would have been approximately $50 billion higher, or some $125 billion.

The SPR may have other costs that are more difficult, if not impossible, to quantify. For example, by helping to protect consumers and refiners from oil market disruptions, the SPR may have reduced both the need for private sector entities to maintain their own inventories and the incentives for consumers to increase their ability to shift fuels in times of oil shortages (Koplow and Martin 1998, 4.17). In fact, private stocks have declined by several hundred million barrels since the SPR was established, although this drop may have other causes as well (see Figure 3.5).

Economic Cooperation with Other Consumer Countries

The United States has sought to complement its efforts at home to limit American foreign oil dependence and to buffer the economy against future oil shocks by working with other industrialized countries, most of which have relied even more heavily on imported oil. This cooperation has taken place primarily within the International Energy Agency (IEA), which was founded in 1974 at the initiative of the United States following the first oil shock. Under American leadership, the IEA has developed policies and programs intended to mitigate the impact of supply disruptions and to reduce the level of oil imports over the longer term. Overall, however, these measures have not significantly reduced the economic costs and risks to the United States of foreign oil dependence.

Formation of the International Energy Agency

Soon after the initiation of the Arab oil embargo in October 1973, U.S. officials called for unity among the oil consuming nations. Secretary of State Henry Kissinger in particular hoped to coordinate the energy policies of the advanced industrialized countries as a means of inducing members of the Organization of the Petroleum Exporting Countries (OPEC) to moderate oil prices. To that end, the United States invited a number of major oil consumers to attend an energy conference in Washington in February 1974 (Ikenberry 1988, 10).

One of Kissinger's initial goals was to create a unified consumer-nation bloc that could articulate a common negotiating position and thereby bargain effectively with OPEC. This goal was frustrated, however, by European and Japanese fears of antagonizing the oil producers through an overly confrontational stance. Most of the other consumer countries lacked substantial domestic energy resources to fall back on. As a result, some were seeking to forge bilateral deals with OPEC countries that would guarantee them adequate supplies of oil (Walton 1976, 187; Bohi and Russell 1978, 239; Ikenberry 1988, 88–89; Long 1985, 26).

Nevertheless, there was much on which the oil consuming states could concur. During the next nine months, they developed detailed agreements for an International Energy Program (IEP) and for the establishment of a new international agency, the IEA, which would serve as the organizational mechanism for implementing the provisions of the program. Both agreements were adopted by sixteen member countries of the Organization for Economic Cooperation and Development (OECD) in November 1974 (Willrich and Conant 1977, 200; R. Scott 1994, I).

The IEP contained two main components that were intended to address directly the problems posed by foreign oil dependence. One involved preparations for and responses to possible future supply disruptions. The other concerned longer-term efforts to reduce oil imports.[18]

Provisions for Coping with Oil Supply Disruptions

The highest priority of the states that founded the IEA was to develop collective means for responding to oil supply disruptions. As early as the February 1974 Washington Energy Conference, the United States proposed a set of emergency measures, including the sharing of oil holdings, that could be implemented in the event of another oil shock (Ikenberry 1988, 89; R. Scott 1994, I:45). By November 1974, the main outlines and many of the details of what was called the Emergency Sharing System had been worked out and were included as the first four chapters of the International Energy Program adopted at that time. The Emergency Sharing System consists of treaty-based, obligatory measures for preparing for and responding to short-term supply disruptions. In particular, it requires members (1) to build and maintain substantial levels of oil stocks; (2) to plan and implement, if necessary, measures to reduce oil consumption during interruptions, and (3) to allocate available oil supplies equitably among IEA members in an emergency (R. Scott 1994, II:35, 68–69).

According to the 1974 IEP agreement, members commit themselves to maintain emergency oil reserves equal to sixty days of imports. In 1976, the IEA agreed to raise the required level of stocks to the equivalent of ninety days of imports by 1980 (R. Scott 1994, II:73). The IEP also obligates each member "at all times [to] have ready a program of contingent oil demand restraint measures enabling it to reduce its rate of final consumption." Whenever the group as a whole sustains an oil supply reduction of at least 7 percent, each country must reduce its consumption by that amount. If collective oil supplies are cut by 12 percent or more, each participant must reduce consumption by 10 percent. In the event that only one country is affected, it must implement comparable measures of demand restraint.

Finally, and most significantly, the Emerging Sharing System provides for the allocation of oil supplies during a disruption. Should one or more members or the IEA as a whole suffer a supply reduction of at least 7 percent and reduce consumption accordingly, participants are required to share their supplies so as to equalize the burden of coping with the reduction. In particular, countries suffering a disproportionate loss of oil supplies are entitled to transfers from less affected members (Willrich and Conant 1977, 207; Bohi and Toman 1986, 38; R. Scott 1994, II:84).

The process of activating the Emergency Sharing System assigns a central role to the supranational secretariat of the IEA. It begins when the secretariat makes a finding that a reduction in oil supplies available to the group as a whole or to a participating country of at least 7 percent has occurred or can reasonably be expected to occur. Should the secretariat issue such a finding, activation can be blocked only by a large majority of the members. Thus the process involves a substantial delegation of authority, and implementation does not require a prior political decision by member governments (Willrich and Conant 1977, 209–10; R. Scott 1994, II:86).

For all its innovative features, the original Emergency Sharing System nevertheless suffered from a number of limitations (Bohi and Toman 1986, 44; R. Scott 1994, II:71, 80–82, 90, 125). First, some elements lacked specificity. For example, there were no agreed measures regarding the use of oil stocks and demand restraint, raising questions about how those elements would be implemented and whether they would be effective. Second, the system offered members considerable latitude with regard to how they would meet their commitments. For example, members could use any stocks they held in excess of the required ninety-day emergency reserve to substitute for demand restraint measures. And it provided for no formal sanctions or sanctioning mechanism in the event that members failed to comply with the oil sharing rules.

A third potential problem was the slowness with which the activation process might work. As many as twenty-four days could transpire between the necessary finding by the secretariat and the implementation of emergency measures, during which affected states might have to use a substantial share of their oil stocks. Finally, and most important, the system was not applicable in the event of oil supply disruptions that fell below the 7 percent threshold. The desire to limit the implementation of obligatory demand restraint and oil sharing measures to the most serious instances was understandable. But, as became increasingly clear with time, even disruptions that were too small to trigger activation of the Emergency Sharing System could have substantial negative economic consequences, especially if they generated sharp price increases. As two economists observed, with the system's focus on supply problems rather than on price responses, its ability to moderate price hikes was likely to be limited (Bohi and Toman 1986, 41).

Some of these limitations seemed to be on display during the second oil crisis, which involved the first and only request to activate the Emergency Sharing System. As early as March 1979, following the upheavals in Iran, IEA members had agreed to reduce their demand by two MBD, or approximately 5 percent, but the decision was not legally binding and involved no firm national commitments to implement any particular measures. In the meantime, Sweden had complained that it was suffering a supply shortfall of as much as 17 percent, and in late May, it requested the activation of the Emergency Sharing System, claiming a first-quarter supply reduction of nearly 10 percent after adjusting for seasonal factors. In response, however, the secretariat declined to make the necessary finding, attributing Sweden's problems to special conditions (Keohane 1984, 228–30; R. Scott 1994, II:115, 117).

However justified, the secretariat's refusal to activate the Emergency Sharing System raised questions about its relevance (Cowhey 1985, 271). In the wake of the crisis, there was widespread recognition of the need for more flexible arrangements and procedures, especially the use of stocks and demand restraint, for responding to and managing lesser supply disruptions. During the next five years, the IEA took several steps intended to remedy this deficiency.

In December 1981, it agreed that the Governing Board, the highest-level decision-making body, should meet immediately to address any supply disruption and to consider various measures. In a July 1984 "Decision on Stocks and Supply Disruptions," moreover, it established the Coordinated Emergency Response Measures (CERM) system, which involved a new set of procedural commitments intended to facilitate rapid agreement on measures in response to supply disruptions that fell below the 7 percent threshold and emphasized the early use of oil stocks in a crisis (R. Scott 1994, II:38, 79, 118, 125–26, 135). As a result of these adjustments, concludes an official history of the agency, "the IEA ha[d] become fully armed institutionally to manage a wide range of oil supply disruptions" (R. Scott 1994, II:130).

The first test of the revised system did not occur until the 1991 Gulf War. In early January, the IEA approved a contingency plan that would make 2.5 MBD of oil available to the market within fifteen days. The main goal was not so much to replace any losses as to reassure the markets that adequate oil would be available to meet any shortfall. The plan was activated immediately upon the commencement of hostilities on January 17, but only about half the oil made available was taken up (R. Scott 1994, II:39, 134, 144). Then almost fifteen years later, in the wake of Hurricane Katrina, the IEA agreed to make available to the market the equivalent of 2.0 MBD of oil for an period of thirty days with the goal of offsetting the loss of 1.5 MBD of oil production and 2.0 MBD of refinery capacity in the United States. Europe in particular offered more than 0.5 MBD in finished products such as gasoline, diesel, and fuel oil that were in short supply on the East Coast of the United States.[19]

Despite these improvements and successes, questions remained about the ability of the system to address a serious supply crisis. Of particular concern has been the adequacy of the emergency oil stocks, which have increasingly been expected to play a leading role in addressing supply disruptions. One early analysis noted that "present definitions of reserves are very loose, making it easy for most countries to satisfy a 90-day commitment out of normal working inventories plus fuel-switching capacity and standby oil production" (Willrich and Conant 1977, 206). As a result, a high percentage of the required stocks might not in fact be available for prompt use during an emergency (Plummer and Weyant 1982, 266). In fact, when the Gulf crisis began in August 1990, IEA governments owned or directly controlled stocks equal to only thirty days of consumption, or far fewer than sixty days of imports (R. Scott 1994, II:135). In the mid-1980s, the United States had encouraged other EIA members, especially Japan and Germany, to increase their strategic oil reserves, but this proposal had been strongly resisted due to an unwillingness to undertake the necessary financial burden (DOE 1988, xi; Bohi and Toman 1986, 44) (see Figure 4.5).

Overall, then, it is not clear that the oil supply disruption measures adopted by the IEA have significantly improved the position of the United States. Initially, the oil sharing system might have been expected to benefit the United States as perhaps the most obvious target of a future oil embargo. But as the prospect of a targeted embargo diminished, it became increasingly likely that the United States would be a substantial net contributor in the event that the IEA allocation provisions were activated. Not only was the United States the largest oil producer in the organization, but it also possessed by far the largest strategic oil reserves under government control. Indeed, although total OECD oil stocks grew from 2,588 million barrels in 1973 to more than 4 billion barrels in 2005, much of the increase was accounted for by the creation of the U.S. Strategic Petroleum Reserve (Greene, Jones, and Leiby 1998, 64). Thus, in the 1991 contingency plan, for example, Washington

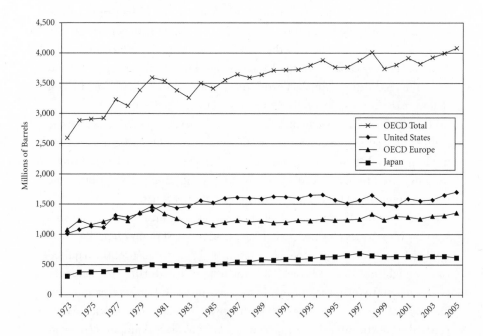

FIGURE 4.5 OECD Oil Stocks, 1973–2005
SOURCE: EIA 2007a, tab. 4.5.

assumed responsibility for meeting nearly 50 percent of the total IEA commitment of 2.5 MBD and nearly 60 percent of the planned stock drawdown by the twenty-four participating countries.[20] Following Hurricane Katrina, moreover, the United States offered half of what the IEA as a whole promised to contribute. In short, the IEA provisions have added little to the U.S. capacity to mitigate unilaterally the economic impact of an oil shock.

Long-Term Measures to Reduce Oil Imports

The second principal component of the IEA's International Energy Program of direct relevance to the problem of foreign oil dependence concerned longer-term efforts to limit oil imports. The IEP itself contained no detailed guidance or commitments, as there had been insufficient time to develop such a plan. But over the remainder of the decade, the members adopted a number of more specific measures, including a comprehensive long-term cooperation program in March 1976, intended to reduce their reliance on imported oil (Willrich and Conant 1977, 212; R. Scott 1994, II:43, 157). These measures took two main forms: the setting of specific import reduction targets and various means for stimulating the development of additional indigenous energy sources.

In February 1975, at the urging of the United States, the IEA established a nonbinding goal of reducing imports by 10 percent, or two MBD, that year (Walton 1976, 194; Cowhey 1985, 257). The following year, the United States began to press the other members to make firm political commitments to reduce their dependence on foreign oil and to increase domestic energy production (Willrich and Conant 1977, 221). This effort led to a 1977 agreement on a group import target of twenty-six MBD in 1985, which represented a four MBD reduction in the level of imports projected for that future year. Nevertheless, U.S. calls for firm national targets were opposed (Keohane 1978, 941; Keohane 1984, 225–26; R. Scott 1994, II:164).

Interest in import reduction goals was rekindled by the 1979 oil crisis, which resulted in a further doubling of prices. At the end of the year, the IEA fixed individual import targets for 1980, and it lowered the previously agreed group target for 1985 to 24.6 MBD (Plummer and Weyand 1982, 266; R. Scott 1994, II:118, 165). According to one observer, however, even these targets were too high to be effectively constraining (Keohane 1984, 231). Indeed, total net imports for the OECD countries, including several non-IEA members, amounted to just seventeen MBD in 1985. And as the second oil shock eased, the renewed interest in setting targets quickly waned. In 1980, U.S. proposals for additional cuts in 1981 and 1985 were opposed, and since then, no further quantitative group or national import goals have been adopted (Keohane 1984, 232; Cowhey 1985, 259 and 273; R. Scott 1994, II:44, 165).

Especially during the 1970s, the IEA, again prodded by the United States, also adopted a number of measures intended to promote domestic energy production as a means of reducing oil imports. The most noteworthy of these was the now forgotten minimum safeguard price (MSP). As early as November 1974, the United States proposed the establishment of a floor for the cost of imported oil in order to protect new investments in alternative energy sources, especially domestic oil production, from the risk of a decline in the price of imports. In March 1975, the IEA members reached an agreement in principle to adopt such a minimum safeguard price. But those countries that lacked significant indigenous energy sources in which to invest were not enthusiastic about the concept, so another year and a half transpired before all the details could be worked out. In order to obtain a consensus, moreover, the MSP was eventually set at just $7 per barrel, which was lower than anyone at the time expected prices would ever fall. In any case, within two years, it was rendered meaningless by the second oil shock and, as a result, has never been invoked (Walton 1976, 194; Willrich and Conant 1977, 213; Keohane 1978, 939–40; Cowhey 1984, 253–54; R. Scott 1994, II:45, 167).

Finally, the United States has sought to use the IEA to promote greater international cooperation in energy research and development. Until 1974, international energy cooperation was largely limited to the exchange of information. Since its establishment, however, the IEA has played an important role in the formation and operation of collaborative projects, to which its founders and early policymakers assigned high priority. By the late 1970s, the total number of specific IEA sponsored project activities had reached approximately fifty, where it remained for at least the next decade and a half (R. Scott 1994, II:228, 258, 260, 282).

Nevertheless, some have expressed considerable doubts as to the significance of these projects and the contributions of the IEA to energy research and development more generally. The United States had initially promoted an umbrella organization to share the risks on difficult projects, but other states rejected common funding. Consequently, the IEA provides no financing, and the projects it approves are fully decentralized, with all activities carried out in member states rather than at IEA facilities (Cowhey 1985, 255–56; R. Scott 1994, II:267, 282). It appears then that many of the projects could have been developed outside the IEA framework, if necessary, and that the agency's research and development efforts have been of relatively little importance in comparison with national programs (Keohane 1978, 943–44).

Thus IEA efforts to reduce member oil imports over the long term have been even less successful than the agency's attempts to develop provisions for dealing with short-term supply disruptions. A reduction in the level of imports was an important initial objective, and some members, led by the United States, were willing to consider highly interventionist measures, such as import targets and the MSP. But few effective operational mechanisms for achieving the goal were ever in fact established. Since the early 1980s, the IEA, like the United States itself, has placed heavy reliance on market forces (Plummer and Weyant 1982, 262; R. Scott 1994, II:24, 158).

In sum, the United States took the lead in creating the IEA and developing its functions and capabilities, especially during the 1970s (Keohane 1978, 945–46). Many IEA activities have paralleled U.S. policy efforts at home to reduce oil consumption and imports and to limit the impact of future oil shocks. Yet the value added of the IEA in these areas is questionable. Certainly, it has done relatively little in comparison with purely national efforts by the United States to reduce the costs of its foreign oil dependence. Although the agency has amounted, as two early observers noted, to something more than a mirage, it never became much more than a modest mechanism for contingent oil sharing and has done little by itself to lower imports (Willrich and Conant 1977, 202; Ikenberry 1988, 10). Instead, the IEA has become best known for its contributions in the area of collecting and disseminating information about energy markets and national energy policies.

Conclusion

Since the oil shocks of the 1970s, the United States has undertaken a number of economic policy measures intended to reduce the costs and risks of foreign oil dependence. Its greatest success has been in the area of mitigating the likely economic impact of future oil shocks, primarily through the creation of a substantial strategic petroleum reserve. In contrast, the United States has done relatively little to limit oil use or imports by American consumers. For example, U.S. gasoline taxes have remained among the lowest in the industrialized world, and the government has provided only very limited support for mass transit and the development of alternative energy sources. The most ambitious government program, for the development of synthetic fuels, made little progress and was soon abandoned.

Instead, the policies that have been most effective at reducing oil consumption have been the removal of price controls on domestic crude oil and petroleum products in the late 1970s and early 1980s and the establishment of fuel economy standards for passenger cars and light trucks. Yet price controls were lifted only belatedly, and even the benefits of the CAFE program have been increasingly undermined by the existence of significantly lower standards for light trucks and the substantial growth in their share of the light-duty vehicle fleet.

The generally modest nature of U.S. economic policy responses can be attributed to a variety of factors. During the 1970s, at the height of the oil crises, government officials proposed a number of often ambitious ideas for reducing oil consumption. But most of these were either never adopted, significantly diluted in the legislative process, or greatly delayed in their implementation. In a few cases, progress was impeded by real conflicts between competing policy objectives, such as the stimulation of domestic oil production and limiting the negative consequences of higher world oil prices, which required maintaining price controls. More often, however, special interests, including both consumer and business groups, exploited the opportunities offered by the American political system to block policies that they opposed but were arguably in the national interest. Also important was the limited capacity of the American government to pursue highly interventionist policies (Ikenberry 1988).

In the 1980s and later, the goal of reducing foreign oil dependence encountered two more sets of obstacles. One was the distinct preference of the Reagan and, arguably, subsequent administrations to rely primarily, if not exclusively, on market forces. As a 1988 Department of Energy review noted:

> The experience of the 1970s shows that massive government intervention, through taxes, regulations, and subsidies, is not the proper response to over-dependence on potentially insecure suppliers. Instead, reliance on the market, supplemented where necessary with prudent government programs, is the best—indeed the only—approach to meeting successfully the challenges ahead. (DOE 1988, 35)

Second, a marked softening of the world oil market in the early 1980s largely ended fears of supply disruptions and sharp price hikes. Indeed, oil prices

TABLE 4.2 Comparison of Oil Consumption in 2005

	Oil Use (million barrels per day)	Oil as % of Total Energy	Oil Use per Capita* (barrels per year)	Oil Intensity (barrels per $1,000 of GDP)
Britain	1.79	36.5	10.8	.359
France	1.96	35.5	11.8	.398
Germany	2.59	37.5	11.5	.381
Japan	5.36	46.6	15.3	.486
U.S.	20.66	40.4	25.3	.612

*Based on population estimates for 2006
SOURCES: BP 2006; CIA n.d.

plummeted in the mid-1980s, further reducing any remaining impetus to limit consumption. Even though global demand thereafter resumed its former upward course, overall production capacity would greatly exceed consumption until the late 1990s or early 2000s, providing a substantial cushion against possible oil shocks.

On the positive side, because the United States has made such limited efforts thus far to limit oil demand, the opportunities for doing so remain largely unexploited. This conclusion is further suggested by a comparison of U.S. oil use with that of other large industrialized countries (see Table 4.2). Oil as a percentage of total energy use is roughly the same, ranging from 35.5 to 46.6 percent, with the United States lying in the middle of the range. Yet U.S. oil consumption per capita is more than double that in Britain, France, and Germany, and nearly two-thirds higher than that in Japan, even though the latter depends on oil to meet a higher percentage of its energy needs. Moreover, U.S. oil intensity—the amount of oil used for every dollar of GDP—varies from 25 to 70 percent higher than in the other countries. Thus the potential to use policy to reduce U.S. consumption in the future would seem to be substantial.

5 U.S. Foreign Policy Responses and Their Costs

> For 60 years, my country, the United States, pursued stability at the expense of democracy in this region here in the Middle East, and we achieved neither.
>
> *Secretary of State Condoleeza Rice, Cairo, Egypt, June 21, 2005*

RATHER THAN rely heavily on domestic policy measures to address the economic costs and risks of foreign oil dependence, the United States has instead made extensive use of external policy instruments. Since the first oil shock, the United States has attempted to develop common policies and programs with other advanced industrialized countries intended to mitigate the impact of supply disruptions and to reduce the level of oil imports over the longer term. The primary targets of outwardly oriented American policies, however, have been actual and potential oil producing states and regions.

The overall objective of these efforts has been to ensure that oil continues to flow dependably and in sufficient quantities to the United States and its economic and security partners so as to maintain oil prices at reasonable levels and to prevent market shocks. Depending on the circumstances, the achievement of this goal has required pursuing one or more specific aims:

1. Convince existing oil producers to refrain from politically motivated embargoes or production cuts and, instead, encourage them to produce at levels that would result in moderate oil prices and to increase production above normal levels whenever necessary to compensate for unexpected supply disruptions;

2. promote the development of previously unexploited oil resources;

3. strengthen and stabilize oil producers in the face of external or internal threats; and

4. if necessary, protect vital oil supplies and transit routes so as to ensure Western access to them.

To these ends, the United States has made use of the full range of external policy instruments, including diplomacy, military and economy assistance, and the U.S. armed forces. The nature and magnitude of American actions have varied from region to region and over time, as both the demand for oil and threats to its supply have waxed and waned. Overall, however, these efforts have been substantial. As one early study of energy security noted, "The dangers and uncertainties accompanying any sizable disruption of oil supplies are so great that it is worth major diplomatic efforts to forestall their occurrence" (Bohi and Quandt 1984, 40). But for the presence of oil and Western need for it, U.S. policy toward actual and potential oil producing regions would arguably have been very different during the past three decades.

What is more, these policies would not have been pursued had they not seemed to be effective. To be sure, it is difficult, if not impossible, to establish precisely what benefits they have yielded. If such efforts had not been made, would oil prices have been higher? Would supply disruptions have been greater in size or more frequent? To answer such questions, one would need to construct elaborate counterfactual arguments based on numerous debatable assumptions. But U.S. policies have enjoyed at least some success in helping to stabilize the world oil market and to ensure Western access to foreign oil supplies.

At least as certain as the benefits, however, are the costs that U.S. external policies in response to foreign oil dependence have entailed, and these costs have at times been considerable. Some have been quite tangible, as when American actions have involved the expenditure of financial, material, and human resources that can be counted in dollars and cents—or lives. These policies have included various forms of military and economic assistance and, on an even larger scale, U.S. military programs and operations aimed at protecting oil producing regions and key transit points.

No less important are the intangible costs of U.S. policies toward actual and potential oil producing regions. These, too, have been substantial, even if they cannot be so easily measured. Not infrequently, the oil-related goals of U.S. policy have conflicted with other valued objectives, such as the promotion of democracy, good governance, respect for human rights, and compliance with international law. Where such conflicts have existed, the latter aims have often received diminished attention, or have been sacrificed altogether.

Thus in its quest for oil security, the United States has often found itself in the awkward position of supporting despotic or authoritarian regimes. It has tolerated practices, such as the repression of political opposition, government corruption, human rights abuses, and the use of illegal weapons, that U.S. policy has ostensibly opposed and that, elsewhere, might have been the object of American scorn. As noted oil analyst Melvin Conant presciently wrote two and a half decades ago, "The oil factor must be more clearly understood as endlessly complicating the attainment of many other objectives" (Conant 1982, xiv). These conflicts and compromises have arguably grown only more intense with the passage of time.

More generally, the imperative to ensure reliable Western access to adequate quantities of foreign oil at reasonable prices has limited America's freedom of action.[1] As a 1987 U.S. Department of Energy study frankly admitted, "Increased dependence on insecure oil supplies reduces flexibility in the conduct of U.S. foreign policy" (DOE 1987, 68, cited in Greene and Leiby 1993, 49). A 1996 government report echoed this view, noting, "The United States and its allies may be constrained from pursuing foreign policy actions for fear of alienating oil producing nations and provoking them into actions that would increase world oil prices" (GAO 1996, 31).

This chapter examines general U.S. foreign policy efforts toward different actual and potential oil producing regions of the world. The chapter pays particular attention to the Persian Gulf, but it also looks at three other regions of increasing importance to the United States: Latin America, the Caspian Sea, and sub-Saharan Africa. The next chapter focuses more narrowly on U.S. military policy responses and their costs, which have been so substantial as to merit a separate discussion.

The Persian Gulf

The principal geographical focus of oil-related U.S. foreign policy efforts has been the Persian Gulf, and for good reason. Since the early 1970s, the Persian Gulf has been the single most important oil producing and exporting region in the world. Yet oil production and exports there have been subject to periodic, and occasionally severe, disruptions. Consequently, the United States has been highly motivated to take measures designed to prevent disruptions and, beyond that, to encourage regional producers to supply the world market with adequate quantities of oil at reasonable prices (see Map 5.1).

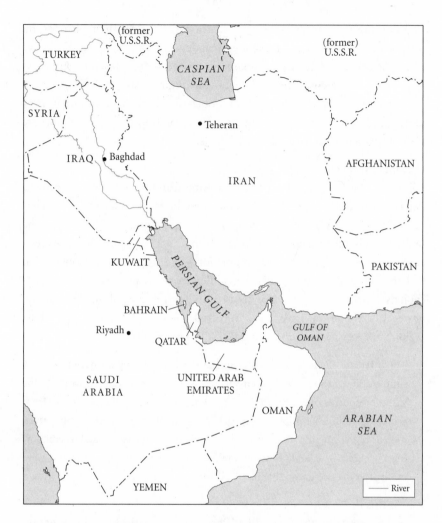

MAP 5.1 Persian Gulf

Commensurate with the magnitude of these efforts, nowhere have the external policy costs of U.S. foreign oil dependence been more prominently on display. These costs have included direct financial outlays, primarily in the form of overt or covert military assistance. But with the primary exception of Iraq in the 1980s, the states that the United States has sought to help or influence have enjoyed substantial financial resources, thanks to their high levels of oil exports. Instead, the costs of U.S. policy have primarily assumed more intangible forms that do not lend themselves to easy measurement.

At a minimum, they have involved constraints, often considerable ones, on American freedom of action, as foreign oil dependence has limited the range of options that U.S. decision makers have been willing to consider (GAO 1996, 5). And frequently, they have entailed compromising and even sacrificing other important U.S. foreign policy objectives in the region, such as promoting democracy, protecting human rights, and limiting arms sales, where these have conflicted with oil-related goals.

U.S. Interests in the Persian Gulf

Oil has not been the sole factor guiding American foreign policy toward the Persian Gulf. U.S. interests have also included the security of Israel, which has been threatened by various countries in the region, and, especially since the 1970s, resolving the various Arab-Israeli conflicts. Thus an important American objective has been gaining support for—or at least reducing opposition to—the existence of Israel and the Middle East peace process in the region's capitals. During the past several decades, indeed for most of the postwar era, however, U.S. interests have largely revolved around or been derivative of the region's oil. As veteran Gulf analyst Gary Sick has written:

> The interests of the United States in the Persian Gulf region have been very simple and consistent: first, to ensure access by the industrialized world to the vast oil resources of the region; and second, to prevent any hostile power from acquiring political or military control over these resources. . . . Other objectives, such as preserving the stability and independence of the Gulf states or containing the threat of Islamic fundamentalism, were derivative concerns and were implicit in the two grand themes of oil and containment.[2]

Why is this the case?

By any measure, the Persian Gulf has played a critical role in global oil markets since well before the first oil shock. It more than any other single region has determined oil prices and whether world supplies were adequate to meet demand. Since the mid-1960s, the region's share of global oil production has averaged approximately 30 percent. This figure grew steadily after World War II, reaching an all-time high of 37 percent in the mid-1970s. Following a sharp decline to less than 20 percent in the mid-1980s, it returned to around 30 percent in the mid-1990s, where it has stayed ever since (see Figure 5.1).

As impressive as these figures are, the Persian Gulf has been even more important as a source of exports. The region's share of world oil exports peaked at nearly 70 percent in the late 1970s. As in the case of production, this figure

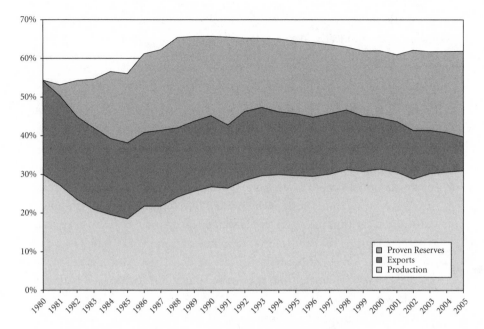

FIGURE 5.1 Persian Gulf Shares of World Oil Production, Exports,
             and Reserves, 1980–2005
SOURCE: BP 2006.

dropped dramatically in the early 1980s, to a low of 38 percent. But since the
mid-1980s, it has remained between 40 and 47 percent. Thus over the years,
the United States and its oil-dependent allies and trading partners have relied
heavily on the countries of the Persian Gulf to meet their energy needs.

Most impressive of all has been the Persian Gulf's share of proven oil reserves. Since at least the mid-1960s, this figure has stood at more than 50 percent. Because of significant upward revisions in the reserve estimates for all
the major regional producers in the 1980s, it grew to as high as two-thirds of
the world total and has remained at more than 60 percent ever since. Although
reserves cannot be immediately translated into oil production and exports,
they have served as a powerful indicator of the region's future importance as
a source of oil.

During the first decades after World War II, another important American
interest was ensuring that U.S.-based oil companies were able to play a major
role in developing the region's energy resources. But by the mid-1970s, most of
these holdings had been or were in the process of being nationalized (Yergin

1991; Little 2002, 72). Thus since the first oil shock, the United States has had one overriding concern: to ensure that the region remained a reliable supplier of oil at reasonable prices and in quantities sufficient to meet world demand (Long 1985, 25; Kolko 2002, 19).

During the past three decades, this interest has faced two main threats. On the one hand, oil producing states in the region might choose to withhold oil from the world market or particular consumers for political purposes, as exemplified by the 1973 Arab oil embargo. On the other hand, their ability to supply oil might be disrupted for reasons beyond their control. Unintended supply disruptions could result from internal conflicts and upheavals within the oil producing states, such as the Iranian Revolution. Alternatively, inter-state conflicts within the region could shut down oil production and exports, as occurred during the Iran-Iraq War and Iraq's invasion of Kuwait. Or countries in the region could be subjected to external threats and aggression, as was feared might emanate from the Soviet Union during the last decades of the cold war.

From these threats have followed a set of more specific U.S. foreign policy goals in the region. First, the United States has sought to discourage producing countries from withholding oil from the market and, conversely, to encourage them to provide oil in sufficient quantities so as to keep prices stable and at reasonable levels. In particular, Washington has wanted Gulf producers to increase output as necessary to compensate for supply disruptions, wherever they might occur. A second aim has been to prevent any external power, most notably the Soviet Union, from controlling or exerting significant influence over region. Third, the United States has sought to prevent any single Persian Gulf state from dominating its neighbors or disrupting the region's oil supplies. And it has tried to strengthen friendly oil producers so that they could better deal with various internal and external threats.

Phases of U.S. Policy

Since the first oil shock, when the extent of the economic costs and risks of U.S. foreign oil dependence first became manifest, American policy toward the Persian Gulf has consistently aimed at achieving these strategic goals. Nevertheless, one can discern several distinct phases in U.S. policy, reflecting shifting concerns and, correspondingly, operational priorities.

The first phase corresponded roughly with the 1970s. During this period, U.S. policymakers sought to avoid a repeat of the first oil embargo and to obtain the help of regional producers in stabilizing the nominal price of oil, which had quadrupled in 1973 (Yergin 1991, 642–43). At the same time, under the Nixon Doctrine, the United States had chosen to rely heavily on regional powers to exclude Soviet influence following the British withdrawal from the Gulf in 1971, a policy that was continued under presidents Gerald Ford and Jimmy Carter. The two largest oil producers, Saudi Arabia and especially Iran, were designated as the principal protectors of U.S. interests, in what became known as the "twin pillars" strategy (Brzezinski 1983, 357; Sick 1985, 24; Kupchan 1987, 34–37; Teicher and Teicher 1993, 23; Little 2002, 145).

The second phase corresponded with the 1980s. It was bracketed at one end by the 1979 Iranian Revolution, which undermined the twin pillars strategy and necessitated a complete overhaul of U.S. policy, and at the other by the 1990 Iraqi invasion of Kuwait. Under the Carter Doctrine, which was declared in response to the 1979 Soviet invasion of Afghanistan, and the subsequent Reagan Corollary, the United States indicated a new willingness to intervene militarily to prevent any outside power—but especially the Soviet Union—from gaining control of the region's oil resources. The Iran-Iraq War, which broke out in 1980, quickly introduced a new imperative: that of preventing any hostile regional power, in this case Iran, from dominating the Persian Gulf (Sick 1983, 77; Long 1985, 66; Teicher and Teicher 1993, 112, 145).

The third phase corresponded with the 1990s. The end of the cold war put a definitive end to the Soviet threat to the region's oil supplies. But following the Gulf War, the United States had to regard both Iran and Iraq as potential problems. Accordingly, it adopted a policy of "dual containment," which was intended to prevent either adversary from disrupting the region. At the same time, the United States had to contend increasingly with potential internal threats to stability, especially in Saudi Arabia.

The beginning of the War on Terror in 2001 and, especially, the U.S. invasion of Iraq in 2003 marked the beginning of a new phase in U.S. policy toward the Persian Gulf. As of this writing, the longer-term outlines of this phase remain unclear. Much will depend on what happens in Iraq and, of course, how dependent the United States remains on foreign oil.

Thus over the years, U.S. policy toward the region has focused on three states: Iran, Iraq, and Saudi Arabia. Not only have these been the most populous and the most militarily powerful countries in the Persian Gulf. But Iran and Saudi Arabia have consistently been the two largest oil producers, and although Iraq has often lagged well behind as a result of the relatively late

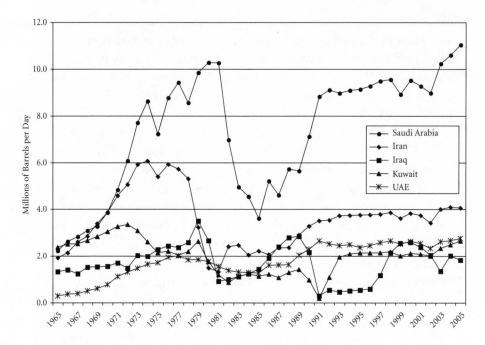

FIGURE 5.2 Persian Gulf Oil Production, 1965–2005
SOURCE: BP 2006.

development of its oil fields, the damage sustained in two wars, and UN sanctions, it has had the potential to rank among the region's biggest producers. Also important to consider, however, is U.S. assistance to the Afghan resistance in the 1980s insofar as it was motivated by concern about threats to Persian Gulf oil supplies (see Figure 5.2).

Iran in the 1970s

The principal focus of U.S. oil-related diplomacy in the 1970s was Iran. During that period, Iran was easily, after Saudi Arabia, the second largest producer and exporter in the Gulf, averaging more than 5.7 million barrels per day (MBD) of output between 1973 and 1978. As such, it enjoyed an influential voice within the Organization of the Oil Exporting Countries (OPEC). The United States strongly backed the shah of Iran, who became the largest purchaser of American weapons. But this support came at the price of conflicts with other U.S. foreign policy objectives, especially during the Carter administration, such as limiting arms sales and promoting human rights, and of reduced freedom of action, which limited the ability of the United States to anticipate and respond to the events that eventually brought about the fall of the shah.

U.S. Interests and Policy Objectives in Iran

To be sure, American interests in Iran—and thus U.S. reasons for supporting the shah—were not limited to oil, and they predated the first oil shock (Dumbrell 1993, 161). In particular, under the Nixon Doctrine, the United States relied heavily on Iran to serve as a regional stabilizer and bulwark against Soviet influence. In 1968, Great Britain, the traditional external power in the region, had announced its intention to withdraw all its forces in the Gulf by 1971. Because of the continuing conflict in Vietnam and declining American support for foreign engagements, however, the incoming administration of Richard N. Nixon was unwilling to see the United States assume the British mantle. Instead, it turned to its closest friends in the region, Iran and Saudi Arabia, to fill the power vacuum created by the British departure. Because of Iran's much larger population and armed forces and its location adjacent to the Soviet Union, however, the Nixon administration placed primary emphasis on building up and using that country as a U.S. proxy, a policy that was continued under presidents Ford and Carter.[3]

Iran's assumption of this key role in U.S. strategy led to several more specific American interests. In the early 1970s, the United States set up electronic listening posts in northern Iran for the purpose of monitoring Soviet missile tests. As U.S. arms sales rapidly grew, the United States increasingly relied on Iran to provide a market for American-made weapons systems. And especially in the late 1970s, the United States sought the shah's support for and assistance with the recently inaugurated Middle East peace process (Sullivan 1981, 124).

Underlying Iran's importance to the United States in the 1970s, however, was the region's oil wealth and the West's growing dependence on it. For this reason, the first oil shock further enhanced Iran's strategic significance. Henceforth, it would be all the more essential to maintain order in the region, to exclude Soviet influence, and, more generally, to ensure continued Western access to Persian Gulf oil. Yet of all the states in the region, only Iran was seen as being capable of playing this multifaceted role (Rubin 1981, 186–87; Vance 1983, 314; Brzezinski 1983, 354–56).

Following the first oil shock, the United States had two more specific oil-related objectives vis-à-vis Iran. One was to see that the country maintained a

high level of oil production. In the mid-1970s, Iran was easily the fourth largest producer and, after Saudi Arabia, the second largest exporter in the world.
Fortunately, for the United States, the achievement of this goal was never in
doubt. Iran under the shah was, if nothing else, a reliable supplier. The shah
had refused to join the 1973 embargo and could be counted on not to use oil
as a political weapon. To the contrary, he preferred to maintain a high level
of output in order to maximize oil revenues. But this preference complicated
the achievement of the second American goal: bringing about a moderation
in the cost of oil. During the early to mid-1970s, the shah was a leading advocate of ever-higher prices. In 1975, for example, Iran championed a further 25
percent increase in the posted price of OPEC oil (Vance 1983, 317; Yergin 1991,
644; Miglietta 2002, 79).

U.S. Actions

U.S. leaders repeatedly urged the shah to reconsider his position on oil prices
(Bill 1988, 204; Sullivan 1981, 117–200; Vance 1983, 314–15). But in view of Iran's
strategic and economic importance, the hallmark of U.S. policy toward the
country during the 1970s was strong and largely unconditional support for the
shah. This support began during the Nixon administration, which initiated
the policy of relying on Iran to promote U.S. interests in the Persian Gulf. But
it continued largely unmodified during the first years of the Carter administration, virtually right up to the end of the shah's reign in 1979. As Sick, who
served in the administration, has written, the overriding consideration for
U.S. policy toward Iran under Carter was that the cooperative relationship be
preserved and that Iran remain a strong, reliable, and friendly ally (Sick 1985,
24–25; see also Vance 1983, 317; Bill 1988, 226). Thus Carter offered only praise
for the shah during his December 1977 visit to Tehran, and the administration
refrained from any public criticism for most of the following year, even as
mounting public protests against the regime triggered bloody, but ultimately
ineffectual, military responses. U.S. verbal and moral support for the shah
continued until the very end (Rubin 1981, 201–2; Keddie 1981, 254).

The most tangible aspect of U.S. support during this period was the massive sale of American arms to Iran. During a visit to Tehran in May 1972,
President Nixon agreed to permit the shah to purchase virtually any type
of conventional weaponry that he desired. The U.S. Department of Defense
objected to such an open-ended offer, arguing that it was not necessary for
the defense of Iran. In response, however, Henry Kissinger, then the national

security advisor, indicated that decisions on purchases of U.S. military equipment would be left primarily to the government of Iran, effectively exempting them from the usual arms sales review processes (Vance 1983, 315; Litwak 1984, 141; Sick 1985, 13–15; Bill 1988, 200–201; Gasiorowski 1991, 113; Teicher and Teicher 1993, 23; Little 2002, 145).

As a result of this decision, U.S. arms sales to Iran ballooned during the following years. From 1950 to 1970, they had totaled less than $800 million, and even during the next two years, they had averaged just $400 million per year. Between 1973 and 1978, following the Tehran meeting, however, Iran placed orders for some $16 billion in military equipment, accounting for about one-third of all U.S. arms sales during that period (Rubin 1981, 59; Ramazani 1982, 47–48; Bill 1988, 202–3; Miglietta 2002, 71; K. Pollack 2004). The arrival of American arms was accompanied by dramatic growth in the presence of U.S. military advisers and civilian contractors, who were needed to train the Iranians to operate and maintain the more advanced weaponry. Between 1973 and 1978, their numbers increased from 3,600 to some 10,000, while the total number of Americans in the country grew to 50,000 (Miglietta 2002, 69, 76).

In addition to their unrivaled size, U.S. military sales to Iran were distinguished by the sophisticated nature of the weaponry involved. In January 1974, the Nixon administration approved the sale of F-14 fighter aircraft, which the United States itself had placed in service only the previous year.[4] Then in 1975, the Ford administration announced plans to sell to the shah 160 F-16 fighters, which would not even be delivered to the U.S. air force until 1979.[5]

As a sign of his support for the shah, Carter chose to continue the policy of offering virtually unlimited access to U.S. conventional weaponry. During its first months in office, in early 1977, the new administration reaffirmed the earlier decision to sell the F-16. Even more significantly, Carter agreed to seek congressional approval to provide Iran with the highly advanced Airborne Warning and Control System (AWACS) aircraft. Not until late 1977 did Carter ask the shah to reduce his breathtaking arms requests. But when confronted with the latter's insistence that even more F-14s and F-16s were needed, the president reluctantly agreed to consult the Congress rather than anger his ally (Sullivan 1981, 20; Brzezinksi 1983, 257; Vance 1983, 318, 322–23; Sick 1985, 22–23; Bill 1988, 228; Gasiorowski 1991, 114; Little 2002, 148; K. Pollack 2004, 122).

The proposed AWACS sale in particular became a major test of the Carter administration's commitment to maintain the special security relationship with Iran. The sale faced widespread opposition from elements of the administration, especially in the Department of State and the Central Intelligence Agency, as well as Congress. Although he had already reduced the proposed number of aircraft from ten to seven, Carter was still forced to withdraw his request temporarily. After negotiating additional assurances with the shah and adding some minor modifications to the request, however, members of the administration, including the president, engaged in intense lobbying, meeting with and calling congressional leaders repeatedly until they were able to obtain a slim majority for approval in the House of Representatives (Rubin 1981, 198; Sullivan 1981, 114–16; Vance 1983, 319–21; Sick 1985, 26–27; Bill 1988, 229).

Why was Carter willing to pay such a high political price to please the shah? The answer to this question has much to do with U.S. oil interests. As a major oil supplier and protector of regional stability, Secretary of State Cyrus Vance explained, Iran needed and deserved the AWACS. "The AWACS aircraft would fill an important defense requirement and would strengthen our relations with Iran at a time when we were trying to persuade the Shah to moderate increases in oil prices" (Vance 1983, 320; see also Rubin 1981, 198).

Benefits of U.S. Policy

In fact, at least until the fall of the shah, U.S. policy toward Iran did appear to be paying dividends. It is difficult to say how events would have unfolded if the United States had not supported the shah so unreservedly. By most accounts, however, this central component of the Nixon Doctrine was, until 1978, a success. Iran was able to provide a defensive bulwark against Soviet influence in the Persian Gulf and enhanced the region's overall stability (Litwak 1984, 143).

In addition, U.S. hopes that the shah would help to arrest the upward trend in oil prices were eventually rewarded. Daniel Yergin has written that the shah was already having second thoughts about the value of pushing for higher prices (Yergin 1991, 645). Nevertheless, it was only after Vance reassured the shah about continued U.S. support during a May 1977 visit to Tehran that the Iranian government began to talk about moderating its stance on the issue. And after Carter pressed the shah during the latter's November 1977 visit to Washington to support a price freeze at the OPEC meeting scheduled for the following month, the shah agreed to urge the organization to "give Western nations a break" and publicly promised to oppose any further price hikes at the meeting (Yergin 1991, 645–46; Sullivan 1981, 129; Vance 1983, 321–22).[6] Thus the shift in Iranian policy would appear to be more than a mere coincidence, uninfluenced by U.S. policy efforts.

Costs of U.S. Policy

At the same time, U.S. policy toward Iran during this period entailed substantial costs. First, it conflicted with the Carter administration's policy of restraining the transfer of American arms abroad. During the presidential election campaign, Carter had criticized Nixon and Ford for presiding over an enormous increase in U.S. arms sales. Total U.S. military sales agreements had mushroomed from less than $1.2 billion in 1970 to more than $13 billion per year in the middle of the decade. Thus in May 1977, Carter issued a presidential directive calling for a reduction in the dollar volume of new commitments and placing strict limits on the transfer of newly developed advanced weapons systems. Only countries with which the United States had special treaty obligations, namely members of NATO, Japan, Australia, and New Zealand, would be exempted.[7]

One problem with this policy was that it contravened a basic tenet of the Nixon Doctrine, which was to provide regional proxies with all the weapons they needed. By this time, moreover, the unimpeded flow of arms had become a litmus test of U.S. support for Iran under the shah. Thus Carter chose to make an exception, and on the very day that the directive was issued, Vance reassured the shah that the United States would continue to meet his country's presumed military needs. In the end, the new policy had little practical effect on U.S. arms transfers to Iran, even though the provisions restricting the sale of advanced weapons could be construed as applying to both the F-16 and AWACS aircraft (Rubin 1981, 196; Vance 1983, 319; Bill 1988, 229; Teicher and Teicher 1993, 28). As the *Washington Post* soon editorialized, the sale of the AWACS in particular was an embarrassment to Carter's intent to reduce the U.S. role as the world's leading arms merchant (Rubin 1981, 199).

Just as important, U.S. support for the shah resulted in conflicts in the area of human rights. The promotion of human rights had not received much attention from the Nixon and Ford administrations, but this situation was expected to change under Carter. As with arms transfers, Carter had made human rights a major issue during the campaign, and he gave the theme a prominent place in his inaugural address, noting, "Our commitment to human rights must be absolute."[8] In a subsequent statement, he pronounced, "As long as I am President, the Government of the United States will continue, throughout the world, to enhance human rights. No force on earth can separate us from that commitment" (W. Buckley 1980, 790).

There is some evidence that the administration did in fact engage the shah on the subject of human rights. According to the U.S. ambassador to Iran, Carter asked him to try to persuade the shah to improve Iran's human rights performance. And at various times, the president protested excesses committed by Iranian security forces and reportedly asked the shah to consider using less repressive measures (Sullivan 1981, 22; Vance 1983, 317; Little 2002, 149, 224).

Others have argued, however, that the Carter administration put no serious pressure on the shah to respect human rights (for example, Keddie 1981, 231; Bill 1988, 227–28; Kemp 1994, 24; K. Pollack 2004, 139). Instead, according to one examination of the relationship, it pursued the same basic approach to Iran as had the administrations of Nixon and Ford and resisted efforts by human rights advocates in the Department of State and Congress to compel the shah to undertake political liberalization (Gasiorowski 1991, 100). In Iran, at least, "U.S. human rights policy was little more than a gesture" (Dumbrell 1993, 172), and "human rights were defended at the abstract level only" (Cottam 1988, 160). As a result, according to one observer, the Carter administration spent more time defending than criticizing the shah's record. For example, the 1977 State Department report on human rights emphasized that Iran was trying to improve its performance in the area, while the following year's report, which appeared after the violent revolutionary events of 1978, was only slightly more critical (Rubin 1981, 193–95).

Nor was much emphasis placed on human rights in the high-level bilateral meetings that took place between members of the Carter administration and the shah. Although Vance subsequently wrote that he had stressed the importance of human rights as a key element of U.S. policy during his May 1977 visit to Tehran, he appears to have offered no specific criticisms of the situation in Iran, noting instead that the United States was encouraged by recent Iranian steps to improve the treatment of prisoners (Vance 1983, 318–19; K. Pollack 2004, 122). The subject of human rights was also conspicuously absent from the list of U.S. objectives for Carter's meeting with the shah in Washington in November 1977 (Vance 1983, 322; Bill 1988, 232–33). When the president returned the visit at the end of the year, moreover, he made no mention of human rights either in his New Year's toast or in the thank you letter that he composed the next day (Cottam 1988, 163; Dumbrell 1993, 164).

As further evidence, critics of the Carter administration's approach toward human rights in Iran have cited the administration's response to the revolutionary events as they unfolded in 1978. In August, Vance approved the shipment of crowd-control equipment, including tear gas, over the objections of the State Department's human rights bureau, which opposed giving any assistance to the shah in suppressing opposition (Sullivan 1981, 148; Vance 1983, 325). That fall, the United States offered further support for the shah, encouraging him to take a tough stance, even after hundreds of civilians had been killed in clashes with Iranian troops (K. Pollack 2004, 139).

Commentators have offered various reasons for the Carter administration's restrained approach on human rights in Iran. For example, Sick has suggested that modest reform measures introduced by the shah in 1976 and 1977 provided a rationale for not significantly revising the policies of the previous five years. James Bill has written that although human rights were a genuine concern of the Carter administration, the issue was certainly not to take precedence over security and economic issues. Others, however, have identified a more direct link between U.S. oil interests and human rights policy. In particular, the failure to make more of an issue of human rights in Iran has been attributed, at least in part, to the U.S. desire for the shah's assistance on oil prices. It seems likely, in the view of Nikki Keddie, that the Carter administration promised to downplay human rights issues as well as to continue the flow of arms in return for a softening of Iran's previously hawkish stance. As the shah saw it, according to Daniel Yergin, he was offered precisely such a quid pro quo by Carter at their November 1977 meeting (Sick 1985, 24; Bill 1988, 227–28; K. Pollack 2004, 122; Keddie 1981, 234; Yergin 1991, 646).

More generally, U.S. policy toward Iran engendered an excessive dependence on the shah and a corresponding loss of freedom of action. As Sick has written, the United States "was dependent on the shah to protect U.S. interests in a region that was becoming increasingly important to the very survival of the Western industrial system" (Sick 1985, 18; see also Little 2002, 225). Indeed, a report by the inspector general of the U.S. foreign service concluded as early as the summer of 1976 that Iran exerted the determining influence in the bilateral relationship with the United States. In Sick's colorful metaphor, "Iran was the regional tail wagging the superpower dog" (Sick 1985, 21; see also Miglietta 2002, 94). Thus Vance and others argued that the United States could not afford to alienate the shah (Bill 1988, 231). Despite the Carter administration's interest in limiting arms sales and promoting human rights, the overriding consideration was to preserve the cooperative relationship and to ensure that Iran remained a strong and reliable ally (Sick 1985, 24–25).

Given these objectives, it is ironic that a further consequence of the U.S. loss of leverage was a surprising level of ignorance about developments inside Iran. The shah was annoyed by and suspicious of American contacts with opposition groups. Because successive administrations did not want to offend him, the Department of State and CIA sharply curtailed intelligence gathering within the country. U.S. diplomats and intelligence operatives had little or no contact with reformist and other opposition elements, tending instead to rely solely on Iranian government officials and the internal security service, SAVAK, for information. According to one estimate, by the early 1970s, the volume of CIA political reporting had dropped below that of the 1940s. Thus knowledge in Washington about unfavorable developments was sketchy, and U.S. intelligence underestimated in particular the degree and scope of opposition to the regime. The civil unrest of 1978 caught U.S. officials largely by surprise, and the United States was unprepared to respond effectively to the situation (Keddie 1981, 253; Vance 1983, 316; Sick 1985, 32; Gasiorowski 1991, 100; Miglietta 2002, 87; Rathmell, Karasik, and Gompert 2003, 3).

Iraq in the 1980s

In the 1980s, much of the focus of U.S. diplomacy shifted to Iraq. The country had been a major source of American concern in the Persian Gulf since at least 1967, when it broke diplomatic relations because of its hostile attitude toward the United States and ties to the Soviet Union. Subsequently, the United States had listed Iraq as a state sponsor of terrorism and imposed an arms embargo on it. But in a stunning reversal, Iran became the main threat to U.S. interests in the Gulf following the Islamic revolution. "With [the shah's] departure and the arrival of a hostile Islamist regime in Tehran, the United States was left strategically naked in the Persian Gulf, with no safety net" (Sick 2003, 293). For want of better alternatives, the United States soon settled on Iraq as a prime vehicle for protecting its regional interests.

American support for Iraq was triggered most directly by the Iran-Iraq War. Iraq had initiated the conflict in September 1980, hoping to exploit the continuing turmoil in Iran for political and territorial gain. But Iran had managed to halt the initial Iraqi offensives, and beginning in 1982, it made a series of gains on the battlefield that raised the prospect of an Iraqi defeat. U.S.

officials believed that an Iranian victory would be a major blow to American interests in the region, since it would allow Iran to threaten Saudi Arabia and the other Persian Gulf oil kingdoms. Thus preventing such an undesirable outcome became a U.S. policy imperative (Hiro 1989, 119; Dobbs 2002; Tyler 2002; K. Pollack 2004, 206–7, 234).

Although the official U.S. stance toward the war was one of neutrality, the United States in fact began to tilt increasingly toward Iraq by 1982. American assistance took several forms. The first steps occurred in the diplomatic arena. In February 1982, the Department of State removed Iraq from the list of terrorist supporting countries, and in November 1984, the United States restored full diplomatic relations. These highly symbolic measures also had important practical implications; they allowed the U.S. government to offer various forms of financial assistance and to loosen export controls (Jentleson 1994, 33, 48; K. Pollack 2002, 18–19).

Starting in 1983, the United States began to provide economic aid in the form of loan guarantees for the purchase of U.S. agricultural goods. The value of these guarantees rose rapidly, from $400 million in 1983 to $513 million in 1984 and then to as much as $675 million in 1985 and 1986, when they represented nearly one-quarter of the entire program (K. Pollack 2002, 18; Jentleson 1994, 42, 55; Hiro 1989, 161). Through 1988, when the Iran-Iraq War finally ended, the United States had provided Iraq with some $2.8 billion in agricultural products under the credit-guarantee program, and in 1989, the new Bush administration further increased the amount of available guarantees to about $1 billion per year (Waas 1991, 93).

In addition, the U.S. Export-Import Bank provided Iraq with various forms of financing. Between 1984 and 1987, it extended approximately $200 million in short-term loan guarantees for the purchase of American goods (Waas 1991, 94–95; Jentleson 1994, 61). In 1984, moreover, it provisionally guaranteed $485 million of the estimated $570 million cost of building an Iraqi pipeline through Jordan to the Gulf of Aqaba, which amounted to one of the single largest commitments ever made by the bank (Hiro 1989, 159; Jentleson 1994, 44).

Other forms of American assistance were covert. As early as mid-1982, the United States began to provide Iraq with military intelligence, primarily in the form of satellite photos of Iranian troop deployments, and the U.S.-Iraqi intelligence relationship steadily strengthened over the following years. The United States established a direct link between the CIA and the embassy in

Baghdad in order to make its intelligence available to Iraq on a regular basis. By 1987, according to White House officials, the United States was providing Iraq with targeting information as well as assistance with planning long-range air attacks in Iran, and American military officers were offering tactical military advice on the battlefield (Hiro 1989, 160; Teicher and Teicher 1993, 207, 391; A. Friedman 1993, 27, 38; Jentleson 1994, 46; K. Pollack 2002, 18; Tyler 2002).

Not least important, the Reagan administration played a major role in arming Iraq during and immediately after the conflict (Waas 1991, 85). It did so in three ways. First, although U.S. policy prohibited the sale of defense items to Iraq, the administration provided Iraq with "dual-use" goods, ostensibly civilian items that could nevertheless be converted to military applications. In 1982, for example, Iraq was allowed to purchase sixty helicopters that were a civilian version of a type that had been widely used in the Vietnam War. And in 1984, the State Department approved the sale of forty-five more helicopters that had been originally designed for military purposes (Waas 1991, 90; A. Friedman 1993, 37). Beginning in 1985, moreover, the Commerce Department began to issue export licenses for high-technology goods that had previously been denied, including computers, other electronics, and machine tools. Between 1985 and 1990, the department approved as many as 771 licenses for the sale of dual-use items valued at $1.5 billion to Iraq, sometimes over the objections of the Pentagon, and Iraq spent some $782 million on related purchases. As Commerce Department officials later told government investigators, few foreign policy controls were placed on exports to Iraq during the 1980s (Waas 1991, 90; GAO 1994, 5; see also Jentleson 1994, 62).

Second, the Reagan White House allegedly authorized the secret transfer of U.S. military equipment from third countries, in violation of the Arms Export Control Act. Such arms shipments were made regularly through Jordan, Egypt, Saudi Arabia, and Kuwait. For example, the Saudis transferred American-made bombs to Iraq, an action that almost certainly could not have been taken without American approval. In addition, the United States reportedly shipped military supplies stored in Europe to Iraq, especially spare parts and various specialty items (Waas 1991, 85, 87; A. Friedman 1993, 24, 33–34, 38–39; Phythian 1997, 35).

Third, the Reagan administration encouraged other countries—notably Britain, France, Germany, and Italy—to sell weapons to Iraq (Waas 1991, 87; Jentleson 1994, 45; Phythian 1997, 36). For example, the French government, with the knowledge of the United States, secretly sold Iraq $1.4 billion in howitzers (Waas 1991, 88). One former high-level U.S. intelligence official has been quoted as saying that "the billions upon billions of dollars of shipments from Europe would not have been possible without the approval and acquiescence of the Reagan administration" (Waas 1991, 87).

Arguably, the Regan administration's assistance to Iraq in the 1980s helped to prevent an Iranian victory, with all the dangers that that would have entailed to American interests in the Persian Gulf. But it also involved nontrivial costs, not to mention likely violations of U.S. law. The total amount of assistance provided by the United States to Iraq, including food credits, technology, and industrial products, has been estimated at more than $5 billion (Kolko 2002, 34). In addition, U.S. assistance may have enabled Iraq to pose a greater military threat to its neighbors and even to the United States itself in later years.

Also important were the intangible costs. In its eagerness to help Iraq, the Reagan administration tolerated a variety of transgressions by Saddam Hussein that might otherwise have drawn sharp American criticism and even economic sanctions. According to some reports, Iraq continued to support international terrorism, at least to much the same extent that it had when it was on the State Department list of state sponsors. At a minimum, it continued to play host to alleged terrorists, such as the Palestinian Abu Abbas (Waas 1991, 94; Teicher and Teicher 1993, 275, 330; Dobbs 2002). Even more seriously, U.S. officials largely looked the other way while Iraq engaged in the extensive use of chemical weapons, in clear violation of international law. By 1983, the United States was aware of the fact that Iraq was launching chemical attacks against Iranian forces. But the Reagan administration did not actually condemn Iraq until a March 1984 UN report had provided incontrovertible documentation, and this pro forma denunciation was not backed by any reduction in U.S. support (K. Pollack 2002, 20; K. Pollack 2004, 208; Everest 2004, 103). In the words of Kenneth Pollack, who spent seven years in the CIA as a Persian Gulf analyst, "The United States was willing to ignore whatever Iraq thought was necessary to hang on" (K. Pollack 2004, 208; see also Tyler 2002).

Yet U.S. tolerance continued even after the wartime imperatives had abated. In 1987 and 1988, as hostilities between Iran and Iraq were winding down, Saddam Hussein launched a scorched-earth campaign against Iraq's Kurds. Chemical weapons were used against Kurdish villages in the northern part of the country, killing thousands. Once again, however, the Reagan administration took no action other than to issue a verbal condemnation, and it actively resisted congressional efforts to impose sanctions on Iraq (Waas 1991, 93; Tei-cher and Teicher 1993, 393; Jentleson 1994, 69; Dodd 2002; Everest 2004, 112–14).

Saudi Arabia

When it comes to oil, by far the most important U.S. bilateral relationship has been with Saudi Arabia. Fortunately for policymakers in Washington, Ameri-can and Saudi interests with regard to oil production and pricing have over-lapped considerably. As a result, the United States has not needed to engage in substantial diplomatic efforts to achieve its principal objectives vis-à-vis the Saudis. As in the case of Iran in the 1970s, the main tool used to further U.S. oil-related interests has been the sale of military goods and services. On several occasions, these sales have created apparent conflicts with other American goals in the region, especially the security of Israel. But the princi-pal cost of U.S. dependence on Saudi Arabia's oil resources has taken the form of American forbearance toward potentially threatening Saudi policies and developments within the country.

U.S. Interests and Goals

U.S. interests in Saudi Arabia have derived first and foremost from the coun-try's unrivaled oil resources (Long 1985, 117). Since the 1970s, Saudi Arabia has possessed between 20 and 25 percent of the world's proven oil reserves. Thanks to this abundant resource endowment, Saudi Arabia has consistently ranked among the three largest oil producers in the world, along with the United States and the former Soviet Union, and since the early 1990s, follow-ing the collapse of Soviet production, it has held the top position. Between 1974 and 2005, Saudi oil output averaged over eight MBD, or more than 12 percent of the world total. Of this, a high percentage has been available for sale abroad, making the country by far the largest exporter. Perhaps most im-portant, Saudi Arabia has maintained the greatest amount of excess produc-tion capacity, which has typically amounted to half or more of the world total. Thus the kingdom has been uniquely positioned to influence the world oil market by raising or lowering production in response to changing political and economic conditions. For all these reasons, it came as no surprise when President George H. W. Bush assured the Saudi king, just hours after the Iraqi invasion of Kuwait in 1990, that "the security of Saudi Arabia is vital—basi-cally fundamental—to U.S. interests and really to the interests of the Western world" (Bush and Scowcroft 1998, 330).

In view of Saudi Arabia's unrivaled oil wealth, the primary objective of U.S. policy toward the country since the first oil shock has been to enlist Saudi help in stabilizing the international oil market and moderating prices. As Secretary of the Treasury William Simon wrote on the eve of an August 1974 visit to the country:

> For the U.S. the primary interest is our continued access to Saudi Arabian oil in adequate quantities . . . at an acceptable political as well as economic price. We wish to assure that the Saudis continue to exercise their growing power in oil and monetary matters with moderation and in ways that are consistent with our own objectives. (Ottaway and Kaiser 2002)

The achievement of this goal has required that Saudi Arabia maintain production at levels sufficient to meet demand and, in particular, that it increase output in response to unexpected supply disruptions elsewhere in the world. It has also required that Saudi Arabia exercise restraint with respect to oil prices.

A second important oil-related goal has been to ensure that Saudi Arabia was strong enough to defend itself against potential threats, both external and internal, and that it was able to contribute more generally to the security of the region. After all, nothing would do more to disrupt the world oil market than an attack on the country or a violent domestic upheaval. This goal first became prominent under the Nixon Doctrine and the twin pillars strategy of the 1970s, when the United States greatly increased its military sales to Saudi Arabia. Following the fall of the shah and the loss of Iran as a U.S. ally, however, Saudi Arabia acquired even more strategic significance, and the modernization and expansion of the Saudi military became yet more imperative (Cordesman 2003, 112). During the 1990s and early 2000s, the country arguably served as the linchpin of the U.S. policy of containing both Iran and Iraq by hosting significant numbers of American forces and continuing to strengthen its own.

It should be noted that the United States has had several other important objectives vis-à-vis Saudi Arabia that have not been directly related to the goals of oil market stability and price moderation. One has been to reduce the U.S. balance of payments deficit by means of Saudi purchases of American goods and services and investments in the United States. Another has been to gain and maintain Saudi backing for the Middle East peace process. Given Saudi Arabia's influence within the Arab world, Washington has viewed Saudi support as critical to the success of its efforts to resolve the Arab-Israeli conflict (Long 1984, 138). More generally, the United States has sought to cultivate Saudi Arabia as a moderate voice among the Arab states. And especially since September 2001, Washington has looked to the Saudis for help in the global War on Terror.

Fortunately for the United States, the Saudis have largely shared U.S. oil-related objectives. As Clifford Chanin and F. Gregory Gause have noted, "For the most part, Saudi Arabia has exercised its oil power in ways consistent with American interests in stable supply and stable pricing" (Chanin and Gause 2003, 122). Saudi Arabia has repeatedly emphasized its commitment to be a reliable supplier of oil and to respond to U.S. and Western oil needs (for example, Safran 1985, 400; Larson 2003; Ignatius 2003).

As evidence of this commitment, one can point first to the fact that Saudi Arabia has not suspended exports to the United States or any other industrialized country since the Arab oil embargo was lifted in early 1974. During the remainder of the 1970s and into the early 1980s, moreover, it consistently sought to limit increases in the price of oil charged by OPEC. Initially, the Saudis wanted the price to lag behind inflation so as to help the world economy recover from the recession of 1974–75, and they were opposed more generally to sudden, steep, and unpredictable price hikes (Rustow 1982, 183, 195–96, 201). Thus in 1976, the Saudis initially blocked a 15 percent increase demanded by Iran and Iraq, and when a majority of OPEC members finally approved it over Saudi objections, they threatened to defy the decision by increasing production to full capacity (Safran 1985, 268–70). Similarly, when price hawks exploited the turmoil triggered by the Iranian Revolution to raise contract prices to as high as $40 per barrel, the Saudis increased their price only gradually, so that it did not reach $24 per barrel until late 1979 and $32 per barrel until late 1980 (Rustow 1982, 187; Long 1985, 29). Overall, Saudis policymakers have striven to keep the price of oil at a level that would allow them to maximize their revenues over a period of decades (J. Pollack 2002, 83).

Perhaps most important, Saudi Arabia has on several occasions increased production in an attempt to compensate for supply disruptions elsewhere, thereby helping to stabilize the oil market and keep prices at reasonable levels. This first occurred during the Iranian Revolution, when in response to the sudden drop in Iranian production, the Saudis initially increased their output to 10.4 MBD in December 1978. This level was reduced to 9.8 MBD during the first quarter of 1979 and then just 8.8 MBD during the next three months in order to make room on the market for renewed Iranian production. But when these levels proved insufficient to prevent additional jumps in the spot price of oil, the Saudis agreed at U.S. urging to restore production to 9.8 MBD in July 1979 (Safran 1985, 301–3, 307, 402–4; Quandt 1981, 131; Rustow 1982, 199; Long 1985, 27–28).[9]

When the outbreak of the Iran-Iraq War suddenly removed up to 4 MBD from the world market in late 1980, the Saudis again raised the level of production to as high as 10.4 MBD and kept it at significantly more than 10 MBD for nearly a year.[10] Likewise, when the Iraqi invasion of Kuwait cut off more than 4 MBD in exports from those countries almost exactly one decade later, Saudi Arabia quickly increased output by as much as 3 MBD. And during the first months of 2003, the Saudis expanded production by some 1.5 MBD above previous levels to compensate for losses from Venezuela, Nigeria, and then Iraq, following the outbreak of hostilities there.[11]

U.S. Actions Toward Saudi Arabia

The United States has not been willing to rely entirely on this coincidence of interests to ensure that its objectives were achieved, however. In mid-1974, immediately after the embargo, the United States and Saudi Arabia signed an agreement on economic and military cooperation that called for substantial U.S. assistance in return for Saudi help in meeting the energy needs of the United States and its allies (Safran 1985, 173–74; Miglietta 2002, 275). Subsequently, Washington has at times appealed directly to the Saudis to increase oil production and to work to control oil prices (for example, Long 1985, 29; Ikenberry 1988, 92).

Especially in times of uncertainty, the United States has offered pledges of support and protection intended to reassure the Saudis and, in the bargain, to enhance U.S. influence with them. In early 1979, for example, when crises in the Gulf, the Yemens, and the Arab-Israeli arena simultaneously came to a head, Carter administration officials pledged to defend Saudi Arabia against external threats, and the United States deployed naval and air forces to the region "in order to impress the Saudis with its willingness and ability to protect their security interests" (Safran 1985, 278, 303–4). During the Iran-Iraq War, the Carter administration quickly dispatched four AWACS aircraft to deter attacks on Saudi oil fields, and the Reagan administration indicated that it was prepared to use force to protect Saudi interests in the Gulf (Kupchan 1987, 132; Long 1985, 67). And of course, President George H. W. Bush promised to defend Saudi Arabia immediately following the Iraqi invasion of Kuwait (Bush 1991a).[12]

A more concrete aspect of U.S. policy has been the sale of American arms and military services to Saudi Arabia. Between 1973 and 1999, U.S. arms sales agreements with the Saudis totaled approximately $68 billion, or more than 20 percent of all such agreements worldwide. To put this figure into perspective, it helps to note that the United States sold only about $43 billion in arms to Israel and Egypt combined during the same period, and less than $100 billion worth to all its NATO allies during the entire postwar era. U.S.-Saudi military construction agreements during this period came to another $17 billion, most of which were concluded in the 1970s, or approximately 85 percent of the global total (DOD 1999). In the estimation of one expert on the subject, "The importance of these arms transfers overshadowed all other facets of the interaction between the two countries" (Miglietta 2002, 232).

This massive transfer of U.S. military goods and services has been intended to serve several interrelated purposes (Miglietta 2002, 264). Most directly, according to Charles Kupchan, the United States sought to use arms sales to influence Saudi oil production and pricing policy during the 1970s. "By providing Saudi Arabia with the weapons they wanted, the United States hoped to convince the Saudis to maintain production levels that would ensure sufficient supplies and reasonable prices" (Kupchan 1987, 57–58). In addition, the sales have greatly helped to strengthen the Saudi armed forces, thereby reducing the need for a U.S. military presence. In the process, the incorporation of some of the most modern weapons systems in the Saudi arsenal has enhanced the country's prestige and reinforced its position of leadership in the Arab world. At the same time, U.S. military sales have facilitated the rapid deployment of substantial American forces, if necessary, to the region by creating infrastructure such as airfields where they could be based and establishing depots of equipment and spare parts upon which they could draw. No less important, the sales have provided tangible evidence of American support, thereby increasing U.S. influence with Saudi Arabia. Especially in the late 1970s and early 1980s, the Saudis perceived "the military relationship with the United States to be the principal test of America's political commitment to the Kingdom" (Miglietta 2002, 230). Finally, the substantial military sales to Saudi Arabia have provided more general economic and military benefits to the United States, by generating, for example, a steady stream of export revenues and lowering the unit production costs of expensive military items (Long 1985, 55, 60).

Average annual U.S. military sales agreements jumped from the tens of millions of dollars in the late 1960s and very early 1970s to the billions of dollars later in the decade as a result of the Nixon Doctrine. Between 1973 and 1979, the value of arms and related military service purchases from the United States averaged more than $4 billion per year (DOD 1979; see also Safran 1985, 296). During this period, roughly half of the sales consisted of military construction projects carried out by the U.S. Army Corps of Engineers, as Saudi Arabia lacked both a modern construction industry and experience with building large military facilities (Quandt 1981, 52). Primary emphasis was placed on strengthening the Saudi Air Force as a means of deterring any hostile power from attacking the country as well as defending the oil fields (Miglietta 2002, 230). Most notably, the United States agreed to sell Saudi Arabia sixty advanced F-15 fighters. In the 1980s, U.S. military sales agreements averaged closer to $2 billion per year, but they included equipment to upgrade the F-15s and sophisticated AWACS aircraft. As a result of the increased threat posed by Iraq, U.S.-Saudi military sales agreements jumped to approximately $10 billion per year in the early 1990s, much of it for ground combat and support vehicles, before returning to an annual average of about $1 billion during the remainder of the decade (DOD 1999).

The Costs of U.S. Policy Toward Saudi Arabia

Arguably, U.S. policy toward Saudi Arabia has contributed to the stability of the Persian Gulf and helped to ensure that Saudi Arabia in particular remained a reliable supplier of oil. As elsewhere in the region, however, these benefits have been attained only at some cost. In the case of Saudi Arabia, these costs have taken two main forms. First, the buildup of the Saudi military has at times conflicted, or at least seemed to conflict, with other U.S. interests, especially the security of Israel, resulting in heated political battles in Washington (Teicher and Teicher 1993, 38). Second, the United States has been reluctant to promote political, economic, and social reforms in Saudi Arabia or to press the government to modify external and internal policies that have raised concerns in Washington.

During the 1970s and 1980s, the importance of Saudi Arabia both as an oil producer and as a defensive bulwark in the Gulf was reflected in a strong U.S. desire to be responsive to Saudi requests for arms, even when American officials had doubts about the wisdom of providing them (Long 1985, 55). It was not always clear whether the Saudi military would be able to make effective use of all the weapons it purchased, and some officials feared that excessive arms sales could contribute to instability inside Saudi Arabia, as they arguably had in Iran (Teicher and Teicher 1993, 42; Cordesman 2003, 115). Of particular concern in those decades, however, was the potential threat that the growing Saudi arsenal of advanced weapons posed to Israel. As a result, on at least three occasions a Saudi arms request triggered a major political battle in Washington. It was not until the 1990s that the tightened alliance between the United States and Saudi Arabia resulting from the Gulf War and diminished Israeli concerns removed most of the political obstacles that the Saudis had faced in obtaining sophisticated U.S. arms (Cordesman 2003, 108).

The first controversy arose over a 1977 Saudi request to purchase sixty F-15 fighters (Quandt 1981, 118–20; Cordesman 1984, 205–12; Long 1985, 60; Kupchan 1987, 60–61; Teicher and Teicher 1993, 40–41; Miglietta 2002, 232–37). Despite its policy of limiting arms sales to nonallies, the Carter administration was strongly inclined to honor the request. Not only would the F-15s greatly enhance Saudi air defenses, but the Saudi leadership also attached considerable political importance to the sale. Indeed, for the Saudis, the sale of the F-15s became a litmus test of their relationship with the United States as well as of the U.S. commitment to the security of the Gulf. Thus, as national security advisor Zbigniew Brzezinski later acknowledged, the sale of the jets was "absolutely necessary" to retain U.S. credibility with the Saudis (Brzezinksi 1983, 247).

Nevertheless, the request quickly ran up against stiff opposition in Congress, where it would have to be approved by either the House of Representatives or the Senate. Both the Israeli government and pro-Israeli groups mounted a major effort to block the sale on the grounds that the F-15 was not necessary for the defense of Saudi Arabia and that it could pose a threat to Israel. Thus in order to secure congressional passage, the Carter administration was forced to make significant compromises. It placed restrictions on the configuration, deployment, and equipment of the F-15s that would limit their attack capabilities, and it linked the deal to a larger military assistance package that included the sale of thirty-five F-15s and seventy-five F-16s to Israel.

An even more bitter dispute over U.S. arms sales to Saudi Arabia erupted just three years later.[13] In 1981, following the outbreak of the Iran-Iraq War, the Saudis asked to purchase AWACS aircraft, fuel tanks that would give the F-15s greater range, and tanker aircraft for aerial refueling as well as advanced air-to-air missiles and related ground equipment (Safran 1985, 327; Long 1985, 64–65; Kupchan 1987, 144–47; Miglietta 2002, 239–41; Laham 2002). This time, it fell to the new Reagan administration to make the case. In addition to the types of political and military benefits attributed to the previous F-15 sale, this so-called Air Defense Enhancement Package would enable the United States to deploy up to 140 fighter aircraft to the Gulf in an emergency, since it meant Saudi Arabia would have in place all the basing, service facilities, refueling capabilities, spare parts, and key munitions needed by such a force. According to one military expert, "No conceivable improvement in U.S. airlift and [U.S. Air Force] rapid deployment and 'bare basing' capability could come close to giving the U.S. this rapid and effective reinforcement capability" (Cordesman 1984, 326).

Despite these ostensibly considerable benefits, the proposed sale was once again viewed by many as undermining Israel's security and consequently encountered strong resistance. Indeed, Israeli Prime Minister Menachem Begin and other senior Israeli officials lobbied Congress, and at one point, a majority in both houses was on record as opposing the sale. It required an all-out effort by the administration to win Senate acceptance by a thin margin, and by then the struggle between Reagan and Begin had seriously strained U.S.-Israeli relations (Cordesman 1984, 331–35; Long 1985, 65; Laham 2002).

A third major episode, in 1985, had a different outcome. This time, the Saudis sought further to enhance their air defense capability by upgrading the F-15s that they already owned, purchasing an additional forty of the aircraft (with eight more to be stored in the United States as a reserve), and expanding their arsenal of advanced air-launched missiles. Once again, the request triggered sharp criticism and lobbying by Israel and pro-Israeli groups, but this time, the critics prevailed. Such was the level of opposition—fifty-one Senators had signed a letter opposing the sale even before the administration had announced its terms—that the Reagan administration never formally submitted a proposal. In frustration, the Saudis decided to turn instead to the British for a new fighter aircraft (Miglietta 2002, 263–65; Cordesman 1988, 269–308).

Of even greater significance, however, have been the costs of what the United States has *not* done because of its dependence on the Saudis. Few pairs of countries have been less alike than the United States and Saudi Arabia. Until recently, the kingdom possessed no representative bodies or meaningful elections. To the contrary, criticism of the royal family, the Saudi government, and religious leaders has been legally forbidden and strictly monitored, and those who have dared to challenge the regime or its policies have been punished (Hanson 2002, 24; Zunes 2002, 16). In addition, Saudi Arabia has lacked religious freedom for non-Muslims and even for Muslims who do not follow the official interpretation of Islam, Wahhabism. And it has placed restrictions on the public and professional roles of women (Chanin and Gause 2003; see also Hanson 2002, 23–24). As one particularly harsh critic has contended, "No country in the world is more hostile to the American idea of religious tolerance, free speech, constitutional government, and sexual equality" (Hanson 2002, 27).

Arguably, almost any other country with such characteristics would have been the object of sharp U.S. criticism and pressures to change. But Saudi Arabia has not. Rather, the United States has exhibited a perhaps remarkable degree of forbearance toward the al-Saud regime. It has not pressed the royal family very hard for democratic reforms. It has been largely silent on the question of women's rights. And it has turned a blind eye to what is taught in Saudi schools and mosques. Indeed, according to one longtime case officer, the CIA's Directorate of Intelligence pointedly avoided writing National Intelligence Estimates on Saudi Arabia (Baer 2003, 36). Another critic concludes that the United States pays more deference to the Saudis than to any other government in the world (Singer 2003).

To be sure, there have sometimes been good reasons for this American quiescence. Certainly, pushing too hard for democratic reforms could be counterproductive (for example, Gause 2002). But to many observers, this exceptional degree of tolerance has owed more than anything else to Saudi Arabia's uniquely critical role in the world oil market (for example, *Washington Post* 2001, 21; T. Friedman 2002; Hanson 2002, 25; T. Friedman 2003a; Mandelbaum 2003; Kalicki and Goldwyn 2005, 5).

Since September 11, 2001, particular attention has been devoted to the question of how hard the United States has pressed the Saudis to provide assistance in the fight against terrorism. Although some have accused the Saudi government of directly supporting Islamic terrorists and other violent forms of Islam, the real issue is whether the regime has done all it could to help further U.S. objectives both before and after 9/11. In this area as well, successive administrations have been accused of closing their eyes to problems in Saudi Arabia, muting concerns about threatening developments there, and failing to confront the Saudis or apply much pressure on them (for example, *New York Times* 2001; Brisard and Dasquie 2002, 93; T. Friedman 2002; Benjamin and Simon 2002, 415).

This reticence first appeared in the mid-1990s, when the United States attempted to investigate terrorist attacks against American targets in Saudi Arabia. So sensitive were U.S.-Saudi relations that the CIA instructed officials at its Riyadh station not to collect intelligence on Islamic extremists—even after the 1996 Khobar Towers bombing killed fourteen U.S. military personnel—for fear of upsetting their hosts (Kaplan, Ekman, and Latif 2003). The 1998 attacks on the U.S. embassies in Kenya and Tanzania prompted the United States to conduct missile strikes against al Qaeda training camps in Afghanistan and to press for international sanctions on that country. Yet the administration of President Bill Clinton looked the other way as the Saudi government continued to send money and free oil to the Taliban regime there (Banerjee 2001a). And both the Clinton and George W. Bush administrations allegedly placed restrictions on FBI and military intelligence investigations of members of the bin Laden family and other prominent Saudis (Palast and Pallister 2001). Even after the attacks of September 11, 2001, in which a majority of the participants were Saudi nationals, the Bush administration was unwilling to criticize Saudi Arabia for its refusal to provide passenger lists for flights to the United States (Banerjee 2001a).

Most important of all has been the issue of terrorist financing. There is little evidence that the Saudi government or senior officials have themselves directly provided funds to terrorist organizations. But many would agree that the government "has been less than vigilant in preventing financial contributions by Saudi citizens to Usama bin Laden's al Qaeda and groups like it, in allowing front groups for violent Islamist extremists to collect contributions from Saudi citizens under the pretext of soliciting for charity, and in not properly monitoring the overseas activities of branches of what are otherwise legitimate charities" (Gause 2002, 46). "Without this money," opined the *New York Times*, "Al Qaeda would have had trouble financing some of its most ambitious attacks" (*New York Times* 2004b).[14]

Yet before September 2001, according to one detailed investigative report, U.S. officials did painfully little to confront the Saudis not only on terrorist financing but on backing Muslim extremists abroad more generally. American officials knew about the role of Saudis in funding terrorist groups by 1996, but for years Washington did almost nothing to stop it. Examining the Saudi role, according to a senior intelligence analyst interviewed for the report, was "virtually taboo." Even after the embassy bombings in Africa, moves by counterterrorism officials to act against the Saudis were repeatedly rebuffed by senior staff at the State Department and elsewhere who felt that other foreign policy interests outweighed fighting terrorism (Kaplan, Ekman, and Latif 2003; see also Coll 2004, 511–12).

Afghanistan in the 1980s:
Support for the Mujahideen

Before leaving the Persian Gulf, one other U.S. policy episode merits mention: American assistance to the resistance fighters in Afghanistan during the 1980s. Immediately after the Soviet invasion of December 1979, President Carter authorized the CIA to provide weapons and ammunition to the mujahideen. This covert effort was continued by the Reagan administration, which later expanded both the financial resources devoted to it and the types of weapons and other forms of military assistance that were provided. By the time of the Soviet withdrawal in 1988, the United States had spent several billion dollars on the program.

The United States supported the Afghan resistance for several reasons. There were the usual cold war objectives of preventing the expansion of Soviet influence and wearing down the Soviet Union, in this case by making its involvement in Afghanistan as costly as possible. Also important, however, were particular concerns about the threat that the Soviet military presence in the country posed to Persian Gulf oil supplies. This theme was sounded most urgently by Carter administration officials, who were already preoccupied by the impact of the Iranian Revolution on the stability of the region (Vance 1983, 386 and 391; Acharya 1989, 46; J. Scott 1996, 43; Little 2002, 151–53; Coll 2004, 50–51). As an authoritative history of the Afghan conflict notes, the invasion provided new credibility to warnings that Moscow would use Afghanistan as a springboard for seizing control of the area's energy resources (Cordovez and Harrison 1995, 49). Indeed, a special National Intelligence Estimate completed in the last months of the Carter administration concluded that the Soviets were developing plans for military contingencies in Iran, including a large-scale invasion as far as the south-central part of the country (Gates 1996, 130). But concern about the threat to Persian Gulf oil was also shared by members of the subsequent Reagan administration, especially CIA Director William Casey (J. Scott 1996, 43; Coll 2004, 97).

Before the United States could aid the Afghan resistance to any substantial extent, it first had to secure the help of Pakistan, through which most weapons and other forms of military assistance would have to pass. During the first three years of the Carter administration, U.S.-Pakistan relations had reached a low point. A military coup, American concerns about human rights abuses, and Pakistan's insistence on acquiring a nuclear reprocessing facility had prompted the United States to cut off all but food aid. Immediately after the Soviet invasion, however, the Carter administration quickly offered a $400 million package equally divided between military and economic assistance. This initial offer was rejected by Pakistan as inadequate. But the following year, the Reagan administration was able to obtain a positive response when it proposed $1.7 billion in economic and $1.5 billion in military aid. Included in the deal were forty advanced F-16 fighter-bombers, which the United States had previously supplied only to NATO allies, Israel, and Japan.[15]

The initial disagreement over American aid did not prevent cooperation between the CIA and the Pakistani intelligence service. U.S. weapons shipments began as early as January 1980 and continued for a decade. For the first several years, the program was funded at a modest annual level of about $30 to $40 million. In the mid-1980s, however, the amount of funding expanded considerably, reaching more than $100 million in 1984, $250 million in 1985, $470 million in 1986, and $630 million in 1987 (Gates 1996; J. Scott 1996; Weinbaum 2003; Coll 2004). A critical watershed was passed in March 1985, when President Reagan signed National Security Decision Directive (NSDD) 166 authorizing the CIA to support the mujahideen with "all means possible" (J. Scott 1996, 59; see also Teicher and Teicher 1993, 326; Cordovez and Harrison 1995, 161; Lansford 2003, 128). By the end of the 1980s, the CIA had funneled approximately $3 billion in aid to the resistance, making U.S. involvement in Afghanistan "the most extensive and expensive covert warfare operation since Vietnam" (Weinbaum 2003, 449; see also Kolko 2002, 48; Cogan 1993, 78; Weaver 1995, 41–42; Weaver 1996, 26; J. Prados 1986, 361).

Not only did the overall level of funding increase, but so did the range of weapons and other forms of military assistance that were sent to the mujahideen. Initially, the CIA supplied only items that were used by the Soviets or their allies or were already commonly available in Afghanistan. In order to make it difficult for the Soviets to prove U.S. involvement, no arms or equipment made in the United States or typically associated with the West were provided (Kux 2001, 252; Yousaf and Adkin 2001, 81–83). The 1985 NSDD removed the previous restrictions, however, and the CIA began to supply an array of more sophisticated weapons, including mine-clearing devices, satellite-targetable mortars, "mule-mobile" rocket launchers, helicopter detectors, and even rudimentary cruise missiles (Kuperman 1999; Cordovez and Harrison 1995, 160; Coll 2004, 135). Most notable was the administration's decision, in early 1986, to provide the mujahideen with shoulder-fired Stinger

surface-to-air missiles (Kuperman 1999; Gates 1996, 350). In addition, the CIA
shared satellite photos and maps, tactical information from radio intercepts,
and advice on technical matters, and Americans began to play a more active
role in operational planning (Teicher and Teicher 1993, 326; J. Scott 1996, 59;
Yousaf and Adkin 2001, 93–94; Lansford 2003, 128).[16]

Overall, the American investment in the mujahideen appears to have
been a highly cost-effective one. At a total financial cost to the United States
of less than $6 billion, including the aid to Pakistan, the program first pre-
vented an early defeat of the resistance and then raised considerably the price
tag of the war for the Soviets, although just how much is uncertain. By one
estimate, the dollar cost to Moscow ranged between approximately $5 and $7
billion per year during the early 1980s (J. Prados 1986, 359), and shortly after
the Soviet withdrawal, then Soviet foreign minister Eduard Shevardnadze put
the total cost of the Soviet intervention at $96 billion (Cogan 1993, 81). The
introduction of the Stingers in particular complicated the Soviet war effort.
The missiles forced a change in Soviet military tactics, making it necessary
to fly at higher altitudes, spend less time over any one target, and avoid some
missions altogether. In turn, these tactical adjustments made it easier for the
resistance to bring supplies into the country and to conduct large-scale combat operations (Cordovez and Harrison 1995, 198–99; Lansford 2003, 128–29).

Yet on the larger question of whether U.S. assistance brought about or even
hastened the Soviet withdrawal, there has been much debate. Members of the
Reagan administration and others have argued that the U.S. effort, especially
the provision of Stinger missiles, had a major, even decisive, impact (for example, Shultz 1993, 692; J. Scott 1996, 77; Bergen 2001, 73). And a former Pakistani
intelligence officer who worked closely with the U.S. program concluded a decade after the Soviet departure that without the CIA contributions, the Soviets would still be in Afghanistan (Yousaf and Adkin 2001, 96). Other analyses
have concluded, however, that the escalation of U.S. aid in the mid-1980s was
not crucial to the rebels' survival nor a critical determinant of Soviet decision
making (Kuperman 1999; see also Cordovez and Harrison 1995, 199–201).

The costs to the United States of the program, moreover, were not limited
to dollars and cents. In the first place, Washington was temporarily forced to
compromise some of its other foreign policy goals vis-à-vis Pakistan, especially its prior firm opposition to Islamabad's nuclear program (Cordovez and
Harrison 1995, 66; J. Scott 1996, 80). In addition, the United States lost control of a valuable military technology and weapons system in the form of the

Stingers. Before the Stinger decision, concerns had been raised that missiles would fall into the hands of the Soviets, terrorists, or other enemies of the United States, such as Iran, and this in fact happened. According to the most detailed published analysis of the issue, Pakistan skimmed off a percentage of the Stingers, with some reportedly winding up on the black market. Of those that reached the mujahideen, perhaps half were sold for cash, given to allies such as Iran, lost in ambushes, or hoarded for future conflicts. Although the CIA initiated a buyback program in the 1990s, some three to six hundred missiles of the one thousand or more provided to the resistance remain unaccounted for (Kuperman 1999, 253–55; see also Cordovez and Harrison 1995, 195–98; J. Scott 1996, 61 and 80; Bergen 2001, 74; Coll 2004, 11).

Latin America

Although U.S. foreign policy efforts intended to stabilize and expand the world oil market have often been directed at the Persian Gulf, that is not the only area that has been of concern to American policymakers. Especially in more recent years, the United States has also had a strong interest in promoting oil production in other parts of the world, and it has sometimes employed considerable diplomatic efforts and other means of influence to do so. Indeed, the 2002 National Security Strategy called for expanding "the sources and types of global energy supplied, especially in the Western Hemisphere, Africa, Central Asia, and the Caspian region" in order to enhance U.S. energy security.[17] Yet just as in the Persian Gulf, these efforts have not been without costs, especially in the form of compromises with other foreign policy objectives.

Overall, the second most important oil exporting region after the Persian Gulf has been Latin America. Since the early 1980s, Latin America's proven oil reserves have stood at between 10 and 15 percent of the world total, and the region has accounted for between 11 and 14 percent of global oil production. During the past decade, it has consistently produced between 10 and 10.5 MBD, or 13 and 14 percent of world output.

In some respects, however, these figures understate the significance to the United States of Latin America, which has provided a disproportionately large share of American imports. After World War II, Venezuela became the first major source of U.S. oil imports, and since 1980 it and Mexico have consistently ranked among the top four foreign providers of oil along with Canada and Saudi Arabia. Latin American countries have typically exported more than half of their oil to the United States, and in 2004, one-third of all U.S. petroleum imports came from the region. Since September 2001, maintaining unhindered access to the region's oil has assumed even greater importance for U.S. policymakers, given heightened concerns about the stability of Persian Gulf oil supplies (Stokes 2005, 124–25).

Fortunately, American access to Latin American oil has been largely un-problematic, at least until the last few years. Although the oil industries in the two largest exporters were nationalized—Mexico in the 1930s and Venezuela in the mid-1970s—both countries have been generally interested in achieving and maintaining high levels of production and exports in order to maximize revenues. Neither country has faced significant external threats, nor has the shipment of oil to the United States posed any problems. Tankers do not have to pass through any vulnerable choke points and, given the proximity of the region, U.S. naval forces can easily protect the relevant sea lanes. With only two recent exceptions, moreover, regional oil production has not been severely disrupted by internal conflicts. The upshot of these favorable circumstances is that Latin American countries have been among the most reliable U.S. sup-pliers (Larson 2003). The United States has not needed to exert much effort to secure its energy interests in the region, and these have rarely conflicted with other policy priorities (see Figure 5.3).

Mexico

Mexico in particular has been an ideal energy partner since the first oil shock. Mexican production grew rapidly during the decade following the Arab oil embargo, surpassing that of Venezuela in the early 1980s. Petroleum output rose from just 525,000 barrels per day in 1973 to 3 MBD in 1982, where it re-mained for a dozen years. Since 1995, production levels have climbed even higher, reaching more than 3.8 MBD in 2004. Mexican exports grew apace, from nothing in 1973 to approximately 1.85 MBD in 1982. Between 1986 and 1999, exports fluctuated around 1.5 MBD, but have since expanded to nearly 2 MBD (BP 2006).

Significantly, most Mexican petroleum exports have gone to the United States, ensuring the latter of an extremely secure and reliable source of oil. Although Mexico has cooperated at times with OPEC to stabilize oil prices since the late 1990s, it has remained outside the organization and has never used oil as a political weapon. Nor has Mexican oil production ever been se-verely disrupted by domestic disturbances. The only note of concern in this otherwise rosy picture has been a steep downward slide in Mexico's stated oil

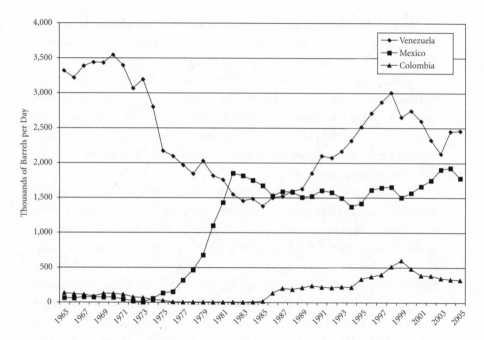

FIGURE 5.3 Latin American Oil Exports, 1965–2005
SOURCE: BP 2006

reserves, from nearly fifty billion barrels in the mid-1990s to less than four-teen billion barrels in 2005, due to a change in how they are calculated.[18] The resulting reserves-to-production ratio is lower than even that of the United States, raising questions about Mexico's ability to maintain, let alone increase, its current level of output.

Venezuela

Equally important to the United States has been Venezuela, which possesses the largest proven reserves outside of the Persian Gulf and by far the largest in Latin America. The current estimate for conventional oil—about 80 bil-lion barrels—does not include even more substantial deposits of extra-heavy oil and bitumen, for which estimates of recoverable reserves range as high as 270 billion barrels.[19] Although Venezuela was overtaken by Mexico in the early 1980s as the region's largest producer, it has remained, except for a half a dozen years in the 1980s, the greatest source of exports in Latin America. In recent years, it has ranked as the fourth or fifth largest exporter in the world, after Saudi Arabia, Russia, Norway, and, occasionally, Iran.

Overall, the governments of the United States and Venezuela enjoyed good relations between the late 1950s and the late 1990s. In particular, they experienced few, if any, serious disagreements on energy issues. Venezuela was willing to supply large amounts of oil—more than half of its exports— to the United States at reasonable prices. It took no part in the 1973 oil embargo and regularly exceeded the OPEC production quotas that were first established in the early 1980s. For its part, the United States accepted without protest Venezuela's nationalization of the petroleum industry in the mid-1970s (Romero 2004, 132–34).

Since Hugo Chávez assumed the presidency in 1999, however, U.S.-Venezuela energy relations have been marked by a number of tensions. First, Chávez quickly assumed a militant role within OPEC, supporting production cuts as a means of raising oil prices (Romero 2004, 144, 148). In addition, he signaled a desire to reduce Venezuela's dependence on oil sales to the United States, most obviously by signing agreements to open Venezuela's oil and gas fields to China (C. Buckley 2004; Romero and Ellsworth 2005). And Chávez took a series of measures that tended to discourage foreign investment and have thus diminished the long-term prospects for oil production.

In the 1990s, Venezuela had reopened the upstream oil sector—exploration, development, and production—to international oil companies. By 2005, foreign companies accounted for roughly 1.2 MBD, or 40 percent, of Venezuela's production (Romero and Ellsworth 2005). In 2001, however, a new hydrocarbon law substantially raised the royalty rate that would have to be paid on new investments and stipulated that all future projects must take the form of joint ventures in which the state-owned oil company, Petróleos de Venezuela S.A. (PdVSA), would hold a majority share (Forero 2001; Mommer 2004, 141). And in 2005, the Chávez government announced that the new law would apply retroactively to a number of the preexisting foreign operations and that international oil companies owed $4 billion in back taxes.[20]

Notwithstanding these irritants, of perhaps greatest concern to U.S. policymakers has been the prospect of political instability in Venezuela, with its negative implications for the country's ability to remain a major oil producer and exporter. In April 2002, disaffected sectors of Venezuelan society and the military staged an unsuccessful coup against Chávez. A subsequent government crackdown on coup supporters prompted massive work stoppages, including a two-month-long strike by PdVSA workers. As a result, production plummeted from nearly 3 MBD to just 700,000 barrels per day in January

2003, and exports to the United States dropped to 426,000 barrels per day, a far cry from the average of some 1.5 MBD in previous years.[21] Since then, the Chávez government has moved to exercise tighter control over PdVSA, which had come to be regarded by many as an unaccountable state within the state. The government has used a substantial share of the company's earnings—roughly $4 billion in 2004—for social programs and public projects. Whatever its social virtues, this diversion has raised doubts about whether PdVSA will have sufficient funds to invest in exploration and development.[22]

Thus far, the United States has responded cautiously to these challenges to its energy interests in Venezuela. While some observers have averred that Washington afforded tacit support to the coup leaders (for example, Rutledge 2005, 94–96), "the preponderance of the evidence suggests that the Bush administration refused to be involved" (Romero 2004, 145). It remains to be seen what, if anything, the United States will do, should Venezuelan oil production and exports undergo a prolonged decline.

Colombia

The other principal challenge to U.S. regional energy interests has occurred in Colombia. Although a much smaller oil producer and exporter than either Mexico or Venezuela, Colombia has become increasingly important in the last decade. During the 1990s, it was believed to have the fourth largest proven reserves in the region, after Venezuela, Mexico, and Brazil. Oil production more than doubled in the late 1980s and then again in the 1990s, rising from 407,000 barrels per day in 1989 to a high of 838,000 barrels per day in 1999. During the same period, Colombia's exports increased dramatically, to approximately 600,000 barrels per day, making it the third largest Latin American exporter. In 1999, Colombia provided the United States with more than 4.3 percent of the latter's imports, temporarily making it the seventh largest U.S. supplier.[23]

Meanwhile, however, Colombia has been riven by a long-standing civil war. In recent years, a principal tactic of the antigovernment forces has been to attack oil pipelines and installations in the interior of the country. In 2001, for example, a major pipeline was bombed 170 to 180 times, shutting it down for 240 days and preventing the delivery of an estimated 24 million barrels of crude oil. During the first half of this decade, these and other attacks caused a substantial decline in Colombia's output, to just 550,000 barrels per day in 2004. Likewise, total exports dropped by nearly 50 percent, and exports to the United States fell even more sharply, to just 176,000 barrels per day in 2004.[24]

In addition, the conflict in Colombia may threaten stability in neighboring countries such as Venezuela (Stokes 2005, 125).

In response to this threat to American energy interests, the United States has stepped up its support for the Colombian government. After providing less than $100 million per year in economic and military assistance through most of the 1990s, it sharply increased the total to more than $1 billion in 2000 and, with the exception of 2001, provided more than half a billion dollars of aid in each of the following years. In 2002, the Bush administration acknowledged that one of its objectives was to help the Colombian government protect oil pipelines from guerilla sabotage, and it specifically requested $98 million for the purpose of training and equipping two brigades of Colombian troops that would be dedicated to providing pipeline security (Klare 2004a, 141; Stokes 2005, 125–26). That same year, the United States dispatched approximately seventy U.S. Army special forces instructors to the area in which much of the guerilla activity has taken place in order to help train those units (Klare 2004a, 142; Forero 2004b; Rutledge 2005, 101). Although these efforts have been followed by a decline in the number of successful attacks on the oil infrastructure, they have increased the risk of direct U.S. involvement in the civil war.

The Caspian Sea Region

Since the early to mid-1990s, U.S. policymakers have also shown considerable interest in the oil resources of the Caspian Sea region. The area around the city of Baku, which is located on the southwestern shore of the Caspian, was the first in the world to achieve large-scale oil production, in the late 1800s. For nearly seventy-five years, however, the region lay within the boundaries of the Soviet Union, and thus outside the reach of Western influence. That all changed in 1991 with the breakup of the USSR and the subsequent establishment of a handful of new independent states with substantial energy resources—Azerbaijan, Kazakhstan, Turkmenistan, and Uzbekistan—on or near the Caspian littoral (see Map 5.2).

The Region's Oil Potential
Outside observers were quick to tout the energy potential of the Caspian basin, although estimates of the amount of oil that might be pumped out of the ground have varied substantially. During the 1990s, the authoritative U.S. Energy Information Administration (EIA) set the region's proved oil reserves at between 16 and 32 billion barrels, but it also attributed another 160 to 200

MAP 5.2 Caspian Sea Region

billion barrels in possible reserves to the region. Meanwhile, more conservative sources put the total amount of proven reserves at as few as 8 billion (*Oil
& Gas Journal*) to 16 billion (British Petroleum/BP) barrels (Bahgat 2003, 143;
Klare 2004b, 7; Rutledge 2005, 104). In more recent years, thanks primarily to
additional discoveries in Kazakhstan, the EIA has raised its upper estimate of
the region's proven reserves to 44 billion barrels, while the previously more
cautious BP has revised its figure dramatically upward to nearly 48 billion
barrels (BP 2006). If even only a fraction of the estimated possible reserves
were to be confirmed, it would give the Caspian the second largest set of
untapped reserves in the world outside the Persian Gulf. In any case, many
would agree with former U.S. Undersecretary of State Alan Larson that the
region "has tremendous potential" (Larson 2003).

In response to this potential, U.S. and other international oil companies
have become active in the region and have made substantial investments. As

early as 1993, Chevron entered into a joint venture with Kazakhstan's state-owned oil company to develop the Tengiz oil field, which is estimated to hold between six and nine billion barrels. The following year, a consortium of eight companies promising to invest more than $7 billion signed a production sharing agreement with Azerbaijan to develop several offshore oil fields with estimated reserves of up to five billion barrels. And in 2000, another consortium discovered a new field (Kashagan) off the coast of Kazakhstan that has been described as the largest outside of the Middle East and the fifth largest in the world, with an estimated nine to thirteen billion barrels of recoverable reserves. By the end of the 1990s, American and other firms had already sunk billions of dollars in new production and transportation facilities and were planning to spend even larger amounts before 2010, when total investment was expected to reach the $50 billion level.[25]

U.S. Interests

Immediately after the dissolution of the Soviet Union, U.S. policymakers showed little interest in the states of the Caspian region, tending to view them as "inconvenient additions to the international scene."[26] As Western oil companies entered the region and the extent of its energy resources became clearer, however, Washington began to pay more attention, especially during the Clinton administration. By the mid-1990s, the United States had come to regard the Caspian as a strategic opportunity to increase and diversify the world's energy supplies, thereby reducing Western dependence on the Persian Gulf and bolstering the energy security of the United States and its allies. Accordingly, American leaders began to place heavy emphasis on the development of the region's energy resources (Klare 2001, 83; Manning 2000; Dekmejian and Simonian 2001, 134–35).

To be sure, doing so was expected to result in other benefits as well. It could strengthen the independence and prosperity of the new states in the region, which were still emerging from the shadow of the former Soviet Union. By establishing stronger economic links among them, moreover, it would mitigate regional conflicts. And it would provide valuable commercial opportunities for U.S. companies. American firms had been the lead players in the Caspian and already held substantial percentages of nearly every major Caspian consortium agreement and rights over almost every major field under exploration or development (Bremmer 1998, 28; Manning 2000, 47).[27] But underpinning all of these interests was the strategic value of the region's oil.

An essential component to the exploitation of the Caspian's energy resources has been the development of new means for bringing its oil and gas to market. The region is landlocked, and preexisting pipelines, dating from the Soviet era, could handle only a fraction of the amount of oil and gas that the area was expected to be able to produce. Thus the construction of multiple pipelines has been a major U.S. foreign policy priority since the mid-1990s, one that has been shared by both the Clinton and Bush administrations (U.S. Congress 1998, 3; Larson 2003; Rutledge 2005, 114).

Not just any new pipelines would do, however. For other strategic reasons, U.S. officials have sought to block the development of new pipelines running south through Iran and to prevent Russia from dominating the export routes, as it previously had (D. Ottaway 2000; see also Dekmejian and Simonian 2001, 136). To this end, the United States has placed particular emphasis on creating an east-west transportation corridor that would reduce the need for energy flows and regional trade and communications along the north-south axis between Iran and Russia (Hill 2001). It has been the main proponent in particular of a large 1-MBD-capacity pipeline from Baku via the Georgian capital of Tbilisi to the Turkish city of Ceyhan on the Mediterranean and another across the Caspian Sea itself (Klare 2001, 102; Bahgat 2003, 167–68; Klare 2004b, 8). Indeed, the Trans-Caspian and Baku-Tbilisi-Ceyhan (BTC) pipelines became the primary focus U.S. policy toward the region (Hill 2001), although for several years in the 1990s, the Clinton administration also took an interest in the efforts an American oil company, Unocal, to build oil and gas pipelines from the region across Afghanistan to Pakistan.

U.S. Policy Efforts

In contrast to the highly interventionist nature of U.S. policy toward the Persian Gulf, American efforts to promote the development of Caspian energy resources and new energy transit routes from the region have been relatively low-key. In the view of American officials, the proper U.S. role has been to facilitate discussions and to serve as a catalyst for financing.[28] Nevertheless, these U.S. efforts have been substantial.

Especially after its decision in 1996 to promote the BTC pipeline, the Clinton administration engaged in frequent high-level diplomatic contacts (Klare 2001, 95; Dekmejian and Simonian 2001, 135–36; Bahgat 2003, 167–68). The leaders of Azerbaijan, Georgia, Kazakhstan, and Uzbekistan all came to Washington for meetings with the president and vice president, and top U.S. officials traveled to each of the region's capitals. In 1999, President Clinton was present as the presidents of Azerbaijan, Georgia, and Turkey signed the legal framework for the construction of that critical transit route. Once construction was underway and further exploration suggested that the largest oil reserves lay on Kazakh territory, the focus of U.S. diplomacy shifted to the realization of the Trans-Caspian pipeline (Larson 2003).

The United States has made clear that it would not directly cover any of the construction costs. Nevertheless, it has used the institutional resources at its disposal to help arrange financing. In 1998, for example, the Clinton administration announced a new Caspian Sea Initiative that would coordinate the efforts of the U.S. Trade Development Administration, Overseas Private Investment Corporation (OPIC), and Export-Import Bank to promote investment in regional energy projects. American contributions would include grants for technical assistance, political risk insurance, loans, and other incentives for potential investors (Hill 2001; Dekmejian and Simonian 2001, 136; Rutledge 2005, 115–16).

At the same time, U.S. policymakers increasingly recognized that Caspian energy resources could not be successfully developed without stabilizing and strengthening the states in the region (Hill 2001). The United States had offered most of them a good deal of economic assistance immediately after they had gained their independence, but American aid levels had generally declined through the mid-1990s. Coincident with U.S. efforts to promote the BTC and Trans-Caspian pipelines, however, the amount of assistance provided jumped sharply. Between fiscal years 1998 and 2001, before U.S. policy in the region became complicated by the War on Terror, economic aid to the five most critical states—Azerbaijan, Georgia, Kazakhstan, Turkmenistan, and Uzbekistan—totaled more than $900 million.[29]

During the Clinton administration, the United States also initiated a number of military assistance programs with Caspian states aimed at strengthening their internal security capabilities. The administration provided arms and training while engaging in exchanges and even conducting joint exercises (Klare 2001, 95–97; Klare 2004a, 133–39; Klare 2004b, 8). The Bush administration continued these policies, pledging additional aid to the countries in the region and even deploying military instructors to Georgia to train special units whose duties would eventually include guarding the Georgian segment of the BTC pipeline (Klare 2004b, 8; see also Rutledge 2005, 117).

One of the more curious episodes in U.S. policy toward the region involved an aborted plan to create energy transit routes across Afghanistan. In 1995, the American oil company Unocal along with a Saudi partner reached a preliminary agreement with Turkmenistan to build a gas pipeline through Afghanistan to Pakistan, which it hoped would be followed by a parallel oil pipeline (IEA 1998a, 39, 40, 251, 258). By the next year, according to one authoritative account, "the United States had taken up Unocal's agenda as its own" (Coll 2004, 310). The United States lobbied Pakistan on behalf of the pipeline (Rashid 2000, 165; Coll 2004, 310). More notably, these commercial plans resulted in a brief flirtation by the Clinton administration with the Taliban itself (Weinbaum 2003, 454). Between 1995 and 1997, it supported the Taliban indirectly through Pakistan and Saudi Arabia, accepting the latter's provision of arms and funding to the movement (Rashid 2000, 176 and 180). In 1996, the United States described the Taliban's military gains as a "positive" development, and it attempted to obtain Uzbek approval for the new Taliban regime in Kabul. Presumably, American officials hoped that the Taliban would create the political stability and provide the security needed to build the pipeline (Mackenzie 1998, 96; Dekmejian and Simonian 2001, 100 and 134).

In 1997, these efforts seemed to be bearing fruit. Unocal, Turkmenistan, and Pakistan entered into a contract to begin construction of the pipeline the following year (Rashid 2000, 160, 172; Dekmejian and Simonian 2001, 38; Coll 2004, 306). In early 1998, the Taliban agreed to the pipeline and pledged to provide security (Dekmejian and Simonian 2001, 100). By then, however, the project's prospects were already fading, as U.S. interest in the Taliban had cooled appreciably. In late 1997, U.S. Secretary of State Madeleine Albright and other top officials criticized the Taliban for human rights violations, especially the treatment of women, and tolerance of drug trafficking (Mackenzie 1998, 90, 101; Coll 2004, 363–65). The coup de grâce was delivered by the bombing of the U.S. embassies in Kenya and Tanzania in August 1998, which triggered U.S. strikes on al Qaeda training camps in Afghanistan and then UN economic sanctions on the country because of the Taliban's refusal to extradite Osama bin Laden.

Costs of U.S. Policy
Clearly, U.S. government efforts to promote the development of Caspian energy resources since the early to mid-1990s have enjoyed some success. Of particular note was the timely completion of the pipeline from Baku to Ceyhan in 2005 (Arvedlund 2005). But U.S. policy has not been without costs. Apart from the relatively modest cost of economic and military assistance, successive administrations have appeared willing to sacrifice other important

U.S. foreign policy objectives, and this tendency has been only reinforced by the priority given to the War on Terror since September 2001. Following the breakup of the Soviet Union, U.S. policy efforts, however limited they may have been, focused initially on promoting democracy, human rights, and socially beneficial economic development. States were treated differently based on the progress they were making toward achieving a democratic transition (Dekmejian and Simonian 2001, 138; U.S. Congress 1998, 40).

Within a few years, however, these objectives were de-emphasized as new priority was given to gaining and ensuring access to the region's energy resources. Indeed, one early account suggests that the Clinton administration made a strategic decision to emphasize the economic stakes in the region rather than the civil strife and human rights violations (Baker 1997). As a result, "Oil company agreements and top-level U.S. government contacts with state governments have entrenched aging regional leaders and helped to transform governments into corrupt oligarchies that have enriched themselves with wealth generated through control of energy resources and suppressed opposition" (Hill 2001). Pressure for democratization, government transparency, and fiscal accountability declined. As Caspian expert Martha Brill Olcott observed as early as 1998:

> Now the behavior of U.S. policy makers sends a different message. Presidents of the energy-rich states are now welcome official visitors in Washington, regardless of how undemocratic their regimes are. Pipeline politics has come to eclipse concerns over sustaining macroeconomic reforms, and fear of political instability has begun to clearly overshadow our commitment to the cause of popular political empowerment. . . . We don't hold leaders accountable when they backslide or make little headway in implementing democratic reforms. (U.S. Congress 1998, 40)

Having failed sufficiently to emphasize political and economic reform in the region, in the view of another observer, the United States had compromised its "core principles" (Kramer 1998).

Particular attention has been paid to the case of Azerbaijan, which has been especially critical to U.S. policy because of its dual role as one of the two largest oil producers in the region and as the point of origin for the BTC pipeline. For a decade, the former Soviet republic was ruled by Heydar Aliyev, an ex-Soviet era communist boss who seized power from the country's first elected government in 1993. Although Aliyev won a presidential election in 1998, the process was widely regarded as rigged, and he routinely allowed the arrest and torture of political opponents, had public protests violently quelled, and suppressed the independent media. In addition, the watchdog group Transparency International has described Azerbaijan as one of the world's most crooked countries, ranking it near the very bottom of its global corruption index (Case 2004; Howden and Thornton 2005). Then in 2003, Aliyev was succeeded by his son, Ilhan, who triumphed in a second disputed election "marred by numerous, serious irregularities" that was followed by renewed protests, repression, and violence.[30] As the organization Human Rights Watch complained in a May 2005 letter to the younger Aliyev, Azerbaijan "has yet to take significant steps to open up its political processes to ensure that a plurality of groups can voice their opinions on political and social issues."[31] Likewise, the Department of State has repeatedly noted in its annual report on human rights practices in Azerbaijan that "the government's human rights record remained poor, and it continued to commit numerous abuses."

Notwithstanding this poor record on democracy, governance, and human rights, the Clinton and Bush administrations, given their desire to establish and maintain close ties with the government, have generally offered only muted criticism even in response to the most egregious abuses (Case 2004; Murphy 2005). Prior to the November 2005 parliamentary election, the United States did encourage the government to hold fair and free elections. Following the vote, it urged the government to conduct credible investigations of what the State Department described as "major irregularities and fraud that are of serious concern," and it condemned subsequent police violence against political protestors.[32] Nevertheless, those most recent problems and Azerbaijan's troubling overall record did not prevent President George W. Bush from inviting the country's leader to the White House in April 2006 (Diehl 2006; Chivers 2006).

Nor were such conflicts among U.S. policy objectives limited to Azerbaijan. By the mid-1990s, American officials had also begun to turn a blind eye toward authoritarianism and the absence of meaningful elections in Turkmenistan, Uzbekistan, and, especially, Kazakhstan (Kramer 1998). At least the human rights community in Kazakstan perceived that U.S. support had wavered. Until then, the American embassy had been very connected to the community and regularly invited non-governmental organizations to meetings. During the following several years, however, U.S. officials seemed to be so interested in making commercial deals that they were reluctant to meet with members of the human rights community for fear of offending government ministers who viewed them as the political opposition. Thus in this case, the U.S. push for economic development primarily in the form of new energy projects was viewed as setting back the cause of human rights.[33]

Like Azerbaijan, Kazakhstan has repeatedly come in for sharp criticism in the State Department's annual human rights reports, which have noted, among other things, that "dissent is suppressed, journalists harassed and power concentrated in the presidency," which has been held since 1991 by Nursultan Nazarbayev (Kessler 2006). Human rights groups have frequently characterized Nazarbayev as a dictator who has "established a hammerlock on his country's oil riches and amassed a fortune at the expense of an impoverished citizenry" (Stodghill 2006). As in the case of Azerbaijan, however, hopes were also raised prior to the December 2005 presidential elections that the United States would place top priority on promoting democracy when Secretary of State Condoleezza Rice toured the region and spoke of the need to hold free and fair elections (Brinkley 2005). Nevertheless, that contest, too, was marred by "widespread irregularities" both before and during the vote, and during the next six months, two opposition politicians were murdered and the government shut down two prominent American democracy organizations working there. Notwithstanding these setbacks, Vice President Richard Cheney conducted a high-profile visit to the country the following May, and President Bush received the Kazakh leader at the White House in September 2006 (Pickett 2006; Greenberg and Kramer 2006; Myers and Greenberg 2006).

Finally, the United States may have been at least temporarily willing to ignore the Taliban's Islamic fundamentalist agenda, its suppression of women, and other human rights abuses while the construction of a pipeline through Afghanistan remained a possibility. According to veteran journalist Ahmed Rashid, not a word of criticism issued from Washington after the Taliban captured the city of Herat in 1995 and threw out thousands of girls from schools. And when the Taliban captured Kabul in 1997, the Clinton administration was initially silent on Taliban's repression of that city's women (Rashid 2000, 176–78; see also Lafeber 2002, 545).

The costs of such tolerance were not limited, moreover, to their immediate negative effects. A number of observers feared that they could have long-term consequences that would redound to the disadvantage of the United States. As one analyst noted, "To the extent that we lose focus on democratization, we could also be risking an affiliation with forces and trends that, if unchecked, could later act to undermine internal and regional security and development in these states" (Blank 2000, 7). Others have pointed out the risks of becoming overly dependent on authoritarian regimes, since the uncertainties associated with future leadership successions could eventually result in U.S. policy being cut adrift (Kramer 1998; Bremmer 1998, 33).

Sub-Saharan Africa: The Gulf of Guinea

The latest oil producing region to hold the attention of U.S. policymakers has been sub-Saharan Africa, notably the states that are located in or along the Gulf of Guinea.[34] Although Nigeria has been a major producer since the early 1970s, the discovery in just the last decade of substantial amounts of oil has greatly raised the region's profile. Especially during the administration of George W. Bush, American officials have shown considerable interest in the development of the region's energy resources. But the realization of this goal has been complicated by the profound political, economic, and social problems, not the least of which is widespread corruption, that have beset the actual and potential oil producing states and have created tensions in U.S. policy (see Map 5.3).

The Region's Oil Resources

As in Latin America and the Caspian Sea region, an important basis for the recent American interest has been the Gulf's substantial oil and gas resources. Largely because of offshore discoveries, the region's proven oil reserves doubled between 1993 and 2003, to more than 50 billion barrels, and some observers expect this total to rise even higher as additional offshore areas are explored (for example, Ndumbe 2004). Likewise, total production in the Gulf has doubled since the late 1980s, reaching five MBD in 2005. And according to various estimates, the region could add another two to three MBD of oil to the market by the end of the decade, an increment that would represent as much as 20 percent of all new worldwide output (Gary and Karl 2003, 9–10; Goldwyn and Morrison 2004, 4; Hueper 2005, 243–47).

Although the Gulf of Guinea and adjacent inland areas boast at least eight actual or potential oil producers, three countries stand out. The first is Nigeria, which easily remains the single largest producer in the region. The country possesses the bulk of the Gulf's proven oil reserves, currently estimated at more than 35 billion barrels, although its share has steadily declined, from 85 percent in 1980 to 70 percent today, as a result of significant discoveries in

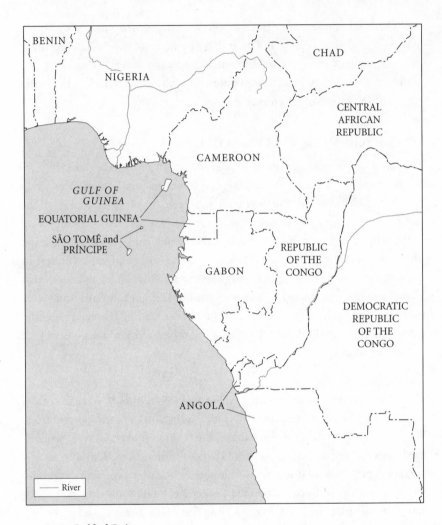

MAP 5.3 Gulf of Guinea

other countries. Nigerian production temporarily peaked at 2.3 MBD during
the second oil crisis, before dropping below 1.5 MBD during most of the 1980s.
Since then, however, output has risen more or less steadily, and it reached an
all time high of 2.6 MBD in 2005, making Nigeria the eleventh largest producer in the world. The government planned to increase production to 3 MBD
in the next year or two and then to 4 MBD in 2010.[35]

Next in importance is Angola, which has enjoyed both the second largest reserves and, since the early 1980s, the second highest level of production

in the region. Even more noteworthy is the fact that, thanks to "a stunning string of deepwater discoveries," the country's proven reserves have tripled in the last decade, to approximately 9 billion barrels, and its actual output has more than doubled, to a high of 1.2 MBD in 2005. Angolan production is expected to continue to rise, reaching 2 MBD within the next few years.[36]

Traditionally, Cameroon, Gabon, and the Republic of the Congo have vied for the honor of being sub-Saharan Africa's third largest oil producer. But in the past several years, all these countries have been surpassed by Equatorial Guinea, which has also been a beneficiary of significant offshore discoveries since the mid-1990s. Between 1994 and 2005, the country's proven reserves increased more than sixfold, to 1.8 billion barrels, and production expanded rapidly, reaching more than 350,000 barrels per day (see Figure 5.4).[37]

U.S. Goals

American interest in the Gulf of Guinea has grown in tandem with the region's oil reserves and production. To be sure, the United States has had a long-standing commercial interest in seeing that American energy firms obtain contracts in the region. In contrast to much of the Persian Gulf and

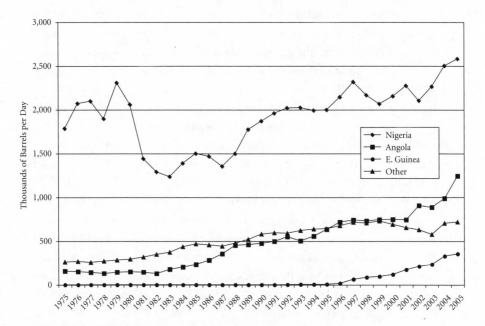

FIGURE 5.4 Sub-Saharan African Oil Production, 1975–2005
SOURCE: BP 2006

Latin America, where state-owned companies predominate, the development of West and Central Africa's oil resources has depended on investment by international oil companies, many of which have been based in the United States. According to a 2001 estimate, total U.S. direct investment in Africa's petroleum sector already stood at about $10 billion, or more than in either Latin America, the Caspian region, or the Middle East, and American firms were expected to invest as much as $50 billion more by 2010 (Lewis 2001, 107). As of 2003, ChevronTexaco alone had invested some $5 billion in the region and planned to invest another $20 billion during the next five years (Melvin and Deans 2003; Gary and Karl 2003, 12). This high level of investment was estimated to generate more than one hundred thousand U.S.-based jobs (Goldwyn and Morrison 2004, 16).

Moreover, American energy firms have played a leading or important role in each of the three largest producing states. They have dominated oil exploration and production in Equatorial Guinea, where they have been awarded most of the concessions to date (Silverstein 2002; Volman 2003, 575). In Angola, ChevronTexaco has been responsible for some 60 to 70 percent of all oil output, and in 2004, it announced that it would invest an additional $11 billion or more in that country alone during the remainder of the decade.[38] Even in Nigeria, where foreign-based Shell has been the top producer, ExxonMobil currently produces around six hundred thousand barrels per day and planned to invest $11 billion in the oil sector between 2003 and 2011 in order to double its output to 1.2 MBD.[39]

What has changed in the past decade is a pronounced new U.S. strategic interest in seeing that the region's energy resources are developed as a means of diversifying the world's oil supplies and reducing dependence on the Persian Gulf in particular. As recently as 1995, a U.S. Defense Department report concluded, "Ultimately, we see very little traditional strategic interest in Africa."[40] By the end of the Clinton administration, however, U.S. officials had begun to note Africa's importance "as a key source of diverse energy supply."[41] This theme assumed even greater prominence in the pronouncements of the Bush administration. The 2001 National Energy Policy report developed under the leadership of Vice President Cheney emphasized the need to ensure reliable access to increasing quantities of oil and gas from foreign sources, notably Latin America and West Africa. And following the terrorist attacks of September 2001, the desire to secure African oil in order to diversify U.S. energy supplies gained even greater impetus (Gary and Karl 2003, 14; Goldwyn and Morrison 2004, 4). Thus by 2002, the assistant secretary of state for African affairs could declare that "African oil is of national strategic interest to us, and it will increase and become more important as we go forward" (Klare 2004a, 143).

This interest has been reflected in the rising level of American oil imports from the region, which have grown from slightly more than 1.0 MBD in the early 1990s to nearly 1.6 MBD in 2004. In recent years, Nigeria has been the fifth largest U.S. supplier, while Angola has ranked ninth. Although the share of total U.S. petroleum imports supplied by the region has fluctuated between 10 and 14 percent during the past decade, a number of observers expect this figure to increase to as much as 20 or 25 percent by 2015 (NIC 2000, 73; Silverstein 2002; Gary and Karl 2003, 14; Goldwyn and Morrison 2004, 15; Goldwyn and Ebel 2004, 12).

U.S. Policy Actions

In view of this growing strategic interest in the Gulf of Guinea, recent U.S. administrations have taken an increasing number of steps to improve American relations with the oil producing states in the region. During the last years of the Clinton administration, the United States undertook several energy-related initiatives, including the first of a series of gatherings of U.S. and African energy ministers. Washington played an active role in supporting the restoration of democracy in Nigeria and initiated a bilateral consultative commission with Angola.[42]

The pace of U.S. energy diplomacy toward the Gulf of Guinea accelerated greatly, however, during the Bush administration, as both the feasibility and desirability of expanding oil production in the region became increasingly clear. Since 2001, American leaders have engaged in a number of high-level contacts with their counterparts in the oil producing states of the Gulf. The assistant secretary of state for African affairs made extensive trips to the region to discuss oil production among other issues, and in 2002, Secretary of State Colin Powell visited Gabon and Angola, where he broke ground for a new $40 million embassy building. That same year, President Bush met at the United Nations with the leaders of all the major oil producing states, and he has hosted several of them, including the presidents of Nigeria and Angola, at the White House. In 2003, Bush himself went to Nigeria as part of a tour of several African states. Although the president of Equatorial Guinea has not been granted such a high-profile reception, he met privately in Washington with Powell and Secretary of Energy Spencer Abraham in 2004, and the Bush administration reopened the U.S. embassy in the capital, Malabo, which had been shuttered since the mid-1990s (Silverstein 2002; Dao 2002b; Vieth 2003; Volman 2003, 578; Gary and Karl 2003, 14, 53; Ndumbe 2004; Eviatar 2004; Maass 2005).

Also during the early 2000s, U.S. economic assistance to Nigeria and Angola grew substantially, averaging approximately $100 million per year for each country. A good deal of this increase could be attributed to other objectives, such as consolidating democracy in Nigeria and rebuilding war-torn Angola as well as basic humanitarian motives. But it also reflected the heightened strategic importance of the region in the eyes of American policy-makers.[43] Moreover, some forms of assistance were directly targeted at the energy sector. OPIC has provided hundreds of millions of dollars in loan guarantees and political risk insurance for such projects as a natural gas liquids facility in Nigeria and a methanol gas plant in Equatorial Guinea, the latter representing the largest-ever loan by the agency for a project in sub-Saharan Africa (Gary and Karl 2003, 55). Similarly, the Export-Import Bank announced in 2002 a $135 million loan guarantee to help finance the construction of a petroleum plant in Nigeria (Vieth 2003).

Finally, the region has witnessed strengthening military ties and an un-precedented level of military contacts with the United States in recent years. The top-ranking generals of the U.S. European Command, which has respon-sibility for the region, have paid visits to several countries (Abramovici 2004). In addition, the Bush administration negotiated access agreements that would allow American troops to use airfields in Cameroon, Gabon, and Equatorial Guinea, among other countries, and has begun to secure rights for the estab-lishment of naval bases in the region, most notably in Nigeria and São Tomé (Volman 2003, 580; Klare 2004b, 9). Most recently, both Angola and Nige-ria became eligible to receive surplus American arms, and the United States conducted its first joint military exercise with Angola in 2005, with another scheduled for Nigeria in 2006 (Klare 2004a, 143; Apps 2005).

Problems in the Region
All this activity, however, has taken place against a troubling background. In addition to their oil wealth, the states of the Gulf of Guinea are well known for extreme poverty, lack of democracy, human rights abuses, and, of particular relevance, fiscal mismanagement and corruption. In most of the region's oil

producing countries, oil revenues have accounted in recent years for a large proportion of gross domestic product, ranging from 40 percent in Nigeria to more than 85 percent in Equatorial Guinea (Huepner 2005, 249). Yet much of this wealth has been squandered, mismanaged, or commandeered by leaders for their own purposes (Lewis 2001, 108). Partly as a result, the vast majority of the citizens of these countries remains near the bottom of every index of human development, and there are good reasons to be concerned that little of the revenue generated by the region's expanding level of oil production will ever benefit them (Goldwyn and Morrison 2004, 1).

A classic example of these problems is Equatorial Guinea, which "has a history marked by extreme levels of repression, human rights violations, rigged elections, and little transparency or accountability" (Gary and Karl 2003, 39). Since 1979, the country has been ruled by Teodoro Obiang Nguema Mbasogo, whose regime is generally considered to rank among the world's worst. In the 1990s, the UN Human Rights Commission reported that torture and political murder were routine and that responsible officials enjoyed "rampant immunity" (Hecht 1999). In 2002, the European Parliament condemned Equatorial Guinea for arrests and unfair trials of opposition leaders (Gary and Karl 2003, 39; see also Silverstein 2002; Maass 2005). In recent years, these criticisms have been joined by widespread allegations of corruption, mismanagement, and misappropriation of the country's rapidly increasing oil revenues, which grew from just $3 million in 1993 to an estimated $725 million in 2003 and are still rising. In 1998, for example, the IMF calculated that the government earned $130 million in royalties from oil, while the regime itself reported receiving just $34 million. The missing sums are widely assumed to be lining the pockets of members of the president's family, some of whom are known for their lavish lifestyles (Gary and Karl 2003, 39; Hecht 1999). In turn, a U.S. government analysis has noted with perhaps some understatement that "the government's failure to direct oil revenues toward development has undermined economic and social progress in the country."[44]

The problems of corruption and mismanagement have existed on an even larger scale in nearby Angola, where oil revenues have been much greater. To be sure, the country's troubles have been exacerbated by the long-standing civil war, which came to a definitive conclusion only in 2002. But, in the words of Global Witness, a non-governmental organization that examines the link between natural resource exploitation and human rights abuses, "It is hard to overstate the scale of state-looting that has taken place in Angola over the past few years."[45] Indeed, according to one observer, "Oil-financed patronage has been a fundamental part of the strategy pursued by President José Eduardo dos Santos for the consolidation and preservation of political power" (Hodges 2004, 161). As a result, much of the fiscal revenue due from the state oil company, Sonangol, has not been paid to the national bank or recorded in budget accounts. According to various estimates, approximately $1 to $1.5 billion, or between one-quarter and one-third of the country's oil revenues, went unaccounted for every year in the late 1990s and early 2000s.[46] In contrast, little of the money has been invested in social and economic-development programs (Hodges 2004, 4). Thus only a small elite has benefited from Angola's oil wealth. The country ranks near the bottom of the UN Human Development Index, with approximately 70 percent of the population living in poverty and 80 percent having no access to medical care (Gary and Karl 2003, 31; Eviatar 2004).

The situation is somewhat brighter in Nigeria, where democracy and civilian rule were restored in 1999, but it is still not very hopeful. In the words of two expert observers, "So overwhelming is the mismanagement and rent-seeking that Nigeria has become virtually synonymous with corruption" (Gary and Karl 2003, 26). The country received more than $300 billion in oil revenues between the late 1970s and early 2000s, yet it performed worse in terms of basic social indicators than sub-Saharan Africa as a whole. Indeed, the percentage of people living in poverty increased from 28 percent in 1980 to 66 percent in 1996 (Gary and Karl 2003, 27). The situation reached its nadir in the 1990s, during the dictatorship of General Sani Abacha, who siphoned off as much as $10 billion (Hueper 2005, 250). Although the elected government of Olusegun Obasanjo that followed made some efforts to achieve political and economic reform, it had, as of 2004, "not yet taken concrete steps to reform procurement, reveal the size of signing bonuses and new contracts, eliminate corruption in the concession of licensing process, or create accurate and complete accounts of government revenue and expenditure" (Goldwyn and Morrison 2004, 3). Thus a 2004 World Bank report concluded that up to 80 percent of oil revenues still accrue to only 1 percent of the population.[47]

Conflicts in U.S. Policy
How has U.S. policy responded to these problems in the context of America's growing strategic interest in seeing that region's energy resources are developed and made available to world markets? American officials have claimed

that they are doing all they can to promote democracy, good governance, economic development, and respect for human rights in their dealings with African leaders (Vieth 2003). As a high-level Bush administration official has noted:

> We have a strong policy interest in assisting oil producing countries to chan-nel their energy resources into solid and sustainable economic development that will benefit their populations. Democratization and the development of responsible governing institutions are particularly important in reducing oil-related conflicts and promoting African supply stability. Substantial foreign direct investment is needed to develop African energy resources both onshore and offshore deepwater. We support this process by encouraging the reforms needed to improve the investment climate. Accountability and transparency are necessary to ensure that oil revenues benefit the population and support development. We have an interest in helping West African nations solve these problems, not just out of altruism, but also self-interest. (Larson 2003; see also Humphries 2000)

In particular, the United States has made some efforts to promote transpar-ency and to curb corruption with regard to the development of energy re-sources. The Department of State has cooperated with American firms in an attempt to delineate corporate security procedures that are compatible with good local community relations and the protection of human rights in Nigeria. When Secretary of State Powell visited Angola in 2002, he reportedly warned that the United States would reduce its bilateral assistance—then roughly $100 million per year—if the regime failed to reduce "corrupt practices in the oil industry" (Gary and Karl 2003, 54; Lewis 2001, 109; Dao 2002b).

But a number of outside observers have claimed that the Clinton and especially the Bush administrations, in their eagerness to promote the devel-opment of the region's oil resources, have sacrificed other important U.S. for-eign policy goals. As the assistant secretary of state for African affairs in the Clinton administration has noted, "Oil seems to be taking precedence over other issues when American officials are trying to elaborate what our interests are in Africa. . . . There's a lot more they could and should be doing" (Vieth 2003). From this alternative perspective, as the strategic value of African oil exports has grown in recent years, so U.S. officials have become increasingly willing to court the leaders of producing countries, regardless of their records on democracy, human rights, and the management of oil revenues (Gary and

Karl 2003, 2, 53, 77; Hodges 2004, 142). The inevitable effect of such behavior, argue Ian Gary and Terry Karl, has been to enhance the legitimacy of those leaders and to validate the status quo (Gary and Karl 2003, 54). Likewise, the Bush administration in particular has been frequently criticized for an unwillingness to pressure U.S. oil companies to report the payments they make to host governments and for failing to support strongly international initiatives to promote transparency (Vieth 2003; Gary and Karl 2003, 54; M. Ottaway 2005).

In Nigeria, some of this reluctance may be attributed to an understandable desire not to undercut the new democratic regime. Even during the previous Abacha dictatorship, however, although the United States took some tough diplomatic measures, it stopped short of imposing sanctions on oil companies, as it had in the cases of Iran and Libya. For its part, the repressive and corrupt Obiang regime in Equatorial Guinea has received little or no public criticism. To the contrary, one former ambassador to the country has accused Bush administration officials of being "big cheerleaders for the government" (Maass 2005). Indeed, hardly had Equatorial Guinea been censored by the European Union than the United States announced in 2003 that it would soon reopen its embassy there (Melvin and Deans 2003). And in 2006, Secretary of State Rice warmly greeted Obiang in Washington as a "good friend" (Kessler 2006). But even the Clinton administration certified Equatorial Guinea as making progress toward labor standards, despite serious labor and human rights problems in the country as documented by the State Department itself (Gary and Karl 2003, 55).

For many observers, however, U.S. policy toward Angola has been particularly troubling. Although the State Department has condemned the regime's "persistent financial mismanagement and corruption," the United States has, at least publicly, remained quiet about the uses of Angola's oil money. Indeed, in 2003, the Bush administration deemed Angola eligible for trade preferences, based on a set of criteria that were supposed to include corruption-related policies. When President dos Santos visited Washington in May 2004, moreover, U.S. officials said little to the press about the need for more transparency with regard to Angola's oil revenues (Eviatar 2003; *New York Times* 2004a). In the meantime, it has been reported that the United States has significantly reduced the aid that it previously provided to local pro-democracy and independent media organizations in the country, which offered the greatest hope for generating internal pressure for reform (Eviatar 2003; Eviatar 2004).

Conclusion

Especially since the shocks of the 1970s highlighted the potentially high economic costs of foreign oil dependence, considerations of oil have exerted significant influence over U.S. policy toward not only the Persian Gulf but also several other actual and potential oil producing regions of the world. The United States has made noteworthy efforts to shape the oil-related policies, especially production and pricing, of many of the countries in these regions. In a number of cases, it has also sought to strengthen the military capabilities of key regional actors, such as Iraq and Saudi Arabia, that would be relied upon to defend themselves and their neighbors against potential external threats to oil supplies. And it has occasionally tried to help producing countries cope with internal sources of instability.

The overall goal of these policies has been to make sure that oil would be reliably available to the United States and its economic and security partners in adequate amounts and at stable and affordable prices. Just how effective were they? Given the numerous determinants of oil supplies and prices, it is nigh impossible to provide an overall assessment of the impact of U.S. policy, although one can point to particular examples of success. For instance, although Iran and Saudi Arabia may have had their own reasons for seeking to slow the rise of oil prices in the mid- and late 1970s, American pleas and inducements were almost certainly a factor in their decisions to do so.

At least as visible, however, have been the various costs that these policies have entailed. In some cases, these costs have consisted of financial outlays for economic and military assistance. In others, they have entailed reduced diplomatic flexibility and a reluctance to pursue other valued foreign policy goals, such as the promotion of democracy, the protection of human rights, good governance, and economic development. And in yet others, they have taken the form of increased entanglement, or risk thereof, in local and regional conflicts. Some of these costs and the policies from which they have issued may not be entirely attributable to U.S. foreign oil dependence, but neither can it be ruled out as an important contributory cause.

Nor do they represent the sum total of the costs of external U.S. policy responses to foreign oil dependence. A large component is due to the various and substantial military efforts that the United States has undertaken to protect oil supplies and ensure Western access to them, which are the subject of the next chapter.

6   U.S. Military Responses and Their Costs

Each year the U.S. expends enormous military resources protecting the
chronically vulnerable oil production and distribution network while also
preparing to guarantee international access to key oil producing regions.
Energy Security Leadership Council, 2006

U.S. POLICYMAKERS have not regarded diplomacy and various
forms of assistance as sufficient to secure American energy interests abroad. Especially since the late 1970s and early 1980s, when first the
Iranian Revolution and then the Iran-Iraq War disrupted the flow of oil from
the Persian Gulf and when the Soviet invasion of Afghanistan raised the spec-
ter of external attempts to gain control of the region's resources, the United
States has employed its military power to help protect foreign oil supplies and
ensure access to them. This dimension of U.S. policy was first emphasized
by President Jimmy Carter, who in response to the Soviet action declared in
what became known as the Carter Doctrine, "An attempt by any outside force
to gain control of the Persian Gulf region will be regarded as an assault on
the vital interests of the United States of America, and such an assault will be
repelled by any means necessary, including military force."[1] But it has figured
prominently in every subsequent administration.[2] Indeed, as Michael Klare
argues, American leaders have placed ever greater reliance on the use of military force to protect the global production and transport of oil (Klare 2005).
Although difficult to substantiate, such an assessment is consistent with U.S.
military spending trends.

What military policies has the United States adopted in response to foreign
oil dependence, and what have been their costs? To answer these questions,
it is useful to focus on the Persian Gulf. This is the oil producing region toward which by far the most substantial military efforts have been directed

and thus for which the military costs have been greatest. Initially, the United States maintained only a token military presence in the Persian Gulf and concentrated on increasing its ability to deploy forces rapidly to the region in the event of a crisis. Beginning in the early 1990s with the Gulf War, however, it stationed a significant combat force there and redoubled its efforts to improve its capabilities for quickly reinforcing that presence with units from the United States and elsewhere. And twice in the last two decades, the United States has sent hundreds of thousands of troops to the Gulf to fight wars that arguably might never have occurred if not for the concentration of so much oil there.

Perhaps not surprisingly, these costs have been substantial. The United States has spent several billions of dollars per year or more on additional military capabilities and routine operations that have been directly, and often exclusively, associated with the defense of U.S. oil-related interests in the Persian Gulf. More important, a substantial share of the outlays for U.S.-based general purposes forces, on the order of tens of billions of dollars per year, can be attributed to the mission of maintaining access to the region's oil from the early 1980s through the early 2000s. To this must be added much of the expense of the increasingly costly major military operations that the United States has mounted in the Gulf, culminating in the ongoing war in Iraq.

How, precisely, should the costs of U.S. military policies due to foreign oil dependence be determined? In some cases, it may be possible to attribute a particular action entirely to the goal of protecting and maintaining access to oil supplies. Often, however, relevant U.S. military programs and operations have arguably been intended to serve one or more other purposes as well. In such cases, it would not be accurate to attribute the entire costs of those activities to foreign oil dependence.

Even in the Persian Gulf, which has figured most prominently in American efforts to reduce the economic costs and risks of foreign oil dependence, the United States has had multiple objectives. Other aims of U.S. policy have included preserving regional stability, preventing the emergence of hegemonic powers, and ensuring the security of Israel and moderate Arab states in the region (Fuller and Lesser 1997; see also Bush 1990, 13). To these goals might be added resisting Soviet expansion prior to the end of the cold war and, especially since September 11, 2001, the suppression of terrorism (Acharya 1989, 16; Byman and Wise 2002, 2).

When U.S. military policies cannot be attributed entirely to the goal of mitigating the economic consequences of foreign oil dependence, how should the costs be apportioned? The simplest approach would be to divide them evenly among the various objectives. A more sophisticated method, suggested by David Koplow and Aaron Martin, is known as Ramsey pricing, whereby "costs are allocated based on the relative strength of demand for the products co-produced" (Koplow and Martin 1998, 4.12). Nevertheless, this approach requires judging each objective's relative share of the total demand, which may itself be a very difficult, if not impossible, task.

At least in the central case of the Persian Gulf, however, U.S. objectives, with the principal exception of ensuring the security of Israel, may boil down almost entirely to maintaining reliable access to oil at reasonable prices. Certainly, a number of regional experts and other informed observers have suggested as much. In former CIA and National Security Council official Kenneth Pollack's words, which are representative of a number of other statements, "America's primary interest in the Persian Gulf lies in ensuring the free and stable flow of oil from the region to the world at large" (K. Pollack 2003; see also Delucchi and Murphy 1996, 3; Fuller and Lesser 1997, 42; Byman and Wise 2002, 2–3). As the U.S. Defense Planning Guidance for fiscal years 1994–99 stated, "In the Middle East and Southwest Asia, our overall objective is to remain the predominant outside power in the region and preserve U.S. and Western access to the region's oil."[3] Indeed, even during the cold war, when the Soviet threat loomed especially large, the Joint Chiefs of Staff wrote that among the U.S. interests of oil security, regional stability, and Soviet containment, "continued access to oil on reasonable political and economic terms is the most important to U.S. and allied security" (Delucchi and Murphy 1996, 4). Thus even when American officials have offered other rationales for U.S. military actions in the region, such as the 1990–91 Persian Gulf War and, especially, the 2003 invasion of Iraq, it is important to consider the broader context of U.S. involvement, which is inextricably bound up with the dependence of the United States and its economic and security partners on foreign oil.

Previous Efforts to Measure the Military Costs of Foreign Oil Dependence

Since the early 1980s, the United States has devoted considerable sums on military forces, deployments, and operations intended to prevent disruptions in the production and transport of oil from foreign sources. The lion's share of this spending has focused on protection of the oil exporting states and waters of the Persian Gulf. Unfortunately, the U.S. Department of Defense (DOD) has never provided a breakdown of the defense budget by region (CRS 1992, 23). Nevertheless, especially since the Gulf War, a number of analysts have offered estimates of the costs to the United States of protecting Persian Gulf oil supplies and access to them. These estimates have generally ranged between $20 and $80 billion per year (see Table 6.1). Typically, however, they have been accompanied by no explanation of the methodology employed on or derived from on a small number of original analyses.

Where analysts have described their methods, they have used one of two general approaches to measure these costs. The total cost approach involves dividing the number of basic combat units in each service into the entire

TABLE 6.1   Estimates of Annual Military Expenditures for Defending Middle East Oil Supplies

Source	Year of Estimate	Amount in Billions of Dollars (fiscal year)
Rowen and Weyant (1982)	1980s	$30–40 (1980)
Tonelson and Hurd (1990)	NA	$40–45 (NA)
Copulos (1990)	FY1988	$40 (1988)
Kaufmann and Steinbruner (1991)	FY1990	$64.5 (1992)
Ravenal (1991)	FY1992	$50 (1992)
GAO (1991)	1980–1990	$27.3 (1990)
CRS (1992)	NA	$6.4 (1990)
Greene and Leiby (1993)	1980–1990	$10.8 (1990)
Delucchi and Murphy (1996)	NA	$20–40 (1996)
GAO (1996)	NA	Several to $65 (NA)
Fuller and Lesser (1997)	NA	$30–60 (NA)
Ravenal (1997)	FY1997	$82 (1997)
Koplow and Martin (1998)	1995	$10.5–23.3 (NA)
Losman (2001)	1990s	$30–60 (NA)
Conry and Peña (2003)	NA	$80 (NA)
Copulos (2003)	2003	$49.1 (2003)
Amidon (2005)	1991–2004	$60 (NA)
ICTA (2005)	2005	$39–98.5 (NA)

manpower and budget of that service and then multiplying the cost of each unit by the number of units attributable to a particular mission. The marginal cost approach involves identifying the specific programs, capabilities, and activities that have been undertaken for a particular purpose and then adding up their costs (Ravenal 1991, 49–50; see also Koplow and Martin 1998, 4.3). As a means of measuring the military costs of protecting and ensuring access to foreign oil supplies, each approach has distinct strengths and weaknesses.

Total Cost Approach

Most published efforts to measure the costs of defending the Persian Gulf have used the total cost approach. Methodologically, this approach is the least demanding, as it requires much less data. It also ensures that the additional overhead and support costs generated by dedicated combat units are taken into account.

In 1991, the U.S. General Accounting Office (GAO, now called the Government Accountability Office) prepared an estimate of the military costs of protecting U.S. interests in Southwest Asia. The GAO described these interests as "maintaining the uninterrupted flow of Persian Gulf oil, ensuring the security of Israel, and promoting a comprehensive resolution of the Arab-Israeli conflict" (GAO 1991, 8). Using DOD estimates for the eleven-year period encompassing fiscal years (FY) 1980 to 1990,[4] it reported that the United States had invested a total of $300 billion, or approximately $27.3 billion per year. This estimate included $27.2 billion for military programs and activities directly related to Southwest Asia-specific missions or primarily Southwest Asia-oriented missions as well as another $272.6 billion for programs that were motivated by the need to develop capabilities that would enable the United States to defend its interests not only in Southwest Asia but also in other regions (GAO 1991, 11). More than 99 percent of these other defense expenditures were for strategic airlift ($49.5 billion) and the bulk of the forces available to the U.S. Central Command ($220.3 billion), which had been assigned responsibility for the region.. Given the other potential uses for these general contingency forces, a subsequent estimate by Greene and Leiby based on the GAO report attributed only one-third of their cost to the defense of Southwest Asia, yielding a revised total of $118.3 billion, or $10.8 billion per year (Greene and Leiby 1993).

Also in 1991, Earl Ravenal of the Cato Institute explicitly applied the total cost approach to generate an estimate of the costs of defending the Persian Gulf. Assuming that the assignment of ground forces provided an adequate representation of those for tactical air wings and surface vessels, he multiplied the total cost of general purpose forces by a fraction representing the active land divisions (both army and marine) attributable to the region. Judging that the U.S. government attributed four of the seventeen active land divisions to Persian Gulf defense in the FY1992 budget, he calculated that four-seventeenths of the $215 billion intended for general purposes forces, or $50 billion in 1992 dollars, could be plausibly considered to be devoted to that purpose (Ravenal 1991, 50–51).

Six years later, Ravenal provided an updated estimate. By that time, the United States maintained only thirteen active land divisions—ten U.S. Army and three Marine Corps—of which he attributed five (four army and one marine) to the defense of the Persian Gulf/Middle East. Given that the FY1997 defense budget contained $217 billion in budget authority for general purpose forces, Ravenal calculated the annual cost of defending the Gulf at approximately five-thirteenths of that amount, or $82 billion in 1997 dollars (Ravenal 1997).

Finally, in a third 1991 study, William Kaufmann and John Steinbruner of the Brookings Institution offered an estimate of the amount of budgetary authority allocated to the Middle East/Persian Gulf force planning contingency in FY1990. Suggesting that the Persian Gulf contingency package consisted of more than six army divisions, the equivalent of nine fighter wings, three carrier battle groups, and at least one marine amphibious force, they pegged the cost at as much as $64.5 billion per year in 1992 dollars. They noted, moreover, that the figure did not include any of the substantial funds ($19.2 billion) allocated to national intelligence and communications that year (Kaufmann and Steinbruner 1991, 8, 14–15).

As helpful as these estimates might be, they still leave much to be desired. By lumping ground, air, and naval forces together, Ravenal's methodology is extremely crude, and the other sources do not spell out in any detail the steps used to arrive at their results. With the exception of Greene and Leiby's refinement of the GAO estimate, moreover, none accounts for the other uses to which Persian Gulf-oriented contingency forces might be put. By requiring that every combat unit be assigned to a particular mission or region, they may overestimate the costs of preparing for those missions (although as the Gulf War and Iraq War have also revealed, forces beyond those assigned might also be pressed into service in a given region). Finally, these estimates are all dated, most having been generated about the time of the Gulf War. As a result, they may underestimate some of the costs insofar as the Persian Gulf has assumed even greater prominence in U.S. military planning in more recent years.

Marginal Cost Approach

Perhaps owing to the difficulty of assembling all the relevant details, attempts to identify the marginal costs of U.S. military programs intended to ensure access to foreign oil have been infrequent, and these have invariably been made by the Department of Defense rather than by independent analysts or non-governmental bodies. In 1983, the Pentagon provided detailed figures to the Congressional Budget Office (CBO) for the direct and indirect costs of the Rapid Deployment Joint Task Force (RDJTF), which amounted to $2.55 billion in FY1983 dollars. Adding the costs of airlift programs that were closely associated with the RDJTF, the CBO derived a total annual budgetary figure of $4.1 billion (CBO 1983).

A 1991 GAO study reported Pentagon estimates of the costs of protecting U.S. interests in Southwest Asia for the period FY1980–90. These costs included $21.4 billion for military programs "dedicated" to Southwest Asia, such as construction, prepositioning of equipment and supplies, operation of U.S. Central Command, and military exercises, and $5.8 billion for programs "oriented" toward the region as well as $200 million for protecting Kuwaiti tankers during the Iran-Iraq War. The total came to an average of $3 billion per year. Nevertheless, DOD maintained that two of the most expensive "dedicated" programs, the maritime prepositioned squadron at the island of Diego Garcia ($0.8 billion) and a carrier battle group in the Indian Ocean ($16.1 billion), as well as all the "oriented" programs, including fast sealift ships ($1.2 billion), the two other maritime prepositioned squadrons ($1.7 billion), and nearly two-thirds of the related military construction ($0.7 billion), would probably or certainly have been funded even if the U.S. military were relieved of its Southwest Asia mission. This left only $4.7 billion in true marginal costs for the eleven-year period (GAO 1991, 10–11; see also Delucchi and Murphy 1996, 9–10).

These marginal cost studies also suffer from important limitations, however. First, in view of their brevity, it is not clear whether they have identified all the relevant military programs. Second, given when they were written, the analyses fail to capture the costs of the many additional Persian Gulf-oriented military programs that were initiated after the Gulf War. Third, their assignment of none of the costs of programs such as the maritime prepositioned squadrons and the deployment of a carrier battle group in the region are highly questionable, since these programs were undertaken largely with Persian Gulf missions in mind. Even if a program had other possible military purposes, at least a fraction of the cost should be attributed to the Persian Gulf in general and the goal of ensuring access to the region's oil in particular.

In sum, any comprehensive estimate of the costs of U.S. military efforts to protect and ensure access to Persian Gulf oil should include both the costs of the programs and activities that were undertaken primarily, if not exclusively, for that purpose and a share of the costs of the U.S.-based general purpose forces that could have been used in Persian Gulf contingencies but that may have had other assignments as well. The first set of costs can be further subdivided into three categories: (1) the military capabilities that have been acquired and maintained for Persian Gulf missions; (2) the basing facilities and the deployment of forces in the region, and (3) actual military operations. The following analysis does not claim to identify every cost for every year in the period under consideration, but the elements described here are representative of the overall costs.

Additional Military Capabilities

Since the late 1970s, the United States has acquired a number of additional military capabilities largely, if not exclusively, for the purposes of ensuring access to Persian Gulf oil supplies. Most prominent among these are the U.S. Central Command and a wide range of strategic mobility forces, including sealift, airlift, and prepositioned equipment and supplies. In addition, some existing combat units have been restructured and reequipped in preparation for possible missions in the Gulf.

Military Planning and Command Structures

The most important military planning and command structure created for the purpose of intervening militarily in the Persian Gulf is the U.S. Central Command (CENTCOM), which has responsibility for Southwest Asia. Planning for a special regional command began in earnest following the Iranian Revolution in 1979 and was at an advanced stage by the time of the Soviet invasion of Afghanistan at the end of that year, but the latter imparted significant bureaucratic momentum to the procurement and planning process, culminating in the March 1980 creation of the RDJTF (Kupchan 1987, 93). In January 1983, however, the RDJTF was renamed and reconstituted as a unified, multiservice command, which placed the mission in Southwest Asia, at least in organizational terms, on the same level as those in Europe and East Asia (Kupchan 1987, 141–42; Acharya 1989, 53).

Although CENTCOM's area of responsibility has extended from the Horn of Africa to Pakistan and now includes Central Asia, the primary focus almost from its inception has been Southwest Asia and especially the Persian Gulf (CBO 1983, 4; Acharya 1989, 54, 65–66). As the CENTCOM Web page notes, "Today's command evolved as a practical solution to the problem of projecting U.S. military power to the Gulf region from halfway around the world."[5] CENTCOM has had a permanent staff of approximately one thousand military personnel and an annual budget of approximately $100 million.[6]

In order to enable CENTCOM to carry out its mission, the United States has steadily accumulated a variety of other military assets, including combat and support forces tailored for Southwest Asia, mobility capabilities, prepositioned stocks, and bases and facilities both en route to and within the area of operations. And as a result of initiatives undertaken by the Carter and Reagan administrations, the U.S. ability to project military power into the Persian Gulf had improved substantially by the time of the Gulf War (Acharya 1989, 56–57, 84–85). In 1980, it was estimated that the United States would need three months to deploy a single division into the region. Following the Iraqi invasion of Kuwait in 1990, however, it was able to amass in just three weeks the equivalent of more than two divisions (seven brigades), fourteen tactical fighter squadrons, and three carrier battle groups (Freedman and Karsh 1993, 94).

The United States has not created any entirely new major combat units for use in Southwest Asia, but some of the existing units assigned to CENTCOM have been reorganized and reequipped so as to be more effective in that role. Both presidents Jimmy Carter and Ronald Reagan initiated programs to increase both the firepower and mobility of the ground forces. In particular, in the 1980s, an infantry division was transformed into a high-technology motorized division that combined the rapid deployability and sustainability of a light division with the mobility, firepower, and survivability of a heavy division (Acharya 1989, 76–77).

Strategic Mobility Forces: Sealift and Airlift

At least prior to the Iraq War, the United States relied primarily on the rapid deployment of U.S.-based forces to meet contingencies in the region rather than station substantial forces in Southwest Asia. During the 1980s and 1990s, the principal planning goal remained fairly constant: to deploy several army divisions as well as air force and marine units to the Persian Gulf within one month.[7] Over time, however, the units assigned to CENTCOM became heavier, so the means required to transport them to their destination had to grow in tandem.

Strategic mobility forces fall into three categories: airlift, sealift, and prepositioning. Each of these components saw significant expansion during the 1980s and 1990s, and much of this growth was driven by planning for contingencies in the Persian Gulf (CBO 1983, xviii–xix). A 1981 congressionally mandated mobility study evaluated the requirements for four scenarios, three of which involved a conflict in the Persian Gulf (Acharya 1989, 80). And the 1992 DOD Mobility Requirements Study looked at what forces the United States would need to fight two major regional conflicts, including one in the Gulf, in rapid succession (CBO 1997b, 35).

Given the lack of forward bases in the region, the new focus on Southwest Asia greatly enhanced the importance of sealift in U.S. military planning. In order to meet the initial sealift requirements of CENTCOM, the DOD purchased eight high-speed container ships (SL-7) and converted them to a roll-on/roll-off (RO/RO) configuration in the early 1980s. This capability, which cost about $830 million, would enable the army to move a heavy division plus some of its support to the Persian Gulf within fourteen to sixteen days (CBO 1983, 35–36; Acharya 1989, 82). Overall, the United States spent as much as $7 billion to improve its sealift capabilities, including approximately $1.2 billion for fast sealift and $1.0 billion for improvements in the Ready Reserve Force (RRF), between 1980 and 1990 (GAO 1991; Yetiv 2004, 65).

In the 1990s, DOD ordered nineteen large, medium-speed, roll-on/roll-off (LMSR) transport ships, each with approximately 50–100 percent more capacity than an SL-7. This program cost about $6 billion, or an average of $314 million per vessel. Eleven would be used for surge sealift and the remainder to preposition equipment for the army. In addition, the number of RO/RO cargo ships in the Ready Reserve Force was increased from seventeen to thirty-one, with plans for another five, following the Gulf War, at a cost of about $450 million (CBO 1997b, xiv, 25, 33; GAO 1997).

Beginning in the early 1980s, the United States also took a number of steps to increase its strategic airlift capabilities, largely in support of CENTCOM. DOD sought to enhance the capabilities of the existing inventory of seventy C-5 and two hundred thirty-four C-141 inter-theater transports. It replaced the wings of a number of the former and stretched many of the latter so as to increase their cargo capacity, and it placed orders for fifty more C-5s and fifty-six KC-10 tanker/transports, at a total expected cost of some $11.7 billion (CBO 1983, 31–33; M. Johnson 1987, 144; Acharya 1989, 80–81). In addition, the Pentagon laid the groundwork for the eventual acquisition of C-17 long-range transport aircraft to replace the aging fleet of C-141s beginning in the following decade. By 1997, the air force had spent $24.9 billion for the acquisition of forty-eight C-17s, and the Clinton administration requested seventy-two more at an expected cost of $18.3 billion in 1997 dollars (CBO 1997b, xiii).[8]

Prepositioning

The most dramatic change in Persian Gulf-oriented strategic mobility forces occurred in the domain of prepositioning. Since the 1960s, the United States had prepositioned military equipment in Europe for NATO-related contingencies, but nowhere else, and certainly not in Southwest Asia prior to the Iranian Revolution. Beginning in 1979, however, successive administrations have placed a significant amount of military equipment in the Persian Gulf as well, and these efforts were intensified following the 1990–91 Gulf War. As a result, by 2001, the United States had prepositioned four heavy brigade sets, a handful of bare airbase sets, and naval forward logistics sets in several Gulf states and on the island of Diego Garcia in the Indian Ocean.

The first important step in this buildup was the establishment in 1980 of the Near-Term Prepositioning Force (NTPF), which grew to seventeen chartered merchant ships by 1983. Six vessels carried equipment and thirty days of supplies for a 12,500-man Marine Amphibious Brigade (MAB). Five others held ammunition and supplies for army and air force components of CENTCOM, five carried fuel and fresh water, and one served as a hospital ship. In 1982, annual operation and support costs already amounted to $137 million (CBO 1983, 38; M. Johnson 1987; Acharya 1989, 82). Overall, the United States spent $1.6 billion between 1980 and 1991 on this force of prepositioning ships (GAO 1991).

Almost simultaneously, DOD began to acquire a fleet of thirteen specially designed Maritime Prepositioning Ships (MPS) organized into three groups or squadrons, at a total cost of about $1.6 billion. Each squadron carried equipment and thirty days of combat supplies for an entire 16,500-man MAB (later renamed Marine Expeditionary Brigade [MEB] and then Marine Air-Ground Task Force [AGTF]). When ready in the mid-1980s, one squadron was stationed at Diego Garcia, replacing the NTPF ships carrying the equipment and supplies for the MAB. It was expected that the other two groups, which were located in the Mediterranean and Western Pacific, could reach the Persian Gulf in ten days or less (CBO 1983, 39; McNaugher 1985, 67, n. 28; Acharya 1989, 82–83). Including operating costs, the total expense for the MPS program through 1990 amounted to $2.5 billion (GAO 1991). In the mid-1990s, the Marine Corps added one more ship to each squadron, for a total of sixteen, at the cost of a further $360 million (CBO 1997b, 40).

Following the Gulf War, the army also prepositioned combat and support equipment in the region both on land and afloat. In 1993, it began placing enough equipment for a six-thousand-man heavy brigade, support units, and fifteen days of supplies aboard seven RO/RO ships at Diego Garcia, from where they could be delivered to either the Persian Gulf or Korea within fifteen days. Later, this equipment was transferred to some of the LMSRs purchased by the navy. In 2002, the army prepositioned an additional brigade (consisting of only two battalions) on two more LMSRs.[9]

In the mid-1990s, the army deployed an entire heavy brigade set in Kuwait and the equipment for a heavy battalion task force in Qatar. Subsequently, Qatar agreed to host an entire heavy brigade set and the equipment for a divisional headquarters, which were in place by 2002, and the army developed plans for storing a third brigade set in the region (CBO 1997b, 37–39; Schmitt and Shanker 2002). According to one unofficial estimate, each prepositioned brigade set cost $263 million (Copulos 2003a, 33). In addition, although Kuwait "paid most of the costs of warehousing, maintaining, and exercising the heavy brigade set prepositioned there," the army expected that operating and supporting the brigade and division base sets in Qatar without host-nation support would cost roughly $70 million per year in 1997 dollars, on top of more than $100 million in construction expenses.[10]

Even before the Gulf War, Saudi Arabia had allowed the U.S. Air Force (USAF) to preposition enough equipment to support at least five tactical aircraft squadrons with a total of 10,800 personnel.[11] After the war, the air force expanded its equipment holdings there so as to be able to support at least fifteen squadrons of twenty-four aircraft each (CBO 1997b, 37). Oman has hosted three USAF prepositioning sites with support equipment for twenty-six thousand personnel as well as the equipment and fuel needed for three airbases.[12] The air force has additional war reserve material storage facilities in Qatar and Bahrain.[13] In the late 1990s, it planned to be able to set up as many as five bare bases in the region (CBO 1997b, 37).

Foreign Facilities and Overseas Deployments

Just as important as the increase in U.S. military capabilities for Southwest Asian contingencies that occurred in the 1980s and 1990s was the acquisition of bases and other installations from which American forces could operate. Prior to the Iranian Revolution, the United States had relied heavily on other states, first Great Britain and then Iran and Saudi Arabia, to provide for the physical defense of the Persian Gulf and its oil wealth. It maintained no military forces or bases of its own in the region, with just two minor exceptions. First, the U.S. Navy stationed a modest Middle East Force (MIDEASTFOR) consisting of a command ship and two to three small surface combatants, based at Bahrain. Second, in the mid-1970s, the Ford administration decided to send naval task forces from the Pacific Fleet into the Indian Ocean three times per year, with every other task force to include an aircraft carrier. To support these deployments, the United States also began to expand and upgrade the facilities at the base on Diego Garcia, which it had leased from Great Britain after the latter withdrew its military forces from the region (Sick 1983, 65, 67; Kupchan 1987, 39, 55–56; Teicher and Teicher 1993, 24).

The 1980s

Beginning in 1979, after the fall of the shah in January and then the Soviet invasion of Afghanistan in December, the U.S. military began to play a more direct and substantial role in the defense of the Persian Gulf. The Carter Doctrine, articulated early the following year, committed the United States more firmly than ever to the security of the region. Likewise, the Reagan administration focused on improving the U.S. ability to act unilaterally to protect its vital interest in Persian Gulf oil and to counter Soviet aggression in the area. As longtime National Security Council staffer Howard Teicher later wrote, "It was important to convince the Soviet Union that the United States had the willingness and ability to use force" (Teicher and Teicher 1993, 126).

To this end, the United States acquired an extensive set of facilities and maintained a larger naval presence in the region. The normal strength of MIDEASTFOR was increased to five ships, and at the height of the Iran-Iraq War, it was expanded even further, while the number of naval personnel in Bahrain grew to more than eight hundred. At particularly critical moments, such as during the Iranian hostage crisis, as many as thirty ships and two aircraft carriers were deployed in the region.[14] As a result of this buildup in the U.S. naval presence, the average number of ships on patrol increased from about three and a half in the late 1970s to nearly sixteen in the 1980s, and at least one carrier battle group was almost always on station in the Indian Ocean or North Arabian Sea at a cost of approximately $1.5 billion per year (GAO 1991).[15]

Simultaneously, the United States negotiated agreements with several countries, including Oman, Kenya, and Somalia, that provided access to facilities in the region or at locations along critical sea and air lines of communication.[16] It also accelerated improvements at the multipurpose base on Diego Garcia in the Indian Ocean, which "became the hub of U.S. efforts to project power into the Gulf region" (Acharya 1989, 96). Through the mid-1980s, the United States spent approximately $1.5 billion to expand and upgrade those various facilities, including more than $600 million for Diego Garcia and smaller amounts in Oman, Egypt, Kenya, Morocco, Portugal, and Somalia.[17]

The 1990s and Early 2000s

After the Gulf War, the American military presence in the Persian Gulf underwent an even bigger increase. With the simultaneous end of the cold war, the primary objective was now to contain Iraq and, secondarily, Iran and to make sure that neither adversary posed a threat to its oil-rich neighbors. Despite Iraq's weakened state, however, it soon became clear that the achievement of this goal would require troops on the ground. Thus U.S. Army and Air Force combat units were based in the region for the first time since the early 1960s, with American military personnel stationed on Saudi and Kuwaiti soil. By the late 1990s, the United States would routinely maintain some twenty to twenty-five thousand military personnel in the Gulf (Klare 2001, 71; Byman and Wise 2002, 40–41; Priest 2003, 84; Rathmell, Karasik, and Gompert 2003, 4).

In January 1991, MIDEASTFOR was absorbed into U.S. Naval Forces Central Command (NAVCENT), which established its headquarters in Bahrain in 1993. During the 1990s, the average size of the American naval presence was significantly greater than it had been during the previous decade. Typically, NAVCENT forces in the area of the Persian Gulf consisted of as many as sixteen thousand personnel (one thousand ashore) and twenty-five ships, including a carrier battle group, an amphibious readiness group, mine countermeasure vessels, and sealift.[18]

To this naval deployment the United States added a virtually permanent U.S. Army presence of approximately five thousand troops, primarily in Kuwait. Following the Gulf War, ground force units were withdrawn from the region, but the army would exercise the equipment prepositioned in Kuwait at least twice a year with battalion task forces flown in for the purpose. In the mid-1990s, however, the Kuwaiti government agreed to a continuous operational presence of U.S. ground forces in Kuwait, with different units rotating in for periods of four months at a time. In 1999, the principal army facility there, Camp Doha, became the standing headquarters of a brigade-sized unit.[19]

Like the army, the U.S. Air Force initially reduced its numbers in the region after the Gulf War, to no more than eighty aircraft and thirty-five hundred personnel in mid-1992, but it was soon required to maintain a standing presence in order to patrol the no-fly zone established that year over southern Iraq. The size of this force was increased, to more than one hundred seventy aircraft and six thousand personnel, in response to aggressive Iraqi moves in the mid-1990s. Subsequently, the air force stationed approximately one hundred twenty aircraft and five to six thousand personnel in the theater, primarily at Prince Sultan Air Base in Saudi Arabia with smaller contingents in Kuwait, the United Arab Emirates, and Oman.[20]

The incremental annual cost of stationing U.S. forces in Southwest Asia rather than at home is difficult to determine with any accuracy, although a rough estimate is possible. According to a 1998 calculation by Michael O'Hanlon of the Brookings Institution, the budgeted cost for operations and maintenance (O&M) per service member in the armed forces was approximately $51,000 per year (O'Hanlon 1998, 141–42). Assuming a presence of twenty thousand military personnel in the Persian Gulf, the total yearly cost would be slightly more than one billion dollars. This number corresponds closely to the amount requested by the Department of Defense in fiscal years 2000–2002, which averaged about $1.2 billion, to support activities in Southwest Asia based on a troop strength of approximately eighteen thousand (OSD 2001, 82–83).

U.S.-Based Combat Forces and Strategic Lift

Since 1980, a significant percentage of U.S.-based combat forces and strategic lift capabilities has been available for missions in the Persian Gulf, and many of these have been deployed to and seen action there. Yet the substantial outlays associated with operating, maintaining, and staffing those forces have often been excluded from estimates of the military costs of protecting and ensuring access to the region's oil supplies. The principal reason for this exclusion is that all of the combat units and much of the lift existed prior to the definition of the mission and the establishment of the RDJTF and then CENTCOM to carry it out. Rather, most of the forces that were originally assigned to CENTCOM already had other commitments, primarily to the North Atlantic Treaty Organization (NATO) and Korea (CBO 1983, 1). As a result, even if CENTCOM had been disbanded, many if not all of these forces might still have been maintained for other purposes (CBO 1983, 56).

Nevertheless, since a central mission, if not *the* central mission, of many of these forces has been the defense of American interests in the Persian Gulf, at least some share of their costs should arguably be included in any comprehensive attempt to measure the costs of U.S. military efforts to protect and ensure access to the region's oil. Indeed, a case could be made for incorporating some of the costs of forces not usually assigned to CENTCOM, since many of them have been used in the region in operations Desert Shield/Desert Storm and Iraqi Freedom.

The 1980s

During the 1980s, a large number of units were assigned to CENTCOM for planning purposes. Descriptions of the assigned forces vary, but they generally included three to five army divisions and one independent brigade, one Marine Amphibious Force (MAF)—consisting of a ground combat division, a tactical air wing, sustaining support, and approximately forty-five thousand troops (CBO 1983, xv)—and one Marine Amphibious Brigade (MAB), seven or more tactical fighter wings, and three carrier battle groups, three amphibious ready groups, and one surface action group, for a total of more than 290,000 military personnel (see Table 6.2).

Most of these units had already been earmarked for use in time of crisis, either in a primary or reinforcing role, in other strategic theaters, especially Europe (Acharya 1989, 74). Nevertheless, as Secretary of Defense Caspar Weinberger noted in 1981, the threats facing NATO as well as Northeast Asia appeared to be less urgent than those in Southwest Asia (CBO 1983, 8). Moreover, many of the CENTCOM-assigned ground force units were not well suited for use in Europe because of their lack of armor. Consequently, one careful analysis found that CENTCOM could count on having five divisions even in potential two-front situations involving a conflict in either Europe or Asia as well as in the Persian Gulf and six divisions if there were no competing operations (McNaugher 1985, 69). What was the cost of maintaining these forces, and how much of the cost could be attributed to Persian Gulf missions?

TABLE 6.2 Forces Assigned to CENTCOM for Planning Purposes or
Used in Major Persian Gulf Military Operations

	Army (divisions/ brigades)	Navy (CVBG/ SAG/ARG)	Air Force (tactical fighter wings)	Marine Corps (MAF/MAB)	Total Personnel
1980s	4/1	3/1/3	7+	1/1	290,000
1991 Gulf War	7/2	6/3/3	10	2/1	500,000
2003 Iraq War	4/4	6/–/3	7	1/1	340,000

SOURCES: *1980s*: CBO 1983; McNaugher 1985; Peterson 1986, 154; M. Johnson 1987; Kaufmann 1987, 95; Kupchan 1987, 34. *1991 Gulf War*: DOD 1992; CBO 1997b, 34; Naval Historical Center n.d.; Global Security n.d. *2003 Iraq War*: Bowman 2003; DOD 2003; Keane 2003; CNN.com n.d.; "US Navy Order of Battle: Operation Iraqi Freedom" n.d.

Abbreviations:
ARG: Amphibious Ready Group
CVBG: Carrier Battle Group
MAB: Marine Amphibious (Expeditionary) Brigade
MAF: Marine Amphibious (Expeditionary) Force
SAG: Surface Action Group

Ground Forces

In the mid-1980s, the cost to staff and operate a single division ranged between approximately $1.1 billion and $1.8 billion per year.[21] Estimates of the acquisition cost of a division ranged from $1.9 to $6.4 billion for a mechanized division and $8.7 billion for a MAF, not including ships.[22] Thus assuming a fifteen-year average service life for equipment and other assets (Epstein 1986, 27, tab. 15), the average annual investment cost per division ranged from $130 to $580 million, depending on the type. This yields a total cost per division of roughly $1.3 to $2.3 billion per year.[23] Assuming that only half the cost of the approximately six division-equivalents assigned to CENTCOM could be attributed to missions in Southwest Asia, the total annual cost of U.S. Army and Marine Corps ground forces for Persian Gulf contingencies lay somewhere between $3.9 and $6.9 billion.

Air Forces

In the early to mid-1980s, the U.S. Air Force spent $12 billion per year to operate, support, and procure selected aircraft for thirty-six tactical air wings, not including indirect costs (CBO 1984). At least seven of these wings were assigned to CENTCOM. Attributing half the cost of these seven wings to Persian Gulf missions, the total cost was approximately $1.2 billion. An alternative and perhaps more accurate calculation begins with the observation that the average acquisition cost of tactical aircraft was $32 million, or $2.3 billion for a wing of seventy-two aircraft, not including spare parts. Assuming an operation and support cost factor of 13 percent, the annual operation and support cost was another $300 million per wing. Assuming a service life of twenty years, the annual investment cost was $115 million per wing, for a total annual cost per wing of $415 million.[24] Attributing half of the cost of the more than eight wings—seven air force and one and one-third Marine Corps—assigned to CENTCOM results in an estimate of $1.7 billion per year for Persian Gulf missions.

Naval Forces
In the mid-1980s, the average annual operating cost of a carrier battle group was approximately $3.6 billion and the annual replacement cost was approximately $500 million—$18.6 billion spread over thirty-five years—for a total yearly cost of about $4 billion (Kaufmann 1986). Given that of the three carrier battle groups assigned to CENTCOM, one was almost always present in the region, it is reasonable to attribute the cost of two to the Persian Gulf mission, or approximately $8 billion per year.

Strategic Lift
Total spending on airlift and sealift grew rapidly in the 1980s, from just $2.3 billion in 1980 to a peak of $7.6 billion in 1986, before declining in the last years of the decade. CBO estimated that the overall program to expand mobility resources would cost more than $13 billion in FY1983 dollars by 1988 (CBO 1983, 29). Overall, the United States spent $53.2 billion in FY1983 dollars on airlift and sealift between 1980 and 1990, or an average of $4.8 billion per year.[25]

Spending on lift had averaged less than $2.6 billion per year in FY1983 dollars from 1973 to 1979. Thus much of the growth during the 1980s can be attributed to the new Southwest Asia mission. In contrast to Europe and Northeast Asia, where U.S. forces could count on substantial local infrastructure, they would have to rely much more heavily on supplies brought in by air and sea in order to operate in the Persian Gulf. Moreover, Southwest Asia was simply farther away than either other theater. Therefore one can conservatively attribute one-third to one-half of the total cost of strategic lift, or an average of $1.6 to $2.4 billion per year, to Persian Gulf missions in the 1980s.

The 1990s and Early 2000s
During the decade following the end of the cold war and the Gulf War, U.S. military planning was guided largely by the Bottom-Up Review conducted by

the Clinton administration in 1993. Most important, the review argued that the United States should "maintain sufficient military power to be able to win two major regional conflicts that occur nearly simultaneously." Although a number of scenarios were examined during the review, the two focused on most closely involved the Persian Gulf and Korea (Aspin 1993). Indeed, concluded a RAND study, "The Gulf became the central theater in U.S. strategic thinking and force planning. From then on, the requirement to conduct large-scale expeditionary warfare in the Persian Gulf, spurred on by both Iran and Iraq's use of asymmetric military strategies, has accounted for a large share of total U.S. military operating, force-structure, and investment costs" (Rathmell, Karasik, and Gompert 2003, 3).

The forces required for a single major regional conflict (MRC) were estimated at four to five army divisions, four to five marine brigades, ten air force fighter wings, one hundred heavy bombers, and four to five carrier battle groups.[26] The review also found that the United States would need up to three divisions, one marine brigade, one to two wings of aircraft, and one to two carrier battle groups for smaller-scale operations, such as peacekeeping, peace enforcement, and other forms of intervention, but these capabilities could for the most part be drawn from the general purpose forces maintained for larger operations. Likewise, fielding forces sufficient to win two MRCs would provide a hedge against the emergence of a larger-than-expected threat in the future. Taking into account the need to maintain a sizable (one carrier battle group) and nearly continuous naval presence in Southwest Asia, Northeast Asia, and Europe, the review set overall U.S. active force requirements at ten army divisions, three Marine Expeditionary Forces (MEF) of one division and one air wing each, eleven carriers (one reserve), and thirteen fighter wings (Aspin 1993; see also Larson, Orietsky, and Leuschner 2001).

On this basis, one can conservatively estimate that at least one-third of U.S. active force requirements—three and one-third army divisions, one MEF, four carrier battle groups, four and one-third fighter wings, and their corresponding support units—were generated by the need to defend U.S. interests in the Persian Gulf. How much did these forces cost to field?

Ground Forces

For the U.S. Army, in FY1998, approximately 310,000 (or 63 percent) of the 495,000 soldiers in the active duty force were assigned to deployable combat and support units, and the remaining 185,000 to the "institutional" army.[27] At the same time, army outlays for military personnel and O&M amounted to $17.2 billion and $19.1 billion, respectively (OUD 1999, tab. 6–6). Assuming that personnel and O&M costs per soldier in combat and support units are no higher than average, they come to $7.7 billion ($2.3 billion per division) for the requirements generated by Southwest Asia missions.[28] A similar calculation yields a cost of approximately $1.6 billion for the one MEF, for a total of $9.3 billion for ground forces. Similarly, O'Hanlon estimated the annual operating and support costs and procurement costs of an active army division at $2 billion and $300–400 million, respectively, for a total of approximately $8 billion for three and one-third divisions (O'Hanlon 1995, 34 and 38).[29] Alternatively, Kaufmann put the annual cost of an army division at $3.35 billion ($11.2 billion for three and one-third divisions) and a marine division (excluding air assets) at $1.7 billion, for a combined total of $12.9 billion in FY1993 dollars (Kaufmann 1992, 70, tab. 6–10).

Air Forces

In the early 1990s, Kaufmann estimated the average incremental cost of an active air force fighter-attack wing as being at about $1.1 billion in FY1993 dollars.[30] At the same time, he gave the average cost of a land-based tactical air wing as a share of the entire budget as $2.0 billion for the U.S. Air Force and $2.3 billion for the Marine Corps in FY1993 (Kaufmann 1992, 70, tab. 6–10). In the mid-1990s, however, O'Hanlon estimated the annual operating and support costs and procurement costs of a tactical combat wing to be one-third of a billion dollars each, for a total of approximately $3 billion for four and one-third wings (O'Hanlon 1995, 34, 38; see CBO 1990 for similar estimates). Thus a conservative estimate for the annual cost attributable to Persian Gulf missions was approximately $3 to $4.8 billion or more for the air force and $700 million to $1.1 billion or more for Marine Corps air assets.

Naval Forces

Kaufmann also estimated the cost of a carrier battle group at $4.15 billion in FY1993 (Kaufmann 1992, 70). In contrast, O'Hanlon put the annual operating and support costs and procurement costs of a carrier battle group at just $1 billion and $700–800 million, respectively (O'Hanlon 1995, 34, 38). Thus the annual cost attributable to Persian Gulf requirements in the 1990s were somewhere between $7 and $16.6 billion.

Strategic Lift

From 1991 to 2001, the United States obligated approximately $110 billion on airlift and sealift, an average of $10 billion per year in FY2000 dollars (OUD

1999, tab. 6–5). From 1995 to 2001, however, spending on lift averaged more than $11 billion per year in FY2000 dollars. Alternatively, Kaufmann put the cost of airlift, sealift, and prepositioning ships at $11.1 billion and $2.6 billion in FY1993, respectively (Kaufmann 1992, 70). Assuming that approximately one-third of the lift requirement derived from Southwest Asia contingencies, the cost share was at least $3 to $4 billion per year.

In sum, the share of the cost of U.S.-based combat forces and strategic lift capabilities that can be attributed to missions in the Persian Gulf since 1980 must be measured in the tens of billions of dollars per year (see Table 6.3). The admittedly rough calculations above suggest that, during the 1980s, the total annual cost came to between $15 and $19 billion. This amount then increased to between $23 and $39 billion in the 1990s. It should be noted that these figures are not adjusted for inflation, so the costs in recent (2006) dollars would be considerably higher: approximately $28 to $36 billion for the 1980s and $30 to $51 billion during the following decade. In addition, they do not include any costs for other regular or reserve forces that might have been used in the Persian Gulf or, in most cases, any share of the more general military infrastructure that was required to maintain them. Thus these figures may well underestimate the full cost of the share U.S.-based forces that could be attributed to Persian Gulf missions.

TABLE 6.3 Annual Cost of U.S.-Based General Purpose Forces and Strategic Lift Attributable to Persian Gulf Missions (billions of nominal dollars)

	1980–1990	*1991–2001*
Army	3.9–6.9	7.7–11.2
Air Force	1.7	3.0–4.8
Navy	8.0	7–16.6
Marine Corps	Included in Army and Air Force totals	Ground: 1.6–1.7 Air: 0.7–1.1
Strategic Lift	1.6–2.4	3–4
Total (2006 dollars)	15–19 (28–36)	23–39 (30–51)

NOTE: Estimates in 2006 dollars are obtained by assuming that the figures for the two time periods were calculated in 1985 and 1995 dollars, respectively, and multiplying them by the respective CPI inflators, 1.87 and 1.32. To achieve rough comparability between the two time periods, the figures for 1980–90 should be multiplied by a factor of approximately 1.4.

Major Military Operations

Drawing on these military assets, the United States has conducted a number of noteworthy military operations in the Persian Gulf since the 1980s. The most important of these have been the protection of Gulf shipping during the Iran-Iraq War, the Gulf War, the operations associated with the enforcement of UN Security Council resolutions on Iraq during the 1990s and early 2000s, and the U.S. invasion and occupation of Iraq. Although American officials have usually offered other rationales, arguably, the ultimate purpose of each of these operations was, directly or indirectly, to protect U.S. and Western oil interests in the Persian Gulf. Certainly, it is easy to imagine that none of them would have occurred but for the importance of the region's oil supplies. Most of these operations, including the Gulf War, have had only a limited budgetary impact. The Iraq War, however, has already cost hundreds of billions of dollars and may eventually rank as the most expensive in the postwar era.

Operation Earnest Will, 1987–1988

The first major military operation—Earnest Will—took place late in the Iran-Iraq War and has been described as a "fundamental turning point" because it was the first time that the United States had assumed an operational role in the Persian Gulf since World War II (Sick 2003, 295). During the mid-1980s, Iranian torpedoes and mines had damaged dozens of oil tankers, including at least fifteen from Kuwait. In response, the United States offered in early 1987 to reregister eleven Kuwaiti tankers as American vessels and to provide naval protection for them. By the time the U.S. Navy began to escort the reflagged tankers in July of that year, its presence in or near the Gulf had grown to roughly thirty-three vessels, including an aircraft carrier and a battleship. During the course of the operation, which involved nearly one hundred separate escort missions, American forces sank or badly damaged two Iranian frigates and several smaller warships, destroyed several of Iran's offshore oil platforms, and captured an Iranian minelayer. In addition, an American frigate, the *U.S.S. Stark*, was struck by Iraqi missiles, which killed thirty-seven sailors and injured twenty-one, and a U.S. cruiser mistakenly shot down an Iranian passenger jet, claiming the lives of all 290 civilians on board (McNaugher 1990; Teicher and Teicher 1993, 391; Little 2002, 250–51; K. Pollack 2004, 224–26). The Department of Defense estimated the total incremental cost of the fifteen-month operation at $240 million, although outlays had run as high as $30 million per month (GAO 1991, 12; Cordesman 1988, 396).

The Reagan administration had multiple motives for undertaking Earnest Will. These included reassuring Kuwait, aiding Iraq in its struggle with Iran, minimizing Soviet influence in the Gulf, and demonstrating American resolve (McNaugher 1990, 114; Hunter 1990, 68; Jentleson 1994, 62). But the most immediate goal was to protect the flow of oil out of the Gulf by deterring Iranian attacks on shipping and the oil producing states. As Secretary of Defense Weinberger later acknowledged, U.S. decision makers unanimously agreed that Persian Gulf oil exports were a vital U.S. interest and had to be defended (Weinberger 1990, 389–92; see also K. Pollack 2004, 226, 234–35; Yetiv 2004, 80).

Operations Desert Shield and Desert Storm, 1990–1991
Just two years after the reflagging operation, U.S. forces went into action once again, albeit on a much larger scale, in response to the 1990 Iraqi invasion of Kuwait. This time, the United States deployed forces from all four services, including seven army divisions and two armored cavalry regiments, two marine divisions and a Marine Expeditionary Brigade, nearly thirteen hundred combat and combat-support aircraft, and six carrier battle groups, for a total of more than five hundred thousand military personnel in the theater (see Table 6.2, above).[31] The coalition air forces conducted more than one hundred thousand sorties during the forty-three–day bombing campaign, while the land forces routed the Iraqi army in a four-day ground offensive. Despite the massive size of the deployment, the number of U.S. casualties was relatively small: approximately three hundred dead and another five hundred wounded. The DOD estimated the incremental cost of the two operations to be $61 billion. But the United States received some $53 billion in cash and in-kind contributions from Saudi Arabia, Kuwait, Japan, Germany, and other countries, resulting in a net outlay of only $8 billion (DOD 1992, 725). The next time the United States undertook such an extensive operation in the Gulf, it would not be so lucky.

Once again, a number of motives lay behind the U.S. action, among them confronting naked aggression and upholding international law. But as one of the best histories of the episode notes, "While it was never the case that the Gulf crisis was solely about oil, oil infused every aspect" (Freedman and Karsh 1993, 180). It was bad enough that, with the occupation of Kuwait, Iraq controlled some 20 percent of the world's oil reserves. "With access to Kuwaiti reserves," President George H. W. Bush's leading advisors argued, "Saddam [Hussein] would be able to wield unprecedented influence over the world oil market" (Freedman and Karsh 1993, 76). If unchecked, moreover, the Iraqi leader was poised to dominate Saudi Arabia and the other oil producing countries of the region through the threat or actual use of force. "He was clearly in a position to be able to dictate the future of worldwide energy policy," warned Secretary of Defense Richard Cheney, "and that gave him a stranglehold on our economy and on that of most of the other nations of the world as well" (quoted in Klare 2004b, 6; see also Freedman and Karsh 1993, 180; Little 2002, 255, 259).

The stakes for the United States could hardly have been higher. As two key national security documents written at the time noted, "Access to Persian Gulf oil and the security of key friendly states in the area are vital to U.S. national security. . . . The United States remains committed to defending its vital interests in the region, if necessary through the use of military force, against any power with interests inimical to our own."[32] President Bush himself cautioned, "Our jobs, our way of life, our own freedom and the freedom of friendly countries around the world would all suffer if control of the world's great oil reserves fell into the hands of Saddam Hussein."[33] Thus, he concluded, "We cannot permit a resource so vital to be dominated by one so ruthless. And we won't."[34]

Post–Gulf War Operations

Following the Gulf War, a small but significant U.S. combat force remained in the theater. It served both to deter possible further aggressive moves by Iraq against its oil-rich neighbors and to enforce the UN sanctions that had been imposed on the country after the war. U.S. naval forces made up much of the multinational Maritime Interception Force (MIF) operating in the Gulf that enforced the embargo on Iraqi imports and oil exports. Army units repeatedly exercised the prepositioned equipment in Kuwait as a show of force under operations Vigilant Warrior and Desert Spring, and both U.S. Army and Marine Corps forces conducted frequent exercises.

Most extensive of all were the air operations intended to enforce the no-fly zones imposed over northern and southern Iraq. In the fall of 2000, according to O'Hanlon, the U.S. presence in the Gulf region was largely devoted to those missions (O'Hanlon 2001, 55–56). The smaller Operation Northern Watch, which succeeded Operation Provide Comfort in 1996, involved approximately fifty aircraft and one thousand U.S. military personnel based in Turkey.[35] Operation Southern Watch, which began in August 1992, was conducted by the approximately one hundred twenty combat aircraft stationed in Saudi Arabia and seventy carrier-based aircraft in the Persian Gulf. By the time the operation ended in 2003, U.S. pilots had flown some 286,000 missions.[36]

The cost of these and related operations, such as the extensive air strikes in December 1998 against Iraq (Operation Desert Fox), averaged around $1 billion per year.[37] In November 1998, just before Desert Fox, a DOD spokesman stated that expanded military operations and crisis buildups in the Persian Gulf since the war had cost a total of $6.9 billion, much of which represented the costs of enforcing the no-fly zones (A. Prados 2002, 9; see also Myers 1999). A later calculation found that from the end of the Gulf War in 1991 until the start of the 2003 Iraq War, the DOD had incurred about $11.5 billion in expenses in containing Iraq and providing humanitarian aid to the Kurds in the northern part of the country (Katzman 2003, 14). Former Undersecretary of Defense Paul Wolfowitz has put the figure for containing Iraq somewhat higher, at about $30 billion (Ricks 2006, 17).[38]

Operation Iraqi Freedom

By far the most expensive military operation mounted by the United States in the Persian Gulf has been the 2003 invasion of Iraq and following occupation. A high percentage of U.S. ground combat and support units, both active and reserve, have deployed to the theater, many for as long as one year or more, and many more than once. Shortly after President George W. Bush declared the end of major combat operations in May 2003, sixteen of the army's thirty-three active brigades as well as a marine division and special forces were in Iraq, for a total of more than 190,000 ground force personnel in the region. In addition, fifteen air wings, six carrier battle groups, three amphibious ready groups, and a number of other ships participated in the initial phase of combat operations (see Table 6.2, above). The number of troops in Iraq was temporarily drawn down to approximately 130,000 in 2004, but was then increased again in 2005 to 160,000 in order to provide security in the face of the persistent insurgency.[39]

In contrast to its experience during the Gulf War, this time the United States would have to bear the financial as well as the human costs of the operation largely by itself, and these costs would both prove to be substantial. By the end of 2006, the number of military personnel who had died in Iraq stood at three thousand, and several times as many had been maimed or badly wounded.[40] In comparison with other military operations, the budgetary burden imposed on the United States was even greater. Through the end of 2006, the Congress had authorized approximately $380 billion for military operations and reconstruction, and the costs were continuing to mount at a rapid clip. Spending on military operations alone had risen from about $5 billion per month in 2003 and 2004 to $8 billion per month in 2006, and the costs of repairing and replacing damaged or destroyed military hardware, or what is known as "reset," was running an additional $20 billion per year.[41]

Based on such figures, the Congressional Budget Office and other independent analysts projected that spending on operations and equipment would eventually reach $600 to $700 billion, rivaling the cost of the Vietnam War ($600 billion in 2005 dollars) and dwarfing that of the Korean War ($430 billion). Yet these amounts do not include the additional outlays associated with providing medical care, disability pay, and other benefits to veterans as well as financing the war through deficit spending, which could increase the total by hundreds of billions of dollars. Also to consider are the economic costs of lives lost and injuries to U.S. soldiers as well as possible macroeconomic effects. Thus, as one headline suggested, Operation Iraqi Freedom could well become "the Trillion-Dollar War."[42]

Of course, of all the military operations that the United States has conducted in the Persian Gulf since 1980, the Iraq War is also perhaps the most difficult to attribute to concerns about foreign oil dependence. The Bush administration has offered a number of justifications, among which the need to protect or maintain access to oil supplies was conspicuously absent. Indeed, Secretary of Defense Donald Rumsfeld insisted that the conflict had "nothing to do with oil, literally nothing to do with oil" (Everest 2004, 248). Instead, during the runup to the invasion, the president and other high-level officials emphasized the threat to U.S. national security posed by Iraq's alleged possession of weapons of mass destruction and links to international terrorists. They claimed that Iraq was armed with biological and chemical weapons as well as missiles to deliver them and that it was actively developing a nuclear capability. In addition, they maintained that Iraq had long-standing and continuing ties to terrorist groups, including al Qaeda. These two factors in turn raised the troubling prospect that Iraq might one day provide weapons of mass destruction to terrorists, who would not hesitate to use them against the United States.

Subsequently, of course, the threat allegedly posed by Iraq to the United States was shown to be exaggerated. Iraq lacked any usable weapons of mass destruction, and its capabilities for building them were rudimentary or nonexistent. The claims of ties to al Qaeda and other terrorist groups turned out to be even more baseless. Although debate still rages over whether and the degree to which the Bush administration may have intentionally offered a distorted view of the threat, it is now clear that U.S. intelligence agencies and some administration officials were in possession of evidence that conflicted with or cast doubt on many of the claims that were made in public. Even if one is sympathetic to the further arguments that the war was necessary to promote democracy in the Middle East or to eliminate a tyrannical regime that had trampled on human rights, one must still ask why Iraq was singled out among the many brutal autocracies in the world.

These observations suggest that it is worth considering what role oil-related concerns may have played in the decision to invade Iraq. It will be years before the memoirs of key participants are available and even longer before we have access to internal documents. Thus the case that the war owes at least in part to U.S. foreign oil dependence must be based on circumstantial evidence, but it is nevertheless a strong one. It begins with the fact that Iraq is located in the center of the world's largest oil producing region and that the country itself possesses the second or third largest proven oil reserves after Saudi Arabia and Iran. As a result, Iraqi policy has major implications for the world's oil supply.

And for many years, these implications had been almost exclusively negative. Iraq continued to pose a serious potential threat to its oil-rich neighbors, with or without nuclear weapons. Moreover, Iraq's own oil production had been artificially suppressed by the destruction wrought in two wars, UN sanctions, a lack of investment, and Saddam Hussein's own attempts to manipulate the level of production for political advantage.

Thus by invading Iraq and deposing Saddam Hussein, the United States could have expected to ease the costs and risks of foreign oil dependence in at least two ways. First, regime change would likely have eliminated the danger that Iraq might once again disrupt world oil supplies by attempting to dominate, whether successfully or not, the vast oil resources of the Gulf. Second, it could free up Iraq's own substantial oil production potential, thereby helping to ease the world's increasingly tight supplies and providing an additional buffer against possible supply disruptions elsewhere. Both of these changes could in turn have been expected to ease upward pressure on oil prices and to increase the stability of world oil markets in the medium to long term, if not immediately (Duffield 2005; see also Morse and Jaffe 2001; Everest 2004; Rutledge 2005).

Finally, it may be instructive to consider the counterfactual, complicated and problematic though it may be. What if the Persian Gulf had never possessed significant amounts of oil? In that case, it is difficult to imagine something like the Iraq War ever having occurred. Even if oil-related considerations played no role in the decision to invade, one can see the war as the logical culmination of a series of prior steps that were taken largely, if not exclusively, because of the region's strategic importance to the United States. Thus it seems appropriate to assign at least part of the massive cost of the war and occupation to U.S. foreign oil dependence.

Conclusion

For at least a quarter of a century, U.S. military planning, preparations, and actions have increasingly centered on the Persian Gulf. These policies have been justified on a number of grounds: deterring Soviet adventurism, protecting neutral shipping, upholding international law, enforcing UN Security Council resolutions, and fighting terrorism, to name only a handful. But underlying all of these rationales has been the region's strategic importance as the leading source of oil production and exports in the world.

This focus on the Persian Gulf began modestly enough, with an increased naval presence and efforts to improve the ability of the United States to project military power to the region in a crisis. It later took the form of a long-term deployment of ground and air force contingents on the Arabian Peninsula. And it ultimately involved the two largest U.S. military operations since the Vietnam War: Desert Shield/Desert Storm and Iraqi Freedom.

The cumulative cost of these military efforts has been enormous. The United States has spent on the order of several billions of dollars per year on additional military capabilities and routine operations that have been directly, and often exclusively, associated with the defense of U.S. oil interests in the Persian Gulf. These expenses include the establishment and operation of CENTCOM, the acquisition of dedicated sea- and airlift capabilities, the prepositioning of equipment in or near the Gulf, the improvement of military facilities in the region, and the stationing of active naval, ground, and air force units there on a semipermanent basis.

To these marginal costs must be added a significant share of the outlays for the U.S.-based general purpose forces and strategic lift whose maintenance and augmentation has been increasingly justified in terms of Persian

Gulf contingencies. Drawing on a variety of authoritative sources, I have estimated these additional annual costs at roughly $15–19 billion in the 1980s ($28–36 billion in 2006 dollars) and $23–39 billion in the 1990s and early 2000s ($30–51 billion in 2006 dollars). Finally, there is the matter of the major military operations that the United States has conducted in the Persian Gulf since the late 1980s. Most of these operations, including the Gulf War, have had only a limited budgetary impact. The recent invasion and occupation of Iraq, however, has already cost several hundred billion dollars and may eventually rank as the most expensive military operation of the postwar era.

It should be recognized that a good deal of uncertainty surrounds these estimates. Cost data are not readily available for some programs, and in other cases, experts have offered figures that differ by as much as a factor of two. Nevertheless, the above analysis provides a reasonable approximation of the costs of the Persian Gulf-oriented military policies that the United States has undertaken in response to foreign oil dependence, and they have been substantial.

7 Unintended Consequences of U.S. External Policy Responses

Increasing the Threat

> The events of September 11 were the direct result of over fifty years of American involvement in the [Middle East] region, the consequence of actions and policies that have destabilized the arc of nations extending from the Mediterranean to South Asia.
>
> *Gabriel Kolko,* Another Century of War

THE FOREIGN and military policies that the United States has pursued toward oil producing countries and regions since the 1970s in response to foreign oil dependence have generated substantial material and nonmaterial costs. American policymakers have been—or could reasonably have been expected to be—aware of many of the costs, such as outlays for military forces, and consciously agreed to assume them. But these policies have resulted in significant additional costs that were not intended or anticipated by their authors.

The unintended consequences of U.S. external policies have taken three broad forms. American actions have undermined nominally friendly regimes, however distasteful they may have been, thereby contributing to greater regional instability. They have generated new enemies by creating anti-American attitudes or strengthening preexisting ones. And in some cases, they have helped to empower hostile actors, be they states or nonstate entities. The overall effect has been to increase the severity of the threats to U.S. interests, oil and otherwise, and to the physical security of the United States itself. Not surprisingly, the majority of these unintended consequences are to be found in the Persian Gulf and adjacent areas, because this region has been the principal focus of the foreign and, especially, the military policies undertaken in response to U.S. foreign oil dependence.

Undermining "Friends": Creating
Instability in the Persian Gulf

Two important and closely related goals of U.S. policy have been to strengthen regimes in oil producing regions that were seen as vital to protecting American interests and, if necessary, to defend key oil exporting states against external threats. To these ends, the United States has provided various forms of assistance to countries in and around the Persian Gulf, and it has deployed substantial military forces there. In the short term at least, these efforts have appeared to yield the desired results. But at times they have been counterproductive, serving to undermine the very regimes that the United States sought to support. The fate of the shah of Iran provides the clearest example of this perverse dynamic. But American policy has contributed to serious tensions and challenges with Saudi Arabia as well.

The Shah of Iran

The first instance of U.S. policy inadvertently weakening a nominal ally occurred in Iran under the shah. The shah was not an especially popular leader to begin with. He had been placed on the Peacock throne by foreign powers and had subsequently pursued policies that had alienated many sectors of Iranian society, especially Muslim clerics.[1] But U.S. policy toward Iran during the 1970s exacerbated this situation in various ways, eventually helping to set the stage for the revolution that toppled the shah.

To be sure, some have questioned just how much the United States was to blame for the shah's demise, if at all. As Kenneth Pollack recently argued, "The shah brought the Iranian Revolution on himself. At the strategic level, his many mistaken policies created tremendous animosity against his regime across the breadth of Iranian society. At a tactical level, he mishandled the manifestations of that unhappiness from start to finish in 1977–1978" (K. Pollack 2004, 137). In an assessment of the situation prepared for President Carter in late 1978 just before the culmination of the revolution, however, venerable diplomat George Ball drew a different conclusion: "We made the shah what he has become. We nurtured his love for grandiose geopolitical schemes and we supplied him with the hardware to indulge his fantasies" (Ball 1982, 459). At a minimum, many would agree with Steven Yetiv that "it seems obvious that U.S. support of the repressive Shah contributed to his downfall" (Yetiv 2004, 62). But how exactly did it do so? And what particular contributions were made by U.S. policy in the 1970s, motivated as it was by a heightened concern about the economic costs and risks of foreign oil dependence?

The root of the problem was the considerable degree to which the shah became associated with the United States during the 1970s. Previously, the U.S. government had not sought particularly close relations with his regime. Beginning with the Nixon administration, however, the United States closely embraced the shah. This embrace resulted in significant benefits for him (see Chapter 5), but it also had several negative consequences (Ramazani 1982, 53).

First, close ties to the United States left the shah vulnerable to charges of being an American stooge and thus a leader who was unlikely to defend the interests and preserve the integrity of the Iranians (Acharya 1989, 32; Little 2002, 223; Yetiv 2004, 62). Not surprisingly, the Ayatollah Khomeini among others believed that he was a puppet who had been installed and supported by the United States (K. Pollack 2004, 157). At the same time, the shah's conspicuous ties to Washington were seen by many in Iran—but especially among the Muslim clergy—as evidence of a "pernicious and heretical embrace of the West" (Klare 2001, 60). This association of the shah's regime with Western culture, commodities, and vices brought on a traditionalist reaction (Keddie 1981, 182). Thus the alliance with the United States eroded the shah's nationalist credentials and political legitimacy (Hunter 1990, 32).

Another set of problems was caused by the shah's virtually unrestricted purchase of U.S. arms and the resulting influx of American military and civilian advisors, which further fueled unrest in Iran (Gasiorowski 1991, 114). The elevated levels of military spending contributed to inflation, while the effort to absorb so many new weapons systems in such a short time resulted in economic bottlenecks, supply shortages, and social dislocation. "Many potentially productive Iranians, including a high percentage of the technically trained, were increasingly concentrated in the armed services and in building projects for army and naval bases and for facilities to transport and house military equipment."[2] It seems reasonable to conclude that if the United States had placed greater limits on its arms sales to the shah, some of these problems would have been avoided or at least attenuated.

Mark Gasiorowski has argued that U.S. policy further contributed to the shah's downfall by making the Iranian state less dependent on and thus less responsive to Iranian society (Gasiorowski 1991, 223–24). Especially with the staggering revenues that followed the oil price increases of 1973, the shah was able to obtain most of the goods and technologies he desired from outside the country. In the process, he greatly increased Iran's economic dependence on the West, especially the United States (Keddie 1981, 143–44). Under these circumstances, it would not be surprising if the shah might have paid less attention to domestic problems until they had become impossible to ignore, and possibly too late to address.

Saudi Arabia

The other Persian Gulf regime that U.S. policy has inadvertently destabilized the most is that of Saudi Arabia. To be sure, many of the charges that have been leveled at the House of Saud by its opponents, including Osama bin Laden, have had little or nothing to do with the United States. Through the 1990s, these criticisms included the regime's alleged flouting of Islamic law, government corruption, the extravagance and lavish lifestyles of members of the royal family, and the country's increasingly poor economic and social conditions (Bergen 2001, 88; Anonymous 2002, 49–51). But some of the most incendiary reproaches have been the result of U.S. actions.

As in the case of Iran, some problems have simply followed from the regime's close ties to the United States. According to one account, they subjected the royal family to growing pressure from Arab radicals as early as the late 1960s (J. Pollack 2003, 82). But bin Laden, perhaps the regime's most outspoken critic, has argued that throughout the rule of the al-Saud family, Saudi foreign policy has been an expanding record of the un-Islamic alignment with Christians and Jews (Anonymous 2002, 116).

The ultimate sin was the government's 1990 decision, at the behest of the United States, to allow the deployment of thousands of American troops on Saudi soil. In the view of Dore Gold, "No event had a greater impact on internal developments in Saudi Arabia in the past quarter century than the 1991 Gulf War" (Gold 2003, 157). For many Saudis, the presence of U.S. forces during and after the war was a source of humiliation and resentment (K. Pollack 2003). More seriously, the arrival of the Americans was in the eyes of many a sacrilege. As such, "it exposed the ruling family to criticism on religious grounds [as well as] for failing in its responsibility to provide for the defense of the country" (Benjamin and Simon 2002, 106; see also Byman and Wise 2002, 54). For all these reasons, the "American occupation" remained a touchstone for opponents of the royal family (J. Pollack 2003).

The fundamentalists in the Saudi religious establishment viewed the American presence as a direct threat. With the recent collapse of the Soviet

Union, they believed that the United States was now the power that could most induce undesirable secular trends in Saudi Arabia, and thereby undermine its Wahhabi religious orientation. Consequently, although the vast majority of U.S. forces departed Saudi Arabia following the end of combat operations in 1991, a religious backlash ensued nonetheless. It began as early as May 1991 with a "Letter of Demands to King Fahd" that was signed by 400 members of the Saudi community of recognized Islamic scholars, or *ulama*, and professors from Saudi universities regarding changes they wanted to see in the kingdom's policies. Then a "Memorandum of Advice" that was sent to the king by 109 Islamic scholars the following year insisted on giving the religious leadership a greater share of power. This second document also challenged the foreign policy that the government had adopted following the Gulf War and "was particularly scathing regarding the kingdom's reliance on arms supplies from the United States" (Gause 2003, 366; Gold 2003, 161–63). Yet other criticisms of the regime by religious authorities followed. Clearly, the U.S. military presence had undermined the government's legitimacy and contributed to "increasingly open challenges" to the royal family's control (Rouleau 2002, 77; Gerth 2002).

The American military presence in the Gulf has also been the focal point of Osama bin Laden's indictment of the Saudi regime (Gause 2003, 8). Although bin Laden had already been critical of the ruling family for not doing enough to serve the Muslim community, the arrival of U.S. forces in Saudi Arabia itself was the last straw (Anonymous 2002, 116). It convinced him that the United States was now seeking to dominate the Muslim world and that the regime was complicit in this American gambit (Gause 2002, 39). By permitting this non-Muslim presence, the Saudi regime had revealed its apostate nature, violating the Prophet Muhammad's injunction "let there be no two religions in Arabia" (Byman 2003, 144).

Following Saudi Arabia's withdrawal of bin Laden's nationality in 1994, he issued public denunciations of the regime based on this premise. In a 1995 "Open Letter to King Fahd," he charged that the king had tied Saudi foreign policy "to the Crusaders and despotic Muslim countries" and called on Fahd to resign (Gold 2003, 171). Even in his 1996 "Declaration of Jihad against the Americans," which was primarily intended to mobilize Muslims against the U.S. enemy, he subjected the royal family to withering criticism. For bin Laden, the House of Saud had lost its last shred of legitimacy and forfeited its right to rule (Anonymous 2002, 115–17; J. Pollack 2003; Danner 2005, 48).[3]

Making Enemies: Fomenting Anti-Americanism

The previous section suggests the prior existence of a considerable amount of anti-Americanism in the Persian Gulf, which had made close ties to the United States a liability for regimes in the region. This may be true, although the magnitude and sources of such sentiment have varied greatly from place to place. It is difficult to separate anti-Americanism from broader negative attitudes toward the West that have roots in the Crusades and were reinforced by the later experiences of European imperialism and the exploitation of the region's natural resources by Western oil companies. Where anti-Americanism has specifically American causes, these have often been matters over which the U.S. government could exercise little or no control, such as the spread of American commercialism and liberal values. In addition, a significant amount can be attributed to policies, such as strong American support for Israel, that have nothing to do with oil. But the policies pursued by the United States since the early 1970s in response to foreign oil dependence have only made the situation worse.

This section considers two examples of such dynamics at work. The first concerns Iran, where U.S. policies in the 1970s and 1980s contributed to the hostility exhibited by the Islamic regime that took power following the fall of the shah. The second regards the Arabian Peninsula, where American support for corrupt, authoritarian regimes, a prolonged U.S. military presence beginning in 1990, and related military actions have laid the foundation for an unprecedented level of anti-Americanism there and in the broader Arab and Muslim worlds.

Revolutionary Iran

Certainly, Iranian grievances toward the United States began long before the 1970s. They stemmed particularly from the U.S. role in the coup that overthrew the popular government of Muhammad Mosaddeq in 1953 and that of the CIA in establishing the dreaded internal security service, SAVAK (see, for example, Keddie 1981, 140–41, 144; Cottam 1988, 157). In addition, Ayatollah Khomeini's own anti-Americanism dates to at least 1963, when he criticized the shah for what he termed "Westoxification"—the indiscriminate imitation of things Western—and the granting of special rights and privileges to Americans in Iran (Sick 1985, 10–11). But U.S. policies toward Iran in the 1970s and 1980s that were driven largely by oil-related considerations exacerbated these preexisting resentments and further laid the groundwork for the intense hostility toward the United States that has characterized the revolutionary Islamic regime.

The overarching source of anti-Americanism was the strong U.S. backing of the shah during the last years of his reign. The United States provided the shah with virtually everything he asked for. Through this support, it became identified with what was widely regarded as an illegitimate and repressive authoritarian government (Ramazani 1982, 52; Bill 1988, 190; Hunter 1990, 46; Kemp 1994, 24; K. Pollack 2004, 98, 155–56). Likewise, Khomeini's "hatred of the Shah was matched only by his detestation of the United States, which he regarded as the main prop of the Pahlavi regime" (Yergin 1991, 675).

The policy of virtually unqualified support for the shah led in turn to several more specific grievances. Some grew out of the unbridled sale of U.S. arms and the concomitantly growing numbers of American military and civilian advisors, which seriously damaged "the historical goodwill of the politically aware Iranians" (Ramazani 1982, 52). By the time of the revolution, many Iranians felt that they had been defrauded by the United States, which had siphoned off their oil revenues in return for advanced military hardware that they were unable to operate (Rubin 1981, 136). At the same time, the presence of so many advisors only added to the anti-American feelings. Their behavior sometimes caused offense, and the much higher living standards that they enjoyed triggered envy and resentment, especially where their spending drove up the cost of housing and other goods (Rubin 1981, 136–37; Keddie 1981, 176–77).

No less an important source of anti-Americanism among Iranians was disappointment over U.S. human rights policy. Carter's rhetoric raised hopes that his administration would do more to promote human rights in their country. When it appeared that the United States would not follow through on this rhetorical commitment, however, many Iranians once again felt betrayed. This process of growing disillusionment culminated in September 1978, when Carter and his national security advisor, Zbigniew Brzezinski, seemed to condone the deaths of hundreds of protestors in Tehran at the hands of the army. After that, both liberal and Islamic opposition leaders stepped up their attacks on the United States (Cottam 1988, 162, 176; Dumbrell 1993, 164, 172; K. Pollack 2004, 124).

Following the revolution, in the 1980s, anti-American sentiment in Iran was reinforced by U.S. support for Iraq in the war between the two countries and American naval operations in the Gulf (Teicher and Teicher 1993,

239; Kemp 1994, 24–25). According to Kenneth Pollack, the Iranians believed that "the United States was encouraging or ordering its Iraqi puppet to use [chemical weapons]" (K. Pollack 2004, 208). When Washington tried to shift the blame for the fatal 1987 attack on the *U.S.S. Stark* to Iran for creating a hostile environment in the Gulf, the Iranians viewed it as "just more proof that America would stoop to any level to destroy the Islamic Republic." And they assumed that the accidental U.S. downing of an Iranian civilian airliner in 1988, resulting in the loss of 290 lives, had in fact been intentional (K. Pollack 2004, 225, 232).

In sum, oil-related U.S. policies and actions helped to turn Iran into one of America's most implacable foes, by both undermining the shah and aggravating anti-American sentiment.[4] Even during the 1970s, Americans in the country became targets of violence (Bill 1988, 191). Then in 1979, when a group of students overran the U.S. embassy and took dozens of American diplomats and marines hostage, the new Islamic regime gave its assent. Subsequently, throughout the 1980s and 1990s, Iran challenged U.S. interests virtually across the board, supporting terrorist attacks against Israel, attempting to topple Persian Gulf monarchies and other moderate Arab regimes, opposing the Middle East peace process, and generally trying to drive the United States out of the region (K. Pollack 2004, passim).

The Arabian Peninsula

Although it is difficult to minimize the problems posed by revolutionary Iran to the United States, of even greater concern now and, most likely, in the future is how oil-driven U.S. policies toward the Arabian Peninsula have fomented anti-Americanism there and in the broader Arab and Muslim worlds. As a senior U.S. intelligence official argued in an anonymously published book, "Policies pursued by the United States and the West for decades in the Middle East and the Muslim world generally are seen by many Muslims as anti-Islamic. . . . That the United States is attacking the religion, sanctities, resources, children, and dignity of Islam . . . is a view increasingly held by Muslims around the world."[5]

To be sure, the U.S. government alone is not entirely to blame for this state of affairs, and as in the case of Iran, the policies in question do not all have their roots in U.S. foreign oil dependence. Anti-American attitudes among Arabs and Muslims in the region have multiple causes, including the sometimes exploitative practices of U.S. oil companies and other businesses, strong and largely unquestioning American support for what many Arabs view as a militaristic and expansionist Israel, the apparent failure of the United States to live up to its avowed principles concerning justice, self-determination, and human rights, and, instead, its predilection to apply a double standard in the region. Thus, Islamists ask, why is only Israel allowed to possess nuclear weapons and why did Iraq's aggression against Kuwait have to be addressed immediately by force while Israel's occupation has been relegated to diplomacy and negotiations over a period of decades (Haddad 2003, 468, 473–74)?

Nevertheless, U.S. policies motivated primarily or largely by oil-related considerations have contributed substantially to the growth of anti-American sentiment in the region. Among these, three stand out: (1) U.S. support for repressive and corrupt regimes, especially in Saudi Arabia; (2) the prolonged American military presence on the Arabian Peninsula beginning in 1990, and (3) direct U.S. military actions, including the prosecution of the Gulf War, the enforcement of UN sanctions and no-fly zones in Iraq, and the 2003 invasion and subsequent occupation of the country.

In its quest for stability in the Persian Gulf, the United States has typically backed the prevailing authoritarian regimes, regardless of how repressive, corrupt, or incompetent at economic management they may have been. Not surprisingly, this support has been held against the United States by local critics of those regimes, turning them into antagonists or even enemies of the United States itself (Banerjee 2001b; Zunes 2002, 6–7; Benjamin and Simon 2002, 415; Byman 2003, 144; Anonymous 2004, 12). The clearest example of this phenomenon at work is Saudi Arabia, where American support of the al-Saud regime has angered many Saudis, damaged its image throughout the Middle East, and helped to make it a target of terrorist attacks (see, for example, *New York Times* 2001; Banerjee 2001a; Martin 2002; Bandow 2003, 545). This hostility is intensified by the fact that some view U.S. protection and support as indispensable to the survival of these authoritarian regimes. Thus attacking the United States is seen as an effective way of driving illegitimate rulers from power (Klare 2001, 76; Zunes 2002, 46–47; Anonymous 2004, 139; Benjamin and Simon 2005, 18–19).

A second important source of anti-American sentiment has been the presence of U.S. military forces in the region. This became an issue as early as the 1970s, with the arrival of growing numbers of defense-related personnel in Saudi Arabia. In the 1980s, the Egyptian government's decision to grant access to military facilities fueled anti-American feelings in that country (Acharya

1989, 31 and 106). But the issue was truly joined with the massive deployment of U.S. combat forces to Saudi Arabia in 1990 and 1991. The subsequent American military presence, which ended only in 2003, was perceived as a standing affront to Muslims in their own heartland and characterized as "the ultimate American sin" (Rouleau 2002, 77; J. Pollack 2003; Byman 2003, 144).[6]

Why has the U.S. military presence provoked such a strongly negative reaction? One reason is that, at least for critics of the al-Saud regime, it has been the most prominent symbol of American support for the government and its ties to the West (Zunes 2002, 65; Zepezauer 2003, 114). A second has been the concern of conservative religious authorities that the presence of so many Americans and their Western mores would liberalize and corrupt Saudi society (J. Pollack 2003). Largely for that reason, the Saudi government increasingly sought to minimize contact between U.S. military personnel and ordinary Saudis, concentrating the former on isolated bases and restricting their off-base movements. An even more commonly heard grievance was that the stationing of U.S. and other non-Muslim Western forces in Saudi Arabia, the location of Islam's holiest sites, constituted a religious offense. It involved trespassing on the heart of the Muslim holy land (Fuller and Lesser 1997, 46; Klare 2001, 54; Byman 2003, 144; Mead 2003). Indeed, such was the magnitude of the offense that it confirmed, for many, the long-standing belief that the United States was by nature the unalterable enemy of Islam and that the American presence was part of a larger Western design to dominate the whole of the Arab and Muslim worlds (Bergen 2001, 77–78; Benjamin and Simon 2002, 107).

Since the Gulf War, the U.S. military presence in Saudi Arabia, or what he has termed "the Land of the Two Holy Places," has been bin Laden's primary grievance against the United States (Gold 2003, 173; Bergen and Reynolds 2005). In reaction to the arrival of the American troops, he reportedly declared, "Never has Islam suffered a greater disaster" (Anonymous 2002, 115; see also Everest 2004, 209). Subsequently, this complaint has been at the heart of each of bin Laden's major anti-American pronouncements. In his August 1996 "Declaration of Jihad Against the Americans," for example, he described the U.S. "occupation" of Saudi Arabia as "the latest and greatest" Western transgression against Islam and the worst calamity since the death of Muhammad (Bergen 2001, 93–94; Benjamin and Simon 2002, 140–41; J. Pollack 2003). In a second "fatwa" against the United States ("Declaration of the World Islamic Front for Jihad Against the Jews and the Crusaders"), he equated the occupation with a declaration of war on God, Muhammad, and Muslims (Bergen 2001, 95–96; Benjamin and Simon 2002, 147–49; Coll 2004, 380–81).

The problem did not stop, however, with the mere presence of U.S. combat forces, which for many Saudis and Muslims was offensive enough. Since then, the hostility toward the United States has been greatly compounded by the series of military actions in which those forces have engaged. The 1991 Gulf War, subsequent U.S. efforts to enforce the UN sanctions and no-fly zones imposed on Iraq, and the ongoing Iraq War and occupation have all further inflamed the anti-Americanism that the initial deployment of American troops had stirred.

The troubles began almost right away with Operation Desert Storm, which commenced in January 1991, just five months after the first U.S. combat forces had arrived. For many Arabs and Muslims, the very act of launching an attack, even with UN authorization, was troubling. It marked the first time that the United States had waged war so directly on a Muslim country. And Iraq, as one of the most forceful advocates of Arab nationalism, was not just any Arab state. Even among the many Arabs and Muslims who opposed Iraq's conquest of Kuwait, the U.S.-led operation was seen as avoidable, unnecessary, and more of an excuse to consolidate American hegemony in the region than a genuine effort to resist aggression and uphold international law (Everest 2004, 209; Zunes 2002, 82 and 85). The majority of Islamists, who were more critical to begin with, "saw U.S. intervention as a continuation of colonial policies designed to rob Arabs and Muslims of their wealth, to foster the dismemberment of the Muslim peoples by maintaining their division into nation-states, and to destroy Arab power in order to maintain Israel's supremacy in the area" (Haddad 2003, 474).

Arabs and Muslims were also shocked by the devastating impact that the war had on Iraq's civilian population. The UN Security Council imposed comprehensive economic sanctions, including a ban on all trade, that caused food shortages. And coalition air strikes, most of which were conducted by American forces, went well beyond purely military targets. They also destroyed or severely damaged refineries and other oil facilities, rail and road bridges, and most of the country's electricity generating plants. The lack of power in turn disabled water pumping and sanitation systems where these were not directly affected by the bombing. A postwar study of the air campaign acknowledged that many targets were selected to amplify the economic and psychological effects of the economic sanctions and to do great harm to Iraq's ability to support itself as an industrial society. Although the most precise Iraqi figures put the number of civilian dead and wounded at less than twenty-three hundred and six thousand, respectively, the strategic bombing campaign produced a general dislocation of civilian life. There was little or no electricity or running water in Baghdad and Iraq's other major cities, and the residents faced the threat of cholera and typhoid epidemics as well as widespread dysentery and diarrhea as a result of the contamination of water supplies by untreated sewage. A UN report concluded that "most means of modern life [had] been destroyed or rendered tenuous" (Freedman and Karsh 1993, 321–22, 326, 329; Alnasrawi 2001, 208–10; Nagy 2001; Gordon 2002; Zunes 2002, 83–84 and 91; Everest 2004, 170–75).

For both of these reasons, U.S. prosecution of the war inflamed preexisting hatreds of the United States and created new ones in the Muslim world. "Even Saddam's most strident critics were offended at the level of overkill" (Zunes 2002, 83). The United States may have defeated Saddam Hussein's army and liberated Kuwait, but it now faced tens of millions of Arabs, both inside and outside Iraq, who were more hostile to America than they had previously been. From among such people Osama bin Laden later found many supporters and willing recruits (Zunes 2002, 85; Everest 2004, 209).

As if the military actions during the Gulf War were not enough, the conflict was followed by what was widely regarded as a prolonged series of further American insults to Arab and Muslim sensibilities. Even after the termination of combat operations, the United Nations maintained stringent economic sanctions and imposed a tough inspections regime in order to ensure that Iraq eliminated its weapons of mass destruction and complied with other requirements of the cease-fire agreement. In addition, the United States along with Britain and France established no-fly zones over northern and southern Iraq in which the use of fixed-wing aircraft was prohibited.

For several years, Iraq could sell no oil, and it could import only food and other humanitarian goods. Although the sanctions were gradually eased beginning in the mid-1990s and Iraq was allowed to export increasing amounts of oil and to buy an expanding range of nonmilitary items, living conditions for many Iraqis remained difficult or worse, as documented in a series of reports by the United Nations, non-governmental organizations, and others. A 1991 UN mission estimated the cost of restoring prewar conditions at $22 billion. Yet until the latter part of the decade, Iraq lacked the foreign currency to pay for needed imports, even food, and it was unable to obtain many of the spare parts required to repair damaged electrical power, water, and sewage treatment systems and other civilian infrastructure. Consequently, malnutrition and preventable diseases were widespread, with young children being especially hard hit. Estimates of the number of Iraqis who died prematurely as a result of these conditions have ranged from 250,000 to well over one million, the majority being under the age of eighteen (Alnasrawi 2001, 210–14; Gordon 2002; Zunes 2002, 90–92; Zepezauer 2003, 20; Everest 2004, 175–85).

Who was responsible for this human catastrophe? In the United States, it was common to pin the blame on Saddam Hussein. After all, had he not failed to comply fully with the disarmament demands of the UN Security Council? Did he not reject early UN offers to allow Iraq to sell oil to pay for needed imports? And was he not using Iraq's revenues to reward his supporters and secretly to acquire technology and materials for military purposes? But however great Saddam's culpability may have been, in the Middle East the United States was seen as the principal culprit. Washington was the leading advocate of maintaining tough sanctions, even as international support dwindled, and the chief enforcer. As a result, the sanctions resulted in widespread anger throughout the Arab and Muslim worlds, and their impact was frequently cited by bin Laden and other Islamic radicals.[7] As veteran Persian Gulf analyst F. Gregory Gause has concluded, "The sanctions policy only strengthen[ed] the belief that the United States is not opposed to Arab dictators per se, but to Arabs and Muslims in general" (Gause 2002, 41; see also Benjamin and Simon 2005, 33).

To make matters worse, the United States along with Britain conducted a number of air and missile attacks against Iraq to enforce the no-fly zones and to punish Iraq for its failure to cooperate with UN weapons inspectors, especially in the late 1990s. The most significant of these was Operation Desert Fox in December 1998, which involved the use of more than one thousand cruise missiles and laser-guided bombs over several days. But during the following months, U.S. and British aircraft bombed hundreds of additional targets. Although these strikes were more narrowly targeted against military installations than those during the Gulf War, they nevertheless produced further civilian casualties and stirred up yet more resentment in Arab and Muslim communities (Myers 1999; Zunes 2002, 88; Everest 2004, 202–3, 212; Ricks 2006, 19).

All in all, these U.S. policies have resulted in a more or less steadily rising tide of anti-Americanism on the Arabian Peninsula and elsewhere in the Islamic world, especially since 1990.[8] This sentiment has been manifested in public opinion, whether measured in formal surveys or through informal demonstrations on the street, and in the declarations of Islamic religious figures. In 1998, for example, the imam of the mosque dedicated to Muhammad in the holy city of Medina criticized the presence of American troops and called for their withdrawal, while groups of clerics in Afghanistan and Pakistan issued fatwas declaring jihad against the United States (Bergen 2001, 99–100).

Anti-Americanism has found its most virulent expression in the hostility of Osama bin Laden and his widespread popularity in the Muslim world. In the mid-1990s, bin Laden defined the expulsion of the Americans from Saudi Arabia as the overriding objective and effectively declared war against the United States (Ottaway and Kaiser 2002; Brisard 2002, 10; Zunes 2002, 65; Anonymous 2002, 228; Gause 2002, 39; Coll 2004, 380–81). In his 1996 declaration, he proclaimed that "warding off the American enemy is the top duty after faith and nothing should take priority over it" (Anonymous 2002, 53). In his 1998 fatwa, which has become perhaps the most famous of jihadist texts, he pronounced that killing "the Americans and their allies—civilians and military—is an individual duty for every Muslim who can do it in any country in which it is possible to do it" (Benjamin and Simon 2005, 34). To this end, bin Laden's al Qaeda organization carried out a series of attacks against American targets, culminating in the shocking events of September 11, 2001. Among these operations were the simultaneous bombings of the U.S. embassies in Kenya and Tanzania on August 8, 1998, the eighth anniversary of the arrival of American combat forces in Saudi Arabia. And he has inspired what appears to be a growing number of unaffiliated radical Islamists to strike at Americans and other Westerners, both before and after the destruction of the World Trade Center.[9]

Empowering Hostile Actors

The third mechanism by which U.S. policy in response to foreign oil dependence has inadvertently increased the threat to the United States and its interests is by unintentionally empowering and enabling actual or potential enemies. One example of this pattern is Iran, where the Islamic Republic inherited all of the advanced U.S. weaponry that had been acquired by the shah. During the 1980s, the Iranian Air Force was seen as posing a serious threat to Saudi Arabia and its oil facilities and was cited by U.S. officials as a principal justification for helping the Saudis to upgrade their air defenses. In that case, however, the magnitude of the threat was mitigated by the fact that Iran had not yet fully mastered some of the weapons systems, and it could obtain the spare parts needed to keep them running only from the United States. In at least two other instances, however, U.S. assistance to nominally friendly actors helped to lay the groundwork for serious threats with which the United States would later have to contend.

U.S. Assistance to Iraq in the 1980s

One episode involves Iraq in the 1980s. In trying to build up the country as a bulwark against Iran, the United States provided Saddam Hussein's regime with technologies and materials that would make it a more formidable foe in the future. Beginning in 1985, the Reagan administration began to issue licenses for the export to Iraq of high-tech civilian goods that could potentially be used for military purposes. During the next five years, the Department of Commerce approved hundreds of license applications and denied very few. Many of the exported items were used, however, to advance Iraq's unconventional weapons programs (Waas 1991, 86–87; Jentleson 1994, 62, 88, 118–19; K. Pollack 2002, 19; Zunes 2002, 55). Indeed, according to what is perhaps the most comprehensive collection of data on the subject, the Reagan and Bush administrations approved dozens of export licenses that allowed American and foreign firms to ship sophisticated U.S. dual-use equipment to weapons factories controlled by Iraq's Ministry of Industry and Military Industrialization (MIMI) that Washington knew were involved in Iraq's clandestine weapons of mass destruction and missile programs (Hurd 2000).

Perhaps the biggest inadvertent U.S. contribution to the Iraqi threat was in the area of biological and chemical weapons. A 1994 Senate investigation identified dozens of biological materials that were shipped to Iraq between 1985 and 1990 by private American suppliers pursuant to application and licensing by the Commerce Department. Among them were highly toxic bacteria and viruses, such as those responsible for anthrax, botulism, tetanus, bubonic plague, and West Nile disease. Typically, these microorganisms were not attenuated or weakened and thus were capable of reproduction, and some were identical to those recovered later by UN weapons inspectors from Iraq's biological weapons program (Jentleson 1994, 89; Blum 1998; Hurd 2000; Dobbs 2002). During the same period, U.S. businesses also supplied Iraq with precursor chemicals necessary for the manufacture of nerve gas. And the Commerce

Department approved the export of insecticides to Iraq, despite widespread suspicions that they were being used for chemical warfare (Waas 1991, 91; Dobbs 2002; Everest 2004, 102).

In addition, U.S. goods were used to advance Iraq's nuclear weapons and long-range ballistic missile programs. According to a 1991 report by the House Committee on Government Operations, the Commerce Department authorized the sale of computer equipment that went directly to an Iraqi research center that was linked with ballistic missile development. Subsequent weapons inspections reportedly found that 40 percent of the equipment at the center had originally come from the United States. Other approved exports, which went to Iraq's medium-range SCUD missile program procurement agency, allowed Iraq to extend the range of the missile far enough to hit targets in Saudi Arabia and Israel (Hurd 2000).

Islamist Jihadists: Blowback from U.S. Support for the Mujahideen in Afghanistan

A second example of how U.S. policies in response to foreign oil dependence have helped to empower potentially hostile actors concerns the unintended consequences of American assistance to the Afghan resistance during the 1980s. Inadvertently, the CIA "helped to train and fund what eventually became an international network of highly disciplined and effective Islamic militants—and a new breed of terrorists as well" (Weaver 1996, 26; see also Danner 2005, 96). In what has been termed "one of the cruelist ironies of the cold war" (Little 2002, 316), some of the same fighters who used U.S. arms and funds to defeat the Soviets in the 1980s later turned against the United States and led the most important opposition to it after the mid-1990s (J. Scott 1996, 79; Kolko 2002, 45). Among these militants was Osama bin Laden. It was during this period, as part of the U.S.-backed war effort, that he received the training and made the contacts that eventually led to the formation of the al Qaeda network in the early 1990s (Zunes 2002, 176; Kolko 2002, 16).

As Peter Bergen, a leading authority on al Qaeda, cautions, it may be too much to claim that bin Laden and the future Islamic jihadists were American creations. In Bergen's view, the real source of the problem was insufficient U.S. oversight of and control over the use of its funds (Bergen 2001, 63, 67). During the conflict, the CIA allowed Pakistan to determine which of the various Afghan factions would receive assistance, and the Pakistani leadership exhibited a distinct preference for the most conservative resistance groups. As a result, anti-Western fundamentalists received between two-thirds and three-quarters of all the external funds. By the most cautious estimates, a total of more than $1 billion in weapons and other aid, including $600 million from the United States, went to the party headed by Gulbuddin Hekmatyar, an Islamist zealot who later sided with Iraq during the Gulf War. Thus the groups that received the bulk of U.S. funding were as hostile to the United States as they were to the Soviet Union (Weiner 1994, 54; J. Scott 1996, 76; Yousaf and Adkin 2001, 105; Bergen 2001, 68).

According to various estimates, the mujahideen received enough money to train and equip at least eighty thousand fighters, and twenty-five thousand or so non-Afghan Islamic militants from some thirty countries fought in the war. Therefore, after the CIA funding ended, tens of thousands of well-trained and well-armed Arab and other fighters were available for new jihads, and many of them harbored an intense hatred of the United States (Weaver 1995, 42, 44; Weinbaum 2003, 449). To make matters worse, Afghanistan remained an international center for the training and indoctrination of terrorists. In the five years after the Soviets withdrew, tens of thousands of "Islamic radicals, outcasts, visionaries and gunmen from some 40 nations" came there to learn the lessons of jihad (Weiner 1994, 53–54). Thus it seems reasonable to conclude that the United States helped to create the conditions in which al Qaeda and a broader transnational force of Arab militants could flourish (Bergen 2001, 63, 67, 75; G. Friedman 2004, 59).

Putting It All Together: The Iraq War

The 2003 invasion and subsequent occupation of Iraq and their direct human and financial costs can be attributed, at least in part, to U.S. foreign oil dependence (see Chapter 6). Insofar as this is the case, we must also consider the unintended consequences of the conflict. And with the possible exception of the decision to station U.S. forces in the Arabian Peninsula during the 1990s and early 2000s, perhaps no other American policy or action in the Persian Gulf—or elsewhere, for that matter—has done as much to increase the threat to the United States. The war has only intensified anti-American sentiments in the Muslim world, and it has created opportunities for the strengthening of radical Islamic forces bent on inflicting as much damage as possible on the United States. As a former senior intelligence official has written, "There is nothing bin Laden could have hoped for more than the American invasion and occupation of Iraq. The invasion of Iraq is Osama bin Laden's gift from America" (Anonymous 2004, 212).

The U.S. invasion of Iraq has resulted in a new low in attitudes toward the United States in the Arab and Muslim worlds and a further radicalization of Muslim sentiment. As a mid-2003 survey concluded, "The bottom has fallen out of support for America in most of the Muslim world. Negative views of the U.S. among Muslims, which had been largely limited to countries in the Middle East, have spread to Muslim populations in Indonesia and Nigeria."[10] Just before the outbreak of the war, bin Laden warned that the United States was preparing to "occupy a former capital of Islam, loot Muslims' wealth, and install an agent government which would be a satellite for its masters in Washington and Tel Aviv" (Benjamin and Simon 2005, 33). And this is how the operation was indeed perceived in large parts of the Muslim world. As one American expert on Arab politics has noted, "The Iraq war has convinced 'many Muslims around the world, perhaps a majority, that the war on terrorism is in fact a war against Islam.'"[11]

As a result, the war prompted a number of Muslim clerics to issue fatwas calling for a defensive jihad against the U.S.-led invaders. One authority has characterized them as equally or even more virulent than the fatwas that greeted the 1979 Soviet invasion of Afghanistan. Even religious leaders who had denounced bin Laden and condemned the attacks of September 11, 2001, gave their blessing to those who wished to fight against the occupation of Iraq (Anonymous 2004, 14, 182; Bergen and Reynolds 2005).

Although it is difficult to detail the effects that the war has had in various countries, it has clearly produced a strong negative reaction in Saudi Arabia. A July 2003 poll found that 70 percent of Saudi respondents held an unfavorable view of the American people, up from 51 percent just the year before (J. Pollack 2003). A 2005 study revealed that of the hundreds of Saudis who had joined the insurgency in Iraq, few had shown signs of militancy or been terrorist sympathizers before the war. Most were motivated by "revulsion at the idea of an Arab land being occupied by a non-Arab country" and "were radicalized almost exclusively by the coalition invasion" (Evans 2005; see also Benjamin and Simon 2005, 39).

Thus the war has created fertile ground for radicalizing ever more Muslims and enlisting them in a jihad against the United States (*New York Times* 2006). In the view of former NSC counterterrorism officials Daniel Benjamin and Steven Simon, "America's image in the Muslim world has never been more battered, and the jihadist claim that the United States seeks to oppress Muslims has never seemed more plausible" (Benjamin and Simon 2005, xiv). As al Qaeda expert Bergen has noted, sadness and anger about Iraq, even among moderate Muslims, is being harnessed and exploited by terrorist and extremist groups worldwide to grow in strength, size, and influence (Bergen 2004). Even then CIA director Porter Goss admitted in 2005 that "Islamic extremists are exploiting the Iraqi conflict to recruit new anti-U.S. jihadists."[12]

Not only have the war and occupation provided another justification for striking the United States, but they have also created new opportunities for preparing future attacks. As a result of the elimination of the repressive Baathist regime and the breakdown of central authority, Iraq has become open to terrorists in ways and to an extent that they could previously only dream of (Bergen 2004; Reuter 2004, 45–46). As Benjamin and Simon have argued, "The new battlefield that is Iraq has given the radicals a place to train, experiment with tactics, and select the most capable fighters. They have acquired access to almost limitless caches of arms, and in the ungovernable regions of the country they have gained a new sanctuary in which to plan attacks."[13] Indeed, the former National Security Council officials conclude, "The terrorists have found in Iraq a better sanctuary, training ground, and laboratory than they ever had in Afghanistan" (Benjamin and Simon 2005, xiv). Moreover, as Mark Danner has noted, Iraq has provided a televised stage from which the struggle of radical Islam against the "crusader forces" can be broadcast throughout the Islamic world (Danner 2005).

Such a development would be bad enough if the United States possessed unlimited resources with which to prosecute the "global war on terrorism." But its resources are finite and some particularly valuable military and intelligence assets for counterterrorism operations are in short supply. Thus, to make matters worse, the war in Iraq resulted in the diversion of scarce resources and political attention away from Afghanistan and the hunt for bin Laden. By early 2002, many critical assets were already being transferred from Central Asia for operations in and around Iraq. According to Bergen, substantial numbers of Arabic speakers at the CIA and National Security Agency were directed to focus on Iraq rather than the destruction of al Qaeda, and Special Operations Forces were pulled out of Afghanistan in the spring of 2002 to search for Scud missiles in western Iraq (Bergen 2004; see also Benjamin and Simon 2005, 175–77). As of mid-2007, bin Laden remains at large, and al Qaeda and the Taliban appear to be enjoying a resurgence in Afghanistan.

In all these ways, then, the war and occupation of Iraq have resulted in an increase in the terrorist threat to the United States. By mid-2004, according to Bergen, a consensus was already emerging among a wide range of intelligence and counterterrorism officials that the invasion had not only failed to help the war on terrorism but also represented a substantial setback (Bergen 2004). America's actions in Iraq, write Benjamin and Simon, have "provided the ideological fuel and the weaponry for a vastly expanded terrorist campaign" (Benjamin and Simon 2005, 46). Indeed, they have dramatically reshaped and energized the jihad in ways that have surprised even those who warned of the negative consequences of invasion (Benjamin and Simon 2005, 31). Foreign volunteers fighting U.S. troops in Iraq today will look for new targets around the world after the war ends (Bergen 2004), while "what had been a relatively small conspiratorial organization has mutated into a worldwide political movement, with thousands of followers eager to adopt its methods and advance its aims" (Danner 2005). Thus, Bergen concluded, "The current war in Iraq will generate a ferocious blowback of its own, which—as a recent declassified CIA assessment predicts—could be longer and more powerful than that from Afghanistan." As evidence of this troubling prospect, he noted that the number of significant terrorist attacks reached a two-decade high in 2003 and then, astonishingly, tripled in 2004 (Bergen 2004). Nor did the situation improve over the following years. An April 2006 National Intelligence Estimate (NIE) representing the consensus view of sixteen U.S. intelligence services also found that the American actions in Iraq had helped spawn a new generation of Islamic radicalism. It stated, according to one U.S. intelligence official, "that the Iraq war has made the overall terrorism problem worse" (Mazzetti 2006).

Conclusion

Since the 1970s, the United States has adopted a range of foreign and military policies intended to help alleviate the economic problems posed by foreign oil dependence. These policies have imposed substantial costs, some quantifiable and some not, of which their architects were generally aware or could have been expected to anticipate. In addition, however, these policies have had considerable unintended consequences.

It is not possible to put a price tag on these unexpected costs. But the overall impact has been to reduce U.S. security, perhaps significantly. American policies have done so in at least three ways, especially in the Persian Gulf. They have sometimes weakened regimes, notably in Iran under the shah and Saudi Arabia, on which the United States has relied to protect American interests. They have fomented anti-Americanism in Iran, Arabia, and the broader Islamic world, helping to turn onetime allies such as Iran into implacable opponents. And in at least a few cases, they have enhanced the ability of actual or potential adversaries, notably Iraq and Islamic jihadists, to threaten the United States and its interests. In sum, U.S. foreign and military policy toward the Persian Gulf has left a costly legacy with which the United States will have to contend for some time.

8 Conclusion

Reducing the Costs of U.S. Foreign Oil Dependence

> By applying the talent and technology of America, this country can . . .
> move beyond a petroleum-based economy, and make our dependence
> on Middle Eastern oil a thing of the past.
> *President George W. Bush, January 31, 2006*

THE UNITED STATES has long been dependent on foreign oil, certainly since it became a net importer in the late 1940s. For some
two decades thereafter, however, U.S. foreign oil dependence had few, if any,
negative consequences. In the event of a supply disruption anywhere in the
world, the United States and friendly oil producing states were able to increase
their output and to redirect available supplies rapidly enough to prevent shortages and sharp price increases both in the United States and elsewhere. Of
greater concern was the fact that abundant cheap oil from abroad depressed
prices, thereby hurting U.S. domestic producers.

The generally benign character of U.S. foreign oil dependence came to an
end in the late 1960s and early 1970s. Rapidly rising global demand began to
outstrip supply, and American producers were forced to pump oil as fast as
they could, leaving no surplus production capacity in the United States. Since
then, foreign oil dependence has imposed substantial economic costs and
risks. American consumers have often had to pay significantly higher prices
on average for oil and petroleum products than they had been accustomed to
during the first decades of the postwar era, and the U.S. economy has been
subject to periodic supply disruptions and price shocks.

In response, the United States has pursued a number of policies both at
home and abroad intended to reduce the economic costs and risks of foreign
oil dependence. Overall, these policy responses have helped to an extent. But

they have imposed additional costs of their own, and some of these further costs have been substantial.

Exactly what, in sum, have been the costs of U.S. foreign oil dependence? How large are these costs likely to be in the future, assuming no fundamental reorientation of American policy? And what can be done to reduce them?

The Costs of U.S. Foreign Oil Dependence: A Summary

Past Costs

The costs of U.S. foreign oil dependence can be grouped into two broad categories: (1) the actual and potential economic costs, and (2) the costs of the various policies that have been adopted in order to reduce these economic costs and risks. Both types of costs have been substantial (see Table 8.1).

The actual and potential economic costs of U.S. foreign oil dependence can take two general forms. Some are the routine and recurring costs associated with paying for oil imports, such as the transfer of wealth abroad and a decrease in potential domestic economic output. Altogether, by one estimate, Americans sent more than $2 trillion abroad for oil purchases between the mid-1970s and the early 2000s (Lovins et al. 2004, 15). Of this amount, according to several other calculations, significantly more than $1 trillion represented a net transfer of wealth to foreign oil producers. This wealth transfer and higher-than-competitive prices resulted in a loss of economic output (GDP) amounting to more than $1 trillion dollars, and possibly two to three times that amount. Given recent high oil prices, moreover, these figures are rapidly growing.

Other economic costs have resulted from unexpected oil supply disruptions and accompanying price increases. Estimates for the total macroeconomic adjustment costs imposed by oil shocks for the period 1970–2000 have ranged from one to several trillion dollars. The lion's share of these costs, however, were incurred in the 1970s and early 1980s following the two oil crises of that decade.

In view of the magnitude of these economic costs and risks, the United States has over the years adopted a number of policies intended to reduce them. A large and diverse set of measures has aimed at limiting oil imports and overall oil consumption. These have included, at various times, a federal

TABLE 8.1 Benefits and Costs of U.S. Foreign Oil Dependence

	Benefits	Costs
Import and Market Dependence	Lower oil prices Extended life of U.S. oil reserves	Wealth transfers abroad: >$1 trillion Loss of potential GDP: >$1 trillion Costs of oil shocks: >$1 trillion Total: approx. $8 trillion (1970–1999) in 2005 dollars
Policy Responses		
Economic Policies 1) CAFE standards	Lower U.S. gasoline consumption (25%)	<$1 billion per year
2) SPR	Insurance against oil shocks	$1–$5 billion per year

Foreign and Military Policies	Increased foreign oil production/lower oil prices
	
	Greater oil market stability/ less volatile prices
	
	Greater influence over oil producers
		Foreign Policy Costs:
		Outlays for economic and military assistance
		Reduced diplomatic flexibility
		Conflicts with other U.S. foreign policy objectives
		
		Military Policy Costs:
		Additional dedicated military capabilities
		Foreign facilities
		Overseas deployments
		U.S.-based combat forces and strategic lift
		    1980s: $28–36 billion per year
		    1990s: $30–51 billion per year
		Major military operations
		
		Negative Unintended Consequences:
		Undermining friends/creating instability
		Making enemies/fomenting anti-Americanism
		Empowering hostile actors

speed limit, taxes on vehicles with low gas mileage, funding for mass transit, the promotion of synthetic fuels, subsidies for the production and use of alcohol transportation fuels, tax deductions for alternative fuel and hybrid vehicles, incentives for domestic oil production, and investment in energy research and development. Each of these measures, however, has been either short-lived or modest in nature. For example, the U.S. government has never imposed a substantial gasoline tax or oil import fee, and it has never invested heavily in mass transit for the purpose of limiting energy demand in the transportation sector. Since the early 1980s, moreover, the use of economic instruments to reduce foreign oil dependence has rarely, if ever, assumed a high priority. Instead, U.S. policy has tended to rely primarily on market forces to determine the production and allocation of energy resources.

The principal exception to this pattern and the measure that has had by far the biggest impact was the establishment of fuel economy standards for passenger cars and light trucks, which account for most of the vehicles sold in the United States and more than 60 percent of all energy use in the transportation sector. Thanks at least in part to the Corporate Average Fuel Economy (CAFE) program, fuel consumption by such light-duty vehicles is roughly one-third lower than it would have been had fuel economy not improved since 1975. In 2000, this reduction translated into an estimated annual savings of 43 billion gallons of gasoline, or more than 3.6 percent of global oil demand.[1] Just as notably, these gains were achieved at only a small cost to vehicle manufacturers and purchasers, most likely far less than $1 billion per year in the late 1970s and 1980s. Until the mid-2000s, however, the CAFE standards were not significantly raised, and overall fuel economy has actually declined as less fuel-efficient light trucks have captured a growing share of the market.

Other U.S. policies have had the goal of mitigating the impact of oil supply disruptions and price shocks independently of any reductions in oil imports and consumption that might be achieved. These have included the maintenance of price controls through the 1970s, the creation of the Strategic Petroleum Reserve (SPR), and the development of an international emergency oil sharing system through the International Energy Agency (IEA). Arguably, the most successful of these measures has been the SPR. Although rarely used, it has provided a good deal of insurance against supply disruptions at an average annual cost of approximately one billion to at most several billion dollars in federal outlays. Even the SPR, however, has not been significantly modified to reflect changes in the international oil market, raising the risk that it will not be adequate to deal with future crises.

The most substantial U.S. responses to the economic costs and risks of foreign oil dependence have taken the form of foreign and military policies toward actual or potential oil producing regions and states. These policies have been intended to reduce the size and risk of potential oil supply disruptions and price shocks and, more generally, to ensure reliable access to foreign oil supplies at reasonable prices for the United States and its economic and security partners. Overall, these external policies appear to have enjoyed at least some success in helping to stabilize world oil supplies. Certainly, the last two and a half decades have seen nothing like the oil shocks of the 1970s, although this favorable record can also be attributed at least in part to changes in the global oil market.

Nevertheless, these foreign and military policies have also imposed substantial costs, which are much larger than most people have realized. American diplomacy and various forms of military and economic assistance aimed at strengthening and influencing the policies of oil producing states have involved additional financial expenditures. Perhaps even more important, U.S. foreign policy has also entailed numerous intangible costs. These have included reduced freedom of action and a reluctance to pursue other valued foreign policy goals, such as the promotion of democracy, the protection of human rights, good governance, and economic development, where they have conflicted with oil-related interests. The costs have also taken the form of increased entanglement, or risk thereof, in local and regional conflicts. Such costs have been most prominent in the Persian Gulf, but they have been increasingly present in other regions, such as the Gulf of Guinea and the Caspian Sea (see Chapter 5).

U.S. military policies undertaken in response to foreign oil dependence have made an even larger dent in the federal budget. The United States has spent on the order of several billions of dollars per year on additional military capabilities and routine peacetime operations that have been directly, and often exclusively, associated with the defense of American oil interests in the Persian Gulf. To these marginal costs must be added a share of the costs of the U.S.-based general purpose forces and strategic lift, the maintenance and augmentation of which has been increasingly justified in terms of Persian Gulf contingencies. These additional costs amounted to roughly $28–36 billion per year in the 1980s and $30–51 billion per year in the 1990s and early 2000s (in 2006 dollars). Not to be overlooked are the escalating costs of major U.S. combat operations in the region since the 1980s, which have culminated in the ongoing war in Iraq (see Chapter 6).

It is also important to include in any comprehensive cost accounting the many unintended consequences of these external policies. They have sometimes weakened regimes, notably in Iran under the shah and in Saudi Arabia, on which the United States has relied to protect American oil interests. They have fomented anti-Americanism in Iran, Arabia, and the broader Islamic world, helping to turn onetime partners such as Iran into implacable foes. And, in at least a few cases, they have enhanced the ability of actual or potential adversaries, notably Iraq and Islamic jihadists, to threaten the United States and its interests. The overall effect has been to increase the magnitude of the threats to U.S. interests, oil and otherwise, and to reduce the security of the United States itself (see Chapter 7).

Overall, it would appear that the policies that the United States has adopted in response to foreign oil dependence have been relatively cost-ineffective. Successive U.S. administrations have tended to neglect the opportunities at home to reduce the economic costs and risks of foreign oil dependence by limiting demand. This neglect is suggested by comparing oil consumption in the United States with that in other advanced, industrialized countries, where oil accounts for a comparable percentage of total energy use. We find that U.S. oil intensity, the amount of oil used for every dollar of GDP, ranges from 25 to 70 percent higher than in similar countries such as Britain, France, Germany, and Japan, and that American oil consumption per capita is more than double that in all but Japan, which depends on oil to meet a significantly higher percentage of its energy needs.

Instead, the United States has emphasized relatively costly foreign and military policies intended to prevent oil shocks by promoting the development of new sources of foreign oil, protecting existing supplies, and ensuring Western access to them both. Yet this strategy has proved to be not only highly expensive but also largely unsuccessful. Three decades after the first oil shock of 1973, we find that the international situation is not much improved. The world oil market is tight and likely to remain so for the foreseeable future. Oil prices have recently flirted with the record highs of the early 1980s. And the risk of potentially costly supply disruptions is as great as it has been in many years.

Future Costs

One cannot be certain what the future costs to the United States of foreign oil dependence will be. But assuming no fundamental changes occur in the world political economy of oil or in U.S. policy responses, they are likely to remain high and will probably rise.

There are good reasons to expect that the recurring economic costs to the United States will only increase in future years. First, the U.S. government's own Energy Information Administration (EIA) projects that imports of oil and petroleum products will rise substantially from the current level of more than twelve million barrels of oil per day (MBD) to somewhere between seventeen and twenty-one MBD during the next two and a half decades. Domestic production is projected to decline while consumption is expected to increase, driven largely by rising demand in the transportation sector. By 2030, imports will account for approximately two-thirds of oil use in the United States.

At the same time, prices are likely to remain high, or at least well above historical averages. The basic problem is that global production is likely to have difficulty keeping up with rising demand, resulting in a tight market and continued upward pressure on prices. Thus, using EIA projections for imports and assuming that prices average $50 per barrel, the United States will spend more than $5 trillion dollars on imports in the next two decades.[2]

The costs of future oil shocks are much more difficult to estimate. Economists have calculated the economic costs of a hypothetical supply disruption, which could run in the hundreds of billions of dollars depending on its size and length. But tremendous uncertainty necessarily attends any attempt to predict the magnitude, likelihood, and duration of supply disruptions.

That said, the economic costs of oil shocks can be expected to be at least as high as at any time in the past two and a half decades. Global oil production is becoming increasingly concentrated in the Persian Gulf and the developing world more generally. The EIA has projected that the Persian Gulf's share of world oil production alone will rise to nearly 35 percent in 2025, and that the share of global oil exports coming from the Gulf will reach 66 percent and possibly as high as 76 percent. Yet many of the leading current and future oil exporting countries and regions are characterized by a significant degree of instability, and this situation seems unlikely to improve in the near future, if at all. As a result, the risk of an oil supply disruption is significant and may be increasing.

At the same time, the world's ability to cope with a major supply disruption may be no better and possibly worse than at any time since the early 1980s. On the positive side, the United States and several other countries have established strategic petroleum reserves, and world oil markets have become much more flexible, allowing supplies to be quickly redistributed to where they are most needed, albeit at the cost of potentially higher prices. Rather, the problem lies in the current and likely future lack of a significant amount of spare production capacity that could be drawn on to replace lost output for a prolonged period. A supply disruption of just four MBD, or roughly 5 percent of current global output, could exhaust more than half of the SPR in just three months, assuming no significant reduction in demand.

The most costly U.S. policy responses to foreign oil dependence have taken the form of foreign and military policies toward actual and potential oil producing regions. What these policies—and their costs—will be even just a few years out is extremely difficult to predict. As recently as 2000, who would have anticipated that, in less than three years, the United States would embark on an expensive military campaign in Iraq that can be attributed in no small part to U.S. foreign oil dependence?

Nevertheless, barring a drastic change in U.S. policies, one can also expect with some confidence these costs to remain high and possibly to rise. The trend of the past two decades has been one of growing American involvement and intervention in distant oil producing regions, including the Persian Gulf, the Caspian Sea, and the Gulf of Guinea. To maintain our access to oil, Michael Klare has argued, "We will have to crawl into bed with some of the world's most corrupt and despotic leaders—plying them with ever more arms, military training, technical assistance, diplomatic support, and White House access while ignoring their contempt for democracy and their egregious human rights violations" (Klare 2004a, 183). Likewise, as more and more oil comes from unstable regions and countries, it seems reasonable to expect that American armed forces will be used increasingly to protect foreign oil fields and supply routes. In Klare's provocative words, the U.S. military is becoming a "global oil-protection service" (Klare 2004a, 6–7). Yet U.S. support for unpopular authoritarian regimes and, in some places, an American military presence will continue to engender hostility toward the United States and, especially in the Persian Gulf, to inspire terrorist attacks against American targets.

Thus far, this analysis has assumed that global oil production will continue to grow in tandem with rising demand, even if higher prices are required to stimulate the necessary further investment. But this may not be the case. A growing chorus of voices has argued that total world oil output may soon reach its historic peak and then begin to decline, even as the need for energy, especially in developing countries, accelerates (for example, Deffeyes 2001; Roberts 2004; Goodstein 2004). If this contention is true, then the various costs of foreign oil dependence are sure to be only greater. Prices will rise faster and higher than have been projected. As the supply of oil begins to dry up, moreover, the competition for what remains will intensify, resulting in an increased likelihood of disruptions and higher price volatility (Klare 2004a, 185). In turn, we might expect to see an even greater imperative to use U.S. foreign and military policy instruments to prevent disruptions and to guarantee access to oil supplies and a further rise in their attendant costs.

To make matters worse, the rising costs of foreign oil dependence may be joined by an additional set of costs associated with imports of natural gas. The international trade in natural gas is still small compared with that in oil and petroleum products, but it is rapidly growing. The EIA expects that the mature market economies will rely on imports to meet more than one-third of their natural gas consumption in 2030, up from just 15 percent in 2002, and much of this growth will occur in the United States (EIA 2005c, 38; EIA 2006c, 40). As recently as 2005, the EIA projected that U.S. imports would rise from 3.24 trillion cubic feet (tcf) in 2003 to 8.66 tcf in 2025. As a share of U.S. consumption, natural gas imports would increase from 15 to 30 percent during the same time period (EIA 2005a, 159, tab. A13).

At the same time, a growing fraction of the natural gas trade will consist of liquified natural gas (LNG). After increasing by nearly 8 percent per year since 1980, LNG imports and exports already account for more than one-third of all internationally traded natural gas (Kenderdine and Moniz 2005, 441; BP 2006). Currently, most U.S. natural gas imports come from Canada via secure pipelines. But the EIA has projected that LNG will account for approximately three-quarters of all U.S. natural gas imports—and more than 20 percent of U.S. natural gas consumption—by 2025 or 2030 (EIA 2005a, 159, tab. A13; EIA 2006a, 155). And energy expert Daniel Yergin has predicted that the share of total U.S. demand met by imported LNG could rise to as high as 25 to 30 percent (Yergin 2005, 59).

As a world market in LNG develops, it will be increasingly subject to many of the same vicissitudes as the world oil market (Kenderdine and Moniz 2005, 441). Almost 60 percent of world reserves of natural gas is concentrated in just three countries: Russia (27.5 percent), Iran (16 percent), and Qatar (15 percent). Of the remaining 40 percent, nearly one-fourth is located in other Persian Gulf countries and another quarter lies in Nigeria, Venezuela, and the Caspian Sea region (EIA 2006c, 39). Likewise, as U.S. dependence on natural gas imports, and especially on less secure LNG from more distant regions, grows, it can be expected to impose ever greater economic costs and risks and to elicit policy responses similar to those prompted in the past by foreign oil dependence.

How to Reduce the Costs of Foreign Oil Dependence

Arguably, the costs of U.S. foreign oil dependence and the resulting policy responses have been substantial. Moreover, the costs are likely to continue to be high, if not higher, should the United States remain on its present course. What, if anything, can be done to reduce them?

Clearly, the United States has little or no control over some features of the current situation. Barring a global recession that causes a significant reduction in demand, the world oil market will continue to be tight. As long as the market remains tight, there will be upward pressure on prices. Likewise, the United States can do little about instability in a number of important oil producing countries and regions. And as long as instability persists and supplies are susceptible to disruptions, oil prices will remain volatile and the market will be prone to occasional shocks.

Nevertheless, the United States could take a number of steps to reduce the costs of foreign oil dependence and of its past policy responses. These potential measures can be grouped into three broad categories. First, the United States could make renewed efforts to reduce oil consumption and, indirectly, its oil imports from abroad. Doing so would reduce both the recurring economic costs of foreign oil dependence as well as the potential costs of future supply disruptions and price shocks. Second, the United States could increase its capacity to mitigate, if not neutralize, the impact of future oil shocks. Third, it could modify its foreign and military policies toward oil producing regions with an eye toward ensuring their cost-effectiveness. Since these external policies have been the most costly of all the responses pursued by successive administrations, modifications in them to remove elements that were counterproductive or unnecessary to enhance oil security or to bring the costs in line with the benefits could yield the largest savings.

Before proceeding, it is important to emphasize that my intention is not to prescribe a particular set of policies and policy changes. That task would require a book of its own. Rather, my goal is to suggest the availability of cost-effective means of reducing the costs of U.S. foreign oil dependence and to lay out the major options.

I should note, moreover, that the focus here is on measures that the United States can take by itself, not what it might or should try to get other countries to do. Certainly, the potential for international cooperation is far from exhausted. Much is likely to be gained through concerted efforts to help and encourage others to increase their energy efficiency and reduce oil consumption, to enlarge their strategic stocks and improve the coordination of their use, to strengthen their capabilities for protecting energy supplies and transit routes, and to make the most use of foreign investment and technological advances so as to maximize output in producer countries. But the United States cannot dictate the pacing or control the outcomes of such efforts. As the single largest and most influential political, economic, and military actor in the world oil market, however, what the United States is willing to do by itself will have the largest impact both on its own fortunes and that of other actors. And such U.S. leadership may be necessary to provide the impetus for effective collective action.

Reducing (Foreign) Oil Dependence

Determining the Appropriate Goal

The most straightforward way to reduce the costs of foreign oil dependence is to reduce the level of foreign oil dependence itself. U.S. foreign oil dependence takes several forms: import dependence, market dependence, and indirect dependence by way of the import and market dependence of the principal economic and security partners of the United States. The United States can do little by itself to reduce the latter. To do so would require either inducing its partners to reduce significantly their own direct dependence on foreign oil or to reduce U.S. economic and security ties with those countries so that the United States would be less vulnerable to adverse economic developments within them. Needless to say, neither of these approaches is a realistic option. A number of America's partners are already less dependent on foreign oil than is the United States itself. Likewise, reducing U.S. market dependence is virtually out of the question. Delinking or buffering the American markets for crude oil and petroleum products from the corresponding world markets would be difficult, and as the negative consequences of price controls in the 1970s suggest, the costs could well exceed the benefits.

That would seem to leave only one other option: reducing import dependence. Given the current high and growing level of U.S. imports of crude oil and petroleum products, the United States is almost certain to remain a substantial net importer for the foreseeable future. But the greater the level of imports, the greater the potential for reducing them, as there is no absolute reason why they must remain as high as they are. And a lower level of petroleum imports would, at a minimum, reduce the recurring economic costs of foreign oil dependence—the transfer of wealth abroad and losses in potential gross domestic product.

One frequently suggested approach to cutting imports is to increase the level of oil production in the United States. Indeed, reducing U.S. foreign oil dependence has been a principal justification used by proponents of lifting restrictions on offshore drilling and opening up the Arctic National Wildlife Refuge (ANWR) and other federal lands to oil production. But even an all-out effort to raise domestic output will not make a substantial difference. In the first place, the potential is quite limited. According to several recent estimates, increasing access to all possible reserves would result in at most two to three MBD in additional production, and then only when the new Alaskan production was at its temporary peak (Banerjee 2004; Grumet 2006, 29; ESLC 2006, 48–50; Deutsch and Schlesinger 2006, 39).

In addition, short of the elimination of all imports and the effective isolation of the U.S. oil market, there are sharp limits to how much increased production and concomitantly lower imports alone could reduce the economic costs and risks of U.S. foreign oil dependence. As long as the United States remains a large oil consumer and as long as the prices of oil and petroleum products are ultimately set on world markets, the U.S. economy will be hobbled by high prices and susceptible to the negative consequences of oil supply disruptions, wherever they may occur. As one expert has written, "Our nation's economic vulnerability to oil price shocks is largely a function of how much oil we use and not how much we produce."[3] Thus the most effective way to reduce the economic costs and risks of foreign oil dependence is to reduce U.S. oil dependence more generally, regardless of its source. As a recent report on the subject noted, "in a global market, the benefits of each barrel of increased domestic production are shared by all consumers in all nations through a lower equilibrium price, whereas the benefits of each barrel of reduced consumption accrue fully to those who have lessened their oil use."[4]

Reducing U.S. oil dependence across the board could have a number of economic benefits (see also Alm, Colglazier, and Kates-Garnick 1981, 316). First, it would most likely result in a decline in American imports of oil and petroleum products, since not all of the reduction in demand would be met by a drop in domestic production. Second, it could help to bring down prices, at least temporarily. As by far the largest aggregate consumer of oil and petroleum products, the United States more than any other country determines the prices on world markets. Other things being equal, a decline in U.S. consumption would bring about a larger drop in prices than would a comparable reduction as a percentage of demand by any other consumer country. Both lower import volumes and prices would in turn reduce the recurring economic costs of foreign oil dependence.[5]

Third, a decline in—or at least a lessening in the growth of—U.S. consumption would help to ease the current and foreseeable pressure on the world oil market generated by rising global demand. It could help to create some much needed slack in the market, primarily in the form of a restoration of a meaningful margin of surplus production capacity, which would in turn make oil shocks less likely or shorter in duration. Unless the United States could continue to reduce its demand over a prolonged period, however, this effect might also be only temporary as other consumers responded to lower prices by increasing their consumption and producers responded by investing less in new production capacity.

Finally, a decline in overall U.S. oil dependence, as measured by the oil intensity of the American economy, would reduce the economic costs of future oil shocks (see also Parry 2002, 32). Those costs are directly proportional to the overall level of consumption in the economy. For example, a 10 percent reduction in oil intensity would result in a comparable reduction in the immediate outlays for oil, the long-term loss in potential economic output, and the macroeconomic adjustment costs due to sudden price changes. In other words, noted economist Martin Feldstein has argued, "Reducing our consumption of oil would make the U.S. economy less sensitive to global oil prices and therefore to shocks in foreign global supplies. If oil plays a smaller role in the economy, changes in world oil prices would have less of an impact on the domestic price level and on domestic economic output" (Feldstein 2003, 2; see also Parry 2002, 32).

Before continuing, it is worth noting that reducing U.S. oil consumption could have other positive effects, which would make doing so even more worthwhile. Of particular interest have been the potential environmental benefits, such as lower levels of air pollution and greenhouse gas emissions. Whether such additional benefits are in fact realized, however, would depend on the precise measures that are taken to reduce the oil intensity of the American economy. For example, if oil is simply replaced by other fossil fuels, especially coal, then the net impact on the environment could be small and possibly negative.

The potential to reduce U.S. oil consumption would seem to be substantial. The United States has thus far made only limited efforts to do so. Instead, U.S. policy has tended, at least since the early 1980s, to rely on market forces, which have generally failed to reflect the negative externalities of oil consumption, including many of the costs of foreign oil dependence. Perhaps as a result, the demand for oil and petroleum products in the United States remains much higher both per capita and per unit of GDP than in other large, advanced industrialized countries. Yet other than the greater distances between population centers characteristic of the United States, there are no inherent physical reasons why the level of oil consumption must be so much higher. Consequently, it would seem that the United States could still do much to reduce oil use across the board and, in the process, the economic costs and risks of foreign oil dependence.

Indeed, one goal might be to achieve levels of oil consumption that are comparable to those found in other developed countries. If U.S. oil intensity were as low as in Japan, which ranks second after the United States among the major advanced industrialized countries, then overall oil consumption would be approximately four MBD lower. And if U.S. oil consumption per capita were the same as in Japan, which ranks second in that category as well, then total oil consumption would be some eight MBD, or roughly 10 percent of world production, less. Should the United States seek to achieve the even lower levels of oil intensity and per capita demand found in the major European states, the savings would be correspondingly greater. Alternatively, it might be more realistic to set reduction targets based on the existing rates of oil consumption. At the current level of demand, each 10 percent drop would save roughly two MBD, although this number is expected to grow. Thus, for example, the Natural Resources Defense Council has called on Congress to pass legislation requiring the United States to cut oil use by 2.5 MBD, or approximately 10 percent below projections, by 2015 and by 10 MBD, or roughly 35 percent, by 2025 (NRDC 2005).

What are the most promising approaches for achieving such reductions? The greatest potential for savings lies in the transportation sector. Electric power generation now accounts for only 2 percent of all oil consumption, while another 6 percent goes for residential and commercial applications, especially space and water heating. Approximately one-quarter is used in industry, but much of that takes the form of relatively hard-to-replace feed stocks for the petrochemical industry.[6] In contrast, the transportation sector alone consumes approximately two-thirds of all oil used in the United States, and that figure is projected to climb to more than 70 percent by 2030.

Within the transportation sector, perhaps the largest opportunities for reductions are to be found in the consumption of gasoline by light-duty vehicles. Jet fuel accounts for about 8 percent of transportation oil use, and diesel fuel another quarter. The remaining two-thirds, or about 44 percent of all U.S. oil consumption, takes the form of gasoline use by motor vehicles, including passenger cars, minivans, sport utility vehicles (SUVs), and pickup trucks (CBO 2002, 2; Davis and Diegel 2006, tab. 2.5).

A large number of measures for reducing the U.S. consumption of gasoline (and transportation fuels more generally) have been suggested. Most of these, and certainly the most important of them, can be grouped into four main categories: (1) increasing fuel efficiency, primarily through the exploitation of new technologies, such as hybrid engines, and the establishment of higher fuel economy standards; (2) raising taxes on oil and petroleum products; (3) promoting the use of alternative nonpetroleum fuels such as ethanol and, in the longer term, hydrogen, and (4) adopting cap-and-trade schemes, such as those that have been used to reduce emissions of pollutants.

I do not recommend a particular approach or even seek to present all the relative economic and political merits and demerits. That would require a detailed and often highly technical analysis, one that goes well beyond what is possible in a single chapter. Rather, my goal is simply to show that there may be promising ways of reducing U.S. oil consumption and to identify what some of them are. It should also be emphasized that the following approaches are not mutually exclusive. It would be possible, perhaps even desirable, to pursue several, if not all, of them simultaneously.

Finally, it should be recognized that any effort to reduce U.S. oil consumption significantly will take time and impose costs, perhaps even substantial ones. As a recent study noted, "The enormous magnitude of equipment and facilities that comprise the energy supply and demand system implies that even once technologies begin to be adopted, full replacement of the existing facilities will take several decades" (Deutsch and Schlesinger 2006, 30). But these costs must be weighed against the potential benefits in order to determine the overall cost-effectiveness of the measures taken. Some may conclude that the United States should be willing to spend as much on reducing its oil dependence, and thus the costs attributable to high oil prices and supply disruptions, as it has thus far on policies intended to prevent disruptions and to ensure access to foreign oil supplies, which have cost tens, if not hundreds, of billions of dollars per year. Indeed, some have called for an effort on the scale of the U.S. space program in the 1960s, with its goal of putting a man on the moon before the end of that decade.[7] In contrast to the Apollo project, however, the economic benefits of such an effort would likely be substantial and long-lasting.

Increasing Fuel Efficiency

Until now, the largest reductions in oil use in the transportation sector have been made by increasing fuel efficiency. This remains an area with great potential. "While over time the country is going to need a range of approaches to deal with its growing dependency [on imported oil]," the *New York Times* editorialized, "there is no better short-term answer than a more efficient transportation fleet" (*New York Times* 2005a). In the longer term, energy expert Amory Lovins and his colleagues at the Rocky Mountain Institute estimated in 2004 that if state-of-the-art technologies were fully applied, oil consumption by light vehicles could be reduced by approximately eight MBD, or 28 percent of the total then projected by the EIA, by 2025. Even if the 2025 light-duty vehicle fleet consisted only of the most fuel-efficient vehicles currently available, such as the Toyota Prius and the Ford Escape, Lexus RX 400h, and Toyota Highlander SUVs, then the hypothetical savings would still amount to 4.5 MBD, or 16 percent of forecasted oil use (Lovins et al. 2004, 99).

What specific steps might be taken? A large number of often complementary ways to increase fuel efficiency in the transportation sector have been proposed. They include

- producing lighter vehicles. Two-thirds to three-fourths of fuel consumption is typically weight-dependent (Lovins et al. 2004, 47);
- creating fuel economy standards for replacement tires, which have a 20 percent higher rolling resistance than the tires found on new cars. As a result, replacement tires are about 4 percent less fuel efficient than original tires (NRDC 2001; Grumet 2006);
- mandating the use of more efficient forms of motor oil;
- requiring or encouraging public and private operators of large fleets to purchase more fuel-efficient vehicles, which are driven on average more than personal vehicles (OTA 1991, 22).

Several other proposals have received even more attention.

One is to close the light-truck loophole in the "gas-guzzler" tax, which does not apply to SUVs, minivans, and pickup trucks. The environmental organization Friends of the Earth has estimated that if automakers improved the fuel efficiency of light trucks enough to avoid the tax, annual gasoline savings would reach about five billion gallons, or 3 percent of demand, after just ten years.[8]

Another is to provide further incentives for the production and purchase of relatively fuel-efficient gasoline-electric hybrid vehicles. In 2005, hybrid sales amounted to slightly more than two hundred thousand out of total vehicles sales of about seventeen million, and present production plans would raise the number to only about six hundred thousand by 2009 (Samuelson 2005, 41). From 2000 to 2005, the U.S. government offered a onetime tax deduction of $2,000 for hybrid purchases. The Energy Policy Act of 2005 introduced potentially more valuable variable tax credits ranging from $250 to $3,400, depending on the fuel efficiency of the vehicle, but the credit would be phased out after an automaker had sold sixty thousand vehicles (Peters 2005). The Natural Resources Defense Council (NRDC) has recommended that Congress provide a total of $3 billion in consumer and manufacturer credits during the next five to ten years to spur the development and introduction of hybrids (NRDC 2005), while the Energy Security Leadership Council (ESLC) has proposed that the sixty thousand vehicle cap be lifted while linking any incentives to true improvement in fuel economy (ESLC 2006, 35–36).

Perhaps most consequential of all would be to update or overhaul the existing fuel economy standards. The 1975 CAFE program has arguably done more than any other single policy measure to raise and maintain higher levels of fuel efficiency, and it continues to be widely viewed as the most promising mechanism for reducing oil consumption. As a recent NRDC report concluded, "The single most important action the administration can take to reduce our country's oil dependence is to raise the federal fuel economy standards" (NRDC 2005).

Most of the proposals for improving the CAFE program derive from its past shortcomings. The program has exempted a growing number of vehicles with large appetites for gasoline, those with gross vehicle weight ratings (GVWR) of more than eighty-five hundred pounds.[9] Even more important, the overall fuel economy of those new vehicles that are covered, passenger cars and light trucks, has actually declined since the late 1980s. From the mid-1980s through the mid-2000s, the fuel economy standards remained virtually frozen. Meanwhile, an ever-increasing percentage of vehicles sold has consisted of light trucks, which have been subject to a lower standard than passenger cars. When the standards were created, light trucks were primarily work and cargo vehicles that required extra power, different gearing, and less aerodynamic designs. Today, however, many of them, especially minivans and SUVs, are used almost exclusively for personal transport (CBO 2002, 11).

In the meantime, automobile efficiency has steadily improved. But without an incentive or requirement to increase fuel economy even more, manufacturers have instead used technological advances to make vehicles heavier and more powerful. According to a recent EPA analysis, the average weight of light-duty vehicles increased from 3,220 pounds in 1987 to 4,089 pounds in 2005, a 27 percent gain. During the same period, average horsepower rose from 118 to 212, an 80 percent increase, while average 0-to-60 acceleration time dropped from 13.1 seconds to 9.9 seconds. If the 2005 light-duty vehicle fleet had the same distribution of performance and weight as in 1987, it could have achieved about a 24 percent improvement in fuel economy (Heavenrich 2005, ii and v; see also Wald 2005; Grumet 2006, 31–32).

To remedy these shortcomings, a number of changes to the CAFE program have been suggested.[10] Among the potentially most important are:

- including all vehicles with a GVWR of between 8,500 and 10,000 pounds;
- setting fuel economy standards for medium- and heavy-duty vehicles, which account for nearly one-quarter of all highway transportation energy consumption (Davis and Diegel 2006, tab. 2.4). In the absence of any standards, the fuel economy of heavy trucks was no greater in 2003 than it had been thirty years before (ESLC 2006, 38);
- eliminating or restricting the credits given for the manufacture of flexible-fuel vehicles (FFVs), since these rarely operate on anything but conventional gasoline. Some estimate that the credit has resulted in an overall reduction of 0.5 to 0.9 miles per gallon (mpg) in the average efficiency of vehicles sold (Bamberger 2003, 8);
- narrowing the definition of light-duty trucks to emphasize vehicles that primarily carry cargo in actual practice and, eventually, eliminating altogether the distinction between automobiles and light trucks; and
- boosting fuel economy standards across the board and incorporating an automatic adjustment mechanism to ensure that they increase regularly.

Over the years, a number of studies have found that large additional, cost-effective improvements in fuel economy are feasible. At a minimum, some of the horsepower gains of the past two decades could be traded for improved fuel economy without lightening vehicles, and if vehicle weight could be reduced without compromising safety, for example by using stronger materials, the increases in fuel economy could be even greater (*Consumer Reports* 2005, 23). As early as 1982, the U.S. government's Office of Technology Assessment (OTA) estimated that average fleet fuel economy for new cars could reach at least forty to fifty mpg by the early to mid-1990s and forty-five to sixty mpg by 2000, based on relatively pessimistic expectations about improvements in auto technology. In the mid-1990s, the OTA predicted that a fifty-three mpg car could be sold for just $1,500 more than a thirty-three mpg "business as usual" model (Plotkin and Greene 1997, 1184). And in the early 2000s, a National Academy of Sciences study concluded that it was possible to achieve a more than 40 percent improvement in light-truck fuel economy during a ten- to fifteen-year period at costs that would be recoverable over the lifetime of the vehicle's ownership (Bamberger 2003, 7).

Such economically feasible improvements in fuel economy could result in substantial reductions in oil consumption. The NRDC has estimated that an increase in aggregate fuel economy standards to forty mpg by 2015 and then to fifty-five mpg by 2025 could reduce gasoline consumption by 4.9 MBD by 2025 (NRDC 2005). Likewise, the ESLC has estimated that reforming and strengthening fuel-efficiency standards for light-duty vehicles in various ways could save 4.3 MBD, while the National Commission on Energy Policy has calculated that the United States could cut its gasoline and diesel use by 4.6 MBD in 2025. Improvements in the fuel economy of heavy trucks could yield another 1.1 to 1.3 MBD in savings (ESLC 2006, 32, 37–38; Grumet 2006, 39). Even relatively modest and inexpensive measures could quickly yield noteworthy savings. For example, the Congressional Budget Office (CBO) has estimated that raising the CAFE standards for both cars and light trucks by just 3.8 mpg would reduce gasoline use by new vehicles by 10 percent, at a cost of just $230 per vehicle (Dinan and Austin 2004, 1).

To be sure, overhauling the CAFE program in these ways would not be easy, nor would it offer a panacea. For example, making the transition to a single standard for cars and light trucks could pose difficulties. A unified standard that reflected the current average fuel economy of all new light-duty vehicles sold would benefit manufacturers that produce mainly cars and penalize firms that currently sell a disproportionate number of trucks (CBO 2002, 12). Indeed, the Bush administration has recently moved in the opposite direction, disaggregating light trucks into five or six classes with distinct standards. Even if significantly higher standards were adopted, moreover, it would be some time before their full benefits would be realized, since only about 6 percent of the personal vehicle fleet turns over every year (Yergin 2005, 54–55).

Perhaps more important, higher CAFE requirements may not be the most cost-effective way to reduce oil consumption, because they do not foster all potential gas saving activities (CBO 2002, ix, 10). In particular, they would provide individuals with no incentives to drive less, to use their cars more efficiently, or to shift more quickly to more fuel-efficient vehicles (Feldstein 2001, 61; Stavins 2004; Deutsch and Schlesinger 2006, 37). Indeed, by lowering the cost of operating new vehicles, CAFE-induced improvements in fuel economy could cause their owners to drive longer distances. Researchers generally assume that a 10 percent decline in the fuel-related costs of driving leads to about a 2 percent increase in the number of miles driven (CBO 2002, 15; see also Dinan and Austin 2004, 2). More generally, because CAFE standards do not directly encourage either producers or consumers to decrease gasoline use, they do not offer the flexibility or the incentives for gasoline reductions to occur at the lowest possible economic cost (CBO 2002, 10).

Raising Taxes

This final limitation of the CAFE program helps to account for the interest that economists and others have expressed in another general approach to reducing oil consumption: the imposition of higher taxes. This approach has at least one advantage over fuel economy standards and two other positive attributes. The advantage lies in the greater economic efficiency of taxes. A tax does not dictate how people should save gasoline or other petroleum products. It simply raises the price and allows people to adjust their behavior accordingly. By applying to all possible uses that could be reduced at a cost lower than the tax, it would encourage a range of gas saving and oil saving activities (CBO 2002, ix).

Another virtue of taxes is that they can help to internalize the external costs of oil consumption. This is one of the main rationales for the existing federal gasoline tax, most of which is used to build and maintain highways. But the same principle applies to other externalities, such as the foreign and military policy costs of U.S. foreign oil dependence. Thus not only would taxes discourage consumption and, directly or indirectly, imports, but they could also ensure that the price of gasoline and other petroleum products better reflected the true cost, including the total cost to society.

Finally, to the degree that the world price of oil and petroleum products exceeds the competitive market prices, taxes can reduce the resulting transfer of wealth to foreign producers. Energy taxes would make sure that a higher percentage of the economic surplus associated with oil consumption benefits a country's own citizens rather than exporters (Renshaw 1990, 15). And because the revenues would stay in the United States, they could be used to lower other taxes and to reduce the disproportionate impact of energy price increases on the poor as well as to support additional research, development, and the accelerated deployment of advanced energy options (Holdren 2001, 50).

Over the years, two principal types of taxes have been considered or proposed: an excise tax (tariff) on oil imports and an increase in the federal gasoline tax. Perhaps surprisingly, there has been little discussion of taxing all crude oil and petroleum products.

Proposals for tariffs on imported crude oil and petroleum products date back to at least the mid-1970s. Typically, they have emphasized the benefits of internalizing the social costs of foreign oil dependence and reducing the transfer of wealth to oil producers. "The price paid by U.S. consumers [for oil imports] does not fully reflect the true national cost of imported oil," noted one 1988 analysis, making oil "the principal commodity for which a tariff may well be in the interest of the consuming countries."[11] Thus by accounting for the risks of foreign oil dependence that are borne by all U.S. citizens, "an oil import tariff would align the costs of oil imports to society and to the individual oil user" (CBO 1982, 12; see also GAO 1996, 31). In addition, a tariff would result in lower payments to oil exporters, by both lowering the volume of imports and, in most cases, world prices (Broadman and Hogan 1988, 14). For both these reasons, experts have argued in favor of oil import fees of as much as $10 per barrel (Broadman and Hogan 1988, 16; GAO 1996, 31).

By raising the price to consumers, an import tariff would also have the effect, if only indirectly, of reducing overall oil consumption. Depending on the reaction of foreign oil producers, a 1982 CBO study found that a $10 per barrel tariff would raise the price of all refined products by about 16 to 24 cents per gallon. Such a price hike in turn was expected to reduce imports by 0.4 MBD to 0.6 MBD, at a time when the price of oil was near its all-time high but U.S. imports (5 MBD) were less than half of what they are today and total oil consumption was about 25 percent lower (CBO 1982, 11–12). How much a tariff would reduce overall demand would depend, however, on the response of domestic oil producers, who could be expected to increase their output at least modestly in response to the higher prices.

Much more frequently encountered have been proposals to increase the federal gasoline tax. Economists generally regard a tax as a more efficient and cost-effective means of reducing gasoline consumption than fuel economy standards (Parry 2002, 33; Gerard and Lave 2003, 5). Thus far, however, the U.S. government has not used the federal gasoline tax as a means of reducing consumption or otherwise addressing concerns about foreign oil dependence. To the contrary, the tax has been frozen at just 18.4 cents per gallon since 1993, and its value in real terms is roughly where it was before the first oil shock. National gasoline taxes in other industrialized countries have typically been much higher. In recent years, the overall gasoline tax, including state and local taxes, has averaged around 40 cents per gallon in the United States, in contrast to around $4 per gallon in Europe (Gross 2006). In 2002, before the recent run-up in oil prices, the tax component of the cost of gasoline in most European countries ranged between 60 percent (Spain) and 75 percent (Britain). The comparable figure for the United States was just 22 percent (IEA 2004b, 36–37; see also Davis and Diegel 2004, fig. 10.1).

The last several years have seen a flurry of proposals for raising the federal gasoline tax, from across the political spectrum. Many, including some conservative economists, have called for a fixed increase, typically between $1 and $2 per gallon, possibly phased in over five to ten years. Others, most notably *New York Times* columnist Thomas Friedman, have argued for a variable tax that would keep the price of gasoline somewhere in the range of $3 to $4 per gallon (T. Friedman 2003b, 2004, 2005, 2006a, 2006b, 2006c, and 2006e; Rauch 2002; Feldstein 2003, 7; Easterbrook 2004; Klare 2004a; Samuelson 2004; *New York Times* 2005b; Ikenberry and Slaughter 2006; Mankiw 2006).

In contrast to fuel economy standards, a higher gasoline tax would reduce consumption through a variety of mechanisms. In the short term, it would encourage consumers to drive fewer miles and in ways that were more fuel efficient. In the longer term, it would provide direct incentives for consumers to demand and manufacturers to provide vehicles with better fuel economies. A gasoline tax could also stimulate the development and introduction of alternative fuels and vehicles that use them, making them more competitive in the marketplace (GAO 1996, 68; GAO 2000, 17–18; CBO 2002, 15; NRC 2002, 88 and 93; Gerard and Lave 2003, 6; Feldstein 2003, 7; Dinan and Austin 2004, 2; Deutsch and Schlesinger 2006, 36).

As a result, raising the gasoline tax could lead to substantial savings. According to one rule of thumb, a 10 percent rise in the price of gasoline reduces consumption by 6 to 9 percent in the long run (Plotkin and Greene 1997, 1181–82; CBO 2002, 17; Uchitelle and Thee 2006). Thus both CBO and the U.S. Department of Energy (DOE) have recently estimated that an increase on the order of 50 cents per gallon could eventually cut gasoline use by 10 to 15 percent, or approximately 1 MBD to 1.5 MBD at current rates (Dinan and Austin 2004, 3; Stavins 2004). And one economist has suggested that a $2-per-gallon tax on gasoline selling at $2.50 per gallon would reduce consumption by at least that percentage in the short run and by almost 60 percent over the longer term (Frank 2006).

To be sure, raising the gasoline tax substantially would not be easy politically. Like an external oil shock, it could negatively affect the U.S. economy in the short term unless it were offset by other changes in fiscal or monetary policies (GAO 1996, 69), and some might fear that the extra revenue—approximately $140 billion per year for a tax of $1 per gallon—would be used to finance increased government spending. In addition, it would be a regressive tax, hitting the poor harder than the rich. Nevertheless, the negative effects could be largely countered by using the resulting government revenues to cut other taxes and, in particular, to provide tax breaks or credits to low-income households (Renshaw 1990, 16; *New York Times* 2005b).

Developing Alternative Fuels

A third broad approach to reducing U.S. oil consumption is to develop alternative transportation fuels and forms of transportation. In the short to medium term, the greatest potential lies in increasing the use of biofuels. In the long term, major savings may come from the widespread introduction of hydrogen-fueled vehicles and a combination of land-use planning and the greater reliance on mass transit that higher-density development patterns would facilitate. Since such longer-term developments are necessarily more speculative, this section will focus on the prospects for replacing gasoline with biofuels, especially ethanol, during the next two decades.

American automobile engineers learned early on that alcohol could power internal-combustion engines. The Ford Model T, for example, could be modified to run on either gasoline or pure alcohol. But gasoline soon displaced alcohol because it was cheaper to convert crude petroleum into the former than corn and other grains into the latter (Klare 2004a, 195; DiPardo 2002). Since the late 1970s, however, the United States has encouraged the substitution of renewable alcohol fuels for gasoline and diesel, and the production of ethanol in particular has grown steadily in the past two and a half decades. Consequently, some observers have concluded that the United States will eventually be able to replace most of the gasoline it uses with biofuels (NRDC 2004, v). A 1999 National Research Council study found that 1.6 MBD in biofuels could be profitably produced by 2020. A more recent analysis argues that even newer technologies will permit biofuels, mostly in the form of ethanol, to provide the equivalent of 4.3 MBD in crude oil at under $35 per barrel by 2025 (Lovins et al. 2004, 103–4).

Brazil is often cited as a possible model. Although the country's nearly three-decade-long effort to promote ethanol has experienced ups and downs, today about one-third of the fuel used by automobiles consists of ethanol derived from domestically grown sugarcane. All the gasoline sold in Brazil contains about 25 percent ethanol, and approximately 20 percent of the cars operate on ethanol only. In 2005, the share of new cars that are able to run on any combination of gasoline or ethanol passed the 50 percent mark, and it continues to climb (Lovins et al. 2004, 105; Luft 2005; T. Friedman 2005; Dickerson 2005).

In the United States, most ethanol is produced from corn. During the last several years, corn-based ethanol production has risen rapidly, reaching five billion gallons in 2006, in part because of federal mandates. The 2005 Energy Policy Act requires an increase in the sale of renewable fuels by 700 million gallons per year through 2012, when the total must reach at least 7.5 billion gallons. And in January 2007, President Bush proposed that the target for renewable and alternative fuels be raised to 35 billion gallons in 2017.

Nevertheless, corn-based ethanol's potential to reduce oil consumption is severely limited. Even if the entire U.S. corn crop, which accounts for more than 40 percent of global output, were devoted to making ethanol, it would yield only 30 billion gallons. And because a gallon of ethanol contains only two-thirds as much energy as a gallon gasoline, the gasoline equivalent would be only 20 billion gallons, or just 15 percent of current consumption. Well before such levels of output were reached, moreover, competition with other uses of corn for food both in the United States and abroad and as feed for livestock would drive corn prices to unacceptably high and increasingly un-economical levels. In addition, although estimates vary, corn-based ethanol may provide little more energy than is used, typically in the form of natural gas, in the production process. Finally, the technologies involved in convert-ing corn to ethanol are relatively mature, so while further incremental cost reductions can be expected, no major breakthroughs that could bring costs down dramatically are anticipated (DiPardo 2002; IEA 2004a, 67; Grumet 2006, 36; ESLC 2006, 40–41; Schnepf 2006, 10–11).

Instead, the greatest potential to displace transportation oil demand lies in the production of ethanol from cellulosic biomass, which consists of the leaves, stems, and stocks of plants (NRDC 2004). Cellulosic biomass offers a number of advantages over corn as a source of ethanol. It can draw on a far larger and more diverse supply of domestic feedstocks, including agricultural wastes, dedicated energy crops like switch grass, and the biomass portion of the municipal waste stream. It does not compete with the domestic food sup-ply. It requires less energy to produce. It allows production to be more de-centralized, since cellulosic biomass is available in more places. And it offers protection against the risk that pestilence could wipe out a single crop such as corn (NRDC 2004; ESLC 2006, 41–42; Grumet 2006, 28, 36).

The main impediment to the development of a cellulose-based ethanol industry is the cost of converting cellulosic materials into ethanol. In addi-tion, high production volumes will require improved high-yield energy crops, the integration of cellulosic ethanol production into existing farming activi-ties, and efficiency improvements in the conversion process (Schnepf 2006, 12; Grumet 2006, 36). Nevertheless, a number of recent studies suggest that advances in biotechnology could push the cost of producing cellulosic ethanol below that of corn ethanol sometime during the next decade, and between 2010 and 2020, it could begin to compete with gasoline, even assuming that the price of oil returns to somewhere between $25 and $35 per barrel (IEA 2004a, 68, 79–80, 84). According to one estimate, advanced biofuels produc-tion facilities could produce gasoline alternatives at costs equal to between $0.59 and $0.91 per gallon of gasoline-equivalent by around 2014. In addition, the estimated land requirements could be reduced dramatically through in-creases in crop yields and increases in conversion efficiency. Indeed, it might be possible to use the prairie grass growing naturally on idle crop land to pro-duce enough ethanol to meet a significant share of U.S. transportation energy needs. Thus if the United States were to undertake an aggressive program to develop cellulosic biofuels in the next decade, it could produce the first billion gallons of cellulosic ethanol at competitive prices by 2015 and the equivalent of nearly 7.9 MBD by 2050. These targets could be achieved, moreover, with an investment of as little as $2 billion divided roughly equally between research, development, and demonstration efforts and incentives to producers.[12]

Imports of ethanol could also help to reduce oil consumption in the United States. Of course, a growing reliance on such imports would not be without risks. But it would nevertheless help to diversify U.S. energy supplies, and the additional risk would be minimized by the fact that most U.S imports would probably come from the Western Hemisphere, especially the Caribbean and Brazil, which is the lowest-cost ethanol producer in the world. Currently, however, the United States imposes an import tariff of 54 cents per gallon, which greatly reduces the incentives for U.S. refineries to take advantage of efficient ethanol producers abroad (IEA 2004a, 67; Lovins et al. 2004, 106; Dickerson 2005; Deutsch and Schlesinger 2006, 8, 38).

Additional investments would be needed to create an adequate distribution network for delivering ethanol from producers (and importers) to consumers. Since ethanol is an alcohol, it creates some compatibility problems with the existing infrastructure for transportation, distribution, and retailing. In particular, it has a tendency to degrade commonly used materials. Thus refueling station storage and dispensing equipment may need to be upgraded or replaced (IEA 2004a, 89). The typical cost for converting a retail unit with three underground storage tanks is under $1,000, while that for adding a dedicated storage tank and fuel pump that serves ethanol to an existing refueling station can range from $20,000 to $60,000. The total cost of transporting, storing, and dispensing ethanol ranges from about 5 to 29 cents per gallon, although if ethanol capacity expansion were to occur in lieu of any further gasoline capacity expansion, the incremental cost would probably be in the lower half of that range (EIA 2004a, 90–91).[13] Although the number of refueling sites equipped to handle ethanol has more than quintupled since 2003, in early 2007 they still amounted to just 1,000 out of some 180,000 gas stations in the United States.[14] To hasten this process, the 2005 Energy Policy Act provides a 30 percent tax credit (up to $30,000) for investments in alternative fueling stations, and some have proposed that the federal government require major gasoline companies to provide pumps that dispense ethanol at a high percentage of their retail outlets (for example, ESLC 2006, 42).

In the longer term, hydrogen is seen as another potentially promising substitute for gasoline. It could either be burned in modified internal combustion engines or used in fuel cells to generate electricity. Because of this promise, the current Bush administration has made hydrogen a centerpiece of its energy policy. Nevertheless, a number of significant obstacles will have to be overcome before hydrogen can be widely employed as a transportation fuel. Because it does not exist in a pure state in nature, it must be extracted and purified at considerable expense. Today, hydrogen costs several times as much as gasoline, and the most cost-effective means of generating it require the use of large amounts of fossil fuels. Likewise, hydrogen fuel cells are still many times more expensive than equivalently powered internal combustion engines and nowhere near as reliable. As energy policy expert Joseph Romm has noted, "A major technological breakthrough is needed in transportation fuel cells before they will be practical" (Romm 2004, 2). And hydrogen would necessitate an entirely new infrastructure for storage, transportation, and distribution. Consequently, a National Academy of Sciences panel recently concluded, "In the best-case scenario, the transition to a hydrogen economy will take many decades, and any reductions in oil imports and carbon dioxide emissions are likely to be minor during the next 25 years."[15]

Cap-and-Trade Systems

A fourth general approach to reducing U.S. oil consumption would involve cap-and-trade systems, such as those used to limit the emission of pollutants like sulfur dioxide. A 2002 CBO report analyzed the merits of a cap-and-trade system for total carbon emissions resulting from gasoline combustion, but such a program could apply equally to gasoline itself. Under a cap-and-trade system, the federal government would set a limit on the total number of gallons of gasoline that could be produced or imported and auction off a corresponding number of allowances, which could then be traded. In order to sell gasoline in the United States, companies would have to buy allowances, either from the government or other firms, which would lead to higher prices at the pump (CBO 2002, viii, 17).

Alternatively, a cap-and-trade system could apply directly to consumers. Once again, the government would establish an oil consumption target and distribute an equivalent number of vouchers, perhaps in the form of debit cards. Each voucher would permit the owner to purchase one gallon of gasoline or some other petroleum product, and owners that held more than they needed could sell the extra vouchers. Since the number of vouchers would be less than the number of gallons currently purchased, they would command a positive price, effectively raising the cost of the relevant product (Feldstein 2001; Feldstein 2003).

Either way, a cap-and-trade system would be more effective for achieving a predetermined level of reduction in fuel consumption than would a direct tax. Like a tax, it would provide consumers with an incentive to engage in all possible gas saving activities. But in contrast to a tax, it would automatically limit consumption to the desired amount, whereas a tax might have to be adjusted over time in order to obtain the same result.

Through these and other possible measures, it should be possible to reduce U.S. oil consumption substantially in the next two decades. But it would not be possible to eliminate U.S. oil dependence altogether during that time frame. Even in one best-case scenario, the United States would still be using at least 13 MBD of oil in 2025 (Lovins et al. 2004, 123–25).

Mitigating the Impact of Future Oil Shocks

As long as the U.S. economy remains dependent on oil, it will be vulnerable to the negative effects of oil supply disruptions, particularly sharp price hikes. The United States has made some efforts to mitigate the impact of possible oil shocks, chiefly through the creation of the Strategic Petroleum Reserve. Because the magnitude of U.S. oil dependence will remain significant for the foreseeable future, such measures should continue to be an important component of U.S. energy security policy.

Increasing Fuel Flexibility
One approach for mitigating the impact of oil shocks is to increase the fuel flexibility of the U.S. economy. If consumers could rapidly shift from the use of oil to other energy sources, then they would be less affected by sharp increases in the price of oil. In economic terms, greater fuel switching capability would increase the price elasticity of oil consumption, which in turn would facilitate macroeconomic adjustment to price shocks.

In the wake of the energy crises of the 1970s, a number of oil burning power and industrial plants added dual-fuel capable facilities that could use either oil or natural gas. Today, given the concentration of oil consumption in the transportation sector, the greatest potential for increasing overall fuel flexibility lies in the introduction of large numbers of flexible fuel vehicles (FFVs).

Virtually all cars built in the United States since the early 1980s can run on a gasoline blend that contains as much as 10 percent ethanol (E10). Since the mid-1990s, some five million vehicles, mostly SUVs, that can handle blends of up to 85 percent ethanol (E85) have been manufactured. However impressive, this number represents only about 2 percent of the U.S. light-duty vehicle fleet. In addition, a 2002 DOT study found that less than 1 percent of the fuel consumed by FFVs was E85, although this situation should change as ethanol becomes more widely available.[16]

Thus one approach for increasing U.S. fuel flexibility would be to require manufacturers—or to provide them with incentives—to produce more FFVs. Indeed, a number of energy experts have called for FFVs to become the norm for all new light vehicles during the next decade not long after 2010 (Lovins et al. 2004, 107; ESLC 2006, 43; Khosla 2006). This is already the case in Brazil, where all vehicles can use blends consisting of roughly one-quarter ethanol and three-quarters gasoline, and a rapidly increasing number of so-called total-flex cars are able to run on any combination of the two fuels. Nor should the costs be prohibitive. It is possible to add a flexible fuel capability to automobiles for as little as $100 to $150 per vehicle.

Another proposal is to introduce large numbers of "plug-in" hybrid gasoline-electric vehicles. These cars are much like regular hybrids, but they can be plugged into standard electrical outlets when not in use and travel greater distances using battery power. Since approximately 50 percent of the cars in the United States are driven twenty miles a day or less, a plug-in with a twenty-mile range battery could theoretically reduce fuel consumption by 85 percent on average. Because they can be charged at night when electrical utilities typically have excess capacity, moreover, their widespread use (up to 30 percent of the light-duty vehicle fleet) would not require any additional power generation capability.[17]

The potential savings could be substantial. According to one estimate, if by 2025 all cars on the road were hybrids and half were plug-in hybrid vehicles, U.S. oil consumption would drop by eight MBD. If all of these cars were also FFVs, oil use could be as much as twelve MBD lower.[18] Of course, the full exploitation of large numbers of FFVs would depend on the availability of adequate supplies of ethanol, so that drivers could easily switch back and forth between it and gasoline, depending on relative prices.

Optimizing Strategic Oil Stocks

The other main approach for mitigating the economic impact of future oil shocks is to optimize the size and other characteristics of U.S. strategic oil stocks. By buffering oil supply disruptions and damping sudden price hikes, such reserves "are a direct and effective means for dealing with the risks to economies of persistent supply and price volatility" (Leiby and Bowman 2000b, 1). Since the late 1970s, the United States has relied on the Strategic Petroleum Reserve to perform this function. As one analysis notes, "Private agents cannot justify holding large oil stocks for the long term as a contingency against unlikely, but potentially dramatic, market upheavals or geopolitical struggles. . . . Thus, it is incumbent on the public sector to hold strategic oil reserves since private agents are either unwilling or unable to do so" (Leiby and Bowman 2000b, 1). Moreover, at nearly 700 million barrels, the SPR now accounts for almost half of the government-controlled stocks in the world.[19]

Despite its potential importance, the SPR has been a relatively inexpensive policy response to U.S. foreign oil dependence. Estimates of the total cost during its more than twenty-five-year lifetime range from a low of $25 billion to a high of $125 billion, or just $1 to $5 billion per year. Even in the early 1980s, when the United States was busily filling the reserve and its military involvement in the Persian Gulf was still small, one analysis found that the allocation of resources by the U.S. government was "heavily weighted toward military options rather than stockpile and import reduction options" (Rowen and Weyant 1982, 316).

Over the years, a number of studies have suggested that the size of the SPR should be increased. For example, a 1996 GAO report concluded that it was not large enough to play a significant role in large or long-term disruptions because such disruptions would greatly exceed the capacity of the reserve to affect the world oil market (GAO 1996, 60). Likewise, a more recent analysis by scientists at the Oak Ridge National Laboratory found that the SPR could be effective only against short-lived supply disruptions and that it would have to be as much as thirty times larger to be able to compensate for supply reductions of the magnitude of those seen in the 1970s (Greene and Tishchishyna 2001, 28).

Just how much larger should the SPR be? The original policy goal was to be able to replace all imports for at least ninety days. At the current level of imports (12 MBD), this metric would require increasing the SPR to approximately 1.1 billion barrels. Given the nature of world oil markets, however, the optimal size should be determined primarily by the likely magnitude and duration of potential supply disruptions rather than by U.S. import levels. Using these criteria, a cost-benefit analysis conducted for the DOE in 2000, when the

SPR stood at 580 million barrels, concluded that the efficient reserve size was about 700 to 850 million barrels. Yet that result followed from a number of assumptions that now look optimistic. For example, the study assumed that oil prices would reach only $20 (in 1996 dollars) in about 2006 and then rise gradually to about $24 in 2030, whereas prices have been much higher in recent years. It also assumed that the average oil supply disruption would last 4.5 months, whereas the median length of the eighteen oil market shocks since 1951 had been close to six months. And it assumed that world excess production capacity would never fall below 1.8 MBD, whereas it has in fact been lower in recent years. Indeed, the study acknowledged that if less optimistic assumptions were used, an even larger reserve would be ideal, and it specifically noted that in the case of low excess capacity, an increase in the SPR to more than 1 billion barrels would be cost effective (Leiby and Bowman 2000b).

Perhaps because of such considerations, the Bush administration proposed in January 2007 that the SPR be increased to 1.5 billion barrels. Assuming sufficient underground storage capacity could be found, the capital cost of adding 800 million barrels would be approximately $4 billion, while the annual cost of operations and maintenance would come to another $160 million.[20] Thus by far the biggest expense would be the acquisition of the oil itself. In order to keep outlays to a minimum, especially with oil prices at relatively high levels, the oil could be taken in lieu of royalties from production on federal land. In addition, the United States would need to follow a flexible fill policy so as not to put significant upward pressure on prices at times when the world market is especially tight (Goldwyn and Billig 2005, 521).

In addition to increasing the size of the SPR, the United States should consider three other measures for optimizing its strategic reserves. One would be to increase the drawdown capacity of the SPR. Even an optimally sized reserve would be of limited use if the oil could not be removed rapidly enough in an emergency. A second 2000 analysis for the DOE found that, over a wide range of conditions, expansion of the drawdown capability from the current 4.3 MBD to as much as 7.0 MBD would be economically worthwhile. A higher drawdown capability would be especially valuable if future disruptions are expected to be short and intense (Leiby and Bowman 2000a, 3).

A second measure would be to diversify the SPR to include petroleum products (Goldwyn and Billig 2005, 518). The United States imports ever-growing amounts of refined products, especially gasoline. In 2005, net gasoline imports stood at more than two MBD (EIA 2006b, 131, 135). Yet U.S. refiners lack the spare capacity to quickly compensate for any unexpected reduction in those imports, and the federal government maintains virtually no stocks of refined products. As a result, the United States is increasingly vulnerable to price shocks caused by disruptions in the world supply of petroleum products. Thus it might be highly advisable to create separate government stocks of critical products, as some European countries have done, that could be drawn on in the event of a supply disruption.[21]

Finally, the U.S. government should consider providing incentives to private sector entities to maintain larger commercial inventories. Since the SPR was established, the stocks held by oil refiners, marketers, and consumers have declined, from as much as 1.3 billion barrels in the mid-1970s to less than 1.0 billion barrels in recent years. As one study notes, "Oil-using firms and private customers acting on their own behalf do not have sufficient motivation to adequately insure themselves and the nation against the widespread costs of oil price shocks" (Leiby and Bowman 2000b, 1). In order to encourage companies to maintain higher levels of inventory that would help to maintain a supply cushion in the event of a severe disruption, the United States could offer tax credits to offset part of the cost of additional stocks and storage capacity (Goldwyn and Billig 2005, 522).

Rethinking U.S. Foreign and Military Policy Responses

Perhaps the greatest challenge facing U.S. policymakers concerns how to reduce the costs of the external policies that have been undertaken in response to foreign oil dependence. U.S. foreign and military policies toward oil producing countries and regions are responsible for a substantial portion of the costs attributable to American dependence on oil from abroad. One might therefore expect that this would be an area in which some of the most significant cost savings are to be found.

Yet achieving change in this area might also appear to be the most difficult. U.S. policies toward the Persian Gulf and other oil-rich regions have acquired an air of inevitability. It sometimes seems almost impossible to imagine the United States not remaining or becoming ever more deeply engaged, as it has most recently in Iraq. Plausible alternatives do not readily come to mind. In addition, the connections between U.S. foreign oil dependence and particular policies are not always self-evident. The recent Iraq War, for example, has been justified on any of a number of grounds, but oil has not been among them. A good deal of work may be required to identify the underlying relationship.

Nevertheless, there are also reasons for cautious optimism about the possibility of change. One is simply that the costs of U.S. external policy responses to foreign oil dependence have become so great that they are difficult to ignore. During the 1980s and even the 1990s, the outlays for U.S. military programs and operations intended to protect and secure access to foreign oil supplies could largely be hidden within the overall defense budget, while the financial tab for the 1991 Gulf War was largely picked up by other countries. Even U.S. support for autocratic oil regimes in the 1970s and 1980s could be viewed as part of the broader cold war task of containing Soviet power and influence.

Since at least September 11, 2001, however, the costs have been much more prominently on display. The terrorist attacks of that day caused many Americans to begin to question the wisdom of close U.S. ties to the current Saudi regime. And the recent military operations in Iraq have imposed a heavy burden on the federal budget as well as other, less tangible, costs.

A related reason for believing in the possibility of change is that the circumstances under which the United State embarked on and consolidated these policies have changed. Two particularly influential factors in the 1970s and 1980s are no longer present. One was the cold war. During that period, policymakers could plausibly point to the risk of excessive Soviet influence over or Soviet domination of oil producing regions, especially the Persian Gulf, although the actual level of threat was almost certainly exaggerated. The other factor was the relatively rigid nature of oil markets, which were based on long-term contracts between identifiable producers and consumers. This situation heightened the prospect of supply shortages in the event of an embargo or an unexpected disruption. Today, however, oil markets are much more fluid. Supplies can be quickly rerouted via the price mechanism in response to shortages. Thus although prices are potentially quite volatile, willing consumers will almost always be able to obtain the oil they need. Access to oil, at some price, is virtually assured.

A third reason for optimism is the potential feasibility of revising U.S. foreign and military policies, at least in conjunction with implementation of the types of proposals discussed above. Reducing U.S. oil dependence and increasing the U.S. capacity to weather oil price shocks would make it easier for the United States to tolerate supply disruptions and instability in oil producing regions. This lower degree of vulnerability would in turn reduce the imperative to ensure reliable access to foreign oil supplies at reasonable prices and to prevent disruptions from occurring in the first place, which have been the overall objectives of American policies toward oil producing states and regions. U.S. leaders would be able to take a more relaxed view toward developments in those parts of the world and place greater emphasis on the pursuit of other foreign policy interests.

The Costs of Doing Nothing: Are They Really So High?

Indeed, it may already be the case that the United States could scale back its foreign and military policy efforts. Previously, it was widely assumed that if the United States did not seek to protect foreign oil supplies and to ensure access to them, the economic costs could be unbearable. In fact, the costs of a more laissez-faire approach may not be intolerably high.

Consider the following analysis of the situation confronting the United States immediately after the Iraqi invasion of Kuwait in 1990 (Henderson 1990). In the worst case, Iraqi forces, if unopposed, might have gone on to seize Saudi Arabia and the United Arab Emirates, thereby gaining control of 12.3 MBD of production. In order to maximize its oil revenues, Iraq might then have cut output in the areas under its control by as much as 4 MBD, or 6.7 percent of world production at the time. Assuming a short-run elasticity of demand for oil of -0.15, the price of oil would have risen temporarily by about 50 percent, from $20 to $30 per barrel.[22] Since the United States was importing about 8 MBD at the time, the additional outlays for imports would have amounted to $80 million per day or $29.2 billion per year. In other words, the economic price of not intervening militarily would have been slightly more than 0.5 percent of the U.S. gross national product at the time.

Of course, this 1990 thought experiment neglected other negative economic effects of a sharp price rise, such as the macroeconomic adjustment costs. Nor did it consider the security externalities of a much wealthier Iraq. In other respects, however, the analysis might have overstated the potential economic costs to the United States of Iraqi control of Persian Gulf oil supplies, less those of Iran. For example, a dominant Iraq might not have cut oil production by as much as the analysis assumed. And, as had occurred in the late 1970s and early 1980s, significantly higher oil prices would have stimulated additional domestic production and discouraged consumption, thereby suppressing U.S. imports and helping to bring down the world price of oil.

Whatever the merits of the analysis, it nevertheless underscores an important general point that sometimes appears to have been forgotten by American policymakers: the costs of U.S. external policy responses of foreign oil dependence must be constantly weighed against the expected economic benefits. If the economic costs and risks of U.S. foreign oil dependence can be significantly reduced through purely domestic policy measures, as suggested above, then so can the foreign and military policy efforts that have been undertaken in response to those costs and risks in the past.

General Principles

Should the costs of U.S. external policy responses be found to outweigh the economic benefits, how might these policies be modified? Before offering any specific suggestions, it is important to set out some general principles.

The first is that the United States should attempt to treat oil no differently than any other commodity. Since World War II, oil has come to occupy a unique place among traded goods in U.S. policy. As Michael Klare has convincingly argued, U.S. leaders "have chosen to *securitize* oil—that is, to cast its continued availability as a matter of 'national security,' and thus something that can be safeguarded through the use of military force" and they have "turned to the U.S. military to provide insurance against the hazards associated with [oil] dependency" (Klare 2004a, 12, 15, also xiv).

Thus the first step in rethinking U.S. policy is to "desecuritize" oil. The United States should no longer allow its foreign and military policies to be dictated by the desire to maintain reliable access to adequate amounts of oil at reasonable prices. Doing so would allow these instruments to be used more consistently to pursue other valued American goals and interests. As a U.S. undersecretary of state recently argued, "We must ensure that the United States can pursue its foreign policy and national security interests without being constrained by energy concerns" (Larson 2003).

A second general principal and corollary of the first is that the United States should stop treating oil exporting states differently from other countries. As Klare has also observed, the United States has effectively entered into a number of "oil-for-protection" arrangements with what have often been unsavory regimes. In fact, the problem goes beyond such arrangements insofar as the United States has used other means in its efforts to influence the policies of oil producing states and to protect access to oil supplies. In the process, the United States has sacrificed or been willing to compromise other important values, such as democracy, economic development, human rights, good governance, and respect for international law.

Instead, the United States should scale back or terminate such oil-for-protection arrangements and reserve security guarantees and assistance for countries that share American values and institutions. As Klare argues, "The U.S. government needs to impose a blanket proscription on any security commitment whose primary purpose is to ensure our access to a country's energy deposits" (Klare 2004a, 189; see also 186, 192). Concomitantly, it should accord higher priority to promoting democratization, real economic development, respect for human rights, good governance, the rule of law, and other traditional American goals in oil producing countries as it does elsewhere.

In the short term, this approach may—is even likely to—result in greater instability in the world oil market and a higher risk of oil supply disruptions. These dangers may be exaggerated, however, as all leaders and regimes in oil producing states will have an interest in developing and selling their oil resources, albeit not necessarily at past levels. And in the long run, this approach should have the opposite effect, as political and economic development is more likely to lead to the effective, responsible, and sustainable exploitation of oil resources. As a result, supplies will become less subject to disruptions, and the market will become more stable.

Specific Policy Reforms

These principals would seem to be most directly applicable to U.S. policy toward the Persian Gulf, which, arguably, has been short-sighted. In its attempts to ward off the most immediate threats to the region's oil supplies, the United States has allowed underlying sources of instability to fester and has even created new problems. It has helped to keep in power corrupt, despotic, and repressive regimes and to foment a backlash of anti-Americanism. If the United States is interested in promoting long-term stability in countries like Saudi Arabia, then it must show less forbearance toward the misuse of oil revenues, the denial of basic rights, and the preaching of intolerance and instead press harder for political, economic, and social reform (*New York Times* 2004b; Anonymous 2004, 247; Clawson and Henderson 2005, xi–xii). At the same time, it should reduce its military presence in the region, or even withdraw it entirely (K. Pollack 2003; Klare 2004a, 191). As one analysis maintains, "It is the American role in the Gulf that makes the United States the enemy in the eyes of millions of Muslims, some of whom are willing to join the ranks of al-Qaeda and other terrorist organizations. A less visible and less militarized role would likely mean improved relations and provide greater security" (Zunes 2002, 105).

The case of the Persian Gulf is perhaps the most important one, but one should not overlook the possibilities for change in U.S. policy toward other oil producing regions. Indeed, the opportunity for the United States to exercise a positive influence may be even greater in other areas, given their relative economic backwardness and lack of wealth. Consider sub-Saharan Africa, although many of the following points may apply to other regions as well. Important oil producing countries such as Nigeria, Angola, and Equatorial Guinea have been characterized to varying but often substantial degrees by extreme poverty, lack of democracy, human rights abuses, fiscal mismanagement, and corruption. Thus far, the United States, in its eagerness to see that the region's oil resources are developed, has been frequently criticized for tolerating governmental abuses and not addressing these problems.

Nevertheless, former assistant secretary of energy David Goldwyn and others have made a convincing case that the United States can and should do more. They argue that Washington must use its leverage "to press governments to become transparent, spend their revenues for the betterment of their people, and respect human rights and the rule of law." In particular, the United States "should make transparency in governance a benchmark by obliging governments to tell their citizens, in a comprehensive and highly visible manner, what revenues the government earns and where it spends them." In cooperation with other developed countries and by using international institutions, it should create a system of carrots and sticks to push for reforms in the resource-rich countries of the region (Goldwyn and Ebel 2004, 6–8, 22; see also Goldwyn 2003; Deutsch and Schlesinger 2006, 9–10). In this connection, much attention has been focused on efforts, such as the Extractive Industries Transparency Initiative (EITI) and the Publish What You Pay campaign, intended to encourage or require governments and energy companies to disclose revenues and payments and to improve accounting of the uses to which they are put.

These experts have identified a number of specific tools for achieving these goals. One would be to offer "debt-for-transparency" swaps. "If host governments agree to adopt public budgeting, making income and expenditures accessible to the broad public, and negotiating a domestic investment program with the World Bank," argue Goldwyn and Ebel, "creditor governments should agree to conditional long-term rescheduling of sovereign debt or even debt forgiveness." But, they continue, "debt relief must be structured [and] [g]overnments should take irreversible public steps on transparency and governance before they earn significant relief" (Goldwyn and Ebel 2004, 18; also 15).

A second approach would be to place conditions on trade finance. "Given the political uncertainty in the region," note Goldwyn and Ebel, "nearly all significant investments require sovereign risk insurance or trade financing." And just as there is now widespread acceptance of the need to assess the environmental impact of proposed projects, "it may be worth adding a developmental impact statement for projects in underdeveloped countries. To obtain financing, countries would need to demonstrate a commitment to using the proceeds of the resources for national development and agree to transparent monitoring and auditing of project income" (Goldwyn and Ebel 2004, 16, 19).

A third potential tool is capacity building. As Goldwyn and Ebel observe, "Most African nations lack the human capital to prepare, audit, and monitor public finance and to manage their petroleum reserves. [Thus] the United States and other nations must provide long-term capacity-building programs to train national officials in these essential skills." Additional programs could focus on "capacity building for civil society and local NGOs that are interested in monitoring government revenue and expenditure" (Goldwyn and Ebel 2004, 18).

The opportunities to employ such tools in sub-Saharan Africa and elsewhere are not unlimited, however. As Goldwyn and Ebel have warned, "The leverage the United States can muster, [even] in coalition with others, is not overwhelming" (Goldwyn and Ebel 2004, 7). In a global market, moreover, actual and potential oil producers can choose among investors. Indeed, in a perhaps misplaced quest for greater energy security, China and other emerging economies have been aggressively strengthening their ties with oil producers such as Angola and Sudan. And given the size of the investments that have been made in recent years, some countries may soon be awash with oil revenues, further limiting U.S. influence (Goldwyn and Ebel 2004, 12, 15). Thus if the United States does not act quickly to promote reform, it may soon be too late, at least in some places.

None of this is to say that altering the trajectory of U.S. policy toward oil producing regions over the past three to four decades will be easy, or that doing so may not create other problems. Of particular concern is the possibility that a more laissez-faire policy will have negative security externalities. For example, a successful Iraqi conquest of Kuwait, and even of the entire

southern littoral of the Persian Gulf, in 1990 may not have imposed unbearable economic costs on the United States and its oil-dependent partners. But
the resulting increase in oil revenues might have facilitated Iraq's acquisition
of a military capability, including nuclear weapons, that could have posed a
grave threat to non-oil-related U.S. interests, such as the security of Israel.
Derivative threats of this nature would have to be addressed through traditional mechanisms like extended deterrence. But if the United States is more
successful in promoting democratization, economic development, rule of law,
good governance, and respect for human rights as a result of a reorientation
of its policy toward oil producing regions, then such threats may be less likely
to arise in the first place.

We must also be conscious of the limits of what the United States can ac-
complish by itself through a reorientation of its external policies. Striving to
"desecuritize" oil and to treat oil exporting states no differently from others
will not transform the world overnight. The United States alone may not be
able to offer sufficient threats, inducements, or resources to achieve its goals.
Instead, it will often require the cooperation, or at least the acquiescence, of
other major powers, and that cooperation or acquiescence will not always
be forthcoming. Some states will not share U.S. goals at all, or they will be
tempted to pursue parochial commercial and security interests at the expense
of global public goods.

But the existence of such constraints is not a sufficient reason for inaction,
and the United States is still uniquely situated to make a difference. A perhaps
all-too-common viewpoint is that "as the world's only superpower . . . [the
United States] must accept its special responsibilities for preserving access to
worldwide energy supplies."[23] Yet the logic underlying this position is questionable, and to embrace it would involve perpetuating a status quo that is as
unnecessary as it is untenable. Indeed, the fact that American power remains
unrivaled suggests a very different policy implication: that the United States
has a special responsibility to take the lead in attempting to transcend the
traditional politics of oil and to create a new world order in which foreign oil
dependence is not a crippling liability.

REFERENCE MATTER

Notes

Chapter 1

1. Unfortunately, the study provided no data on total GDP, so the percentage effect on GDP cannot be determined.

2. Available at http://www.jimmycarterlibrary.org/documents/speeches/su80jec.phtml (accessed July 21, 2004). Nearly a year earlier, in February 1979, in a statement that went largely unremarked, Secretary of Defense Harold Brown had declared that the flow of oil from the Persian Gulf was "clearly part of our vital interests," which would be defended "with whatever means are appropriate, including military force where necessary" (*New York Times*, Feb. 26, 1979, A12, cited in Acharya 1989, 50).

Chapter 2

1. Unless otherwise specified, the terms "oil" and "petroleum" are used to refer to crude oil and natural gas liquids (NGL), which include ethane, propane, butane, and other liquids that are removed from natural gas. Currently, NGLs account for nearly one-third of U.S. oil production.

2. EIA, "U.S. Energy Consumption by Energy Source" (Aug. 2005), available at http://www.eia.doe.gov/cneaf/solar.renewables/page/trends/table1.html (accessed Nov. 20, 2006).

3. Just one year earlier, the EIA had projected that total petroleum demand would reach 27.9 MBD in 2025, for an annual growth rate of 1.5 percent, and that petroleum products supplied to the transportation sector would rise to 19.8 MBD in 2025 in the reference case (EIA 2005a, 183, tab. C4).

4. All production figures include both crude oil and natural gas liquids. They do not include the gains in volume that typically occur during the refining process.

5. BP 2006. See also EIA, "U.S. Crude Oil, Natural Gas, and Natural Gas Liquids Reserves Report" (Nov. 30, 2006), available at http://www.eia.doe.gov/oil_gas/ natural_gas/data_publications/crude_oil_natural_gas_reserves/cr.html (accessed Dec. 2, 2006).

6. EIA 2006a, 179, tab. C4. The figure includes crude oil and NGLs but not refinery processing gain or other domestic sources, such as liquids from coal. Similarly, Sieminski estimates that U.S. petroleum production will fall at a rate of about 2 percent per year during the 2000–2030 period, to a level of just 5.4 MBD (Sieminski 2005, 32).

7. Just one year earlier, the EIA projected that net petroleum imports would increase at an average annual rate of 2.4 percent in the reference case, reaching 15.4 MBD in 2015 and more than 19 MBD in 2025, when they would meet more than two-thirds of U.S. demand (EIA 2005a, 120, tab. 37).

8. WTRG Economics, "Oil Price History and Analysis" (n.d.), available at http:// www.wtrg.com/oilprice.htm (accessed Mar. 22, 2005).

9. Deutsch and Schlesinger 2006, 15. There have, of course, been exceptions to this rule. For example, the spike in gasoline prices following Hurricane Katrina in 2005 was primarily due to the temporary shutdown of pipelines and loss of refining capacity along the U.S. Gulf Coast.

10. Because of declining production in the North Sea, Britain is poised to become once again a net importer before the end of the decade.

Chapter 3

1. The concepts gross national product and gross domestic product are closely related. Gross national product (GNP) is the total value of final goods and services produced in a year by a country's nationals, including profits from capital held abroad. Gross domestic product (GDP) is the total value of final goods and services produced within a country's borders in a year. See "Measures of National Income and Output," available at http://en.wikipedia.org/wiki/Measures_of_national_income_and_ output.

2. In 2004, for example, the EIA projected that net imports would rise to between 16.6 and 23.3 MBD in 2025, and in 2005, it put this figure at between 17.0 and 21.2 MBD (EIA 2004a, 95, tab. 26; EIA 2005a, 120, tab. 37).

3. EIA 2006c, 87, 122. See also EIA 2005c, 175; EIA 2005a, 2; IMF 2005b, 165; Sieminski 2005, 38–31; Mouawad 2005a. Just one year before, the EIA projected that global consumption would reach 119 MBD in 2025. EIA 2005c, 93.

4. According to one estimate, the major oil companies have reduced their exploration budgets by more than one-quarter in recent years, notwithstanding higher prices (Stevens 2004).

5. According to one calculation, oil revenue per capita in the Persian Gulf states, including Saudi Arabia, was lower in 2003 than it had been in 1972, before the first significant price increase (Rutledge 2005, 168).

6. The relationship between spare capacity and oil shocks is discussed below.

7. For detailed descriptions of these disruptions, see Bohi and Toman 1996, 31–38; Yergin 1991, passim.

8. Other producers increased output by 600,000 barrels per day, resulting in a net supply reduction of about 4.4 MBD.

9. One recent authoritative study suggests the following estimates: demand will decline by just 0.08 percent, and supply will increase by just 0.05 percent for each 1.0 percent increase in the price of oil (Huntington 2005, 5–6).

10. Greene and Leiby 1993, 44–47. See also Greene, Jones, and Leiby 1998, 60; Greene and Tishchishyna 2001, 24. Similarly, a 2003 study by the National Defense Council Foundation put the total cost of past oil shocks at $2.2 to $2.5 trillion, or an average of $74.8 to $82.5 billion per year (Copulos 2003a; Copulos 2003b).

11. This comes to $512 billion in 1980 dollars and more than $1.2 trillion in 2006 dollars.

12. The Persian Gulf includes Oman, which is not a member of OPEC. Nevertheless, Oman's share of Persian Gulf oil production has always been less than 5 percent.

13. During the entire two-month period of the supply disruption, the average gross supply shortfall averaged only 2.0 MBD. See EIA, "Global Oil Supply Disruptions Since 1951," available at http://www.eia.doe.gov/emeu/security/distable.html (accessed Dec. 22, 2005).

14. EIA, "Global Oil Supply Disruptions Since 1951," available at http://www.eia .doe.gov/emeu/security/distable.html (accessed Dec. 22, 2005); OTA 1991, 9, tab. 2–2; Goldwyn and Ebel 2004, 13.

15. Aljazeera.com, "Al Qaeda Calls for Attacks on Saudi Oil Sites" (Dec. 19, 2004), available at http://www.aljazeera.com/me.asp?service_ID=6274 (accessed Dec. 3, 2006).

16. Hersh 2001; Lovins et al. 2004, 10; Baer 2003, xvii–xix. Indeed, in February 2006, terrorists linked to al Qaeda attempted, albeit unsuccessfully, to destroy the Abqaiaq facility. See Fattah 2006.

17. For a detailed list, see the "Iraq Pipeline Watch," maintained by the Institute for the Analysis of Global Security (IAGS) at http://www.iags.org/iraqpipelinewatch .htm.

18. Morse and Jaffe 2001, 10; Mouawad 2005a; Boussena 2004; Kalicki and Goldwyn 2005, 2; Goldwyn and Billig 2005, 515; *Economist* 2005; IMF 2005a, 9–10, 14. According to the EIA, OPEC spare production capacity reached historic low levels in 2005, at around 1.0–1.5 MBD, all of which was concentrated in Saudi Arabia. See EIA, "Short-Term Energy Outlook" (Nov. 2005), available at http://www.eia.doe.gov/pub/ forecasting/steo/oldsteos/novo5.pdf (accessed Dec. 9, 2006).

19. Bahree 2006. Likewise, the IMF has said a level of spare capacity in excess of three to four MBD might be needed. See IMF 2005a, 18.

20. For similar expressions of concern, see also IMF 2005a, 18; IMF 2005b, 171; Deutsch and Schlesinger 2006, 17; Barnes and Jaffe 2006, 145.

21. Goldwyn and Billig 2005, 517. Beccue and Huntington (2005, 15) put the chance that no spare capacity would be available at slightly more than 55 percent.

Chapter 4

1. Light-duty vehicles include passenger cars and light trucks, such as sport utility vehicles, vans, and pickup trucks, that weigh less than eighty-five hundred pounds.

2. Informative discussions of U.S. energy policy debates in the 1970s and early 1980s can be found in Goodwin 1981; Cowhey 1985; and Ikenberry 1988.

3. In 2001, excise taxes on gasoline brought more than $20 billion into the Highway Trust Fund (CBO 2002, 4).

4. Davis and Diegel 2004, tab. 4.18, gives slightly higher figures—26.2 mpg in 1987 and 24.5 mpg in 1999—but the downward trend is the same.

5. NRC 2002, 19, 23; GAO 2000, 4, 5; Bamberger 2003, 6; Davis and Diegel 2004, tabs. 4.8, 4.9; Rutledge 2005, 200. Between 1985 and 2001, the share of light trucks in the total light-vehicle output of the Big Three U.S. automakers became even more lopsided, increasing from 27 to 63 percent (Rutledge 2005, 122).

6. Davis and Diegel 2006, tabs. 4.1, 4.2. Heavy trucks account for most of the remaining VMT and fuel use.

7. The other federal tax subsidies are the alcohol mixture (blender's) tax credit, the tax credit for small ethanol producers, and the alternative fuels production tax credit, all of which have been little used (Lazzari 1995; Lazzari 1999).

8. For highway use of ethanol, see Davis and Diegel 2006, tab. 2.9. Detailed ethanol production data can be found at "EIA-819 Monthly Oxygenate Report," available at http://www.eia.doe.gov/oil_gas/petroleum/data_publications/monthly_oxygenate_telephone_report/motr.html.

9. EIA 2006b, 127, tab. 5.1. According to one recent estimate, subsidies to the oil industry worth 10 percent of the current price of oil would increase the world's oil supply by only about 0.2 percent, or 0.17 MBD (Metcalf 2006, 30–32).

10. Since the mid-1970s, under the terms of the International Energy Program of the International Energy Agency, the United States has been obligated to maintain oil inventories equivalent to ninety days of net imports, although the total can include privately owned stocks.

11. Bohi and Russell 1978, 244; Alm, Colglazier, and Kates-Garnick 1981, 326; Goldwyn and Billig 2005, 509; EIA, "Country Analysis Briefs: United States," available at http://www.eia.doe.gov/emeu/cabs/Usa/Full.html (accessed Jan. 26, 2007).

12. Congressional Digest 2000, 295–96; EIA, "Country Analysis Briefs: United States."

13. In the mid-1990s, one facility had to be closed due to problems with oil leakage, reducing the total storage capacity to 680 million barrels (Delucchi 1998, 63–64; Koplow and Martin 1998, 4.17).

14. EIA, "Country Analysis Briefs: United States"; DOE, "Strategic Petroleum Reserve—Profile," available at http://www.fe.doe.gov/programs/reserves/spr/index.html (accessed Dec. 15, 2006).

15. EIA, "Country Analysis Briefs: United States."

16. In September 2005, the United States also drew on the SPR after Hurricane Katrina devastated the oil production, distribution, and refining industries in the Gulf

of Mexico regions of Louisiana and Mississippi. It loaned 9.8 million barrels to affected companies and offered another 30 million barrels for sale, of which 11 million barrels were actually purchased, as part of a coordinated emergency response with the International Energy Agency. See DOE, "Releasing Crude Oil from the Strategic Petroleum Reserve," available at http://fossil.energy.gov/programs/reserves/spr/spr-drawdown.html (accessed Dec. 12, 2006); "Strategic Petroleum Reserve Hurricane Katrina Exchange Contracts Summary Fact Sheet," available at http://www.fossil.energy.gov/programs/reserves/spr/katrina_exchange_summary.pdf (accessed Dec. 12, 2006).

17. ICTA 2005, 4; DOE, "U.S. Strategic Petroleum Reserve—Profile."

18. The "Agreement on an International Energy Program" is available at http://www.iea.org/Textbase/about/IEP.PDF (accessed Dec. 15, 2006).

19. IEA press releases (05)14 (Sept. 2, 2005) and (05)15 (Sept. 7, 2005).

20. Figures derived from table in R. Scott 1994, II:141–42.

Chapter 5

1. See also Bohi and Toman 1996; Lugar and Woolsey 1999; Bergsten 2004; Deutsch and Schlesinger 2006, 19.

2. Sick 2003, 291. See also A. Friedman 1993, xvi; Kolko 2002, 19. This observation applies as well to the U.S. financial interest, especially during the 1970s but also increasingly of late, in seeing that Persian Gulf oil revenues were reinvested in the United States in order to prevent a global liquidity crisis and to alleviate the U.S. balance of payments deficit (Long 1985, 81).

3. For descriptions of Iran's role in the Nixon Doctrine, see Ramazani 1982, 25; Vance 1983, 314–15; Long 1985, 55; Gasiorowski 1991, 100; Teicher and Teicher 1993, 29; Miglietta 2002, 59. On its continuation under Carter, see Sullivan 1981, 20–21; Vance 1983, 314–15; Brzezinski 1983, 257; Sick 1985, 24–25; Little 2002, 147–48.

4. Litwak 1984, 210, n. 45; Federation of American Scientists, "F-14 Tomcat," available at http://www.fas.org/man/dod-101/sys/ac/f-14.htm (accessed Dec. 21, 2006).

5. Rubin 1981, 175; Federation of American Scientists, "F-16 Fighting Falcon," available at http://www.fas.org/man/dod-101/sys/ac/f-16.htm (accessed Dec. 21, 2006).

6. OPEC did raise the price of oil from $11.46 to $12.70 at its December 1977 meeting, but this 11 percent increase was well below the level of inflation since the previous price hike.

7. Rubin 1981, 196; Vance 1983, 316, 319; Kupchan 1987, 62; Bill 1988, 229; Teicher and Teicher 1993, 28. The directive, Presidential Directive/NSC-13, is available at http://www.jimmycarterlibrary.org/documents/pddirectives/pd13.pdf (accessed Dec. 21, 2006).

8. Miller Center of Public Affairs, "Jimmy Carter Speeches: Inaugural Address (January 20, 1977)," available at http://millercenter.virginia.edu/scripps/diglibrary/prezspeeches/carter/jec_1977_0120.html (accessed Dec. 21, 2006).

9. Some sources report slightly lower levels for Saudi production. Where the sources disagree, I rely on the figures published in EIA, "Monthly Energy Review," available at http://www.eia.doe.gov/emeu/mer/contents.html.

10. Long 1985, 29; EIA, "Monthly Energy Review," Apr. 2007, tab. 11.1a, Crude Oil Production: OPEC Members, available at http://tonto.eia.doe.gov/merquery/mer_data.asp?table=T11.01a (accessed May 12, 2007).

11. Chanin and Gause 2003; EIA, "Country Analysis Briefs: Saudi Arabia" (Aug. 2005), available at http://www.eia.doe.gov/emeu/cabs/saudi.html (accessed Jan. 26, 2007).

12. The actual military actions taken by the United States in the Persian Gulf are discussed in Chapter 6.

13. In the estimation of Charles Kupchan, "Never before had a single arms agreement stimulated such controversy in Washington" (Kupchan 1987, 144).

14. The role of Saudis in funding al Qaeda and other terrorist organizations is examined in Brisard 2002; Greenberg 2003; Greenberg 2004; and NCTAUS 2004.

15. Tahir-Kheli 1982, 99, 104; Cordovez and Harrison 1995, 57, 65–66; Kux 2001, 245–51, 256–61. The F-16s intended for Iran were never delivered.

16. For a complete list of the CIA tasks, see Yousaf and Adkin 1991, 95–96.

17. The National Security Strategy of the United States of America, Sept. 19–20, 2002, available at http://www.whitehouse.gov/nsc/nss.html (accessed Oct. 31, 2005).

18. Ed Morse, e-mail message to author, Sept. 28, 2005.

19. EIA, "Country Analysis Briefs: Venezuela," Sept. 2006, available at http://www.eia.doe.gov/emeu/cabs/Venezuela/Full.html (accessed Dec. 22, 2006).

20. Ellsworth 2005; EIA, "Country Analysis Briefs: Venezuela," Sept. 2006, available at http://www.eia.doe.gov/emeu/cabs/Venezuela/Full.html (accessed Dec. 22, 2006).

21. EIA, "Country Analysis Briefs: Venezuela," Sept. 2006, available at http://www.eia.doe.gov/emeu/cabs/Venezuela/Full.html (accessed Dec. 22, 2006).

22. Forero 2004a; EIA, "Country Analysis Briefs: Venezuela," Sept. 2005, available at http://www.eia.doe.gov/emeu/cabs/Venezuela/Full.html (accessed Sept. 26, 2005).

23. BP 2006; EIA, "Monthly Energy Review" (Aug. 2005).

24. Klare 2004a, 128, 140–42; EIA, "Monthly Energy Review" (Aug. 2005), 53.

25. Klare 2001, 86; EIA, "Country Analysis Briefs: Kazakhstan," Oct. 2006, available at http://www.eia.doe.gov/emeu/cabs/Kazakhstan/Full.html (accessed Dec. 22, 2006); EIA, "Country Analysis Briefs: Azerbaijan," Aug. 2006, available at http://www.eia.doe.gov/emeu/cabs/Azerbaijan/Full.html (accessed Dec. 22, 2006). In 2006, the EIA projected that investments in Kazakhstan and Azerbaijan alone would total significantly more than $100 billion. See EIA, "Kazakhstan: Major Oil and Natural Gas Projects," Oct. 2006, available at http://www.eia.doe.gov/emeu/cabs/Kazakhstan/kazaproj.html (accessed Dec. 22, 2006); EIA, "Azerbaijan: Production-Sharing Agreements," June 2006, available at http://www.eia.doe.gov/emeu/cabs/Azerbaijan/azerproj.html (accessed Dec. 22, 2006).

26. Martha Brill Olcott in U.S. Congress, Senate 1998, 37.

27. For official statements of U.S. objectives during the second term of the Clinton administration, see Marc Grossman in U.S. Congress, Senate 1998; Testimony by Ambassador Richard L. Morningstar, Special Advisor to the President and Secretary

of State for Caspian Basin Energy Diplomacy, before the Senate Subcommittee on International Economic Policy, Exports and Trade Promotion, Mar. 3, 1999, available at http://www.treemedia.com/cfrlibrary/library/policy/morningstar.html (accessed Sept. 15, 2005); John Wolf in "Wolf on Caspian Region 'Oil and Gas Story' at Senate Hearing," Apr. 12, 2000, available at http://www.usembassy-israel.org.il/publish/press/congress/archive/2000/April/uc10413.htm (accessed Jan. 31, 2007).

28. Testimony by Ambassador Richard L. Morningstar.

29. See USAID, "U.S. Overseas Loans and Grants (Greenbook)," available at http://qesdb.cdie.org/gbk/ (accessed Sept. 16, 2005). See also Klare 2001, 95–96.

30. U.S. Department of State, "Country Reports on Human Rights Practices—2003: Azerbaijan," Feb. 24, 2004, available at http://www.state.gov/g/drl/rls/hrrpt/2003/27826.htm (accessed Dec. 22, 2006).

31. Human Rights Watch, "Azerbaijan: Ensure Freedom of Assembly for the Opposition," May 24, 2005, available at http://hrw.org/english/docs/2005/05/24/azerba110115_txt.htm (accessed Dec. 22, 2006).

32. Diehl 2005; Chivers 2005a; Chivers 2005b; Jeffrey Thomas, "Improvements Seen, but Azerbaijan Election Said to Fall Short," Nov. 7, 2005, available at http://usinfo.state.gov/eur/Archive/2005/Nov/07-749512.html (accessed Dec. 22, 2006).

33. Testimony of Ms. Maureen Greenwood, Advocacy Director for Europe and the Middle East, Amnesty International, before the Senate Subcommittee on East Asia and Pacific Affairs, Mar. 3, 1999, available at http://asiep.free.fr/asiecentrale/mercaspienne-hearing-3–99.html (accessed Sept. 15, 2005).

34. The principal actual and potential oil producing states in the region are Angola, Cameroon, Equatorial Guinea, Gabon, Nigeria, the Republic of the Congo (Brazzaville), and São Tomé and Príncipe. In addition, landlocked Chad has recently begun to export oil via a pipeline through Cameroon.

35. Dao 2002a; BP 2006; EIA, "Country Analysis Briefs: Nigeria," Mar. 2006, available at http://www.eia.doe.gov/emeu/cabs/Nigeria/Full.html (accessed Dec. 22, 2006).

36. Hodges 2004, 144, 147; BP 2006; EIA, "Country Analysis Briefs: Angola," Jan. 2006, available at http://www.eia.doe.gov/emeu/cabs/Angola/Full.html (accessed Dec. 22, 2006).

37. BP 2006; EIA, "Country Analysis Briefs: Equatorial Guinea," May 2006, available at http://www.eia.doe.gov/emeu/cabs/Equatorial_Guinea/Full.html (accessed Dec. 22, 2006).

38. Eviatar 2004; Hodges 2004, 145; EIA, "Country Analysis Briefs: Angola," Jan. 2006, available at http://www.eia.doe.gov/emeu/cabs/Angola/Full.html (accessed Dec. 22, 2006).

39. EIA, "Country Analysis Briefs: Nigeria," Mar. 2006, available at http://www.eia.doe.gov/emeu/cabs/Nigeria/Full.html (accessed Dec. 22, 2006).

40. Office of International Security Affairs, Department of Defense, "U.S. Security Strategy for Sub-Saharan Africa," *Defense Issues* 10, no. 78 (Aug. 1995), available at

http://www.defense.link.mil/speeches/1995/s19950801–report.html (accessed Dec. 22, 2006).

41. Statement of Calvin R. Humphrey, Principal Deputy Assistant Secretary for International Affairs, Department of Energy, in U.S. Congress, House 2000, 30.

42. Ibid.

43. See, for example, the discussions of Nigeria and Angola in FY2006 Congressional Budget Justification for Foreign Operations, available at http://www.state.gov/s/d/rm/rls/cbj/ (accessed Oct. 5, 2005).

44. EIA, "Country Analysis Briefs: Equatorial Guinea," May 2006, available at http://www.eia.doe.gov/emeu/cabs/Equatorial_Guinea/Full.html (accessed Dec. 22, 2006).

45. Prepared Statement of Global Witness in "Weak States in Africa: U.S. Policy in Angola," hearing before the Subcommittee on African Affairs of the Committee on Foreign Relations, United States Senate, 107th Congress, 2d session, Oct. 16, 2002, p. 15.

46. Eviatar 2003; Gary and Karl 2003, 32; Hodges 2004, 165; EIA, "Country Analysis Briefs: Angola," Jan. 2006, available at http://www.eia.doe.gov/emeu/cabs/Angola/Full.html (accessed Dec. 22, 2006).

47. EIA, "Country Analysis Briefs: Nigeria," Apr. 2005, p. 6, available at http://www.climatelaw.org/gas.flaring/report/section3/doc3.1.pdf (accessed Dec. 22, 2006).

Chapter 6

1. Jimmy Carter, "State of the Union Address 1980," Jan. 23, 1980, available at http://www.jimmycarterlibrary.org/documents/speeches/su80jec.phtml (accessed Dec. 22, 2006). Nearly a year earlier, in February 1979, in a statement that went largely unremarked, Secretary of Defense Harold Brown had declared that the flow of oil from the Persian Gulf would be defended "with whatever means are appropriate, including military force where necessary" (*New York Times*, Feb. 26, 1979, A12, cited in Acharya 1989, 50; see also Brzezinski 1983, 443).

2. See, for example, National Security Directive 45, "U.S. Policy in Response to the Iraqi Invasion of Kuwait," Aug. 20, 1990, available at http://bushlibrary.tamu.edu/research/nsd/NSD/NSD%2045/0001.pdf (accessed May 25, 2004); Clinton 2000.

3. "Excerpts from Pentagon's New Plan," *New York Times*, Mar. 8, 1992. See also Gellman 1992.

4. Since the mid-1970s, the U.S. federal budgetary fiscal year has begun on October 1. Thus FY2005 included the last three months of calendar year 2004 and the first nine months of 2005.

5. Jay E. Hines, "US CENTCOM History," available at http://www.centcom.mil/sites/uscentcom1/Shared%20Documents/History.aspx (accessed Oct. 12, 2006).

6. Acharya 1989, 67–69; Delucchi and Thomas 1996, 4. In 1991, the GAO provided an estimate of $600 million between 1980 and 1990, plus an additional $600 million for training and $300 million for joint combined exercises (GAO 1991). Others have placed the cost at as much as $1 billion per year (R. Johnson 1989, 157–58, n. 126).

7. On the 1980s, see CBO 1983, 30. On the 1990s, see CBO 1997b, 79; O'Hanlon 1998,

58. Under the Strategic Mobility Plan developed after the Gulf War, the army ultimately hoped to be able have a full five-division corps with its accompanying support and sustainment units in place within seventy-five days.

8. With the growth in the C-17 fleet from 48 to 120 planes, annual operation and support costs for that aircraft alone were expected to rise from less than $400 million to more than $1 billion in 1997 dollars (CBO 1997b, xiii).

9. CBO 1997b, 29, 37; Global Security, "Army Prepositioned Stock (APS-3)," available at http://www.globalsecurity.org/military/agency/army/aps-3.htm (accessed Jan. 5, 2006).

10. CBO 1997b, 43; Global Security, "Camp as Sayliyah," available at http://www.globalsecurity.org/military/facility/camp-as-sayliyah.htm (accessed Jan. 5, 2006).

11. A 1991 study gives a total figure of $1 billion for the cost of air force prepositioning and bare-base sets in the region through 1990 (GAO 1991).

12. Global Security, "Oman Facilities," available at http://www.globalsecurity.org/military/facility/oman.htm (accessed Jan. 5, 2006).

13. Global Security, "Manama, Bahrain," available at http://www.globalsecurity.org/military/facility/manama.htm (accessed Jan. 5, 2006).

14. Acharya 1989, 112, 129; Hiro 1989, 12; Naval Historical Center, "Overview: The Role of the Navy," available at http://www.history.navy.mil/wars/dstorm/ds1.htm (accessed Oct. 12, 2006).

15. Naval presence figures are derived from Palmer 1992, 107. A typical entry in the annual *Military Balance* published by the authoritative International Institute for Strategic Studies (IISS) lists one carrier battle group, including six surface combatants, and the MIDEASTFOR of four combatants and a command ship.

16. A detailed description is provided in Acharya 1989, chap. 5. See also Brzezinski 1983, 446; Sick 1983, 72–74; Kupchan 1987, 129; Teicher and Teicher 1993, 84.

17. Acharya 1989, 93; CBO 1983, 59. The GAO (1991) gave a slightly lower figure—$1.1 billion—for the total cost of military construction for Southwest Asia dedicated and oriented programs, while Kupchan (1987, 144) reports that the United States funneled $2 billion into improving regional facilities during that period.

18. IISS 2002, 25; Yetiv 2004, 69; Global Security, "Manama, Bahrain" available at http://www.globalsecurity.org/military/facility/manama.htm (accessed Jan. 5, 2006); U.S. Naval Forces Central Command and 5th Fleet, "COMUSNAVCENT History," available at http://www.cusnc.navy.mil/Orders%20to%20Command/pages/history_navcent.htm (accessed Jan. 5, 2006).

19. Global Security, "Operation Vigilant Warrior," available at http://www.globalsecurity.org/military/ops/vigilant_warrior.htm (accessed Oct. 12, 2006); Global Security, "Exercise Intrinsic Action," available at http://www.globalsecurity.org/military/ops/intrinsic_action.htm (accessed Oct. 12, 2006); Global Security, "Desert Spring," available at http://www.globalsecurity.org/military/ops/desert_spring.htm (accessed Oct. 12, 2006); Priest 2003, 84.

20. IISS 2002; Schmitt 2003; Bandow 2003, 544; Priest 2003, 84; Global Security, "Operation Vigilant Warrior."

21. The lower figure is derived from CBO 1983, 25. Epstein 1986, 27, provides an estimate of $1.8 billion for the annual cost of operating and supporting an armored division.

22. The $1.9 billion figure appears in CBO 1983. The higher figures are from Kaufmann 1987, 88.

23. A 1990 CBO analysis yielded a similar range of $1.5 to $2.3 billion per division, depending on whether or not overhead costs were included.

24. Figures derived from Epstein 1986, 27. Kaufmann placed the cost of an F-16 wing at $2.0 billion and that of an F-15 wing at $6.0 billion (Kaufmann 1987, 88). A 1990 CBO study offered a slightly higher annual estimate of $500 million per wing, not including institutional overhead costs of another $200 million per wing.

25. Calculated from OUD 1999, tab. 6–4.

26. Similarly, a planning contingency used by the previous Bush administration to generate the "base force" requirements assumed that the United States would use four and two-thirds heavy army divisions, approximately three marine brigades, five fighter-attack wings, four heavy bomber squadrons, and three carrier battle groups to defeat an Iraqi attack on Kuwait and Saudi Arabia (Kaufmann 1992, 50).

27. Calculations based on CBO 1997a.

28. In addition to excluding the personnel and O&M costs of the "institutional" army, this figure does not consider any of the costs associated with National Guard and reserve units, procurement, research, development, testing, and evaluation (RDT&E), military construction, retirement pay, and other categories, which totaled nearly $27 billion in FY1997. Thus it may significantly underestimate the true cost of the forces maintained for Persian Gulf missions.

29. O'Hanlon offers a total procurement cost, including parts and munitions, of $10 billion and assumes a weapons lifetime of twenty-five to thirty years.

30. Kaufmann 1992, 82, tab. 7–4. This figure is based on a cost of $4.8 billion for four wings of F-15s and $5.7 billion for six wings of F-16s.

31. DOD 1992; CBO 1997b, 34. One source lists ten tactical fighter wings as well as a number of other air units. See Global Security, "Operation Desert Storm: Air Forces," available at http://www.globalsecurity.org/military/ops/desert_storm-air .htm (accessed Oct. 12, 2006).

32. National Security Directive 45, "U.S. Policy in Response to the Iraqi Invasion of Kuwait," Aug. 20, 1990, available at http://bushlibrary.tamu.edu/research/ nsd/NSD/NSD%2045/0001.pdf (accessed May 25, 2004); National Security Directive 54, "Responding to Iraqi Aggression in the Gulf," Jan. 15, 1991, available at http:// bushlibrary.tamu.edu/research/nsd/NSD/NSD%2054/0001.pdf (accessed May 25, 2004).

33. Quoted in Yergin 1991, 773. See also Bush 1991a, 196.

34. Quoted in Little 2002, 73. See also Bush and Scowcroft 1998, 399–400. In a similar vein, Secretary of Defense Cheney reportedly said, "We're there because the fact of the matter is that part of the world controls the world supply of oil, and whoever controls the supply of oil, especially if it were a man like Saddam Hussein, with a

large army and sophisticated weapons, would have a stranglehold on the American economy and on—indeed on the world economy" (Koppel 2006).

35. Global Security, "Operation Northern Watch," available at http://www .globalsecurity.org/military/ops/northern_watch.htm (accessed Jan. 5, 2006).

36. Global Security, "Operation Southern Watch," available at http://www .globalsecurity.org/military/ops/southern_watch.htm (accessed Jan. 5, 2006); Schmitt 2003.

37. *Washington Post* reporter Thomas Ricks has estimated that the two no-fly zones cost roughly $1 billion a year, while other U.S. military preparations, such as the exercises in Kuwait, added another $500 million to the bill (Ricks 2006, 15).

38. Some analysts have estimated the costs of these operations and of containing Iraq more generally at between $11.3 and $19.4 billion per year in 2003 dollars (for example, Amidon 2005; Davis, Murphy, and Topel 2006). Where these calculations are made explicit, however, they attribute the entire costs of the forces involved to the operations and may also include the cost of CENTCOM forces located outside the Persian Gulf and thus not directly involved.

39. Ricks 2006, 321–22. The Congressional Budget Office has estimated that the total number of troops involved, including those not stationed in Iraq, peaked at between 240,000 and 300,000 in May 2003 before dropping to a low of 170,000 from late 2003 through late 2004 and then rising again to 260,000 in September 2005 (Belasco 2006, 28–39).

40. As of the end of 2006, more than ten thousand U.S. military personnel had been wounded severely enough that they could not return to duty within seventy-two hours. See "Iraq Coalition Casualty Count," available at http://icasualties.org/oif/ (accessed Dec. 30, 2006). Another source notes that, through the end of 2005, seven thousand servicemen had suffered brain, spinal, amputation, and other serious injuries (Bilmes and Stiglitz 2006, 5).

41. Isenberg 2005; Bilmes 2005; Khalili 2005; Sterngold 2005; Sanger and Schmitt 2005; Belasco 2006; Ricks 2006. In 2006, the Congress authorized $23 billion for reset in FY2007, and the army said it would need an average of $14 billion per year over six years for repairs and replacements. Even the White House reportedly estimated that war costs would reach $110 billion in FY2007 (AP 2006; Shankar and Gordon 2006, A10).

42. Bilmes 2005. See also Khalili 2005; Sterngold 2005; Wallsten and Kosec 2005; Belasco 2006; Bilmes and Stiglitz 2006. A March 2006 estimate by three economists put the total present value of the cost of the war "in the range of 410 billion to 630 billion in 2003 dollars," but by the end of 2006 it was clear that government outlays on operations, equipment, and reconstruction alone would approach the lower figure by the end of FY2007 (Davis, Murphy, and Topel 2006, 2).

Chapter 7

1. See Keddie 1981 for a detailed description.

2. Keddie 1981, 176–77. See also Rubin 1981, 200; Little 2002, 222.

3. Interestingly, bin Laden also damned the kingdom's senior clerics for having approved the entry of Christian troops in the first place (Anonymous 2002, 115).

4. Ayatollah Khomeini in particular "was obsessively—even mindlessly—opposed to the United States." He blocked every effort at reconciliation, sought a total cleansing of U.S. influence from Iran, and blamed America for all of Iran's problems (K. Pollack 2004, 146).

5. Anonymous 2002, 17, 229. See also Anonymous 2004. The official has since been identified as Michael Scheuer, who resigned from the CIA in late 2004.

6. In addition to the regular forces, another thirteen to fourteen hundred U.S. military personnel and civilian contractors were involved in training the Saudi Arabian National Guard (SANG) (Bandow 2003, 544; Priest 2003, 85).

7. Zunes 2002, 96; Haddad 2003, 477; Everest 2004, 218; Anonymous 2004, 212. For bin Laden's statements, see Bergen 2001, 95–96; Anonymous 2002, 28.

8. Indeed, former Undersecretary of Defense Paul Wolfowitz has described "the real price" of containing Iraq in the 1990s as "giving Osama bin Laden his principal talking point . . . his big complaint is that we have American troops on the holy soil of Saudi Arabia and that we're bombing Iraq. That was his big recruiting device, his big claim against us" (quoted in Ricks 2006, 18).

9. Benjamin and Simon 2005, 19–21, provides a list of post–9/11 incidents.

10. Pew Global Attitudes Project, "Views of a Changing World 2003: War With Iraq Further Divides Global Publics," June 3, 2003, available at http://pewglobal.org/reports/display.php?ReportID=185 (accessed Jan. 5, 2007). See also FT 2003. Subsequent surveys found that the number of respondents in Jordan, Turkey, Indonesia, and Nigeria expressing a favorable view of the United States increased but remained below prewar levels.

11. Quoted in Bergen 2004. See also Benjamin and Simon 2005, 31–32.

12. Porter J. Goss, "Global Intelligence Challenges 2005: Meeting Long-Term Challenges with a Long-Term Strategy," Testimony before the Senate Select Committee on Intelligence, Feb. 16, 2005, available at https://www.cia.gov/cia/public_affairs/speeches/2005/Goss_testimony_02162005.html (accessed Jan. 5, 2007).

13. Benjamin and Simon 2005, 50, see also 42 and 46–47. Likewise, in 2005, a National Intelligence Council study described Iraq as the primary training ground for the next generation of terrorists, and the U.S. Department of State acknowledged that "foreign fighters appear to be working to make the insurgency in Iraq what the resistance movement to the Soviet occupation of Afghanistan was to the earlier generation of jihadists—a melting pot for jihadists from around the world, a training ground, and an indoctrination center." See Mazzetti 2006; DOS 2005, 7.

Chapter 8

1. A recent report by the Energy Security Leadership Council estimated that savings due to CAFE now amount to sixty billion gallons per year (ESLC 2006, 32).

2. Projections based on EIA 2006a, tab. 1. For a similar estimate, see Klare 2004a.

3. Grumet 2006, 29. Likewise, the 1991 National Energy Strategy acknowledged

that "our vulnerability to price shocks is not determined by how much oil we import . . . [but] how oil dependent our economy is" (quoted in NRDC 2001). See also Feldstein 2001, 61; Klare 2004a, 193.

4. ESLC 2006, 14. See also Ikenberry and Slaughter 2006.

5. Deutsch and Schlesinger 2006, 21–22, estimate that, in the current tight oil markets, a 10 percent drop in U.S. consumption could cause a temporary decline in global prices of 12 to 25 percent.

6. Nevertheless, Lovins et al. find that the demand for petrochemical feedstocks could be reduced by 0.27–0.51 MBD through plastic recycling and that biomaterials could displace another 0.6–1.2 MBD of crude-oil based petrochemical feedstocks by 2025 (Lovins et al. 2004, 110).

7. See, for example, www.apolloalliance.org (accessed Jan. 22, 2007); http://www .nrdc.org/air/energy/fensec.asp (accessed Jan. 22, 2007); and http://democrats.senate. gov/energy/about.html (accessed Jan. 22, 2007).

8. "Gas-Guzzler Loophole: SUVs and Light Trucks Drive Off with Billions," available at http://www.electrifyingtimes.com/gasguzzlerloophole.html (accessed Dec. 14, 2005).

9. In 2006, this loophole was partially closed, but pickup trucks weighing more than eighty-five hundred pounds and SUVs more than ten thousand pounds continued to be excluded.

10. Many of these are summarized in NRC 2002, 86–93; and ESLC 2006, 35–38.

11. There was little consensus at the time, however, on the size of the gap between the social and private costs. Estimates ranged from as low as $2 per barrel to as high as $124 per barrel (Broadman and Hogan 1988, 8–9).

12. IEA 2004a, 58, 79–80, 84; NRDC 2004, v–vii; Grumet 2006, 37; Woolsey 2002, 32.

13. The $60,000 figure is offered by Set America Free, "A Blueprint for U.S. Energy Security," available at http://www.setamericafree.org/blueprint.pdf (accessed Jan. 26, 2007).

14. Davis and Diegel 2004, tab. 6–4; Alternative Fuels Data Center, "Alternative Fueling Station Counts by State and Fuel Type," available at http://www.eere .energy .gov/afdc/infrastructure/station_counts.html (accessed Jan. 26, 2007).

15. Romm 2004, 2. See also Klare 2004a, 199; Roberts 2004, 272.

16. CBO 2002, 14; Lovins et al. 2004, 105; Associated Press, "Federal Program to Reduce Fuel Use Instead Increased It," *Dallas Morning News*, Jan. 6, 2006, available at http://www.dallasnews.com/sharedcontent/dws/bus/stories/010606dnbusfuel.4fa74d14.html (accessed Jan. 26, 2007).

17. Gaffney 2005; Set America Free, "A Blueprint for U.S. Energy Security."

18. Set America Free, "A Blueprint for U.S. Energy Security."

19. EIA, "International Petroleum Monthly" (Dec. 2006), tab. 1.6, available at http://www.eia.doe.gov/emeu/ipsr/t16.xls (accessed Jan. 26, 2007).

20. These calculations are based on Leiby and Bowman 2000b.

21. European gasoline stocks were drawn on to replenish supplies in U.S. markets that were disrupted by Hurricane Katrina in 2005.

22. In fact, the UN embargo on Iraqi and Kuwaiti oil exports had similar supply and price effects. See Chapter 3.

23. Robert Ebel, *The Geopolitics of Energy Into the 21st Century*, A Report of the CSIS Strategic Energy Initiative, vol. 1 (Washington, DC: Center for Strategic and International Studies, 2002), 24, 30, quoted in Klare 2004a, 14, 184.

Works Cited

Abramovici, P. 2004. United States: The New Scramble for Africa. *Le Monde Diplo-matique* (English edition), July. Available at http://mondediplo.com/2004/07/ 07usinafrica.

Acharya, A. 1989. *U.S. Military Strategy in the Gulf.* London: Routledge.

Alm, A. L., W. Colglazier, and B. Kates-Garnick. 1981. Coping with Interruptions. In *Energy and Security*, ed. D. A. Deese and J. S. Nye. Cambridge, MA: Ballinger.

Alnasrawi, A. 2001. Iraq: Economic Sanctions and Consequences, 1990–2000. *Third World Quarterly* 22(2): 205–18.

Amidon, J. M. 2005. America's Strategic Imperative: A "Manhattan Project" for En-ergy. *Joint Forces Quarterly* (39): 68-77. Available at http://www.ndu.edu/inss/ Press/jfq_pages/editions/i39/i39_essaywin_04.pdf (accessed May 14, 2007).

Andrews, E. 2004. The Oil Question. *New York Times*, May 23.

Anonymous. 2002. *Through Our Enemies' Eyes: Osama bin Laden, Radical Islam, and the Future of America.* Washington, DC: Brassey's, Inc.

Anonymous. 2004. *Imperial Hubris: Why the West Is Losing the War on Terror.* Wash-ington, DC: Brassey's, Inc.

Apps, P. 2005. US Seeks Stronger Ties with Regional Player Angola. *Reuters*, Sept. 15.

Arvedlund, E. E. 2005. Pipeline Done, Oil From Azerbaijan Begins Flowing to Turkey. *New York Times*, May 26.

Aspin, L. 1993. *Report on the Bottom-Up Review.* Oct. Available at http://www.fas.org/ man/docs/bur/ (accessed Aug. 5, 2004).

Associated Press (AP). 2006. Senate, 100–0, Approves Budget for Pentagon. *New York Times*, Sept. 29.

Baer, R. 2003. *Sleeping with the Devil: How Washington Sold Our Soul for Saudi Crude.* New York: Crown.

Bahgat, G. 2001. Managing Dependence: American-Saudi Oil Relations. *Arab Studies Quarterly* 23(1): 1–14.

Bahgat, G. 2003. *American Oil Diplomacy in the Persian Gulf and the Caspian Sea.* Gainesville: University Press of Florida.

Bahree, B. 2006. Investment by Oil Industry Stalls. *Wall Street Journal*, Nov. 8.

Baker, P. 1997. Clinton Courts Head of Oil-Rich Azerbaijan; Aliyev Welcomed Despite Rights Abuses, Dispute With Armenia. *Washington Post*, Aug. 2.

Ball, G. W. 1982. *The Past Has Another Pattern: Memoirs.* New York: W. W. Norton.

Bamberger, R. 2003. *Automobile and Light Truck Fuel Economy: The CAFE Standards.* Issue Brief for Congress. Washington, DC: Congressional Research Service, Library of Congress.

Bandow, D. 2003. The U.S. Alliance with Saudi Arabia. In *Cato Handbook for Congress: Policy Recommendations for the 108th Congress.* Washington, DC: The Cato Institute.

Banerjee, N. 2001a. The High, Hidden Cost of Saudi Arabian Oil. *New York Times*, Oct. 21.

Banerjee, N. 2001b. Military Plans Must Ensure Oil Flow. *New York Times*, Sept. 24.

Banerjee, N. 2004. Would More Drilling in America Make a Difference? *New York Times*, June 20.

Barfield, C. E. 1982. *Science Policy from Ford to Reagan: Change and Continuity.* Washington, DC: American Enterprise Institute for Public Policy Research.

Barnes, J., and A. M. Jaffe. 2006. The Persian Gulf and the Geopolitics of Oil. *Survival* 48(1): 143–62.

Barsky, R. B., and L. Kilian. 2004. Oil and the Macroeconomy Since the 1970s. *Journal of Economic Perspectives* 18(4): 115–34.

Beccue, P. C., and H. G. Huntington. 2005. *An Assessment of Oil Market Disruption Risks.* Oct. 3. Stanford, CA: Energy Modeling Forum, Stanford University. Available at http://www.stanford.edu/group/EMF/publications/doc/EMFSR8.pdf (accessed Dec. 3, 2006).

Belasco, A. 2006. *The Cost of Iraq, Afghanistan, and Other Global War on Terror Operations Since 9/11.* CRS Report for Congress. Washington, DC: Congressional Research Service. Available at http://www.fas.org/sgp/crs/natsec/RL33110.pdf (accessed Dec. 22, 2006).

Benjamin, D., and S. Simon. 2002. *The Age of Sacred Terror: Radical Islam's War on America.* New York: Random House.

Benjamin, D., and S. Simon. 2005. *The Next Attack: The Failure of the War on Terror and a Strategy for Getting It Right.* New York: Times Books/Henry Holt.

Bergen, P. L. 2001. *Holy War, Inc.: Inside the Secret World of Osama bin Laden.* New York: The Free Press.

Bergen, P. L. 2004. Backdraft: How the War in Iraq Has Fueled Al Qaeda and Ignited Its Dream of Global Jihad. *Mother Jones* 29(4). Available at http://www.motherjones.com/news/feature/2004/07/07_401.html (accessed Jan. 5, 2007).

Bergen, P. L., and A. Reynolds. 2005. Today's Insurgents in Iraq Are Tomorrow's Terrorists. *Foreign Affairs* 84(6): 2–6.

Bergsten, C. F. 2004. Foreign Economic Policy for the Next President. *Foreign Affairs* 83(2): 88–101.

Bill, J. A. 1988. *The Eagle and the Lion: The Tragedy of American-Iranian Relations.* New Haven, CT: Yale University Press.

Bilmes, L. 2005. The Trillion-Dollar War. *New York Times*, Aug. 20.

Bilmes, L., and J. E. Stiglitz. 2006. The Economic Costs of the Iraq War: An Appraisal Three Years After the Beginning of the Conflict. Paper prepared for presentation at the ASSA meetings, Boston. Available at http://www2.gsb.columbia.edu/faculty/jstiglitz/cost_of_war_in_iraq.pdf (accessed Dec. 22, 2006).

Blank, S. J. 2000. *U.S. Military Engagement with Transcaucasia and Central Asia.* Carlisle, PA: U.S. Army War College Strategic Studies Institute. Available at http://www.strategicstudiesinstitute.army.mil/pdffiles/PUB113.pdf (accessed Sept. 14, 2005).

Blum, W. 1998. The United States vs. Iraq: A Study in Hypocrisy. Available at http://members.aol.com/bblum6/usvsiraq.htm (accessed Oct. 31, 2005).

Bohi, D. R. 1989. *Energy Price Shocks and Macroeconomic Performance.* Washington, DC: Resources for the Future.

Bohi, D. R. 1991. On the Macroeconomic Effects of Energy Price Shocks. *Resources and Energy* 13(2): 145–62.

Bohi, D. R., and W. B. Quandt. 1984. *Energy Security in the 1980s: Economic and Political Perspectives.* Washington, DC: The Brookings Institution.

Bohi, D. R., and M. Russell. 1978. *Limiting Oil Imports: An Economic History and Analysis.* Baltimore, MD: Johns Hopkins University Press.

Bohi, D. R., and M. A. Toman. 1986. Oil Supply Disruptions and the Role of the International Energy Agency. *The Energy Journal* 7(2): 37–50.

Bohi, D. R., and M. A. Toman. 1996. *The Economics of Energy Security.* Boston: Kluwer Publishers.

Boussena, S. 2004. Oil and Market Stability After 2004. *Middle East Economic Survey* 47(40).

Bowman, S. 2003. *Iraq: U.S. Military Operations.* CRS Report for Congress. Washington, DC: Congressional Research Service. Oct. 2. Available at: fpc.state.gov/documents/organization/25375.pdf (accessed Dec. 22, 2006).

BP. 2006. *BP Statistical Review of World Energy.* London. June. Available at http://www.bp.com/statisticalreview.

Bremmer, I. 1998. Oil Politics: America and the Riches of the Caspian. *World Policy Journal* 15(1): 27–35.

Brinkley, J. 2005. Rice Takes Democracy Call To Central Asian Nations Needing It. *New York Times*, Oct. 14.

Brisard, J.-C. 2002. *Terrorism Financing: Roots and Trends of Saudi Terrorism Financing.* Report prepared for the President of the Security Council, United Nations. New York: JCB Consulting. Dec. 19.

Brisard, J.-C., and G. Dasquie. 2002. *Forbidden Truth: U.S.-Taliban Oil Diplomacy and the Failed Hunt for bin Laden*. New York: Thunder's Mouth Press/Nation Books.

Broadman, H. G., and W. W. Hogan. 1988. Is an Oil Tariff Justified? The Numbers Say Yes. *The Energy Journal* 9(3): 7–29.

Bronson, R. 2006. *Thicker than Oil: America's Uneasy Partnership with Saudi Arabia*. New York: Oxford University Press.

Brzezinski, Z. 1983. *Power and Principle: Memoirs of the National Security Adviser, 1977–1981*. New York: Farrar, Straus and Giroux.

Buckley, C. 2004. Venezuela Agrees to Export Oil and Gas to China. *New York Times*, Dec. 27.

Buckley, W. F., Jr. 1980. Human Rights and Foreign Affairs: A Proposal. *Foreign Affairs* 58(4): 775–96.

Buechner, W. N.d. History of the Gasoline Tax. Available at http://www.artba.org/ economics_research/reports/gas_tax_history.htm (accessed May 17, 2005).

Bush, G. 1990. *National Security Strategy of the United States*. Washington, DC: The White House.

Bush, G. 1991a. In Defense of Saudi Arabia. In *The Gulf War Reader: History, Documents, Opinions*, ed. M. L. Sifry and C. Cerf, 197–99. New York: Random House.

Bush, G. 1991b. *National Security Strategy of the United States*. Washington, DC: The White House. Available at http://www.fas.org/man/docs/918015–nss.htm (accessed May 25, 2004).

Bush, G., and B. Scowcroft. 1998. *A World Transformed*. New York: Alfred A. Knopf.

Byman, D. L. 2003. Al-Qaeda as an Adversary: Do We Understand Our Enemy? *World Politics* 56(1): 139–63.

Byman, D. L., and J. R. Wise. 2002. *The Persian Gulf in the Coming Decade: Trends, Threats, and Opportunities*. Santa Monica, CA: RAND.

Case, D. 2004. The Crude Doctrine. *Mother Jones* 29: 68–74.

Central Intelligence Agency (CIA). N.d. *The World Factbook*. Available at https:// www.cia.gov/cia/publications/factbook/index.html (accessed Dec. 15, 2006).

Chanin, C., and F. G. Gause III. 2003. U.S.-Saudi Relations: Bump in the Road or End of the Road? Report on a Saudi-American Dialogue sponsored by the Rockefeller Foundation. *Middle East Policy* 10(4): 116–25.

Chivers, C. J. 2005a. Crowd Protests Fraud in Azerbaijan Vote. *New York Times*, Nov. 10.

Chivers, C. J. 2005b. Police Break Up Peaceful Demonstration in Azerbaijan. *New York Times*, Nov. 27.

Chivers, C. J. 2006. Azerbaijan Leader, Under Fire, Hopes U.S. Visit Improves Image. *New York Times*, Apr. 19.

Clawson, P., and S. Henderson. 2005. Reducing Vulnerability to Middle East Energy Shocks: A Key Element in Strengthening U.S. Energy Security. Washington Institute for Near East Policy. Washington, DC. Available at http://www .washingtoninstitute.org/html/pdf/PolicyFocus49.pdf (accessed Dec. 3, 2006).

Clinton, B. 1996. *A National Security Strategy of Engagement and Enlargement*. Washington, DC: The White House. Available at http://www.fas.org/spp/military/docops/national/1996stra.htm (accessed May 28, 2004).

Clinton, B. 1998. *A National Security Strategy for a New Century.* Washington, DC: The White House. Available at http://clinton2.nara.gov/WH/EOP/NSC/html/documents/nssr.pdf (accessed May 25, 2004).

Clinton, B. 2000. *A National Security Strategy for a Global Age.* Washington, DC: The White House. Available at http://www.globalsecurity.org/military/library/policy/national/nss-0012.pdf (accessed May 25, 2004).

CNN.com. N.d. War in Iraq: Forces: US & Coalition. Available at http://edition.cnn.com/SPECIALS/2003/iraq/forces/coalition/ (accessed Dec. 22, 2006).

Cogan, C. G. 1993. Partners in Time: The CIA and Afghanistan Since 1979. *World Policy Journal* 10(2): 73–82.

Cohen, L. R., and R. G. Noll. 1991. Synthetic Fuels from Coal. In *The Technology Pork Barrel*, ed. L. R. Cohen and R. G. Noll, 259–319. Washington, DC: The Brookings Institution.

Coll, S. 2004. *Ghost Wars: The Secret History of the CIA, Afghanistan, and bin Laden, from the Soviet Invasion to September 10, 2001.* New York: Penguin.

Conant, M. A. 1982. *The Oil Factor in U.S. Foreign Policy, 1980–1990.* Lexington, MA: D. C. Heath.

Congressional Budget Office (CBO). 1981. *Managing Oil Disruptions: Issues and Policy Options.* A CBO Study. Washington, DC: Congress of the United States, Congressional Budget Office.

Congressional Budget Office (CBO). 1982. *Oil Import Tariffs: Alternative Scenarios and Their Effects.* Staff Working Paper. Washington, DC: Congressional Budget Office.

Congressional Budget Office (CBO). 1983. *Rapid Deployment Forces: Policy and Budgetary Implications.* Washington, DC: Congressional Budget Office.

Congressional Budget Office (CBO). 1984. *Tactical Combat Forces of the United States Force: Issues and Alternatives.* Staff Working Paper. Washington, DC: Congressional Budget Office.

Congressional Budget Office (CBO). 1990. *Budgetary and Military Effects of a Treaty Limiting Conventional Forces in Europe.* CBO Papers. Washington, DC: Congressional Budget Office.

Congressional Budget Office (CBO). 1997a. *An Analysis of the Army's Force Structure: Summary.* Washington, DC: Congressional Budget Office.

Congressional Budget Office (CBO). 1997b. *Moving U.S. Forces: Options for Strategic Mobility.* Washington, DC: Congressional Budget Office.

Congressional Budget Office (CBO). 2002. *Reducing Gasoline Consumption: Three Options.* Washington, DC: Congressional Budget Office.

Congressional Digest. 2000. Strategic Petroleum Reserve: America's Oil Dependence and Its Consequences. 79(12): 289–303.

Congressional Research Service (CRS). 1992. *The External Costs of Oil Used In Transportation.* CRS Report for Congress. CRS Report 92–574 ENR. Washington, DC: The Library of Congress.

Conry, B., and C. V. Peña. 2001. U.S. Security Strategy. In *Cato Handbook for Congress: Policy Recommendations for the 108th Congress.* Washington, DC: The Cato Institute.

Consumer Reports. 2005. Fuel Economy: Why You're Not Getting the MPG You Expect. Oct.

Copulos, M. R. 1990. Our Gulf Giveaway: Why Subsidize Oil for Japan and Europe? *Washington Post,* July 29.

Copulos, M. R. 2003a. *America's Achilles Heel: The Hidden Costs of Imported Oil: A Strategy for Energy Independence.* Washington, DC: The National Defense Council Foundation.

Copulos, M. R. 2003b. The Real Cost of Imported Oil. *Washington Times,* July 22.

Cordesman, A. H. 1984. *The Gulf and the Search for Strategic Stability: Saudi Arabia, the Military Balance in the Gulf, and Trends in the Arab-Israeli Military Balance.* Boulder, CO: Westview Press.

Cordesman, A. H. 1988. *The Gulf and the West: Strategic Relations and Military Realities.* Boulder, CO: Westview Press.

Cordesman, A. H. 2003. *Saudi Arabia Enters the Twenty-First Century: The Military and International Security Dimensions.* Westport, CT: Praeger.

Cordesman, A. H. 2004. Middle Eastern Energy After the Iraq War: Current and Projected Trends. *Middle East Policy* 19(4): 126–47.

Cordovez, D., and S. S. Harrison. 1995. *Out of Afghanistan: The Inside Story of the Soviet Withdrawal.* New York: Oxford University Press.

Cottam, R. W. 1988. *Iran and the United States: A Cold War Case Study.* Pittsburgh, PA: University of Pittsburgh Press.

Cowhey, P. F. 1985. *The Problems of Plenty: Energy Policy and International Politics.* Berkeley: University of California Press.

Danner, M. 2005. Taking Stock of the Forever War. *New York Times,* Sept. 11.

Dao, J. 2002a. In Quietly Courting Africa, U.S. Liked the Dowry: Oil. *New York Times,* Sept. 19.

Dao, J. 2002b. In West African Visits, Powell Seeks to Prime Oil Pumps. *New York Times,* Sept. 6.

Davis, S. C. 2000. *Transportation Energy Data Book: Edition 2000.* ORNL-6959. Oak Ridge, TN: Oak Ridge National Laboratory.

Davis, S. C., and S. W. Diegel. 2004. *Transportation Energy Data Book: Edition 24.* ORNL-6973. Oak Ridge, TN: Oak Ridge National Laboratory.

Davis, S. C., and S. W. Diegel. 2006. *Transportation Energy Data Book: Edition 25.* ORNL-6974. Oak Ridge, TN: Oak Ridge National Laboratory. Available at http://cta.ornl.gov/data/index.shtml.

Davis, S. J., K. M. Murphy, and R. H. Topel. 2006. War in Iraq Versus Containment. NBER Working Paper Series. Cambridge, MA: National Bureau of Economic Research. Available at http://www.nber.org/papers/w12092 (accessed Dec. 22, 2006).

Deffeyes, K. 2001. *Hubbert's Peak: The Impending World Oil Shortage.* Princeton, NJ: Princeton University Press.

Dekmejian, R. H., and H. H. Simonian. 2001. *Troubled Waters: The Geopolitics of the Caspian Region.* London: I. B. Tauris.

Delucchi, M. A. 1998. *Motor-Vehicle Infrastructure and Services Provided by the Public Sector. The Annualized Social Cost of Motor-Vehicle Use in the United States, Based on 1990–1991 Data.* UCD-ITS-RR-96–3 (7). Davis: Institute of Transportation Studies, University of California, Davis. Available at http://www.its.ucdavis .edu/publications/1996/RR-96–03–07.pdf (accessed May 21, 2004).

Delucchi, M. A., and J. Murphy. 1996. *U.S. Military Expenditures to Protect the Use of Persian-Gulf Oil for Motor Vehicles. The Annualized Social Cost of Motor-Vehicle Use in the United States, Based on 1990–1991 Data.* UCD-ITS-RR-96–03(15). Davis: Institute of Transportation Studies, University of California, Davis. Available at: http://www .its.ucdavis.edu/publications/1996/rr-96–03–15.pdf (accessed on May 20, 2004).

De Marchi, N. 1981. Energy Policy under Nixon: Mainly Putting Out Fires. In *Energy in Perspective: Today's Problems, Yesterday's Solutions,* ed. C. D. Goodwin. Washington, DC: The Brookings Institution.

Deutsch, J., and J. R. Schlesinger. 2006. National Security Consequences of U.S. Oil Dependency. Report of an Independent Task Force. New York: Council on Foreign Relations.

Dickerson, M. 2005. Homegrown Fuel Supply Helps Brazil Breathe Easy. *Los Angeles Times,* June 15.

Dickey, C. 2006. The Oil Shield. *Foreign Policy* (May/June).

Diehl, J. 2005. An Oil-Rich Test for Bush. *Washington Post,* Oct. 24.

Diehl, J. 2006. Retreat from the Freedom Agenda. *Washington Post,* Apr. 24.

Dinan, T., and D. Austin. 2004. *Fuel Economy Standards Versus a Gasoline Tax.* Economic and Budget Issue Brief. Washington, DC: Congressional Budget Office.

DiPardo, J. 2002. Outlook for Biomass Ethanol Production and Demand. Washington, DC: Energy Information Administration. Available at http://www.eia.doe .gov/oiaf/analysispaper/biomass.html (accessed on May 20, 2005).

Dobbs, M. 2002. U.S. Had Key Role in Iraq Buildup: Trade in Chemical Arms Allowed Their Use on Iranians, Kurds. *Washington Post,* Dec. 30.

Duffield, J. S. 2005. Oil and the Iraq War: How the United States Could Have Expected to Benefit, and Might Still. *Middle East Review of International Affairs* 9(2): 109–41.

Dumbrell, J. 1993. *The Carter Presidency: A Re-evaluation.* Manchester, England: Manchester University Press.

Easterbrook, G. 2004. The 50¢-a-Gallon Solution. *New York Times,* May 25.

Economist. 2005. Big Oil's Biggest Monster. Jan. 6.

Economist Intelligence Unit. 2004. *Risk Ratings Review (CRS)* (Sept.), Table 2. Available at http://store.eiu.com (accessed April 27, 2005).

Egan, T. 2004. Suddenly, It's Hip to Conserve Energy. *New York Times,* June 20.

Ellsworth, B. 2005. Oil Companies in Venezuela Face More Control by State. *New York Times,* Apr. 15.

Energy Information Administration (EIA). 1999. *Petroleum: An Energy Profile.* DOE/ EIA-0545(99). Available at http://tonto.eia.doe.gov/FTPROOT/petroleum/054599 .pdf (accessed May 19, 2004).

Energy Information Administration (EIA). 2000. *Potential Oil Production from the Coastal Plain of the Artic National Wildlife Refuge: Updated Assessment.* SR/ O&G/2000–02. Washington, DC: U.S. Department of Energy. Available at http:// www.eia.doe.gov/pub/oil_gas/petroleum/analysis_publications/arctic_national_ wildlife_refuge/html/execsummary.html (accessed Mar. 15, 2005).

Energy Information Administration (EIA). 2003. *Annual Energy Outlook 2003: With Projections to 2025.* Washington, DC: Department of Energy.

Energy Information Administration (EIA). 2004a. *Annual Energy Outlook 2004: With Projections to 2025.* DOE/EIA-0383(2004). Washington, DC: Department of Energy. Available at http://www.econstats.com/EIA/AEO2004.pdf (accessed Jan. 26, 2007).

Energy Information Administration (EIA). 2004b. *International Energy Outlook 2004.* DOE/EIA-0484(2004). Washington, DC: Department of Energy.

Energy Information Administration (EIA). 2004c. Top Petroleum Net Exporters, 2003 (Aug. 18). Available at http://www.eia.doe.gov/emeu/security/topexp.html (accessed Nov. 21, 2006).

Energy Information Administration (EIA). 2005a. *Annual Energy Outlook 2005: With Projections to 2025.* EIA/AEO-0383(2005). Washington, DC: U.S. Department of Energy.

Energy Information Administration (EIA). 2005b. *Annual Energy Review 2004.* DOE/ EIA-0384(2005). Washington, DC: U.S. Department of Energy. Available at http:// www.eia.doe.gov/emeu/aer/petro.html (accessed May 19, 2007).

Energy Information Administration (EIA). 2005c. *International Energy Outlook 2005.* DOE/EIA-0484(2005). Washington, DC: U.S. Department of Energy.

Energy Information Administration (EIA). 2006a. *Annual Energy Outlook 2006: With Projections to 2030.* EIA/AEO-0383(2006). Washington, DC: U.S. Department of Energy.

Energy Information Administration (EIA). 2006b. *Annual Energy Review 2005.* DOE/ EIA-0384(2006). Washington, DC: U.S. Department of Energy.

Energy Information Administration (EIA). 2006c. *International Energy Outlook 2006.* DOE/EIA-0484(2006). Washington, DC: U.S. Department of Energy.

Energy Information Administration (EIA). 2006d. Annual Oil Market Chronology (May). Available at http://www.eia.doe.gov/emeu/cabs/AOMC/overview.html (accessed Dec. 7, 2006).

Energy Information Administration (EIA). 2007a. *International Petroleum Monthly* (April). Available at http://www.eia.doe.gov/emeu/ipm/ (accessed May 18, 2007).

Energy Information Administration (EIA). 2007b. *Monthly Energy Review* (April). Available at http://www.eia.doe.gov/emeu/mer/ (accessed May 18, 2007).

Energy Security Leadership Council (ESLC). 2006. Recommendations to the Nation on Reducing U.S. Oil Dependence. Washington, DC: Security America's Energy Future. Available at http://www.secureenergy.org/reports/ESLC_Oil_Report.pdf (accessed Jan. 12, 2007).

Epstein, J. M. 1986. *The 1987 Defense Budget*. Washington, DC: The Brookings Institution.

Evans, D. 2005. Iraq Invasion Radicalized Saudi Fighters. *Reuters*, Sept. 18. Available at http://www.commondreams.org/headlines05/0918–01.htm (accessed Jan. 26, 2007).

Everest, L. 2004. *Oil, Power and Empire: Iraq and the U.S. Global Agenda*. Monroe, ME: Common Courage Press.

Eviatar, D. 2003. Rich in Oil, Poor in Everything Else: Can Profits Promote Democracy in Africa? *New York Times*, Dec. 4.

Eviatar, D. 2004. Africa's Oil Tycoons. *The Nation*. Apr. 12.

Fattah, H. M. 2006. Suicide Bombers Fail to Enter Saudi Oil Plant. *New York Times*, Feb. 25.

Feldstein, M. 2001. Achieving Oil Security: A Practical Proposal. *The National Interest* (65S): 60–65.

Feldstein, M. 2003. Reducing America's Dependence on Foreign Oil Supplies. Annual Meeting of the American Economic Association. New York: American Economic Association. Available at http://www.nber.org/feldstein/oildependenceaea2003 .pdf (accessed Dec. 8, 2005).

Financial Times (FT). 2003. Global Backlash: Washington Is Losing the Battle for Hearts and Minds. June 4.

Frank, R. H. 2006. A Way to Cut Fuel Consumption That Everybody Likes, Except the Politicians. *New York Times*, Feb. 16.

Forero, J. 2001. Venezuela's New Oil Law Is Seen as a Risk to Growth. *New York Times*, Dec. 4.

Forero, J. 2004a. Oil, Venezuela's Lifeblood, Is Now Its Social Currency, Too. *New York Times*, July 24.

Forero, J. 2004b. Safeguarding Colombia's Oil. *New York Times*, Oct. 22.

Franssen, D. H. 2003. Behind the Gas Pump: Implications of Our Dependence on Mideast Oil: U.S. Oil Security and National Energy Policy: Realities and Disconnects. Houston: International Energy Associates. Jan. 17. Available at http://www.beg.utexas.edu/energyecon/documents/behind_the_gas_pump/ HermanFranssen.pdf (accessed Jan. 26. 2007).

Freedman, L., and E. Karsh. 1993. *The Gulf Conflict, 1990–1991: Diplomacy and War in the New World Order*. Princeton, NJ: Princeton University Press.

Friedman, A. 1993. *Spider's Web: The Secret History of How the White House Illegally Armed Iraq*. New York: Bantam Books.

Friedman, G. 2004. *America's Secret War: Inside the Hidden Worldwide Struggle Between America and Its Enemies*. New York: Doubleday.

Friedman, T. L. 2002. Drowning Freedom in Oil. *New York Times*, Aug. 25.

Friedman, T. L. 2003a. Hummers Here, Hummers There. *New York Times*, May 23.

Friedman, T. L. 2003b. The Real Patriot Act. *New York Times*, Oct. 5.

Friedman, T. L. 2004. Should, Would, Can. *New York Times*, May 27.

Friedman, T. L. 2005. Too Much Pork and Too Little Sugar. *New York Times*, Aug. 5.

Friedman, T. L. 2006a. Fill' Er Up With Dictators. *New York Times*, Sept. 27.

Friedman, T. L. 2006b. Gas Pump Geopolitics. *New York Times*, Apr. 28.

Friedman, T. L. 2006c. As Energy Prices Rise, It's All Downhill for Democracy. *New York Times*, May 5.

Friedman, T. L. 2006d. The New Red, White and Blue. *New York Times*, Jan. 6.

Friedman, T. L. 2006e. Who's Afraid of a Gas Tax? *New York Times*, Mar. 1.

Fuller, G. E., and I. O. Lesser. 1997. Persian Gulf Myths. *Foreign Affairs* 76(3): 42–52.

Fund for Peace. 2006. Failed States Index 2006. Available at http://www.fundforpeace .org/programs/fsi/fsindex2006.php (accessed Dec. 21, 2006).

Gaffney, F. 2005. Freedom in Security: A Naked Energy Gap. *National Review*, Mar. 29.

Gary, I., and T. L. Karl. 2003. *Bottom of the Barrel: Africa's Oil Boom and the Poor.* Baltimore, MD: Catholic Relief Services.

Gasiorowski, M. J. 1991. *U.S. Foreign Policy and the Shah: Building a Client State in Iran.* Ithaca, NY: Cornell University Press.

Gaskins, D., and B. Stram 1991. *A Meta Plan: A Policy Response to Global Warming.* CSIA Discussion Paper 91–3. Cambridge, MA: Kennedy School of Government.

Gates, R. M. 1996. *From the Shadows: The Ultimate Insider's Story of Five Presidents and How They Won the Cold War.* New York: Simon & Schuster.

Gause, F. G., III. 2002. Be Careful What You Wish For: The Future of U.S.-Saudi Relations. *World Policy Journal* 49(1): 37–50.

Gause, F. G., III. 2003. *The Approaching Turning Point: The Future of U.S. Relations with the Gulf States.* Analysis Paper Number Two. Brookings Project on U.S. Policy Towards the Islamic World. Washington, DC: The Brookings Institution. Available at http://www.brook.edu/dybdocroot/fp/saban/gause20030430.pdf (accessed June 29, 2004).

Gellman, B. 1992. Keeping the U.S. First: Pentagon Would Preclude a Rival Superpower. *Washington Post*, Mar. 11.

Gerard, D., and L. B. Lave. 2003. *The Economics of CAFE Reconsidered: A Response to CAFE Critics and a Case for Fuel Economy Standards.* Regulatory Analysis 03–10. Washington, DC: AEI-Brookings Joint Center for Regulatory Studies. Available at http://www.aei.brookings.org/publications/abstract.php?pid=394 (accessed Dec. 9, 2005).

Gerth, J. 2002. U.S. Fails to Curb Its Saudi Oil Habit, Experts Say. *New York Times*, Nov. 26.

Gerth, J. 2005a. Big Oil Steps Aside in Battle Over Arctic. *New York Times*, Feb. 21.

Gerth, J. 2005b. Doubts Raised on Saudi Vow for More Oil. *New York Times*, Oct. 27.

Gielecki, M., F. Mayes, and L. Prete. 2001. *Incentives, Mandates, and Government Programs for Promoting Renewable Energy.* Energy Information Administration. Available at http://www.eia.doe.gov/cneaf/solar.renewables/rea_issues/incent. html (accessed Jan. 26, 2007).

Global Security. N.d. Operation Desert Storm: Air Forces. Available at http://www .globalsecurity.org/military/ops/desert_storm-air.htm (accessed Oct. 12, 2006).

Gold, D. 2003. *Hatred's Kingdom: How Saudi Arabia Supports the New Global Terrorism*. Washington, DC: Regnery Publishing, Inc.

Goldwyn, D. L. 2003. *US Energy Security: Latin America and West Africa*. Testimony before the Subcommittee on International Economic Policy, Export and Trade Promotion. House of Representatives. Washington, DC.

Goldwyn, D. L., and M. Billig. 2005. Building Strategic Reserves. In *Energy and Security: Toward a New Foreign Policy Strategy*, ed. J. H. Kalicki and D. L. Goldwyn, 509–29. Washington, DC: Woodrow Wilson Center Press.

Goldwyn, D. L., and R. E. Ebel. 2004. Crafting a U.S. Energy Policy for Africa. In *Rising U.S. Stakes in Africa: Seven Proposals to Strengthen U.S.-Africa Policy*, ed. W. H. Kansteiner, III and J. S. Morrison. Washington, DC: Center for Strategic and International Studies.

Goldwyn, D. L., and J. S. Morrison 2004. *Promoting Transparency in the African Oil Sector*. A Report of the CSIS Task Force on Rising U.S. Energy Stakes in Africa. Washington, DC: Center for Strategic and International Studies.

Goodstein, D. 2004. *Out of Gas: The End of the Age of Oil*. New York: W. W. Norton.

Goodwin, C. D., ed. 1981. *Energy Policy in Perspective: Today's Problems, Yesterday's Solutions*. Washington, DC: The Brookings Institution.

Gordon, J. 2002. Cool War: Economic Sanctions as a Weapon of Mass Destruction. *Harper's*, Nov.

Greenberg, I., and A. E. Kramer. 2006. Cheney, Visiting Kazakhstan, Wades Into Energy Battle. *New York Times*, May 6.

Greenberg, M. R. 2003. *Terrorist Financing*. Report of an Independent Task Force Sponsored by the Council on Foreign Relations. New York: Council on Foreign Relations.

Greenberg, M. R. 2004. *Update on the Global Campaign Against Terrorist Financing*. Second Report of an Independent Task Force on Terrorist Financing Sponsored by the Council on Foreign Relations. New York: Council on Foreign Relations. Available at http://www.cfr.org/pdf/Revised_Terrorist_Financing.pdf (accessed June 21, 2004).

Greene, D. L. 1990. CAFE or Price? An Analysis of the Effects of Federal Fuel Economy Regulations and Gasoline Price on New Car MPG, 1978–89. *Energy Journal* 11(3): 37–57.

Greene, D. L. 1998. Why CAFE Worked. *Energy Policy* 26(8): 595–613.

Greene, D. L., D. W. Jones, and P. N. Leiby. 1998. The Outlook for U.S. Oil Dependence. *Energy Policy* 26(1): 55–69.

Greene, D. L., and P. N. Leiby. 1993. *The Social Costs to the U.S. of Monopolization of the World Oil Market, 1972–1991*. ORNL-6744. Oak Ridge, TN: Oak Ridge National Laboratory. Available at http://www.ornl.gov/webworks/cppr/y2002/rpt/62964 .pdf (accessed June 17, 2004).

Greene, D. L., and N. I. Tishchishyna. 2001. Costs of Oil Dependence: A 2000 Update. *Transportation Quarterly* 55(3): 11–32.

Greenspan, A. 2002. *Monetary Policy and the Economic Outlook*. Washington, DC.

Available at http://www.federalreserve.gov/boarddocs/testimony/2002/20020417/default.htm (accessed Mar. 7, 2004).

Greenspan, A. 2006. Prepared statement before the U.S. Senate Committee on Foreign Relations, June 7. *Energy Diplomacy and Security: A Compilation of Statements by Witnesses Before the Committee on Foreign Relations, United States Senate*, 6–14. Washington, DC: U.S. Government Printing Office.

Gross, D. 2006. Raise the Gasoline Tax? Funny, It Doesn't Sound Republican. *New York Times*, Oct. 8.

Grumet, J. S. 2006. Prepared Statement. In *Energy Diplomacy and Security: A Compilation of Statements by Witnesses Before the Committee on Foreign Relations, United States Senate*, 23–40. Washington, DC: U.S. Government Printing Office.

Haddad, Y. Y. 2003. Islamist Perceptions of U.S. Policy in the Middle East. In *The Middle East and the United States*, ed. D. W. Lesch, 467–90. Boulder, CO: Westview.

Hakim, D. 2005. E.P.A. Holds Back Report on Car Fuel Efficiency. *New York Times*, July 28.

Hamilton, J. D. 1983. Oil and the Macroeconomy Since World War II. *Journal of Political Economy* 91(2): 228–48.

Hanson, V. D. 2002. Our Enemies, the Saudis. *Commentary* (July–Aug.): 23–28.

Heavenrich, R. M. 2005. *Light-Duty Automotive Technology and Fuel Economy Trends: 1975 Through 2005*. EPA420–S–05–001. Washington, DC: U.S. Environmental Protection Agency.

Hecht, D. 1999. Gushers of Wealth, but Little Trickles Down. *Christian Science Monitor*, July 23.

Henderson, D. R. 1990. *Do We Need to Go to War For Oil?* Cato Foreign Policy Briefing No. 4. Washington, DC: The Cato Institute. Available at http://www.cato.org/pubs/fpbriefs/fpb-004.html (accessed Dec. 1, 2005).

Hersh, S. M. 2001. King's Ransom: How Vulnerable Are the Saudi Royals? *The New Yorker*, Oct. 22.

Hickman, B. G., H. G. Huntington, and J. L. Sweeney, eds. 1987. *Macroeconomic Impacts of Energy Shocks*. Amsterdam: North Holland.

Hill, F. 2001. A Not-So-Grand Strategy: U.S. Policy in the Caucasus and Central Asia Since 1991. *Politique Étrangère* (Feb.). Available at http://www.brook.edu/views/articles/fhill/20010200.htm (accessed Jan. 26, 2007).

Hiro, D. 1989. *The Longest War: The Iran-Iraq Military Conflict*. London: Grafton Books.

Hodges, T. 2004. *Angola: Anatomy of an Oil State*. Bloomington and Indianapolis: Indiana University Press.

Holdren, J. P. 2001. Searching for a National Energy Policy. *Issues in Science and Technology* (spring): 43–50.

Hoo, S., and R. Ebel. 2006. An International Perspective on Gasoline Taxes. *Tax Notes* 108: 1565.

Horsnell, P. 2004. Why Oil Prices Have Moved Higher. *Oxford Energy Forum* (58): 10–12.

Howden, D., and P. Thornton. 2005. The Pipeline that Will Change the World. *The Independent*, May 25.

Hueper, P. F. 2005. Sub-Saharan Africa. In *Energy and Security*, ed. J. H. Kalicki and D. L. Goldwyn, 241–57. Washington, DC: Woodrow Wilson Center Press.

Hunter, S. T. 1990. *Iran and the World: Continuity in a Revolutionary Decade*. Bloomington: Indiana University Press.

Huntington, H. G. 2005. The Economic Consequences of Higher Crude Oil Prices. Oct. 3. Stanford, CA: Energy Modelling Forum, Stanford University. Available at http://www.stanford.edu/group/EMF/publications/doc/EMFSR9.pdf (accessed Dec. 7, 2006).

Hurd, N. 2000. U.S. Diplomatic and Commercial Relationships with Iraq, 1980—2 August 1990 (July 15; updated Dec. 12, 2001). Available at http://www.casi.org.uk/info/usdocs/usiraq80s90s.html (accessed Oct. 31, 2005).

Ignatius, D. 2003. Shaping Reform in Saudi Arabia. *New York Times*, Mar. 11.

Ikenberry, G. J. 1988. *Reasons of State: Oil Politics and the Capacities of American Government*. Ithaca, NY: Cornell University Press.

Ikenberry, G. J., and A.-M. Slaughter. 2006. *Forging a World of Liberty Under Law: U.S. National Security in the 21st Century*. The Princeton Project Papers. Princeton, NJ: Princeton University Press. Available at http://www.wws.princeton.edu/ppns/report .html.

International Center for Technology Assessment (ICTA). 1998. *The Real Price of Gasoline*. Washington, DC: International Center for Technology Assessment. Available at http://www.icta.org/projects/trans/realpricegas.pdf (accessed June 18, 2004).

International Center for Technology Assessment (ICTA). 2005. *Gasoline Cost Externalities: Security and Protection Services*. Washington, DC: International Center for Technology Assessment. Available at http://www.icta.org/doc/RPG_security_update.pdf (accessed Mar. 9, 2005).

International Energy Agency (IEA). 1998a. *Caspian Oil and Gas: The Supply Potential of Central Asia and Transcaucasia*. Paris: International Energy Agency.

International Energy Agency (IEA). 1998b. *Energy Policies of IEA Countries: The United States 1998 Review*. Paris: International Energy Agency.

International Energy Agency (IEA). 2003. *World Energy Investment Outlook*. Paris: International Energy Agency.

International Energy Agency (IEA). 2004a. *Biofuels for Transport*. Paris: International Energy Agency.

International Energy Agency (IEA). 2004b. *Energy Policies of IEA Countries: 2003 Review*. Paris: International Energy Agency.

International Energy Agency (IEA). 2004c. *World Energy Outlook 2004*. Paris: International Energy Agency.

International Institute for Strategic Studies (IISS). 2002. *The Military Balance 2002–2003*. London: Oxford University Press.

International Monetary Fund (IMF). 2005a. *Oil Market Developments and Issues*. Washington, DC: International Monetary Fund. Available at http://www.imf.org/external/np/pp/eng/2005/030105.pdf (accessed Dec. 3, 2006).

International Monetary Fund (IMF). 2005b. *World Economic Outlook: Globalization and External Imbalances.* Washington, DC: International Monetary Fund. Available at http://www.imf.org/external/pubs/ft/weo/2005/01/index.htm (accessed Dec. 4, 2006).

International Monetary Fund (IMF). 2006. *World Economic Outlook: Globalization and Inflation.* Washington, DC: International Monetary Fund. Available at http://www.imf.org/Pubs/FT/weo/2006/01/index.htm (accessed May 18, 2007).

Jentleson, B. W. 1994. *With Friends Like These: Reagan, Bush, and Saddam, 1982–1990.* New York: W. W. Norton.

Jimenez-Rodriguez, R., and M. Sanchez. 2005. Oil Price Shocks and Real GDP Growth: Empirical Evidence for Some OECD Countries. *Applied Economics* 37(2): 201–28.

Johnson, M. O. 1987. Rapid Deployment and the Regional Military Challenge: The Persian Gulf Equation. In *U.S. Strategic Interests in the Gulf Region,* ed. W. J. Olson. Boulder, CO: Westview Press.

Johnson, R. H. 1989. The Persian Gulf in U.S. Strategy: A Skeptical View. *International Security* 14(1): 122–60.

Jones, D. W., P. N. Leiby, and I. K. Paik. 2004. Oil Price Shocks and the Macroeconomy: What Has Been Learned Since 1996. *The Energy Journal* 25(2): 1–32.

Kalicki, J. H., and D. L. Goldwyn. 2005. Introduction: The Need to Integrate Energy and Foreign Policy. In *Energy and Security,* ed. J. H. Kalicki and D. L. Goldwyn, 1–16. Washington, DC: Woodrow Wilson Center Press.

Kaplan, D. E., M. Ekman, and A. Latif. 2003. The Saudi Connection. *U.S. News & World Report,* Dec. 15.

Karl, T. L. 1997. *The Paradox of Plenty: Oil Booms and Petro-States.* Berkeley: University of California Press.

Katzman, K. 2003. *Iraq: Weapons Programs, U.N. Requirements, and U.S. Policy.* CRS Issue Brief for Congress. Washington, DC: Congressional Research Service.

Kaufmann, W. W. 1986. *A Reasonable Defense.* Washington, DC: The Brookings Institution.

Kaufmann, W. W. 1987. *A Thoroughly Efficient Navy.* Washington, DC: The Brookings Institution.

Kaufmann, W. W. 1992. *Assessing the Base Force: How Much Is Too Much?* Washington, DC: The Brookings Institution.

Kaufmann, W. W., and J. D. Steinbruner. 1991. *Decisions for Defense: Prospects for a New Order.* Washington, DC: The Brookings Institution.

Keane, G. J. 2003. An Army Update. Available at http://www.globalsecurity.org/military/library/report/2003/VCSA_Presentation_as_of_23Jul03.ppt (accessed Aug. 3, 2004).

Keddie, N. R. 1981. *Roots of Revolution: An Interpretive History of Modern Iran.* New Haven, CT, and London: Yale University Press.

Kemp, G. 1994. *Forever Enemies? American Policy and the Islamic Republic of Iran.* New York: The Carnegie Endowment for International Peace.

Kenderdine, M. A., and E. J. Moniz. 2005. Technology Development and Energy Security. In *Energy and Security: Toward a New Foreign Policy Strategy*, ed. J. H. Kalicki and D. L. Goldwyn, 425–59. Washington, DC: Woodrow Wilson Center Press.

Keohane, R. O. 1978. The International Energy Agency: State Influence and Transgovernmental Politics. *International Organization* 32(4): 929–51.

Keohane, R. O. 1984. *After Hegemony: Cooperation and Discord in the World Political Economy.* Princeton, NJ: Princeton University Press.

Kessler, G. 2006. Oil Wealth Colors the U.S. Push for Democracy. *Washington Post*, May 14.

Khalili, L. 2005. The Rising Economic Cost of the Iraq War. *Christian Science Monitor*, May 19.

Khosla, V. 2006. Prepared Statement. In *Energy Diplomacy and Security: A Compilation of Statements by Witnesses Before the Committee on Foreign Relations, United States Senate*, 15–22. Washington, DC: U.S. Government Printing Office.

Klare, M. T. 2001. *Resource Wars: The New Landscape of Global Conflict.* New York: Henry Holt and Company.

Klare, M. T. 2004a. *Blood and Oil: The Dangers and Consequences of America's Growing Petroleum Dependency.* New York: Henry Holt.

Klare, M. T. 2004b. Bush-Cheney Energy Strategy: Procuring the Rest of the World's Oil. *Foreign Policy in Focus.* Washington, DC, and Silver City, NM: Interhemispheric Resource Center/Institute for Policy Studies/SEEN. Available at http://www.fpif.org/papers/03petropol/politics.html (accessed Apr. 23, 2004).

Klare, M. T. 2005. Imperial Reach. *The Nation*, Apr. 25. Available at http://www.thenation.com/doc/20050525/klare (accessed Dec. 22, 2006).

Kolko, G. 2002. *Another Century of War?* New York: New Press.

Koplow, D., and A. Martin. 1998. *Fueling Global Warming: Federal Subsidies to Oil in the United States.* Washington, DC: Greenpeace. Available at http://archive.greenpeace.org/climate/oil/fdsuboil.pdf (accessed July 15, 2004).

Koppel, T. 2006. Will Fight for Oil. *New York Times*, Feb. 24.

Kramer, D. J. 1998. Pipeline Dreams in the Caspian. *Washington Post*, Dec. 3.

Kupchan, C. A. 1987. *The Persian Gulf and the West: The Dilemmas of Security.* Boston: Allen & Unwin.

Kuperman, A. J. 1999. The Stinger Missile and U.S. Intervention in Afghanistan. *Political Science Quarterly* 114(2): 219–63.

Kux, D. 2001. *The United States and Pakistan, 1947–2000: Disenchanted Allies.* Washington, DC: Woodrow Wilson Center Press.

Lafeber, W. 2002. The Bush Doctrine. *Diplomatic History* 26(4): 543–58.

Laham, N. 2002. *Selling AWACS to Saudi Arabia: The Reagan Administration and the Balancing of America's Competing Interests in the Middle East.* Westport, CT: Praeger.

Lansford, T. 2003. *A Bitter Harvest: US Foreign Policy and Afghanistan.* Aldershot, England: Ashgate.

Larson, A. P. 2003. International Aspects of U.S. Energy Security. Testimony Before the Senate Foreign Relations Committee, Subcommittee on International Economic Policy, Export and Trade Promotion, Apr. 8, Washington, DC. Available at http://www.state.gov/e/rls/rm/2003/19447.htm (accessed June 21, 2004).

Larson, E. V., D. T. Orietsky, and K. Leuschner. 2001. *Defense Planning in a Decade of Change: Lessons from the Base Force, Bottom-Up Review, and Quadrennial Defense Review.* Santa Monica, CA: RAND.

Lauerman, V. 2005. The Fear Premium in World Oil Markets. *CERI Energy Insight* (7): 1–5.

Lazzari, S. 1995. *Tax Incentives for Alcohol Fuels.* CRS Report for Congress 95–261E. Available at http://ncseonline.org/NLE/CRSreports/energy/eng-12.cfm?&CFID= 13165225&CFTOKEN=61811498 (accessed Jan. 29, 2007).

Lazzari, S. 1999. *Alcohol Fuels Tax Incentives.* CRS Report for Congress 98–435E. Available at http://ncseonline.org/NLE/crsreports/transportation/trans-18.cfm (accessed Jan. 29, 2007).

Leiby, P. N., and D. Bowman. 2000a. *The Value of Expanded SPR Drawdown Capability.* SPR Drawdown Capability Study, Final Report, Draft 2. Oak Ridge, TN: Oak Ridge National Laboratory. Available at http://pzl1.ed.ornl.gov/ORNL_SPRDrawReport2v0.pdf (accessed Jan. 29, 2007).

Leiby, P. N., and D. Bowman. 2000b. *The Value of Expanding the U.S. Strategic Petroleum Reserve.* ORNL/TM-2000/179. Oak Ridge, TN: Oak Ridge National Laboratory.

Leiby, P. N., et al. 1997. *Oil Imports: An Assessment of Benefits and Costs.* ORNL-6851. Oak Ridge, TN: Oak Ridge National Laboratory.

Lewis, P. M. 2001. Pursuing U.S. Economic Interests in Africa. In *Africa Policy in the Clinton Years: Critical Choices for the Bush Administration,* ed. J. S. Morrison and J. G. Cooke, 96–119. Washington, DC: Center for Strategic and International Studies Press.

Little, D. 2002. *American Orientalism: The United States and the Middle East Since 1945.* Chapel Hill: University of North Carolina Press.

Litwak, R. S. 1984. *Detente and the Nixon Doctrine: American Foreign Policy and the Pursuit of Stability, 1969–1976.* Cambridge: Cambridge University Press.

Long, D. E. 1985. *The United States and Saudi Arabia: Ambivalent Allies.* Boulder, CO: Westview Press.

Losman, D. 2001. Symposium: Is Protecting Overseas Oil Supplies Worth Risking U.S. Troops? *Insight Magazine,* Sept. 24.

Lovins, A., et al. 2004. *Winning the Oil Endgame: Innovation for Profits, Jobs, and Security.* Snowmass, CO: Rocky Mountain Institute.

Luft, G. 2005. The Sweet Road to Energy Security: *Energy Pulse.* Available at http://www.energypulse.net/centers/article/article_display.cfm?a_id=1072 (accessed Aug. 29, 2005).

Lugar, R. G., and R. J. Woolsey. 1999. The New Petroleum. *Foreign Affairs* 78(1): 88–102.

Maass, P. 2005. A Touch of Crude. *Mother Jones* 30(1): 48–56.

Mackenzie, R. 1998. The United States and the Taliban. In *Fundamentalism Reborn?*

Afghanistan and the Taliban, ed. W. Maley, 90–103. New York: New York University Press.

Mandelbaum, M. 2003. U.S. Faces Dilemma on Saudi Policy. *Newsday*, July 30.

Martin, S. T. 2002. Can a Marriage Born of Oil Be Saved? *St. Petersburg Times* (Florida), July 25.

Mankiw, N. G. 2006. Raise the Gas Tax. *Wall Street Journal*, Oct. 20.

Manning, R. A. 2000. *The Asian Energy Factor: Myths and Dilemmas of Energy, Security, and the Pacific Future*. New York: Palgrave.

Mansfield, E., and J. Snyder. 1995. Democratization and the Danger of War. *International Security* 20(1): 5–38.

Mazzetti, M. 2006. Spy Agencies Say Iraq War Worsens Terrorism Threat. *New York Times*, Sept. 23.

McNaugher, T. L. 1985. *Arms and Oil: U.S. Military Strategy and the Persian Gulf*. Washington, DC: The Brookings Institution.

McNaugher, T. L. 1990. U.S. Policy and the Gulf War: A Question of Means. In *The Persian Gulf War: Lessons for Strategy, Law, and Diplomacy*, ed. C. C. Joyner. Westport, CT: Greenwood Press.

Mead, W. R. 2003. Deadlier than War. *Washington Post*, Mar. 12.

Meckler, L. 2006. Fuel Standards Set for Automakers. *Wall Street Journal*, Mar. 30.

Melvin, D., and B. Deans. 2003. U.S. Has Eye on Africa Oil. *Atlanta Journal-Constitution*, July 11.

Metcalf, G. E. 2006. Federal Tax Policy Towards Energy. Working Paper 12568. Cambridge, MA: National Bureau of Economic Research. Available at http://www.nber.org/papers/w12568 (accessed Dec. 14, 2006).

Miglietta, J. P. 2002. *American Alliance Policy in the Middle East, 1945–1992: Iran, Israel, and Saudi Arabia*. Lanham, MD: Lexington Books.

Mommer, B. 2004. Subversive Oil. In *Venezuelan Politics in the Chávez Era: Class, Polarization, and Conflict*, ed. S. Ellner and D. Hellinger, 131–45. Boulder, CO: Lynne Rienner.

Moore, J. L., C. E. Behrens, and J. E. Blodgett. 1997. *Oil Imports: An Overview and Update of Economic and Security Effects*. CRS Report 98–1. Washington, DC: Congressional Research Service.

Morgenson, G. 2004. The Peril that Trails an Oil Shock. *New York Times*, Aug. 22.

Mork, K. A. 1982. The Economic Cost of Oil Supply Disruptions. In *Energy Vulnerability*, ed. J. L. Plummer, 83–112. Cambridge, MA: Ballinger.

Morrison, K. 2004. Fear Has Put $15 on Oil Price, Says Naimi. *Financial Times*, Nov. 30.

Morse, E. L., and A. M. Jaffe. 2001. *Strategic Energy Policy: Challenges for the 21st Century*. New York: Council on Foreign Relations.

Mouawad, J. 2004. Oil Demands Can Be Met, but at a High Price, Energy Agency Says. *New York Times*, Oct. 28.

Mouawad, J. 2005a. As Geopolitics Takes Hold, Cheap Oil Recedes into Past. *New York Times*, Jan. 3.

Mouawad, J. 2005b. Production Trends Point to Reliance on Imported Oil. *New York Times*, Jan. 3.

Mouawad, J. 2005c. Saudis Aim for Precision, not Surplus, in Meeting Global Oil Demand. *New York Times*, Dec. 6.

Mouawad, J. 2006. As Profits Surge, Oil Giants Find Hurdles Abroad. *New York Times*, May 6.

Mouawad, J., and S. Romero. 2005. Unmentioned Energy Fix: A 55 M.P.H. Speed Limit. *New York Times*, May 1.

Murphy, K. 2005. Caspian Sea Pipeline Has Its Origins in Turbulent Waters. *Los Angeles Times*, June 27.

Myers, S. L. 1999. In Intense but Little-Noticed Fight, Allies Have Bombed Iraq all Year. *New York Times*, Aug. 13.

Myers, S. L., and I. Greenberg. 2006. Balancing Act: U.S. Welcomes Kazakh Leader. *New York Times*, Sept. 28.

Nagy, T. 2001. The Secret Behind the Sanctions: How the U.S. Intentionally Destroyed Iraq's Water Supplies. *The Progressive*, Sept.

National Commission on Terrorist Attacks upon the United States (NCTAUS). 2004. *The 9/11 Commission Report: Final Report of the National Commission on Terrorist Attacks Upon the United States.* New York: W. W. Norton.

National Highway Traffic Safety Administration (NHTSA). 2005. CAFE Overview— Frequently Asked Questions. Available at http://www.nhtsa.dot.gov/cars/rules/cafe/overview.htm (accessed Jan. 29, 2007).

National Intelligence Council (NIC). 2000. *Global Trends 2015: A Dialogue About the Future With Nongovernment Experts.* NIC 2000–02. Available at http://www.cia.gov/nic/NIC_globaltrend2015.html.

National Research Council (NRC). 2001. *Energy Research at DOE: Was It Worth It? Energy Efficiency and Fossil Energy Research, 1978 to 2000.* Washington, DC: National Academy Press.

National Research Council (NRC). 2002. *Effectiveness and Impact of Corporate Average Fuel Economy (CAFE) Standards.* Washington, DC: National Academy Press.

National Science Foundation (NSF). 2004. *Federal R&D Funding by Budget Function: Fiscal Years 2003–05.* NSF 05–303. Arlington, VA: National Science Foundation: Division of Science Resource Statistics.

Natural Resources Defense Council (NRDC). 2001. Reducing U.S. Oil Dependence: A Real Energy Security Policy. Available at http://www.nrdc.org/air/energy/fensec.asp (accessed Jan. 29, 2007).

Natural Resources Defense Council (NRDC). 2004. *Growing Energy: How Biofuels Can End America's Oil Dependence.* New York: Natural Resources Defense Council. Available at http://www.nrdc.org/air/energy/biofuels/contents.asp (accessed Dec. 9, 2005).

Natural Resources Defense Council (NRDC). 2005. *A Responsible Energy Plan for*

America. New York: Natural Resources Defense Council. Available at http://www
.nrdc.org/air/energy/biofuels/contents.asp (accessed Dec. 9, 2005).

Naval Historical Center. N.d. U.S. Navy in Desert Shield/Desert Storm. Available at
http://www.history.navy.mil/wars/dstorm/ds2.htm and http://www.history.navy
.mil/wars/dstorm/ds5.htm (accessed Oct. 12, 2006).

Ndumbe, J. A. 2004. West African Oil, U.S. Energy Policy, and Africa's Development
Strategies. *Mediterranean Quarterly* 15(1): 93–104.

New York Times. 2001. Reconsidering Saudi Arabia. Nov. 11.

New York Times. 2004a. Angola's Elusive Oil Riches. June 15.

New York Times. 2004b. Saudis in Terror's Shadow. June 28.

New York Times. 2005a. Foolishness on Fuel. Aug. 21.

New York Times. 2005b. Gas Taxes: Lesser Evil, Greater Good. Oct. 25.

New York Times. 2006. Declassified Key Judgments of the National Intelligence Estimate on Global Terrorism. Sept. 27.

Norris, F. 2006. Oil Price Soars Again, and the Market Gives Signs of a Lasting Trend.
New York Times, Jan. 21.

Office of the Secretary of Defense (OSD). 2001. Operation and Maintenance Overview: FY2002 Amended Budget Submission. Available at http://www.defenselink
.mil/comptroller/defbudget/fy2002/fy02pb_overview.pdf (accessed May 18, 2007).

Office of Technology Assessment (OTA). 1982. *Increased Automobile Fuel Efficiency
and Synthetic Fuels: Alternatives for Reducing Oil Imports.* Washington, DC: Congress of the United States, Office of Technology Assessment.

Office of Technology Assessment (OTA). 1991. *U.S. Oil Import Vulnerability: The
Technical Replacement Capacity.* OTA-E-503. Washington, DC: U.S. Government
Printing Office.

Office of the Undersecretary of Defense (OUD). 1999. *National Defense Budget Estimates for FY 2000.* Washington, DC: Department of Defense. Available at www.fas
.org/man/docs/fy00/GREEN2000.pdf (accessed Aug. 4, 2004).

O'Hanlon, M. E. 1995. *Defense Planning for the Late 1990s: Beyond the Desert Storm
Framework.* Washington, DC: The Brookings Institution.

O'Hanlon, M. E. 1998. *How to Be a Cheap Hawk: The 1999 and 2000 Defense Budgets.*
Washington, DC: The Brookings Institution.

O'Hanlon, M. E. 2001. *Defense Policy Choices for the Bush Administration, 2001–5.*
Washington, DC: The Brookings Institution.

Ottaway, D. B., and R. G. Kaiser. 2002. Saudis May Seek U.S. Exit: Military Presence
Seen as Political Liability in Arab World. *Washington Post,* Jan. 18.

Ottaway, M. 2005. Tyranny's Full Tank. *New York Times,* Mar. 31.

Palast, G., and D. Pallister. 2001. FBI Claims Bin Laden Inquiry Was Frustrated: Officials Told to "Back Off" on Saudis Before September 11. *The Guardian,* Nov. 7.

Palmer, M. A. 1992. *Guardians of the Gulf: A History of America's Expanding Role in the
Persian Gulf, 1833–1992.* New York: Free Press.

Parry, I. W. H. 2002. Is Gasoline Undertaxed in the United States? *Resources* (148):
28–33.

Perry, G. L. 2001. The War on Terrorism, the World Oil Market and the U.S. Economy. Washington, DC: The Brookings Institution. Available at http://brookings.edu/views/papers/perry/20011024.htm (accessed Jan. 5, 2006).

Peters, J. 2005. Congress Caps Credits for Hybrid Cars. *New York Times*, July 29.

Peterson, J. E. 1986. *Defending Arabia*. New York: St. Martin's Press.

Phythian, M. 1997. *Arming Iraq: How the U.S. and Britain Secretly Built Saddam's War Machine*. Boston: Northeastern University Press.

Pickett, J. 2006. Oiling Kazakhstan's Wheels of Reform. *Foreign Policy (Mar.)*. Available at http://www.foreignpolicy.com/story/files/story3410.php (accessed Dec. 22, 2006).

Plotkin, S. E., and D. L. Greene. 1997. Prospects for Improving the Fuel Economy of Light-duty Vehicles. *Energy Policy* 25(14–15): 1179–88.

Plummer, J. L., and J. P. Weyant. 1982. International Institutional Approaches to Energy Vulnerability Problems. In *Energy Vulnerability*, ed. J. L. Plummer. Cambridge, MA: Ballinger.

Pollack, J. 2002. Saudi Arabia and the United States, 1931–2002. *Middle East Review of International Affairs* 6(3): 77–102.

Pollack, J. 2003. Anti-Americanism in Contemporary Saudi Arabia. *Middle East Review of International Affairs* 7(4): 30–43.

Pollack, K. M. 2002. *The Threatening Storm: The Case for Invading Iraq*. New York: Random House.

Pollack, K. M. 2003. Securing the Gulf. *Foreign Affairs* 82(4): 2–16.

Pollack, K. M. 2004. *The Persian Puzzle: The Conflict Between America and Iran*. New York: Random House.

Prados, A. B. 2002. *Iraq: Former and Recent Military Confrontations With the United States*. Issue Brief for Congress. Washington, DC: Congressional Research Service.

Prados, J. 1986. *Presidents' Secret Wars: CIA and Pentagon Covert Operations Since World War II*. New York: William Morrow.

President's Committee of Advisors on Science and Technology/Panel on Energy Research and Development (PCAST). 1997. *Report to the President on Federal Energy Research and Development for the Challenges of the Twenty-first Century*. Available at http://www.ostp.gov/Energy (accessed June 2, 2004).

Priest, D. 2003. *The Mission: Waging War and Keeping Peace with America's Military*. New York: W. W. Norton.

Public Agenda. 2006. *Confidence in U.S. Foreign Policy Index: Americans Wary of Creating Democracies Abroad*. A Report from Public Agenda. New York: Public Agenda. Available at http://www.publicagenda.org/foreignpolicy/pdfs/foreign_policy_index_winter06.pdf (accessed Nov. 28, 2006).

Quandt, W. B. 1981. *Saudi Arabia in the 1980s*. Washington, DC: The Brookings Institution.

Quandt, W. B. 1982. *Saudi Arabia's Oil Policy*. Washington, DC: The Brookings Institution.

Ramazani, R. K. 1982. *The United States and Iran: The Patterns of Influence.* New York: Praeger.

Rashid, A. 2000. *Taliban: Militant Islam, Oil and Fundamentalism in Central Asia.* New Haven, CT: Yale University Press.

Rathmell, A., T. Karasik, and D. Gompert. 2003. *A New Persian Gulf Security System.* Issue Paper IP-248–CMEPP (2003). Santa Monica, CA: RAND.

Rauch, J. 2002. A Higher Gas Tax Is the Answer. Who'll Ask the Question? *National Journal* 34(6).

Ravenal, E. C. 1991. *Designing Defense for a New World Order: The Military Budget in 1992 and Beyond.* Washington, DC: The Cato Institute.

Ravenal, E. C. 1997. The 1998 Defense Budget. In *Cato Handbook for Congress: 105th Congress.* Washington, DC: The Cato Institute.

Renshaw, E. 1990. Paying for Oil Security. *Challenge* 33(6): 11–16.

Reuter, C. 2004. Al Qaeda's New Recruits. *Internationale Politik* (Transatlantic Edition) 5(2): 45–50.

Ricks, T. E. 2006. *Fiasco: The American Military Adventure in Iraq.* New York: Penguin.

Roberts, P. 2004. *The End of Oil: On the Edge of a Perilous New World.* Boston and New York: Houghton Mifflin Company.

Romero, C. A. 2004. The United States and Venezuela: From a Special Relationship to Wary Neighbors. In *The Unraveling of Representative Democracy in Venezuela,* ed. J. L. McCoy and D. J. Myers. Baltimore, MD: Johns Hopkins University Press.

Romero, S., and B. Ellsworth. 2005. Venezuela Tensions Worry Oil Executives. *New York Times,* Jan. 25.

Romm, J. J. 2004. Testimony for the Hearing "Reviewing the Hydrogen Fuel and Freedom Car Initiatives." House Science Committee. Mar. 3. Available at http://gop .science.house.gov/hearings/full04/mar03/romm.pdf (accessed Jan. 29, 2007).

Rouleau, E. 2002. Trouble in the Kingdom. *Foreign Affairs* 81(4): 75–89.

Rowen, H. S., and J. P. Weyant. 1982. Trade-Offs Between Military Policies and Vulnerability Policies. In *Energy Vulnerability,* ed. J. L. Plummer. Cambridge, MA: Ballinger.

Rubin, B. 1981. *Paved with Good Intentions: The American Experience and Iran.* New York: Penguin Books.

Russett, B., and J. Oneal. 2001. *Triangulating Peace: Democracy, Interdependence, and International Organizations.* New York: W. W. Norton.

Rustow, D. A. 1982. *Oil and Turmoil: America Faces OPEC and the Middle East.* New York: W. W. Norton.

Rutledge, I. 2005. *Addicted to Oil: America's Relentless Drive for Energy Security.* London: I. B. Tauris.

Sachs, S. 2004. Attacks in Mideast Raise Fear of More at Oil Installations. *New York Times,* May 7.

Safran, N. 1985. *Saudi Arabia: The Ceaseless Quest for Security.* Cambridge, MA: Harvard University Press.

Samuelson, R. J. 2004. Oil Fantasies. *Washington Post*, Oct. 6.

Samuelson, R. J. 2005. Why Cheap Gas Is a Bad Habit. *Newsweek*, Sept. 19.

Sanger, D. E., and E. Schmitt. 2005. New U.S. Efforts to Ready Iraqis to Take Control. *New York Times*, Nov. 30.

Schmitt, E. 2003. U.S. to Withdraw. *New York Times*, Aug. 12.

Schmitt, E., and T. Shanker. 2002. American Arsenal in the Mideast Is Being Built Up to Confront Saddam Hussein. *New York Times*, Aug. 19.

Schnepf, R. 2006. *Agricultural-Based Renewable Energy Production.* RL32712. Washington, DC: Congressional Research Service. Available at http://ncseonline.org/NLE/CRSreports/06jun/RL32712.pdf (accessed Jan. 16, 2007).

Scott, J. M. 1996. *Deciding to Intervene: The Reagan Doctrine and American Foreign Policy.* Durham, NC: Duke University Press.

Scott, R. 1994. *History of the International Energy Agency: Major Policies and Actions of the IEA.* 3 vols. Paris: International Energy Agency.

Sennott, C. M. 2002. Doubts Are Cast on the Viability of Saudi Monarchy for Long Term. *Boston Globe*, Mar. 5.

Shankar, T., and M. R. Gordon. 2006. Strained, Army Looks to Guard for More Relief. *New York Times*, Sept. 22.

Shultz, G. P. 1993. *Turmoil and Triumph: My Years as Secretary of State.* New York: Charles Scribner's Sons.

Sick, G. 1983. The Evolution of U.S. Strategy Toward the Indian Ocean and Persian Gulf Regions. In *The Great Game: Rivalry in the Persian Gulf and South Asia,* ed. A. Z. Rubinstein, 49–80. New York: Praeger.

Sick, G. 1985. *All Fall Down: America's Tragic Encounter with Iran.* New York: Random House.

Sick, G. 2003. The United States in the Persian Gulf: From Twin Pillars to Dual Containment. In *The Middle East and the United States,* ed. D. W. Lesch, 291–307. Boulder, CO: Westview.

Sieminski, A. E. 2005. World Energy Futures. In *Energy and Security: Toward a New Foreign Policy Strategy,* ed. J. H. Kalicki and D. L. Goldwyn, 21–50. Washington, DC: Woodrow Wilson Center Press.

Silverstein, K. 2002. U.S. Oil Politics in the "Kuwait of Africa." *The Nation* 274(15).

Simmons, M. 2005. *Twilight in the Desert: The Coming Saudi Oil Shock and the World Economy.* New York: Wiley.

Singer, M. 2003. Saudi Arabia's Overrated Oil Weapon. *The Weekly Standard* 8(46): 22–25.

Spiro, D. E. 1999. *The Hidden Hand of American Hegemony: Petrodollar Recycling and International Markets.* Ithaca, NY: Cornell University Press.

Stavins, R. N. 2004. A Tale of Two Taxes, A Challenge to Hill. *The Environmental Forum.* Nov./Dec. Available at http://www.env-econ.net/stavins/Column_4.pdf (accessed Dec. 1, 2005).

Sterngold, J. 2005. Casualty of War: U.S. Economy. *San Francisco Chronicle*, July 17.

Stevens, P. 2004. The Future Price of Crude Oil. *Middle East Economic Survey* 47(37).

Stodghill, R. 2006. Oil, Cash, and Corruption. *New York Times*, Nov. 5.

Stokes, D. 2005. *America's Other War: Terrorizing Colombia.* London: Zed Books.

Sullivan, W. H. 1981. *Mission to Iran.* New York: W. W. Norton.

Tahir-Kheli, S. 1982. *The United States and Pakistan: The Evolution of an Influence Relationship.* New York: Praeger.

Taylor, J. 2001. No Matter What, the Oil Will Flow. *Los Angeles Times*, Oct. 12.

Taylor, J., and P. Van Doren. 2005. Pumping the Bizarre. *National Review* (May 4). Available at http://www.nationalreview.com/comment/taylor_200505040803.asp (accessed Dec. 2, 2006).

Teicher, H., and G. R. Teicher. 1993. *Twin Pillars to Desert Storm: America's Flawed Vision in the Middle East from Nixon to Bush.* New York: Morrow.

Toman, M. A. 2002. International Oil Security: Problems and Policies. *Brookings Review* 20(2): 20–23.

Tonelson, A., and A. K. Hurd. 1990. The Real Cost of Mideast Oil. *New York Times*, Sept. 4.

Tyler, P. E. 2002. Officers Say U.S. Aided Iraq in War Despite Use of Gas. *New York Times*, Aug. 18.

Uchitelle, L., and M. Thee. 2006. Americans Are Cautiously Open to Gas Tax Rise, Poll Shows. *New York Times*, Feb. 28.

U.S. Congress. House. Committee on International Relations. 2000. Subcommittee on Africa. *Africa's Energy Potential.* 106th Congress, Mar. 16. Washington, DC: U.S. Government Printing Office.

U.S. Congress. Senate. Committee on Foreign Relations. 1998. Subcommittee on International Economic Policy, Export and Trade Promotion. *Implementation of U.S. Policy on Caspian Sea Oil Exports.* 105th Congress, 2d sess., July 8. Washington, DC: U.S. Government Printing Office.

U.S. Department of Defense (DOD). 1979. *Foreign Military Sales and Military Assistance Facts, December 1979.* Washington, DC: Defense Security Assistance Agency.

U.S. Department of Defense (DOD). 1992. *Conduct of the Persian Gulf War: Final Report to Congress.* Washington, DC: U.S. Department of Defense. Available at http://www.ndu.edu/library/epubs/cpgw.pdf (accessed July 30, 2004).

U.S. Department of Defense (DOD). 1999. *Foreign Military Sales, Foreign Military Construction Sales and Military Assistance Facts as of September 30, 1999.* Washington, DC: Defense Security Assistance Agency. Available at http://www.fas.org/asmp/profiles/FMS_FACTS/FMS_9_30_99/fulltext.pdf (accessed Dec. 22, 2006).

U.S. Department of Defense (DOD). 2003. "Ground Troop Rotation Plan: Operation Iraqi Freedom." Briefing Slide. Nov. 4. Available at http://www.defenselink.mil/dodcmsshare/briefingslide%5C59%5C031106-D-6570C-004.jpg (accessed May 18, 2007).

U.S. Department of Energy (DOE). 1987. *Energy Security.* DOE/S-0057, Washington, DC: Department of Energy.

U.S. Department of Energy (DOE). 1988. *United States Energy Policy, 1980–1988.* Washington, DC: Department of Energy.

U.S. Department of State (DOS). 2005. *Country Reports on Terrorism 2004.* Washington, DC: U.S. Department of State. Available at http://www.state.gov/documents/organization/45313.pdf (accessed Dec. 4, 2006).

U.S. Department of Transportation (DOT), Federal Transit Administration. 1996. *1996 Report: An Update.* Available at http://www.fta.dot.gov/library/policy/96/.

U.S. Environmental Protection Agency (EPA). 2005. *Light-Duty Automotive Technology and Fuel Economy Trends: 1975 Through 2005.* EPA420-R-05-001 (July). Washington, DC: Environmental Protection Agency, Office of Transportation and Air Quality. Available at http://www.epa.gov/otaq/cert/mpg/fetrends/420r05001.pdf (accessed May 18, 2007).

U.S. General Accounting Office (GAO). 1991. *Southwest Asia: Cost of Protecting U.S. Interests.* GAO/NSIAD-91–250. Washington, DC.

U.S. General Accounting Office (GAO). 1994. *Iraq: U.S. Military Items Exported or Transferred to Iraq in the 1980s.* GAO/NSIAD-94–98. Washington, DC.

U.S. General Accounting Office (GAO). 1996. *Energy Security: Evaluating U.S. Vulnerability to Oil Supply Disruptions and Options for Mitigating Their Effects.* GAO/RCED-97–6. Washington, DC. Available at http://www.gao.gov/archive/1997/rc97006.pdf (accessed May 20, 2004).

U.S. General Accounting Office (GAO). 1997. *Strategic Mobility: Late Deliveries of Large, Medium Speed Roll-On/Roll-Off Ships.* Letter Report. GAO/NSIAD-97–150. Washington, DC.

U.S. General Accounting Office (GAO). 2000. *Automobile Fuel Economy: Potential Effects of Increasing the Corporate Average Fuel Economy Standards.* GAO/RCED-00–194. Washington, DC.

"US Navy Order of Battle: Operation Iraqi Freedom." Available at http://www.navysite.de/navy/iraqi-freedom.htm (accessed Dec. 22, 2006).

Vance, C. 1983. *Hard Choices: Critical Years in America's Foreign Policy.* New York: Simon & Schuster.

Verleger, P. K., Jr. 1994. *Adjusting to Volatile Energy Prices.* Washington, DC: Institute for International Economics.

Vieth, W. 2003. U.S. Quest for Oil in Africa Worries Analysts, Activists. *Los Angeles Times,* Jan. 13.

Volman, D. 2003. The Bush Administration and African Oil: The Security Implications of US Energy Policy. *Review of African Political Economy* 30 (98): 573–84.

Waas, M. 1991. What Washington Gave Saddam for Christmas. In *The Gulf War Reader: History, Documents, Opinions,* ed. M. L. Sifry and C. Cerf, 85–95. New York: Random House.

Wald, M. L. 2005. Designed to Save, Hybrids Burn Gas in Drive for Power. *New York Times,* July 17.

Wald, M. L. 2006. U.S. Raises Standards on Mileage. *New York Times,* Mar. 30.

Wallsten, S., and K. Kosec. 2005. *The Economic Costs of the War in Iraq.* Washington,

DC: AEI-Brookings Joint Center for Regulatory Studies. Available at http://www
.aei-brookings.org/admin/authorpdfs/page.php?id=1188 (accessed Dec. 22, 2006).

Walton, A.-M. 1976. Atlantic Bargaining Over Energy. *International Affairs* 52(2):
180–96.

Washington Post. 2001. Reconsidering Saudi Arabia. Oct. 14.

Weaver, M. A. 1995. Children of the Jihad. *The New Yorker,* June 12, 40–47.

Weaver, M. A. 1996. Blowback. *Atlantic Monthly* (May): 24–28, 36.

Weinbaum, M. 2003. The United States and Afghanistan: From Marginality to Global
Concern. In *The Middle East and the United States,* ed. D. W. Lesch, 443–58. Boulder, CO: Westview.

Weinberger, C. W. 1990. *Fighting for Peace: Seven Critical Years in the Pentagon.* New
York: Warner Books.

Weiner, T. 1994. Blowback from the Afghan Battlefield. *New York Times Magazine,*
Mar. 13.

West, J. R. 2004. Paying the Pumper. *Washington Post,* July 23.

West, J. R. 2005. Saudi Arabia, Iraq, and the Gulf. In *Energy and Security: Toward a
New Foreign Policy Strategy,* ed. J. H. Kalicki and D. L. Goldwyn, 197–218. Washington, DC: Woodrow Wilson Center Press.

Willrich, M., and M. A. Conant. 1977. The International Energy Agency: An Interpretation and Assessment. *American Journal of International Law* 71(2): 199–223.

Woolsey, R. J. 2002. Defeating the Oil Weapon. *Commentary* (Sept.): 29–33.

Yager, J. A. 1981. The Energy Battles of 1979. In *Energy Policy in Perspective: Today's
Problems, Yesterday's Solutions,* ed. C. D. Goodwin. Washington, DC: The Brookings Institution.

Yankelovich, D. 2006. The Tipping Point. *Foreign Affairs* 85(3). Available at http://
www.foreignaffairs.org/20060501faessay85309/daniel-yankelovich/the-tipping-
points.html (accessed Nov. 28, 2006).

Yergin, D. 1991. *The Prize: The Epic Quest for Oil, Money, and Power.* New York: Simon
& Schuster.

Yergin, D. 2005. Energy Security and Markets. In *Energy and Security: Toward a New
Foreign Policy Strategy,* ed. J. H. Kalicki and D. L. Goldwyn, 51–64. Washington,
DC: Woodrow Wilson Center Press.

Yergin, D. 2006. Statement before the Committee on Energy and Commerce,
U.S. House of Representatives, Washington, DC. May 4. Available at http://
energycommerce.house.gov/108/Hearings/05042006hearing1865/Yergin.pdf (accessed Dec. 5, 2006).

Yetiv, S. A. 2004. *Crude Awakenings: Global Oil Security and American Foreign Policy.*
Ithaca, NY: Cornell University Press.

Yousaf, M., and M. Adkin. 2001. *Afghanistan—The Bear Trap: The Defeat of a Superpower.* Havertown, PA: Casemate.

Zakaria, F. 2005. How to Escape the Oil Trap. *Newsweek* (Aug. 29–Sept. 5). Available
at http://www.msnbc.msn.com/id/9024768/site/newsweek/ (accessed Nov. 28,
2006).

Zepezauer, M. 2003. *Boomerang: How Our Covert Wars Have Created Enemies Across the Middle East and Brought Terror to America.* Monroe, ME: Common Courage Press.

Zunes, S. 2002. *Tinderbox: U.S. Middle East Policy and the Roots of Terrorism.* Monroe, ME: Common Courage Press.

Index